P9-CDP-280

THE HERITAGE SERIES
VOLUME THREE

UP FROM SLAVERY

AN AUTOBIOGRAPHY

BY

BOOKER T. WASHINGTON

WITH SELECTIONS FROM "CHARACTER BUILDING"

INTRODUCTION BY
PROFESSOR ROBERT CUMMINGS Ph.D.
HOWARD UNIVERSITY

Candace
Press

GRAND RAPIDS, MICHIGAN
1996

Copyright © 1996 Candace Press, Incorporated
Cover Design and Illustration © 1996
Introduction © 1996

Candace Press, Inc.,
2215 29th Street, S.E.
Grand Rapids, Michigan 49508

All rights reserved.
No part of this publication may be reproduced,
stored in any retrieval system, or transmitted,
in any form or by any means,
electronic, mechanical, photocopying,
scanning, or otherwise, without
prior permission of Candace Press, Inc.

Library of Congress Catalog Card Number 96-084472

ISBN 1-889073-01-6

CONTENTS

THE HERITAGE SERIES

"If you can control a man's thinking, you do not have to worry about his action, when you determine what a man shall think, you do not have to concern yourself about what he will do. If you make a man feel that he is inferior; you do not have to compel him to accept an inferior status, for he will seek it himself. If you make a man think that he is justly an outcast, you do not have to order him to the back door. He will go without being told; and if there is no back door, his very nature will demand one."

Carter G. Woodson wrote these words around 1930 amidst his lifetime pursuit to make the world see African Americans as an integral part of our history and not just as a by-product of our society. It is a timeless message, as relevant two hundred years ago as today. One hundred and fifty-seven years after the first slave ships arrived at Jamestown, our founding fathers declared autonomy for themselves from British dominance by proclaiming *". . . these truths to be self-evident, that all men are created equal, that they are endowed by their Creator with certain unalienable Rights, that among these are Life, Liberty and the pursuit of Happiness."* This declaration, a promise unique in the world's history, declared the vision and defined the foundation upon which we rest today.

The men and women who authored the twelve volumes of *The Heritage Series* inhaled the essence of these words and the truths that they proclaimed. Since the day the first slave ship arrived, African Americans have had to fight to keep alive their cultural heritage. Rather than yield to a system that sought to eliminate their African heritage of courage and leadership, these few chose to endure until their victory came. Rather than yield their thinking to the control of others, they chose a destiny of their own. And by their choice, the history of America was forever altered.

The American heroes in *The Heritage Series* are greater than their individual words or actions because they represent the aspirations and demands of an entire people who could see and smell, but not taste the fruits of "Life, Liberty, and Happiness." History has failed to capture and record the contributions of many noteworthy African Americans. But through the centuries these few authors have shared their vision and exposed the empty promises of a country which denied even the most basic human rights to an entire race of its citizens.

The vision of the men and women of *The Heritage Series* is as powerful today and perhaps even more meaningful; as inspiring and demanding as it was when it was first proclaimed. The truths that rang out then are still resounding relevance today. Perhaps you will identify some progress since these writings were penned, but we also hope that you will recognize the distance we must still go to realizing the promise of America.

We present a selection of some of the greatest literature in the history of the world. It is the crowning moment of our painstaking effort to portray the fullness of our American and African American heritages. This Series contains autobiographies and novels, philosophy and poetry, politics and plays. Over ten years of searching and researching has allowed us to locate an original first edition for almost every volume, with the oldest book being almost two and a quarter centuries old. Thus, we offer you the pure thoughts and values of the authors as they wrote them. Our hope is that as you read *The Heritage Series* you will be inspired by the words and actions of our mothers and fathers, grandmothers and grandfathers. They are genuine, and through these volumes, they are still with us today to encourage us and to demand that we rise in pride, knowledge, and strength. For your collection we have wrapped their words in elegant bindings and gold. But please do not allow the beauty of the books to blind you to their real worth for the true value is in what lies between the covers. *Read the words. Share the words. Live the words.*

Finally, this series is entitled "Heritage" because it's our ultimate hope that our readers will share the wisdom and history contained within them with the youth of today. It took the works and words of these great men and women to make us the people and the nation we are today. Will it take less for our children? They are the authors of tomorrow's Heritage Series.

"A mind that remains in the present atmosphere never undergoes sufficient development to experience what is commonly known as thinking . . . .

In our so-called democracy, we are accustomed to give the majority what they want rather than educate them to understand what is best for them." – Carter G. Woodson

Eric J. Williams
Publisher

Wayne S. Morehead
Publisher

The Heritage Series is dedicated to my two daughters,

Candace Faith and Otelia Alon Williams.

They would never encounter most of the information
included in these books in their traditional educational
experiences. Yet, they can not fully understand the history of the United States without the knowledge that
these books hold. My prayer is that they and all young
people will learn of the contributions that African Americans have made to our society. And that as they learn
about great people of the past, they will be encouraged
to be great people in the future.

Eric J. Williams

Publisher

IN APPRECIATION

For making the vision of
The Heritage Series a reality

My Wife, Olivia for supporting me.

My Parents, Wardell and Shirley Reynolds,
for believing in me.

To the Team:
Robin Bellingar, Christina Dugan,
Melbourne Cummings, Robert J. Cummings,
J.R. & Kathi Jablonski,
Wayne Morehead, Jean Reid,
Arifah Shakir, Rashidah Shakir
and Shari Shaw

A special thanks to John Kennedy
for having faith in me.

My Lord and God; El Shaddai
(He will Provide)

INTRODUCTION

Up From Slavery: An Autobiography is the life story of the central figure in the period labeled by historian John Hope Franklin as "The Age of Booker T. Washington." William E.B. DuBois had been forced to recognize this 'ordination' as early as 1903 when he wrote, "Easily the most striking thing in the history of the American Negro since 1876 is the ascendancy of Mr. Booker T. Washington."

Booker Taliaferro Washington was born into slavery in Virginia, either in 1858 or 1859. His birth came only a short time before President Abraham Lincoln's Emancipation Proclamation declared the slave population "free" in the several southern states, led by Virginia, that challenged the authority of the Union. A graduate of Hampton Institute, Washington had been raised by his mother together with his two siblings – older brother John and sister Amanda—without ever knowing his father. Fatherless children were simply one of the legacies of America's peculiar institution.

The autobiography of Booker T. Washington was also striking in its open articulation of the world-view of this distinguished African American educator. Washington's *Up From Slavery,* sought to describe from his own perspective his dedication to up-lifting his race from what he perceived to be the dire consequences and legacy of American slavery. In lifting his own people, however, he believed the need no less great to lift white America as well from the bowels of its own destructive creation. To Booker T., America's slavery had been less than kind to all of its residential participants.

North American slavery was an economic system that created and maintained inequality between the races to assure its own survival.

INTRODUCTION

Slavery in its brutality against black people created fear among the whites as well as high economic expectations. The system in its inhumanity reduced the self-image of black people and increased their lack of self-confidence, which increased their dependency and self-hatred. Slavery, in short, was a destructive force on the African American society. It resided in its truest forms and with its legacy of bestiality in the American south.

The negative influences of slavery were not confined, however, to the former slaves. The machinery of the institution was designed to cause labor, as a rule, to be looked upon as a badge of degradation, or inferiority, by southern whites. Hence manual labor was something to escape. The slave system in a large measure took the spirit of self-reliance and self-help out of white people. They unconsciously imbibed the feeling that manual labor was not the proper thing for them to do.

The slave on the other hand had mastered some handicrafts and skills, was unashamed of manual labor, and was quite willing to work. Willing labor thus was a potential primary currency. The former slave could, if directed properly, ride this phenomenon into socio-political and economic empowerment in a *new* South.

To achieve a new foundation upon which change could occur, the whole of southern society had to be lifted, psychologically and educationally, 'up from slavery.' The challenge of this task required someone with not just an idea, but also a strategy. It was necessary that any original idea to challenge the status quo be linked to a strategy that recognized the fears and animosities of the stronger, and more hostile, southern white community.

Booker T. Washington, having grown up in the South, recognized and accepted the dichotomy that was the southern historical legacy of slavery. Blacks and whites, he understood from his vantage point, had not only learned how to live with the challenges of slavery but were forced after the 1880's to face its legacies. Even so, and it needed to be understood further, the associated interactions between black and white had not created within the general slave population bitter feelings towards their slave holders. "In the case of the slaves on our place, this was

INTRODUCTION

. . . true," Washington notes, "and it was (the same) of any large portion of the slave population in the South where the Negro was treated with anything like decency." He continued:

"During the Civil War one of my young masters was killed, and two were severely wounded. I recall the feeling of sorrow which existed among the slaves when they heard of the death of "Mars Billy." It was no sham sorrow, but real. Some of the slaves had nursed "Mars Billy;" others had played with him when he was a child. "Mars Billy" had begged for mercy in the case of others when the overseer or master was thrashing them. The sorrow in the slave quarter was only second to that in the "big house."

The sympathy of the slaves toward their slave holders was shown in many ways and was a part, together with their tenderness, of their "kindly and generous nature." They defended and protected the women and children of the slave masters and were almost never known to betray a specific trust. Yet, Washington said, less "one may get the idea that some of the slaves did not want freedom . . . I have never seen one who did not want to be free, or one who would return to slavery."

Slavery for Booker Washington was not wholly the fault of any one section, north or south, of the United States. Neither area was totally guilty or innocent in the introduction of the institution, and slavery had managed to fasten itself to the social and economic fabric of the U.S. society and was not easily cast off. Rather than laying blame, therefore, it was necessary to pity any nation or people who were so unfortunate as to get entrapped in the institution of slavery. In fact, while not seeking to justify slavery and recognizing the cruelty and moral wrong of slavery, Washington wanted that some consideration be given to the fact that the ten million African Americans who had survived the onslaught of slavery had achieved a stronger condition, materially, intellectually, and morally and religiously in the U.S. than "is true of an equal number of black people in any other portion of the globe."

In his Chicago "Jubilee Week" speech before an audience of some 16,000 or so, including President William McKinley, Booker T. Washington made this appeal to the consciences of white Americans: "When you have gotten the full story of the heroic conduct of the (African American) in the Spanish-American war, have heard it from the lips of Northern soldiers and Southern soldiers, from ex-abolitionists and ex-masters, then decide within yourselves whether a race that is thus willing to die for its country should not be given the highest opportunity to live for its country."

Washington was driven by a fundamental belief that their few years out of slavery had not provided sufficient time or opportunity to pro-duce a competent, competitive African American population. Linked to this position was Washington's belief that the political condition and socio-economic future of black people were connected inextricably to the South and the white people there, who would, someday, freely share themselves and their knowledge. Indeed, he believed in the goodness of the relationship between Southerners, black and white, for ". . . the time will come when the (African American) in the South will be accorded all the political rights which his ability, character and *material possessions* entitle him to. I think, though, that the opportunity to freely exercise such political rights will not come in any large degree through outside or artificial forcing, but will be accorded . . . by the Southern white people themselves, and that they will protect him in the exercise of these rights" (emphasis added).

To achieve the desired results, however, it was necessary for black people to understand the environment in which they lived. The south was engulfed by slavery to the destruction of both black and white communities. Black people were in the inferior minority position and needed to strive to develop themselves without being perceived as a challenge to their white counterparts. Washington believed that black folks could not only survive, but prosper in the South by owning land themselves, managing farms, cultivating high morals, and maintaining good personal and physical manners. He earnestly thought they must save their money and use it wisely to create for themselves the economic infrastructure necessary to lift, and make financially viable, their own community and themselves.

A proud Southerner himself, Booker Washington understood the

INTRODUCTION

South and its inherent animosity and fear toward educated black people. Education, whites believed, was certain to "ruin our good Negroes." It would make black people think themselves as good as white folks and they would therefore demand social equality.

At Tuskegee, President Washington sought to demonstrate to the white South that the educated black person was an asset rather than someone to fear. Education for black people was also good for white people and social equality was not the primary goal of educational instructions at Tuskegee. Service, respect for the law, cooperation with and contribution to the community were the goals of the Tuskegee (Alabama) Normal and Industrial Institute. Washington was certain that the most racist of humanity "will recognize and reward merit, no matter under what colour of skin merit is found." The individual, Booker Washington taught, who can do something that the world wants done will, in the end, make his way regardless of his race.

Industrial education provided opportunity for Tuskegee students to meet most of their own needs for services and facilities, and to supply, through their labor and creative abilities, a positive response to the needs of the white community for wagons, bricks, houses and other such domestic products. The actual sight of a first-class house built by Tuskegee students is "ten times more potent," he observed, "than pages of discussion about a house that he ought to build, or perhaps could build." Indeed, "If the man can supply the need for those (who feel its needs for brick, houses and wagons), then, it will lead eventually to a demand for the first product, and with the demand will come the ability to appreciate it and to *profit* by it" (emphasis added).

The glorification of labor and pride in the products of that labor were used first to reduce white hostility towards the school. It later became the foundation around which Washington organized the whole curriculum of Tuskegee. He taught that "educated labor" for black people was a primary source for the acquisition of personal respect, wealth and profits.

On one occasion, Booker T. spoke of a Tuskegee graduate who had harvested two hundred sixty-six bushels of sweet potatoes from an acre of land. This marvel had occurred in an Alabama community where the average production had been less than fifty bushels per acre. The young agronomist achieved this agricultural feat as a direct result of his knowledge of soil chemistry and improved agricultural methods. White farmers came to his door in search of his "secrets," which he graciously shared. "These white farmers honoured and respected him because he, by his skill and knowledge," Booker T. wrote, "had added something to the wealth and the comfort of the community in which he lives." These and other tangible results of Washington's educational approach forced many white people to withdraw their open criticisms and lend their public support to both the man and his institute.

In his 1895 Atlanta Exposition address, Washington put forth his philosophy of cooperation and accommodation between the races and demonstrated that black people were not demanding anything other than the opportunity to be good citizens and to serve, to their mutual advantage, both the black and white communities. Washington's carefully designed sociological formula proved its relevancy to Southern-based race relations, its capacity to reduce racial tensions, and its power to improve the public image of his race.

The reporter for the *New York World* was most enthusiastic in his article of 18 September, 1895 as he heralded Washington's Atlanta Exposition address as ". . . the beginning of a moral revolution in America."

> ". . . to the white people of the South on behalf of his race, (Washington said) 'In all things that are purely social we can be as separate as the five fingers, yet one as the hand in all things essential to mutual progress,' (and) the great wave of sound dashed itself against the walls, and the whole audience was on its feet in a delirium of applause. . . ." I have heard the great orators of many countries, but not even Gladstone himself could have pleaded a cause with more consummate power than did this angular Negro, standing in a nimbus of sunshine, surrounded by the men who once fought to keep his race in bondage."

Booker T. Washington, however, took his point to its rational conclusion by admonishing black people as well. If African American people would be truly *free,* then they must initially take on a non-threatening

INTRODUCTION

demeanor and a clearly defined set of priorities and goals.

> Those of my race who depend upon bettering their condition in a *foreign land* or who underestimate the importance of cultivating friendly relations with the Southern white man . . . I would say 'Cast down your bucket where you are' – cast it down in making friends in every manly way of the people of all *races by whom we are surrounded. Cast it down in agriculture, mechanics, in commerce, in domestic service, and in the professions.* (emphasis added).

Booker T. Washington both understood the political and socio-economic and environmental circumstances of his people and had effectively divined a strategy that could empower them. The fascinating point is that he articulates his economic development strategy in the public eye of Southern whites and others, and they cheered him on.

Booker Washington, indeed, was a shrewd educator, politician, leader and community advocate. He never argued that black people should only pursue vocational education, rather he felt that certain subjects simply were not practical for the decades immediately after the abolition of U.S. slavery. Washington firmly believed that the conditions of the south required that the black person, as he was surrounded in fact by hostile forces, deport himself modestly, and with circumspect, "depending upon the slow but sure influences that proceed from the possession of property, intelligence, and high character for the full recognition of his . . . rights."

In his evaluation of the "Age of Booker T. Washington," Professor Franklin discussed Washington's idea and strategy for vocational education as a doctrine that was hailed by whites in both the northern and southern regions of the United States. Some northern whites saw Washington's strategy as a "formula for peace in the South with the establishment of a satisfactory economic and social equilibrium between the races." Others saw an extensive labor force and potential market centers for their finished products.

Southern whites moreover, "agreed with his advocacy of a type of education which they believed would consign (African Americans) to an inferior economic and social status in Southern life." Booker T.

INTRODUCTION

Washington's approach to education at Tuskegee Institute demonstrated his understanding of the fragile sensibilities of southern whites. His strategy relieved them of their fear of black activism for political and civil rights and made them comfortable. Washington successfully achieved his primary goal; to garner sufficient white admiration for his work as to reduce open hostility towards his people.[1]

Up From Slavery then is appropriately silent, in light of Washington's carefully developed public image, regarding the author's private and oftentimes anonymous contributions to several early anti-segregation court cases. He also financed, among others, various evolving civil rights organizations.

Booker T. Washington felt that, as a native son, he understood the South. It was there, with its legacy of slavery, that he was best able (1) to link most successfully his idea of advancement for black people within a carefully designed strategy and (2) to follow and actualize this developmental strategy, designed to free his race, by being unintimidatingly *soft in manner, yet strong in action.*

Professor Robert J. Cummings, Ph.D
Chairman, Department of African Studies and The Research Center
Howard University

[1]John Hope Franklin, FROM SLAVERY TO FREEDOM: A HISTORY OF NEGRO AMERICANS, 3rd Edition, New York: Alfred A. Knopf, 1968, 392. Opposition to Washington's strategy came also from both the north and the south and from black and white leaders. One of the leading critics of Booker T. Washington was W.E.B. DuBois.

PUBLISHER'S NOTE

With each book of *The Heritage Series,* Candace Press has endeavored to recover the work of the author as originally written, untainted by later editing or revision. The materials for this series were drawn from the earliest editions we could obtain, some more than 200 years old. Reading these books you will encounter some inconsistencies, unusual words, phrasing, spelling and punctuation. These are either usages common to the time and locale in which the original text was prepared, or they are devices used by the author for emphasis or to express a particular idea.

ORIGINAL
PREFACE

This volume is the outgrowth of a series of articles, dealing with incidents in my life, which were published consecutively in the *Outlook*. While they were appearing in that magazine I was constantly surprised at the number of requests which came to me from all parts of the country, asking that the articles be permanently preserved in book form. I am most grateful to the *Outlook* for permission to gratify these requests.

I have tried to tell a simple, straightforward story, with no attempt at embellishment. My regret is that what I have attempted to do has been done so imperfectly. The greater part of my time and strength is required for the exectuive work connected with the Tuskegee Normal and Industrial Institute, and in securing the money necessary for the support of the institution. Much of what I have said has been written on board trains, or at hotels, or railroad stations while I have been waiting for trains, or during the moments that I could spare from my work while at Tuskegee. Without the painstaking and generous assistance of Mr. Max Bennett Thrasher I could not have succeeded in any satisfactory degree.

Booker T. Washington

UP FROM SLAVERY

BY

BOOKER T. WASHINGTON

CHAPTER I
A SLAVE AMONG SLAVES

I was born a slave on a plantation in Franklin County, Virginia. I am not quite sure of the exact place or exact date of my birth, but at any rate I suspect I must have been born somewhere and at some time. As nearly as I have been able to learn, I was born near a cross-roads post-office called Hale's Ford, and the year was 1858 or 1859. I do not know the month or the day. The earliest impressions I can now recall are of the plantation and the slave quarters—the latter being the part of the plantation where the slaves had their cabins.

My life had its beginning in the midst of the most miserable, desolate, and discouraging surroundings. This was so, however, not because my owners were especially cruel, for they were not, as compared with many others. I was born in a typical log cabin, about fourteen by sixteen feet square. In this cabin I lived with my mother and a brother and sister till after the Civil War, when we were all declared free.

Of my ancestry I know almost nothing. In the slave quarters, and even later, I heard whispered conversations among the coloured people of the tortures which the slaves, including, no doubt, my ancestors on my mother's side, suffered in the middle passage of the slave ship while being conveyed from Africa to America. I have been unsuccessful in securing any information that would throw any accurate light upon the history of my family beyond my mother. She, I remember, had a half-brother and a half-sister. In the days of slavery not very much attention was given to family history and family records—that is, black family records. My mother, I suppose, attracted the attention of a purchaser who was afterward my owner and hers. Her addition to the slave family attracted about as much attention as the purchase of a new horse or cow. Of my father I know even less than of my mother. I do not even know his name. I have heard reports to the effect that he was a white man who lived on one of the near-by plantations. Whoever he was, I never heard of his taking the least interest in me or providing in any way for my rearing. But I do not find especial fault with him. He was simply another unfortunate victim of the institution which the Nation unhappily had engrafted upon it at that time.

The cabin was not only our living-place, but was also used as the kitchen for the plantation. My mother was the plantation cook. The cabin was without glass windows; it had only openings in the side which let in the light, and also the cold, chilly air of winter. There was a door to the cabin – that is, something that was called a door—but the uncertain hinges by which it was hung, and the large cracks in it, to say nothing of the fact that it was too small, made the room a very uncomfortable one. In addition to these openings there was, in the lower right-hand corner of the room, the "cat-hole,"—a contrivance which almost every mansion or cabin in Virginia possessed during the antebellum period. The "cat-hole" was a square opening, about seven by eight inches, provided for the purpose of letting the cat pass in and out of the house at will during the night. In the case of our particular cabin I could never understand the necessity for this convenience, since there were at least half-dozen other places in the cabin that would have accommodated the cats. There was no wooden floor in our cabin, the naked earth being used as a floor. In the centre of the earthen floor there was a large, deep opening covered with boards, which was used as a place in which to store sweet potatoes during the winter. An impression of this potato-hole is very distinctly engraved upon my memory, because I recall that during the process of putting the potatoes in or taking them out I would often come into possession of one or two, which I roasted and thoroughly enjoyed. There was no cooking-stove on our plantation, and all the cooking for the whites and slaves my mother had to do over an open fireplace, mostly in pots and "skillets." While the poorly built

2

cabin caused us to suffer with cold in the winter, the heat from the open fireplace in summer was equally trying.

The early years of my life, which were spent in the little cabin, were not very different from those of thousands of other slaves. My mother, of course, had little time in which to give attention to the training of her children during the day. She snatched a few moments for our care in the early morning before her work began, and at night after the day's work was done. One of my earliest recollections is that of my mother cooking a chicken late at night, and awakening her children for the purpose of feeding them. How or where she got it I do not know. I presume, however, it was procured from our owner's farm. Some people may call this theft. If such a thing were to happen now, I should condemn it as theft myself. But taking place at the time it did, and for the reason that it did, no one could ever make me believe that my mother was guilty of thieving. She was simply a victim of the system of slavery. I cannot remember having slept in a bed until after our family was declared free by the Emancipation Proclamation. Three children—John, my older brother, Amanda, my sister, and myself—had a pallet on the dirt floor, or, to be more correct, we slept in and on a bundle of filthy rags laid upon the dirt floor.

I was asked not long ago to tell something about the sports and pastimes that I engaged in during my youth. Until that question was asked it had never occurred to me that there was no period of my life that was devoted to play. From the time that I can remember anything, almost every day of my life has been occupied in some kind of labour; though I think I would now be a more useful man if I had had time for sports. During the period that I spent in slavery I was not large enough to be of much service, still I was occupied most of the time in cleaning the yards, carrying water to the men in the fields, or going to the mill, to which I used to take the corn, once a week, to be ground. The mill was about three miles from the plantation. This work I always dreaded. The heavy bag of corn would be thrown across the back of the horse, and the corn divided about evenly on each side; but in some way, almost without exception, on these trips, the corn would so shift as to become unbalanced and would fall off the horse, and often I would fall with it. As I was not strong enough to reload the corn upon the horse, I would have to wait, sometimes for many hours, till a chance passer-by came along who would help me out of my trouble. The hours while waiting for someone were usually spent in crying. The time consumed in this way made me late in reaching the mill, and by the time I got my corn ground and reached home it would be far into the night. The road was a lonely one, and often led through dense forests. I was always frightened. The woods were said to be full of soldiers who had deserted from the army, and I had been told that the first thing a deserter did to a Negro boy when he found him alone was to cut off his ears. Besides, when I was late in getting home I knew I would always get a severe scolding or a flogging.

I had no schooling whatever while I was a slave, though I remember on several occasions I went as far as the schoolhouse door with one of my young mistresses to carry her books. The picture of several dozen boys and girls in a schoolroom engaged in study made a deep impression upon me, and I had the feeling that to get into a schoolhouse and study in this way would be about the same as getting into paradise.

So far as I can now recall, the first knowledge that I got of the fact that we were slaves, and that freedom of the slaves was being discussed, was early one morning before day, when I was awakened by my mother kneeling over her children and fervently praying that Lincoln and his armies might be successful, and that one day she and her children might be free. In this connection I have never been able to understand how the slaves throughout the South, completely ignorant as were the masses so far as books or newspapers were concerned, were able to keep themselves so accurately and completely informed about the great National questions that were agitating the country. From the time that Garrison, Lovejoy, and others began to agitate for freedom, the slaves throughout the South kept in close touch with the progress of the movement. Though I was a mere child during the preparation for the Civil War and during the war itself, I now recall the many late-at-night whispered discussions that I heard my mother and the other slaves on the plantation indulge in. These discussions showed that they understood the situation, and that they kept themselves informed of events by what was termed the "grape-vine" telegraph.

During the campaign when Lincoln was first a candidate for the Presidency, the slaves on our far-off plantation, miles from any railroad or large city or daily newspaper, knew what the issues involved were. When war was begun between the North and the South, every slave on our plantation felt and knew that, though other issues were discussed, the primal one was that of slavery. Even the most ignorant members of my race on the remote plantations felt in their hearts, with a certainty that admitted of no doubt, that the freedom of the slaves would be the one great result of the war, if the Northern armies conquered. Every success of the Federal armies and every defeat of the confederate forces was watched with the keenest and most intense interest. Often the slaves got knowledge of the results of great battles before the white people received it. This news was usually gotten from the coloured man who was sent to the post-office for the mail. In our case the post-office was about three miles from the plantation, and the mail came once or twice a week. The man who was sent to the office would linger about the place long enough to get the drift of the conversation from the group of white people who naturally congregated there, after receiving their mail, to discuss the latest news. The mail-carrier on his way back to our master's house would as naturally retail the news that he had secured among the slaves, and in this way they often heard of important events before the white people at the "big house," as the master's house was called.

I cannot remember a single instance during my childhood or early boyhood when our entire family sat down to the table together, and God's blessing was asked, and the family ate a meal in a civilized manner. On the plantation in Virginia, and even later, meals were gotten by the children very much as dumb animals get theirs. It was a piece of bread here and a scrap of meat there. It was a cup of milk at one time and some potatoes at another. Sometimes a portion of our family would eat out of the skillet or pot, while someone else would eat from a tin plate held on the knees, and often using nothing but the hands with which to hold the food. When I had grown to sufficient size, I was required to go to the "big house" at meal-times to fan the flies from the table by means of a large set of paper fans operated by a pulley. Naturally much of the conversation of the white people turned upon the subject of freedom and the war, and I absorbed a good deal of it. I remember that at one time I saw two of my young mistresses and some lady visitors eating ginger-cakes, in the yard. At that time those cakes seemed to me to be absolutely the most tempting and desirable things that I had every seen; and I then and there resolved that, if I ever got free, the height of my ambition would be reached if I could get to the point where I could secure and eat ginger-cakes in the way that I saw those ladies doing.

Of course as the war was prolonged the white people, in many cases, often found it difficult to secure food for themselves. I think the slaves felt the deprivation less than the whites, because the usual diet for the slaves was corn bread and pork, and these could be raised on the plantation; but coffee, tea, sugar, and other articles which the whites had been accustomed to use could not be raised on the plantation, and the conditions brought about by the war frequently made it impossible to secure these things. The whites were often in great straits. Parched corn was used for coffee, and a kind of black molasses was used instead of sugar. Many times nothing was used to sweeten the so-called tea and coffee.

The first pair of shoes that I recall wearing were wooden ones. They had rough leather on the top, but the bottoms, which were about an inch thick, were of wood. When I walked they made a fearful noise, and besides this they were very inconvenient, since there was no yielding to the natural pressure of the foot. In wearing them one presented an exceedingly awkward appearance. The most trying ordeal that I was forced to endure as a slave boy, however, was the wearing of a flax shirt. In the portion of Virginia where I lived it was common to use flax as part of the clothing for the slaves. That part of the flax from which our clothing was made was largely the refuse, which of course was the cheapest and roughest part. I can scarcely imagine any torture, except, perhaps, the pulling of a tooth, that is equal to that caused by putting on a new flax shirt for the first time. It is almost equal to the feeling that one would experience if he had a dozen or more chestnut burrs, or a hundred small pin-points, in contact with his flesh. Even to this day I can recall accurately the tortures that I underwent when putting on one of these garments. The fact that my flesh was soft and tender added to the pain. But I had no choice. I had to wear the flax shirt or none; and had it been left to me to choose, I should have chosen to wear no covering. In connection with the flax shirt, my brother John, who is several years older than I am, performed one of the most generous acts that I ever heard of one slave relative doing for another. On several occasions when I was being forced to wear a new flax shirt, he generously agreed to put it on in my stead and wear it for several days, till it was "broken in." Until I had grown to be quite a youth this single garment was all that I wore.

One may get the idea, from what I have said, that there was bitter feeling toward the white people on the part of my race, because of the fact that most of the white population was away fighting in a war which would result in keeping the Negro in slavery if the South was successful. In the case of the slaves on our place this was not true, and it was not true of any large portion of the slave population in the South where the Negro was treated with anything like decency. During the Civil War one of my young masters was killed, and two were severely wounded. I recall the feeling of sorrow which existed among the slaves when they heard of the death of "Mars' Billy." It was no sham sorrow, but real. Some of the slaves had nursed "Mars' Billy;" others had played with him when he was a child. "Mars' Billy" had begged for mercy in the case of others when the overseer or master was thrashing them. The sorrow in the slave quarter was only second to that in the "big house." When the two young masters were brought home wounded, the sympathy of the slaves was shown in many ways. They were just as anxious to assist in the nursing as the family relatives of the wounded. Some of the slaves would even beg for the privilege of sitting up at night to nurse their wounded masters. This tenderness and sympathy on the part of those held in bondage was a result of their kindly and generous nature. In order to defend and protect the women and children who were left on the plantations when the white males went to war, the slaves would have laid down their lives. The slave who was selected to sleep in the "big house" during the absence of the males was considered to have the place of honour. Any one attempting to harm "young Mistress" or "old Mistress" during the night would have had to cross the dead body of the slave to do so. I do not know how many have noticed it, but I think that it will be found to be true that there are few instances, either in slavery or freedom, in which a member of my race has been known to betray a specific trust.

As a rule, not only did the members of my race entertain no feelings of bitterness against the whites before and during the war, but there are many instances of Negroes tenderly caring for their former masters and mistresses who for some reason have become poor and dependent since the war. I know of instances where the former masters of slaves have for years been supplied with money by their former slaves to keep them from suffering. I have known of still other cases in which the former slaves have assisted in the education of the descendants of their former owners. I know of a case on a large plantation in the South in which a young white man, the son of the former owner of the estate, has become so reduced in purse and self-control by reason of drink that he is a pitiable creature; and yet, notwithstanding the poverty of the coloured people themselves on this plantation, they have for years supplied this young white man with the necessities of life. One sends him a little coffee or sugar, another a little meat, and so on. Nothing that the coloured people possess is too good for the son of "old Mars' Tom," who will perhaps never be permitted to suffer while any remain on the place who knew directly or indirectly of "old Mars' Tom."

I have said that there are few instances of a member of my race betraying a specific trust. One of the best illustrations of this which I know of is in the case of an ex-slave from Virginia whom I met not long ago in a little town in the state of Ohio. I found that this man had made a contract with his master, two or three years previous to the Emancipation Proclamation, to the effect that the slave was to be permitted to buy himself, by paying so much per year for his body; and while he was paying for himself, he was to be permitted to labour where and for whom he pleased. Finding that he could secure better wages in Ohio, he went there. When freedom came, he was still in debt to his master some three hundred dollars. Notwithstanding that the Emancipation Proclamation freed him from any obligation to this master, this black man walked the greater portion of the distance back to where his old master lived in Virginia, and placed the last dollar, with interest, in his hands. In talking to me about this, the man told me that he knew that he did not have to pay the debt, but that he had given his word to his master, and his word he had never broken. He felt that he could not enjoy his freedom till he had fulfilled his promise.

From some things that I have said one may get the idea that some of the slaves did not want freedom. This is not true. I have never seen one who did not want to be free, or one who would return to slavery.

I pity from the bottom of my heart any nation or body of people that is so unfortunate as to get entangled in the net of slavery. I have long since ceased to cherish any spirit of bitterness against the Southern white people on account of the enslavement of my race. No one section of our country was wholly responsible for its introduction, and, besides, it was recognized and protected for years by the General Government. Having once got its tentacles fastened on to the economic and social life of the Republic, it was no easy matter for the country to relieve itself of the institution. Then, when we rid ourselves of prejudice, or racial feeling, and look facts in the face, we must acknowledge that, notwithstanding the cruelty and moral wrong of slavery, the ten million Negroes inhabiting this country, who themselves or whose ancestors went through the school of American slavery, are in a stronger and more hopeful condition, materially, intellectually, morally, and religiously, than is true of an equal number of black people in any other portion of the globe. This is so to such an extent that Negroes in this country, who themselves or whose forefathers went through the school of slavery, are constantly returning to Africa as missionaries to enlighten those who remained in the fatherland. This I say, not to justify slavery – on the other hand, I condemn it as an institution, as we all know that in America it was established for selfish and financial reasons, and not from a missionary motive—but to call attention to a fact, and to show how Providence so often uses men and institutions to accomplish a purpose. When persons ask me in these days how, in the midst of what sometimes seem hopelessly discouraging conditions, I can have such faith in the future of my race in this country, I remind them of the wilderness through which and out of which, a good Providence has already led us.

Ever since I have been old enough to think for myself, I have entertained the idea that, notwithstanding the cruel wrongs inflicted upon us, the black man got nearly as much out of slavery as the white man did. The hurtful influences of the institution were not by any means confined to the Negro. This was fully illustrated by the life upon our own plantation. The whole machinery of slavery was so constructed as to cause labour, as a rule, to be looked upon as a badge of degradation, of inferiority. Hence labour was something that both races on the slave plantation sought to escape. The slave system on our place, in a large measure, took the spirit of self-reliance and self-help out of the white people. My old master had many boys and girls, but not one, so far as I know, ever mastered a single trade or special line of productive industry. The girls were not taught to cook, sew, or to take care of the house. All of this was left to the slaves. The slaves, of course, had little personal interest in the life of the plantation, and their ignorance prevented them from learning how to do things in the most improved and thorough manner. As a result of the system, fences were out of repair, gates were hanging half off the hinges, doors creaked, window-panes were out, plastering had fallen but was not replaced, weeds grew in the yard. As a rule, there was food for whites and blacks, but inside the house, and on the dining room table, there was wanting that delicacy and refinement of touch and finish which can make a home the most convenient, comfortable, and attractive place in the world. Withal there was a waste of food and other materials which was sad. When freedom came, the slaves were almost as well fitted to begin life anew as the master, except in the matter of book-learning and ownership of property. The slave owner and his sons had mastered no special industry. They unconsciously had imbibed the feeling that manual labour was not the proper thing for them. On the other hand, the slaves, in many cases, had mastered some handicraft, and none were ashamed, and few unwilling, to labour.

Finally the war closed, and the day of freedom came. It was a momentous and eventful day to all upon our plantation. We had been expecting it. Freedom was in the air, and had been for months. Deserting soldiers returning to their homes were to be seen every day. Others who had been discharged, or whose regiments had been paroled, were constantly passing near our place. The "grape-vine telegraph" was kept busy night and day. The news and mutterings of great events were swiftly carried from one plantation to another. In the fear of "Yankee" invasions, the silverware and other valuables were taken from the "big house," buried in the woods, and guarded by trusted slaves. Woe be to any one who would have attempted to disturb the buried treasure. The slaves would give the Yankee soldiers food, drink, clothing—anything but that which had been specifically intrusted to their care and honour. As the great day drew nearer, there was more singing in the slave quarters than usual. It was bolder, had more ring, and lasted later into the night. Most of the verses of the plantation songs had some reference to freedom. True, they had sung those same verses before, but they had been careful to explain that the "freedom" in these songs referred to the next world, and had no connection with life in this world. Now they gradually threw off the mask, and were not afraid to let it be known that the "freedom" in their songs meant freedom of the body in this world. The night before the eventful day, word was sent to the slave quarters to the effect that something unusual was going to take place at the "big house" the next morning. There was little, if any, sleep that night. All was excitement and expectancy. Early the next morning word was sent to all the slaves, old and young, to gather at the house. In company with my mother, brother, and sister, and a large number of other slaves, I went to the master's house. All of our master's family were either standing or seated on the veranda of the house, where they could see what was to take place and hear what was said. There was a feeling of deep interest, or perhaps sadness, on their faces, but not bitterness. As I now recall the impression they made upon me, they did not at the moment seem to be sad because of the loss of property, but rather because of parting with those whom they had reared and who were in many ways very close to them. The most distinct thing that I now recall in connection with the scene was that some man who seemed to be a stranger (a United States officer, I presume) made a little speech and then read a rather long paper—the Emancipation Proclamation, I think. After the reading we were told that we were all free, and could go when and where we pleased. My mother, who was standing by my side, leaned over and kissed her children, while tears of joy ran down her cheeks. She explained to us what it all meant, that this was the day for which she had been so long praying, but fearing that she would never live to see.

For some minutes there was great rejoicing, and thanksgiving, and wild scenes of ecstasy. But there was no feeling of bitterness. In fact, there was pity among the slaves for our former owners. The wild rejoicing on the part of the emancipated coloured people lasted but for a brief period, for I noticed that by the time they returned to their cabins there was a change in their feelings. The great responsibility of being free, of having charge of themselves, of having to think and plan for themselves and their children, seemed to take possession of them. It was very much like suddenly turning a youth of ten or twelve years out into the world to provide for himself. In a few hours the great questions with which the Anglo-Saxon race had been grappling for centuries had been thrown upon these people to be solved. These were the questions of a home, a living, the rearing of children, education, citizenship, and the establishment and support of churches. Was it any wonder that within a few hours the wild rejoicing ceased and a feeling of deep gloom seemed to pervade the slave quarters? To some it seemed that, now that they were in actual possession of it, freedom was a more serious thing than they had expected to find it. Some of the slaves were seventy or eighty years old; their best days were gone. They had no strength with which to earn a living in a strange place and among strange people, even if they had been sure where to find a new place of abode. To this class the problem seemed especially hard. Besides, deep down in their hearts there was a strange and peculiar attachment to "old Marster" and "old Missus," and to their children, which they found it hard to think of breaking off. With these they had spent in some cases nearly a half-century, and it was no light thing to think of parting. Gradually, one by one, stealthily at first, the older slaves began to wander from the slave quarters back to the "big house" to have a whispered conversation with their former owners as to the future.

CHAPTER II
BOYHOOD DAYS

After the coming of freedom there were two points upon which practically all the people on our place were agreed, and I find that this was generally true throughout the South: that they must change their names, and that they must leave the old plantation for at least a few days or weeks in order that they might really feel sure that they were free.

In some way a feeling got among the coloured people that it was far from proper for them to bear the surname of their former owners, and a great many of them took other surnames. This was one of the first signs of freedom. When they were slaves, a coloured person was simply called "John" or "Susan." There was seldom occasion for more than the use of the one name. If "John" or "Susan" belonged to a white man by the name of "Hatcher," sometimes he was called "John Hatcher," or as often "Hatcher's John." But there was a feeling that "John Hatcher" or "Hatcher's John" was not the proper title by which to denote a freeman; and so in many cases "John Hatcher" was changed to "John S. Lincoln" or "John S. Sherman," the initial "S" standing for no name, it being simply a part of what the coloured man proudly called his "entitles."

As I have stated, most of the coloured people left the old plantation for a short while at least, so as to be sure, it seemed, that they could leave and try their freedom on to see how it felt. After they had remained away for a time, many of the older slaves, especially, returned to their old homes and made some kind of contract with their former owners by which they remained on the estate.

My mother's husband, who was the stepfather of my brother John and myself, did not belong to the same owners as did my mother. In fact, he seldom came to our plantation. I remember seeing him there perhaps once a year, that being about Christmas time. In some way, during the war, by running away and following the Federal soldiers, it seems, he found his way into the new state of West Virginia. As soon as freedom was declared, he sent for my mother to come to the Kanawha Valley, in West Virginia. At that time a journey from Virginia over the mountains to West Virginia was rather a tedious and in some cases a painful undertaking. What little clothing and few household goods we had were placed in a cart, but the children walked the greater portion of the distance, which was several hundred miles.

I do not think any of us ever had been very far from the plantation, and the taking of a long journey into another state was quite an event. The parting from our former owners and the members of own race on the plantation was a serious occasion. From the time of our parting till their death we kept up a correspondence with the older members of the family, and in later years we have kept in touch with those who were the younger members. We were several weeks making the trip, and most of the time we slept in the open air and did our cooking over a log fire out-of-doors. One night I recall that we camped near an abandoned log cabin, and my mother decided to build a fire in that for cooking, and afterward to make a "pallet" on the floor for our sleeping. Just as the fire had gotten well started a large black snake fully a yard and a half long dropped down the chimney and ran out on the floor. Of course we at once abandoned that cabin. Finally we reached our destination—a little town called Malden, which is about five miles from Charleston, the present capital of the state.

At that time salt-mining was the great industry in that part of West Virginia, and the little town of Malden was right in the midst of the salt-furnaces. My stepfather had already secured a job at a salt-furnace, and he had also secured a little cabin for us to live in. Our new house was no better than the one we had left on the old plantation in Virginia. In fact, in one respect it was worse. Notwithstanding the poor condition of our

16

plantation cabin, we were at all times sure of pure air. Our new home was in the midst of a cluster of cabins crowded closely together, and as there were no sanitary regulations, the filth about the cabins was often intolerable. Some of our neighbours were coloured people, and some were the poorest and most ignorant and degraded white people. It was a motley mixture. Drinking, gambling, quarrels, fights, and shockingly immoral practices were frequent. All who lived in the little town were in one way or another connected with the salt business. Though I was a mere child, my stepfather put me and my brother at work in one of the furnaces. Often I began work as early as four o'clock in the morning.

The first thing I ever learned in the way of book knowledge was while working in this salt-furnace. Each salt-packer had his barrels marked with a certain number. The number allotted to my stepfather was "18." At the close of the day's work the boss of the packers would come around and put "18" on each of our barrels, and I soon learned to recognize that figure wherever I saw it, and after a while got to the point where I could make that figure, though I knew nothing about any other figures or letters.

From the time that I can remember having any thoughts about any-thing, I recall that I had an intense longing to learn to read. I determined, when quite a small child, that, if I accomplished nothing else in life, I would in some way get enough education to enable me to read common books and newspapers. Soon after we got settled in some manner in our new cabin in West Virginia, I induced my mother to get hold of a book for me. How or where she got it I do not know, but in some way she procured an old copy of Webster's "blue-back" spelling-book, which contained the alphabet, followed by such meaningless words as "ab," "ba," "ca," "da." I began at once to devour this book, and I think that it was the first one I ever had in my hands. I had learned from some-body that the way to begin to read was to learn the alphabet, so I tried in all the ways I could think of to learn it,—all of course without a teacher, for I could find no one to teach me. At that time there was not a single member of my race anywhere near us who could read, and I was too timid to approach any of the white people. In some way, within a few weeks, I mastered the greater portion of the alphabet. In all my efforts to learn to read my mother shared fully my ambition, and sympathized with me and aided me in every way that she could. Though she was totally ignorant, so far as mere book knowledge was concerned, she had high ambitions for her children, and a large fund of good, hard, common sense which seemed to enable her to meet and master every situation. If I have done anything in life worth attention, I feel sure that I inherited the disposition from my mother.

In the midst of my struggles and longing for an education, a young coloured boy who had learned to read in the state of Ohio came to Malden. As soon as the coloured people found out that he could read, a newspaper was secured, and at the close of nearly every day's work this young man would be surrounded by a group of men and women who were anxious to hear him read the news contained in the papers. How I used to envy this man! He seemed to me to be the one young man in all the world who ought to be satisfied with his attainments.

About this time the question of having some kind of a school opened for the coloured children in the village began to be discussed by members of the race. As it would be the first school for Negro children that had ever been opened in that part of Virginia, it was, of course, to be a great event, and the discussion excited the widest interest. The most perplexing question was where to find a teacher. The young man from Ohio who had learned to read the papers was considered, but his age was against him. In the midst of the discussion about a teacher, another young coloured man from Ohio, who had been a soldier, in some way found his way into town. It was soon learned that he possessed considerable education, and he was engaged by the coloured people to teach their first school. As yet no free schools had been started for coloured people in that section, hence each family agreed to pay a certain amount per month, with the understanding that the teacher was to "board 'round" – that is, spend a day with each family. This was not bad for the teacher, for each family tried to provide the very best on the day the teacher was to be its guest. I recall that I looked forward with an anxious appetite to the "teacher's day" at our little cabin.

This experience of a whole race beginning to go to school for the first time, presents one of the most interesting studies that has ever occurred in connection with the development of any race. Few people who were not right in the midst of the scenes can form any exact idea of the intense desire which the people of my race showed for an education. As I have stated, it was a whole race trying to go to school. Few were too young, and none too old, to make the attempt to learn. As fast as any kind of teachers could be secured, not only were day-schools filled, but night-schools as well. The great ambition of the older people was to try to learn to read the Bible before they died. With this end in view, men and women who were fifty or seventy-five years old would often be found in the night-school. Sunday-schools were formed soon after freedom, but the principal book studied in the Sunday-school was the spelling-book. Day-school, night-school, Sunday-school, were always crowded, and often many had to be turned away for want of room.

The opening of the school in the Kanawha Valley, however, brought to me one of the keenest disappointments that I ever experienced. I had been working in a salt-furnace for several months, and my stepfather had discovered that I had a financial value, and so, when the school opened, he decided that he could not spare me from my work. This decision seemed to cloud my every ambition. The disappointment was made all the more severe by reason of the fact that my place of work was where I could see the happy children passing to and from school, mornings and afternoons. Despite this disappointment, however, I determined that I would learn something, anyway. I applied myself with greater earnestness than ever to the mastering of what was in the "blue-back" speller.

My mother sympathized with me in my disappointment, and sought to comfort me in all the ways she could, and to help me find a way to learn. After a while I succeeded in making arrangements with the teacher to give me some lessons at night, after the day's work was done. These night lessons were so welcome that I think I learned more at night than the other children did during the day. My own experiences in the night-school gave me faith in the night-school idea, with which, in after years, I had to do both at Hampton and Tuskegee. But my boyish heart was still set upon going to the day-school, and I let no opportunity slip to push my case. Finally I won, and was permitted to go to the school in the day for a few months, with the understanding that I was to rise early in the morning and work in the furnace till nine o'clock, and return immediately after school closed in the afternoon for at least two more hours of work.

The schoolhouse was some distance from the furnace, and as I had to work till nine o'clock, and the school opened at nine, I found myself in a difficulty. School would always be begun before I reached it, and sometimes my class had recited. To get around this difficulty I yielded to a temptation for which most people, I suppose, will condemn me; but since it is a fact, I might as well state it. I have great faith in the power and influence of facts. It is seldom that anything is permanently gained by holding back a fact. There was a large clock in a little office in the furnace. This clock, of course, all the hundred or more workmen depended upon to regulate their hours of beginning and ending the day's work. I got the idea that the way for me to reach school on time was to move the clock hands from half-past eight up to the nine o'clock mark. This I found myself doing morning after morning, till the furnace "boss" discovered that something was wrong, and locked the clock in a case. I did not mean to inconvenience anybody. I simply meant to reach that schoolhouse in time.

When, however, I found myself at the school for the first time, I also found myself confronted with two other difficulties. In the first place, I found that all of the other children wore hats or caps on their heads, and I had neither hat nor cap. In fact, I do not remember that up to the time of going to school I had ever worn any kind of covering upon my head, nor do I recall that either I or anybody else had even thought anything about the need of covering for my head. But, of course, when I saw how all the other boys were dressed, I began to feel quite uncomfortable. As usual, I put the case before my mother, and she explained to me that she had no money with which to buy a "store hat," which was a rather new institution at that time among the members of my race and was considered quite the thing for young and old to own, but that she would find a way to help me out of the difficulty. She accordingly got two pieces of "homespun" (jeans) and sewed them together, and I was soon the proud possessor of my first cap.

The lesson that my mother taught me in this has always remained with me, and I have tried as best I could to teach it to others. I have always felt proud, whenever I think of the incident, that my mother had strength of character enough not to be led into the temptation of seeming to be that which she was not—of trying to impress my schoolmates and others with the fact that she was able to buy me a "store hat" when she was not. I have always felt proud that she refused to go into debt for that which she did not have the money to pay for. Since that time I have owned many kinds of caps and hats, but never one of which I have felt so proud as of the cap made of the two pieces of cloth sewed together by my mother. I have noted the fact, but without satisfaction, I need not add, that several of the boys who were my schoolmates and used to join in the sport that was made of me because I had only a "homespun" cap, have ended their careers in the penitentiary, while others are not able now to buy any kind of hat.

My second difficulty was with regard to my name, or rather *a* name. From the time when I could remember anything, I had been called simply "Booker." Before going to school it had never occurred to me that it was needful or appropriate to have an additional name. When I heard the school-roll called, I noticed that all of the children had at least two names, and some of them indulged in what seemed to me the extravagance of having three. I was in deep perplexity, because I knew that the teacher would demand of me at least two names, and I had only one. By the time the occasion came for the enrolling of my name, an idea occurred to me which I thought would make me equal to the situation; and so, when the teacher asked me what my full name was, I calmly told him "Booker Washington," as if I had been called by that name all my life; and by that name I have since been known. Later in my life I found that my mother had given me the name of "Booker Taliaferro" soon after I was born, but in some way that part of my name seemed to disappear and for a long while was forgotten, but as soon as

I found out about it I revived it, and made my full name "Booker Taliaferro Washington." I think there are not many men in our country who have had the privilege of naming themselves in the way that I have.

More than once I have tried to picture myself in the position of a boy or man with an honoured and distinguished ancestry which I could trace back through a period of hundreds of years, and who had not only inherited a name, but fortune and a proud family homestead; and yet I have sometimes had the feeling that if I had inherited these, and had been a member of a more popular race, I should have been inclined to yield to the temptation of depending upon my ancestry and my colour to do that for me which I should do for myself. Years ago I resolved that because I had no ancestry myself I would leave a record of which my children would be proud, and which might encourage them to still higher effort.

The world should not pass judgement upon the Negro, and especially the Negro youth, too quickly or too harshly. The Negro boy has obstacles, discouragements, and temptations to battle with that are little known to those not situated as he is. When a white boy undertakes a task, it is taken for granted that he will succeed. On the other hand, people are usually surprised if the Negro boy does not fail. In a word, the Negro youth starts out with the presumption against him.

The influence of ancestry, however, is important in helping forward any individual or race, if too much reliance is not placed upon it. Those who constantly direct attention to the Negro youth's moral weaknesses, and compare his advancement with that of white youths, do not consider the influence of the memories which cling about the old family homesteads. I have no idea, as I have stated elsewhere, who my grandmother was. I have, or have had, uncles and aunts and cousins, but I have no knowledge as to where most of them are. My case will illustrate that of hundreds of thousands of black people in every part of our country. The very fact that the white boy is conscious that, if he fails in life, he will disgrace the whole family record, extending back through many generations, is of tremendous value in helping him to resist temptations. The fact that the individual has behind and surrounding him proud family history and connection serves as a stimulus to help him to overcome obstacles when striving for success.

The time that I was permitted to attend school during the day was short, and my attendance was irregular. It was not long before I had to stop attending day-school altogether, and devote all of my time again to work. I resorted to the night-school again. In fact, the greater part of the education I secured in my boyhood was gathered through the night-school after my day's work was done. I had difficulty often in securing a satisfactory teacher. Sometimes, after I had secured some one to teach me at night, I would find, much to my disappointment, that the teacher knew but little more than I did. Often I would have to walk several miles at night in order to recite my night-school lessons. There was never a time in my youth, no matter how dark and discouraging the days might be, when one resolve did not continually remain with me, and that was a determination to secure an education at any cost.

Soon after we moved to West Virginia, my mother adopted into our family, notwithstanding our poverty, an orphan boy, to whom afterward we gave the name of James B. Washington. He has ever since remained a member of the family.

After I had worked in the salt-furnace for some time, work was secured for me in a coal-mine which was operated mainly for the purpose of securing fuel for the salt-furnace. Work in the coal-mine I always dreaded. One reason for this was that any one who worked in a coal-mine was always unclean, at least while at work, and it was a very hard job to get one's skin clean after the day's work was over. Then it was fully a mile from the opening of the coal-mine to the face of the coal, and all, of course, was in the blackest darkness. I do not believe that one ever experiences anywhere else such darkness as he does in a coal-mine. The mine was divided into a large number of different "rooms" or departments, and, as I never was able to learn the location of all these "rooms," I many times found myself lost in the mine. To add to the horror of being lost, sometimes my light would go out, and then, if I did not happen to have a match, I would wander about in the darkness until by chance I found some one to give me a light. The work was not only hard, but it was dangerous. There was always the danger of being blown to pieces by a premature explosion of powder, or of being crushed by falling slate. Accidents from one or the other of these causes were frequently occurring, and this kept me in constant fear. Many children of the tenderest years were compelled then, as is now true, I fear, in most coal-mining districts, to spend a large part of their lives in these coal-mines, with little opportunity to get an education; and, what is worse, I have often noted that, as a rule, young boys who begin life in a coal-mine are often physically and mentally dwarfed. They soon lose ambition to do anything else than to continue as a coal-miner.

In those days, and later as a young man, I used to try to picture in my imagination the feelings and ambitions of a white boy with absolutely no limit placed upon his aspirations and activities. I used to envy the white boy who had no obstacles placed in the way of his becoming a Congress-man, Governor, Bishop, or President by reason of the accident of his birth or race. I used to picture the way that I would act under such circumstances; how I would begin at the bottom and keep rising until I reached the highest round of success.

In later years, I confess that I do not envy the white boy as I once did. I have learned that success is to be measured not so much by the position that one has reached in life as by the obstacles which he has overcome while trying to succeed. Looked at from this standpoint, I almost reach the conclusion that often the Negro boy's birth and connection with an unpopular race is an advantage, so far as real life is concerned. With few exceptions, the Negro youth must work harder and must perform his tasks even better than a white youth in order to secure recognition. But out of the hard and unusual struggle through which he is compelled to pass, he gets a strength, a confidence, that one misses whose pathway is comparatively smooth by reason of birth and race.

From any point of view, I had rather be what I am, a member of the Negro race, than be able to claim membership with the most favoured of any other race. I have always been made sad when I have heard members of any race claiming rights and privileges, or certain badges of distinction, on the ground simply that they were members of this or that race, regardless of their own individual worth or attainments. I have been made to feel sad for such persons because I am conscious of the fact that mere connection with what is known as a superior race will not permanently carry an individual forward unless he has individual worth, and mere connection with what is regarded as an inferior race will not finally hold an individual back if he possesses intrinsic, individual merit. Every persecuted individual and race should get much consolation out of the great human law, which is universal and eternal, that merit, no matter under what skin found, is, in the long run, recognized and rewarded. This I have said here, not to call attention to myself as an individual, but to the race to which I am proud to belong.

CHAPTER III
THE STRUGGLE FOR AN EDUCATION

One day, while at work in the coal-mine, I happened to overhear two miners talking about a great school for coloured people somewhere in Virginia. This was the first time that I had ever heard anything about any kind of school or college that was more pretentious than the little coloured school in our town.

In the darkness of the mine I noiselessly crept as close as I could to the two men who were talking. I heard one tell the other that not only was the school established for the members of my race, but that opportunities were provided by which poor but worthy students could work out all or a part of the cost of board, and at the same time be taught some trade or industry.

As they went on describing the school, it seemed to me that it must be the greatest place on earth, and not even Heaven presented more attractions for me at that time than did the Hampton Normal and Agricultural Institute in Virginia, about which these men were talking. I resolved at once to go to that school, although I had no idea where it was, or how many miles away, or how I was going to reach it; I remembered only that I was on fire constantly with one ambition, and that was to go to Hampton. This thought was with me day and night.

After hearing of the Hampton Institute, I continued to work for a few months longer in the coal-mine. While at work there, I heard of a vacant position in the household of General Lewis Ruffner, the owner of the salt-furnace and coal-mine. Mrs. Viola Ruffner, the wife of General Ruffner, was a "Yankee" woman from Vermont. Mrs. Ruffner had a reputation all through the vicinity for being very strict with her servants, and especially with the boys who tried to serve her. Few of them had remained with her more than two or three weeks. They all left with the same excuse: she was too strict. I decided, however, that I would rather try Mrs. Ruffner's house than remain in the coal-mine, and so my mother applied to her for the vacant position. I was hired at a salary of $5 per month.

I had heard so much about Mrs. Ruffner's severity that I was almost afraid to see her, and trembled when I went into her presence. I had not lived with her many weeks, however, before I began to understand her. I soon began to learn that, first of all, she wanted everything kept clean about her, that she wanted things done promptly and systematically, and that at the bottom of everything she wanted absolute honesty and frankness. Nothing must be sloven or slipshod; every door, every fence, must be kept in repair.

I cannot now recall how long I lived with Mrs. Ruffner before going to Hampton, but I think it must have been a year and a half. At any rate, I here repeat what I have said more than once before, that the lessons that I learned in the home of Mrs. Ruffner were as valuable to me as any education I have ever gotten anywhere since. Even to this day I never see bits of paper scattered around a house or in the street that I do not want to pick them up at once. I never see a filthy yard that I do not want to clean it, a paling off of a fence that I do not want to put it on, an unpainted or unwhitewashed house that I do not want to paint or whitewash it, or a button off one's clothes, or a grease-spot on them or on a floor, that I do not want to call attention to it.

From fearing Mrs. Ruffner I soon learned to look upon her as one of my best friends. When she found that she could trust me she did so implicitly. During the one or two winters that I was with her she gave me an opportunity to go to school for an hour in the day during a portion of the winter months, but most of my studying was done at night, sometimes alone, sometimes under some one whom I could hire to teach me. Mrs. Ruffner always encouraged and sympathized with me in all my efforts to get an education. It was while living with her that I began to get together my first library. I secured a dry-goods box, knocked out one side of it, put some shelves in it, and began putting into it every kind of book that I could get my hands upon, and called it my "library."

Notwithstanding my success at Mrs. Ruffner's I did not give up the idea of going to the Hampton Institute. In the fall of 1872 I determined to make an effort to get there, although, as I have stated, I had no definite idea of the direction in which Hampton was, or of what it would cost to go there. I do not think that any one thoroughly sympathized with me in my ambition to go to Hampton unless it was my mother, and she was troubled with a grave fear that I was starting out on a "wild-goose chase." At any rate, I got only a half-hearted consent from her that I might start. The small amount of money that I had earned had been consumed by my stepfather and the remainder of the family, with the exception of a very few dollars, and so I had very little with which to buy clothes and pay my travelling expenses. My brother John helped me all that he could, but of course that was not a great deal, for his work was in the coal-mine, where he did not earn much, and most of what he did earn went in the direction of paying the household expenses.

Perhaps the thing that touched and pleased me most in connection with my starting for Hampton was the interest that many of the older coloured people took in the matter. They had spent the best days of their lives in slavery, and hardly expected to live to see the time when they would see a member of their race leave home to attend a boarding-school. Some of these older people would give me a nickel, others a quarter, or a handkerchief.

Finally the great day came, and I started for Hampton. I had only a small, cheap satchel that contained what few articles of clothing I could get. My mother at the time was rather weak and broken in health. I hardly expected to see her again, and thus our parting was all the more sad. She, however, was very brave through it all. At that time there were no through trains connecting that part of West Virginia with   eastern Virginia. Trains ran only a portion of the way, and the remainder of the distance was travelled by stage-coaches.

The distance from Malden to Hampton is about five hundred miles.

I had not been away from home many hours before it began to grow painfully evident that I did not have enough money to pay my fare to Hampton. One experience I shall long remember. I had been travelling over the mountains most of the afternoon in an old-fashioned stage-coach, when, late in the evening, the coach stopped for the night at a common, unpainted house called a hotel. All the other passengers except myself were whites. In my ignorance I supposed that the little hotel existed for the purpose of accommodating the passengers who travelled on the stage-coach. The difference that the colour of one's skin would make I had not thought anything about. After all the other passengers had been shown rooms and were getting ready for supper, I shyly presented myself before the man at the desk. It is true I had prac-tically no money in my pocket with which to pay for bed or food, but I had hoped in some way to beg my way into the good graces of the landlord, for at that season in the mountains of Virginia the weather was cold, and I wanted to get indoors for the night. Without asking as to whether I had any money, the man at the desk firmly refused to even consider the matter of providing me with food or lodging. This was my first experience in finding out what the colour of my skin meant. In some way I managed to keep warm by walking about, and so got through the night. My whole soul was so bent upon reaching Hampton that I did not have time to cherish any bitterness toward the hotel-keeper.

By walking, begging rides both in wagons and in the cars, in some way, after a number of days, I reached the city or Richmond, Virginia, about eight-two miles from Hampton. When I reached there, tired, hungry, and dirty, it was late in the night. I had never been in a large city, and this rather added to my misery. When I reached Richmond, I was completely out of money. I had not a single acquaintance in the place, and, being unused to city ways, I did not know where to go. I applied at several places for lodging, but they all wanted money, and that was what I did not have. Knowing nothing else better to do, I walked the streets. In doing this I passed by many food stands where fried chicken and half-moon apple pies were piled high and made to present a most tempting appearance. At that time it seemed to me that

I would have promised all that I expected to possess in the future to have gotten hold of one of those chicken legs or one of those pies. But I could not get either of these, nor anything else to eat.

I must have walked the streets till after midnight. At last I became so exhausted that I could walk no longer. I was tired, I was hungry, I was everything but discouraged. Just about the time when I reached extreme physical exhaustion, I came upon a portion of a street where the board sidewalk was considerably elevated. I waited for a few minutes, till I was sure that no passers-by could see me, and then crept under the sidewalk and lay for the night upon the ground, with my satchel of clothing for a pillow. Nearly all night I could hear the tramp of feet over my head. The next morning I found myself somewhat refreshed, but I was extremely hungry, because it had been a long time since I had had sufficient food. As soon as it became light enough for me to see my surroundings I noticed that I was near a large ship, and that this ship seemed to be unloading a cargo of pig iron. I went at once to the vessel and asked the captain to permit me to help unload the vessel in order to get money for food. The captain, a white man, who seemed to be kind-hearted, consented. I worked long enough to earn money for my breakfast, and it seems to me, as I remember it now, to have been about the best breakfast that I have ever eaten.

My work pleased the captain so well that he told me if I desired I could continue working for a small amount per day. This I was very glad to do. I continued working on this vessel for a number of days. After buying food with the small wages I received there was not much left to add to the amount I must get to pay my way to Hampton. In order to economize in every way possible, so as to be sure to reach Hampton in a reasonable time, I continued to sleep under the same sidewalk that gave me shelter the first night I was in Richmond. Many years after that the coloured citizens of Richmond very kindly tendered me a reception at which there must have been two thousand people present. This reception was held not far from the spot where I slept the first night I spent in that city, and I must confess that my mind was more upon the sidewalk that first gave me shelter than upon the reception, agreeable and cordial as it was.

THE STRUGGLE FOR AN EDUCATION

When I had saved what I considered enough money with which to reach Hampton, I thanked the captain of the vessel for his kindness, and started again. Without any unusual occurrence I reached Hampton, with a surplus of exactly fifty cents with which to begin my education. To me it had been a long, eventful journey; but the first sight of the large, three-story, brick school building seemed to have rewarded me for all that I had undergone in order to reach the place. If the people who gave the money to provide that building could appreciate the influence the sight of it had upon me, as well as upon thousands of other youths, they would feel all the more encouraged to make such gifts. It seemed to me to be the largest and most beautiful building I had ever seen. The sight of it seemed to give me new life. I felt that a new kind of existence had now begun – that life would now have a new meaning. I felt that I had reached the promised land, and I resolved to let no obstacle prevent me from putting forth the highest effort to fit myself to accomplish the most good in the world.

As soon as possible after reaching the grounds of the Hampton Institute, I presented myself before the head teacher for assignment to a class. Having been so long without proper food, a bath, and change of clothing, I did not, of course, make a very favourable impression upon her, and I could see at once that there were doubts in her mind about the wisdom of admitting me as a student. I felt that I could hardly blame her if she got the idea that I was a worthless loafer or tramp. For some time she did not refuse to admit me, neither did she decide in my favour, and I continued to linger about her, and to impress her in all the ways I could with my worthiness. In the meantime I saw her admitting other students, and that added greatly to my discomfort, for I felt, deep down in my heart, that I could do as well as they, if I could only get a chance to show what was in me.

After some hours had passed, the head teacher said to me: "The adjoining recitation-room needs sweeping. Take the broom and sweep it."

It occurred to me at once that here was my chance. Never did I receive an order with more delight. I knew that I could sweep, for Mrs. Ruffner had thoroughly taught me how to do that when I lived with her.

I swept the recitation-room three times. Then I got a dusting-cloth and I dusted it four times. All the woodwork around the walls, every bench, table, and desk, I went over four times with my dusting-cloth. Besides, every piece of furniture had been moved and every closet and corner in the room had been thoroughly cleaned. I had the feeling that in a large measure my future depended upon the impression I made upon the teacher in the cleaning of that room. When I was through, I reported to the head teacher. She was a "Yankee" woman who knew just where to look for dirt. She went into the room and inspected the floor and closets; then she took her handkerchief and rubbed it on the woodwork about the walls, and over the table and benches. When she was unable to find one bit of dirt on the floor, or a particle of dust on any of the furniture, she quietly remarked, "I guess you will do to enter this institution."

I was one of the happiest souls on earth. The sweeping of that room was my college examination, and never did any youth pass an examination for entrance into Harvard or Yale that gave him more genuine satisfaction. I have passed several examinations since then, but I have always felt that this was the best one I ever passed.

I have spoken of my own experience in entering the Hampton Institute. Perhaps few, if any, had anything like the same experience that I had, but about that same period there were hundreds who found their way to Hampton and other institutions after experiencing something of the same difficulties that I went through. The young men and women were determined to secure an education at any cost.

The sweeping of the recitation-room in the manner that I did it seems to have paved the way for me to get through Hampton. Miss Mary F. Mackie, the head teacher, offered me a position as janitor. This, of course, I gladly accepted, because it was a place where I could work out nearly all the cost of my board. The work was hard and taxing, but I stuck to it. I had a large number of rooms to care for, and had to work late into the night, while at the same time I had to rise by four o'clock in the morning, in order to build the fires and have a little time in which to prepare my lessons. In all my career at Hampton, and ever since I have been out in the world, Miss Mary F. Mackie, the head teacher to whom I have referred, proved one of my strongest and most helpful friends. Her advice and encouragement were always helpful and strengthening to me in the darkest hour.

I have spoken of the impression that was made upon me by the buildings and general appearance of the Hampton Institute, but I have not spoken of that which made the greatest and most lasting impression upon me, and that was a great man—the noblest, rarest human being that it has ever been my privilege to meet. I refer to the late General Samuel C. Armstrong.

It has been my fortune to meet personally many of what are called great characters, both in Europe and America, but I do not hesitate to say that I never met any man who, in my estimation, was the equal of General Armstrong. Fresh from the degrading influences of the slave plantation and the coal-mines, it was a rare privilege for me to be permitted to come into direct contact with such a character as General Armstrong. I shall always remember that the first time I went into his presence he made the impression upon me of being a perfect man; I was made to feel that there was something about him that was superhuman. It was my privilege to know the General personally from the time I entered Hampton till he died, and the more I saw of him the greater he grew in my estimation. One might have removed from Hampton all the buildings, class-rooms, teachers, and industries, and given the men and women there the opportunity of coming into daily contact with General Armstrong, and that alone would have been a liberal education. The older I grow, the more I am convinced that there is no education which one can get from books and costly apparatus that is equal to that which can be gotten from contact with great men and women. Instead of studying books so constantly, how I wish that our schools and colleges might learn to study men and things!

General Armstrong spent two of the last six months of his life in my home at Tuskegee. At that time he was paralyzed to the extent that he had lost control of his body and voice in a very large degree. Notwithstanding his affliction, he worked almost constantly night and day for the cause to which he had given his life. I never saw a man who so completely lost sight of himself. I do not believe he ever had a selfish thought. He was just as happy in trying to assist some other institution in the South as he was when working for Hampton. Although he fought the Southern white man in the Civil War, I never heard him utter a bitter word against him afterward. On the other hand, he was constantly seeking to find ways by which he could be of service to the Southern whites.

It would be difficult to describe the hold that he had upon the students at Hampton, or the faith they had in him. In fact, he was worshipped by his students. It never occurred to me that General Armstrong could fail in anything that he undertook. There is almost no request that he could have made that would not have been complied with. When he was a guest at my home in Alabama, and was so badly paralyzed that he had to be wheeled about in an invalid's chair, I recall that one of the General's former students had occasion to push his chair up a long, steep hill that taxed his strength to the utmost. When the top of the hill was reached, the former pupil, with a glow of happiness on his face, exclaimed, "I am so glad that I have been permitted to do something that was real hard for the General before he dies!" While I was a student at Hampton, the dormitories became so crowded that it was impossible to find room for all who wanted to be admitted. In order to help remedy the difficulty, the General conceived the plan of putting up tents to be used as rooms. As soon as it became known that General Armstrong would be pleased if some of the older students would live in the tents during the winter, nearly every student in school volunteered to go.

I was one of the volunteers. The winter that we spent in those tents was an intensely cold one, and we suffered severely—how much I am sure General Armstrong never knew, because we made no complaints. It was enough for us to know that we were pleasing General Armstrong, and that we were making it possible for an additional number of students to secure an education. More than once, during a cold night, when a stiff gale would be blowing, our tent was lifted bodily, and we would find ourselves in the open air. The General would usually pay a visit to the tents early in the morning, and his earnest, cheerful, encouraging voice would dispel any feeling of despondency.

I have spoken of my admiration for General Armstrong, and yet he was but a type of that Christlike body of men and women who went into the Negro schools at the close of the war by the hundreds to assist in lifting up my race. The history of the world fails to show a higher, purer, and more unselfish class of men and women than those who found their way into those Negro schools.

Life at Hampton was a constant revelation to me; was constantly taking me into a new world. The matter of having meals at regular hours, of eating on a tablecloth, using a napkin, the use of the bathtub and of the tooth-brush, as well as the use of sheets upon the bed, were all new to me.

I sometimes feel that almost the most valuable lesson I got at the Hampton Institute was in the use and value of the bath. I learned there for the first time some of its value, not only in keeping the body healthy, but in inspiring self-respect and promoting virtue. In all my travels in the South and elsewhere since leaving Hampton I have always in some way sought my daily bath. To get it sometimes when I have been the guest of my own people in a single-roomed cabin has not always been easy to do, except by slipping away to some stream in the woods. I have always tried to teach my people that some provision for bathing should be a part of every house.

For some time, while a student at Hampton, I possessed but a single pair of socks, but when I had worn these till they became soiled, I would wash them at night and hang them by the fire to dry, so that I might wear them again the next morning.

The charge for my board at Hampton was ten dollars per month. I was expected to pay a part of this in cash and to work out the remainder. To meet this cash payment, as I have stated, I had just fifty cents when I reached the institution. Aside from a very few dollars that my brother John was able to send me once in a while, I had no money with which to pay my board. I was determined from the first to make my work as janitor so valuable that my services would be indispensable. This I succeeded in doing to such an extent that I was soon informed that I would be allowed the full cost of my board in return for my work. The cost of tuition was seventy dollars a year. This, of course, was wholly beyond my ability to provide. If I had been compelled to pay the seventy dollars for tuition, in addition to providing for my board, I would have been compelled to leave the Hampton school. General Armstrong, however, very kindly got Mr. S. Griffitts Morgan, of New Bedford, Mass., to defray the cost of my tuition during the whole time that I was at Hampton. After I finished the course at Hampton and had entered upon my lifework at Tuskegee, I had the pleasure of visiting Mr. Morgan several times.

After having been for a while at Hampton, I found myself in difficulty because I did not have books and clothing. Usually, however, I got around the trouble about books by borrowing from those who were more fortunate than myself. As to clothes, when I reached Hampton I had practically nothing. Everything that I possessed was in a small hand satchel. My anxiety about clothing was increased because of the fact that General Armstrong made a personal inspection of the young men in ranks, to see that their clothes were clean. Shoes had to be polished, there must be no buttons off the clothing, and no grease-spots. To wear one suit of clothes continually, while at work and in the schoolroom, and at the same time keep it clean, was rather a hard problem for me to solve. In some way I managed to get on till the teachers learned that I was in earnest and meant to succeed, and then some of them were kind enough to see that I was partly supplied with second-hand clothing that had been sent in barrels from the North. These barrels proved a blessing to hundreds of poor but deserving students. Without them I question whether I should ever have gotten through Hampton.

When I first went to Hampton I do not recall that I had ever slept in a bed that had two sheets on it. In those days there were not many buildings there, and room was very precious. There were seven other boys in the same room with me; most of them, however, students who had been there for some time. The sheets were quite a puzzle to me. The first night I slept under both of them, and the second night I slept on top of both of them; but by watching the other boys I learned my lesson in this, and have been trying to follow it ever since and to teach it to others.

I was among the youngest of the students who were in Hampton at that time. Most of the students were men and women—some as old as forty years of age. As I now recall the scene of my first year, I do not believe that one often has the opportunity of coming into contact with the world to teach them the need of education. Many of the older ones were, of course, too old to master the text-books very thoroughly, and it was often sad to watch their struggles; but they made up in earnestness much of what they lacked in books. Many of them were as poor as I was, and, besides having to wrestle with their books, they had to struggle with a poverty which prevented their having the necessities of life. Many of them had aged parents who were dependent upon them, and some of them were men who had wives whose support in some way they had to provide for.

The great and prevailing idea that seemed to take possession of every one was to prepare himself to lift up the people at his home. No one seemed to think of himself. And the officers and teachers, what a rare set of human beings they were! They worked for the students night and day, in season and out of season. They seemed happy only when they were helping the students in some manner. Whenever it is written— and I hope it will be—the part that the Yankee teachers played in the education of the Negroes immediately after the war will make one of the most thrilling parts of the history of this country. The time is not far distant when the whole South will appreciate this service in a way that it has not yet been able to do.

CHAPTER IV
HELPING OTHERS

At the end of my first year at Hampton I was confronted with another difficulty. Most of the students went home to spend their vacation. I had no money with which to go home, but I had to go somewhere. In those days very few students were permitted to remain at the school during vacation. It made me feel very sad and homesick to see the other students preparing to leave and starting for home. I not only had no money with which to go home, but I had none with which to go anywhere.

In some way, however, I had gotten hold of an extra, second-hand coat which I thought was a pretty valuable coat. This I decided to sell, in order to get a little money for travelling expenses. I had a good deal of boyish pride, and I tried to hide, as far as I could, from the other students the fact that I had no money and nowhere to go. I made it known to a few people in the town of Hampton that I had this coat to sell, and, after a good deal of persuading, one coloured man promised to come to my room to look the coat over and consider the matter of buying it. This cheered my drooping spirits considerably. Early the next morning my prospective customer appeared. After looking the garment over carefully, he asked me how much I wanted for it. I told him I though it was worth three dollars. He seemed to agree with me as to price, but remarked in the most matter-of-fact way: "I tell you what I will do; I will take the coat, and I will pay you five cents, cash down, and pay you the rest of the money just as soon as I can get it." It is not hard to imagine what my feelings were at the time.

With this disappointment I gave up all hope of getting out of the town of Hampton for my vacation work. I wanted very much to go where I might secure work that would at least pay me enough to purchase some much-needed clothing and other necessities. In a few days practically all the students and teachers had left for their homes, and this served to depress my spirits even more.

After trying for several days in and near the town of Hampton, I finally secured work in a restaurant at Fortress Monroe. The wages, however, were very little more than my board. At night, and between meals, I found considerable time for study and reading; and in this direction I improved myself very much during the summer.

When I left school at the end of my first year, I owed the institution sixteen dollars that I had not been able to work out. It was my greatest ambition during the summer to save money enough with which to pay this debt. I felt that this was a debt of honour, and that I could hardly bring myself to the point of even trying to enter school again till it was paid. I economized in every way that I could think of—did my own washing, and went without necessary garments—but still I found my summer vacation ending and I did not have the sixteen dollars.

One day, during the last week of my stay in the restaurant, I found under one of the tables a crisp, new ten-dollar bill. I could hardly contain myself, I was so happy. As it was not my place of business I felt it to be the proper thing to show the money to the proprietor. This I did. He seemed as glad as I was, but he coolly explained to me that, as it was his place of business, he had a right to keep the money, and he proceeded to do so. This I confess, was another pretty hard blow to me. I will not say that I became discouraged, for as I now look back over my life I do not recall that I ever became discouraged over anything that I set out to accomplish. I have begun everything with the idea that I could succeed, and I never had much patience with the multitudes of people who are always ready to explain why one cannot succeed. I have always had a high regard for the man who could tell me how to succeed. I determined to face the situation just as it was. At the end of the week I went to the treasurer of the Hampton Institute, General J. F. B. Marshall, and told him frankly my condition. To my gratification he told me that

I could reenter the institution, and that he would trust me to pay the debt when I could. During the second year I continued to work as a janitor.

The education that I received at Hampton out of the text-books was but a small part of what I learned there. One of the things that impressed itself upon me deeply, the second year, was the unselfishness of the teachers. It was hard for me to understand how any individuals could bring themselves to the point where they could be so happy in working for others. Before the end of the year, I think I began learning that those who are happiest are those who do the most for others. This lesson I have tried to carry with me ever since.

I also learned a valuable lesson at Hampton by coming into contact with the best breeds of live stock and fowls. No student, I think, who has had the opportunity of doing this could go out into the world and content himself with the poorest grades.

Perhaps the most valuable thing that I got out of my second year was an understanding of the use and value of the Bible. Miss Nathalie Lord, one of the teachers, from Portland, Me., taught me how to use and love the Bible. Before this I had never cared a great deal about it, but now I learned to love to read the Bible, not only for the spiritual help which it gives, but on account of it as literature. The lessons taught me in this respect took such a hold upon me that at the present time, when I am at home, no matter how busy I am, I always make it a rule to read a chapter or a portion of a chapter in the morning, before beginning the work of the day.

Whatever ability I may have as a public speaker I owe in a measure to Miss Lord. When she found out that I had some inclination in this direction, she gave me private lessons in the matter of breathing, emphasis, and articulation. Simply to be able to talk in public for the sake of talking has never had the least attraction for me. In fact, I consider that there is nothing so empty and unsatisfactory as mere abstract public speaking; but from my early childhood I have had a desire to do something to make the world better, and then to be able to speak to the world about that thing.

The debating societies at Hampton were a constant source of

delight to me. These were held on Saturday evening; and during my whole life at Hampton I do not recall that I missed a single meeting. I not only attended the weekly debating society, but was instrumental in organizing an additional society. I noticed that between the time when supper was over and the time to begin evening study there were about twenty minutes which the young men usually spent in idle gossip. About twenty of us formed a society for the purpose of utilizing this time in debate or in practice in public speaking. Few persons ever derived more happiness or benefit from the use of twenty minutes of time than we did in this way.

At the end of my second year at Hampton, by the help of some money sent me by my mother and brother John, supplemented by a small gift from one of the teachers at Hampton, I was enabled to return to my home in Malden, West Virginia, to spend my vacation. When I reached home I found that the salt-furnaces were not running, and that the coal-mine was not being operated on account of the miners being out on a "strike." This was something which, it seemed, usually occurred whenever the men got two or three months ahead in their savings. During the strike, of course, they spent all that they had saved, and would often return to work in debt at the same wages, or would move to another mine at considerable expense. In either case, my observations convinced me that the miners were worse off at the end of a strike. Before the days of strikes in that section of the country, I knew miners who had considerable money in the bank, but as soon as the professional labour agitators got control, the savings of even the more thrifty ones began disappearing.

My mother and the other members of the family were, of course, much rejoiced to see me and to note the improvement that I had made during my two years' absence. The rejoicing on the part of all classes of the coloured people, and especially the older ones, over my return, was almost pathetic. I had to pay a visit to each family and take a meal with each, and at each place tell the story of my experiences at Hampton. In addition to this I had to speak before the church and Sunday-school, and at various other places. The thing that I was most in search of, though, work, I could not find. There was no work on account of the strike. I spent nearly the whole of the first month of my vacation in an effort to find something to do by which I could earn money to pay my way back to Hampton and save a little money to use after there.

Toward the end of the first month, I went to a place a considerable distance from my home, to try to find employment. I did not succeed, and it was night before I got started on my return. When I had gotten within a mile or so of my home I was so completely tired out that I could not walk any farther, and I went into an old, abandoned house to spend the remainder of the night. About three o'clock in the morning my brother John found me asleep in this house, and broke to me, as gently as he could, the sad news that our dear mother had died during the night.

This seemed to me the saddest and blankest moment in my life. For several years my mother had not been in good health, but I had no idea, when I parted from her the previous day, that I should never see her alive again. Besides that, I had always had an intense desire to be with her when she did pass away. One of the chief ambitions which spurred me on at Hampton was that I might be able to get to be in a position in which I could better make my mother comfortable and happy. She had so often expressed the wish that she might be permitted to live to see her children educated and started out into the world.

In a very short time after the death of my mother our little home was in confusion. My sister Amanda, although she tried to do the best she could, was too young to know anything about keeping house, and my stepfather was not able to hire a housekeeper. Sometimes we had food cooked for us, and sometimes we did not. I remember that more than once a can of tomatoes and some crackers constituted a meal. Our clothing went uncared for, and everything about our home was soon in a tumble-down condition. It seems to me that this was the most dismal period of my life.

My good friend Mrs. Ruffner, to whom I have already referred, always made me welcome at their home, and assisted me in many ways during this trying period. Before the end of the vacation she gave me some work, and this, together with work in a coal-mine at some distance from my home, enabled me to earn a little money.

At one time it looked as if I would have to give up the idea of returning to Hampton, but my heart was so set on returning that I determined not to give up going back without a struggle. I was very anxious to secure some clothes for the winter, but in this I was disappointed, except for a few garments which my brother John secured for me. Notwithstanding my need of money and clothing, I was very happy in the fact that I had secured enough money to pay my travelling expenses back to Hampton. Once there, I knew that I could make myself so useful as a janitor that I could in some way get through the school year.

Three weeks before the time for the opening of the term at Hampton, I was pleasantly surprised to receive a letter from my good friend Miss Mary F. Mackie, the lady principal, asking me to return to Hampton two weeks before the opening of the school, in order that I might assist her in cleaning the buildings and getting things in order for the new school year. This was just the opportunity I wanted. It gave me a chance to secure a credit in the treasurer's office. I started for Hampton at once.

During these two weeks I was taught a lesson which I shall never forget. Miss Mackie was a member of one of the oldest and most cultured families of the North, and yet for two weeks she worked by my side cleaning windows, dusting rooms, putting beds in order, and what not. She felt that things would not be in condition for the opening of school unless every window-pane was perfectly clean, and she took the greatest satisfaction in helping to clean them herself. The work which I have described she did every year that I was at Hampton.

It was hard for me at this time to understand how a woman of her education and social standing could take such delight in performing such service, in order to assist in the elevation of an unfortunate race. Ever since then I have had no patience with any school for my race in the South which did not teach its students the dignity of labour.

During my last year at Hampton every minute of my time that was not occupied with my duties as janitor was devoted to hard study. I was determined, if possible, to make such a record in my class as would cause me to be placed on the "honour roll" of commencement speakers. This I was successful in doing. It was June of 1875 when I finished the regular course of study at Hampton. The greatest benefits that I got out of my life at the Hampton Institute, perhaps, may be classified under two heads:

First was contact with a great man, General S. C. Armstrong, who, I repeat, was, in my opinion, the rarest, strongest, and most beautiful character that it has ever been my privilege to meet.

Second, at Hampton, for the first time, I learned what education was expected to do for an individual. Before going there I had a good deal of the then rather prevalent idea among our people that to secure an education meant to have a good, easy time, free from all necessity for manual labour. At Hampton I not only learned that it was not a disgrace to labour, but learned to love labour, not alone for its financial value, but for labour's own sake and for the independence and self-reliance which the ability to do something which the world wants done brings. At that institution I got my first taste of what it meant to live a life of unselfishness, my first knowledge of the fact that the happiest individuals are those who do the most to make others useful and happy.

I was completely out of money when I graduated. In company with other Hampton students, I secured a place as a table waiter in a summer hotel in Connecticut, and managed to borrow enough money with which to get there. I had not been in this hotel long before I found out that I knew practically nothing about waiting on a hotel table. The head waiter, however, supposed that I was an accomplished waiter. He soon gave me charge of a table at which there sat four or five wealthy and rather aristocratic people. My ignorance of how to wait upon them was so apparent that they scolded me in such a severe manner that I became frightened and left their table, leaving them sitting there without food. As a result of this I was reduced from the position of waiter to that of a dish-carrier.

But I determined to learn the business of waiting, and did so within a few weeks and was restored to my former position. I have had the satisfaction of being a guest in this hotel several times since I was a waiter there.

At the close of the hotel season I returned to my former home in

Malden, and was elected to teach the coloured school at that place. This was the beginning of one of the happiest periods of my life. I now felt that I had the opportunity to help the people of my home town to a higher life. I felt from the first that mere book education was not all that the young people of that town needed. I began my work at eight o'clock in the morning, and, as a rule, it did not end until ten o'clock at night. In addition to the usual routine of teaching, I taught the pupils to comb their hair, and to keep their hands and faces clean, as well as their clothing. I gave special attention to teaching them the proper use of the tooth-brush and the bath. In all my teaching I have watched carefully the influence of the tooth-brush, and I am convinced that there are few single agencies of civilization that are more far-reaching.

There were so many of the older boys and girls in the town, as well as men and women, who had to work in the daytime but still were craving an opportunity for some education, that I soon opened a night-school. From the first, this was crowded every night, being about as large as the school that I taught in the day. The efforts of some of the men and women, who in many cases were over fifty years of age, to learn, were in some cases very pathetic.

My day and night school work was not all that I undertook. I established a small reading-room and a debating society. On Sundays I taught two Sunday-schools, one in the town of Malden in the afternoon, and the other in the morning at a place three miles distant from Malden. In addition to this, I gave private lessons to several young men whom I was fitting to send to the Hampton Institute. Without regard to pay and with little thought of it, I taught any one who wanted to learn anything that I could teach him. I was supremely happy in the opportunity of being able to assist somebody else. I did receive, however, a small salary from the public fund, for my work as a public-school teacher.

During the time that I was a student at Hampton my older brother, John, not only assisted me all that he could, but worked all of the time in the coal-mines in order to support the family. He willingly neglected his own education that he might help me. It was my earnest wish to help him to prepare to enter Hampton, and to save money to assist him in his expenses there. Both of these objects I was successful in accomplishing. In three years my brother finished the course at Hampton, and he is now holding the important position of Superintendent of Industries at Tuskegee. When he returned from Hampton, we both combined our efforts and savings to send our adopted brother, James, through the Hampton Institute. This we succeeded in doing, and he is now the postmaster at the Tuskegee Institute. The year 1877, which was my second year of teaching at Malden, I spent very much as I did my first.

It was while my home was at Malden that what was known as the "Ku Klux Klan" was in the height of its activity. The "Ku Klux Klan" were bands of men who had joined themselves together for the purpose of regulating the conduct of the coloured people, especially with the object of preventing the members of the race from exercising any influence in politics. They corresponded somewhat to the "patrollers" of whom I used to hear a great deal during the days of slavery, when I was a small boy. The "patrollers" were bands of white men—usually young men—who were organized largely for the purpose of regulating the conduct of the slaves at night in such matters as preventing the slaves from going from one plantation to another without passes, and for preventing them from holding any kind of meetings without permission and without the presence at these meetings of at least one white man.

Like the "patrollers" the "Ku Klux Klan" operated almost wholly at night. They were, however, more cruel than the "patrollers." Their objects, in the main, were to crush out the political aspirations of the Negroes, but they did not confine themselves to this, because schoolhouses as well as churches were burned by them, and many innocent persons were made to suffer. During this period not a few coloured people lost their lives.

As a young man, the acts of these lawless bands made a great impression upon me. I saw one open battle take place at Malden between some of the coloured and white people. There must have been not far from a hundred persons engaged on each side; many on both sides were seriously injured, among them being General Lewis Ruffner, the husband of my friend Mrs. Viola Ruffner. General Ruffner tried to defend the coloured people, and for this he was knocked down and so seriously wounded that he never completely recovered. It seemed to me as I watched this struggle between members of the two races, that there was no hope for our people in this country. The "Ku Klux Klan" period was, I think, the darkest part of the Reconstruction days.

I have referred to this unpleasant part of the history of the South simply for the purpose of calling attention to the great change that has taken place since the days of the "Ku Klux." To-day there are no such organizations in the South, and the fact that such ever existed is almost forgotten by both races. There are few places in the South now where public sentiment would permit such organizations to exist.

CHAPTER V
THE RECONSTRUCTION PERIOD

The years from 1867 to 1878 I think may be called the period of Reconstruction. This included the time that I spent as a student at Hampton and as a teacher in West Virginia. During the whole of the Reconstruction period two ideas were constantly agitating the minds of the coloured people, or, at least, the minds of a large part of the race. One of these was the craze for Greek and Latin learning, and the other was a desire to hold office.

It could not have been expected that a people who had spent generations in slavery, and before that generations in the darkest heathenism, could at first form any proper conception of what an education meant. In every part of the South, during the Reconstruction period, schools, both day and night, were filled to overflowing with people of all ages and conditions, some being as far along in age as sixty and seventy years. The ambition to secure an education was most praiseworthy and encouraging. The idea, however, was too prevalent that, as soon as one secured a little education, in some unexplainable way he would be free from most of the hardships of the world, and, at any rate, could live without manual labour. There was a further feeling that a knowledge, however little, of the Greek and Latin languages would make one a very superior human being, something bordering almost on the supernatural. I remember that the first coloured man whom I saw who knew something about foreign languages impressed me at that time as being a man of all others to be envied.

Naturally, most of our people who received some little education became teachers or preachers. While among these two classes there were many capable, earnest, godly men and women, still a large proportion took up teaching or preaching as an easy way to make a living. Many became teachers who could do little more than write their names. I remember there came into our neighbourhood one of this class, who was in search of a school to teach, and the question arose while he was there as to the shape of the earth and how he would teach the children concerning this subject. He explained his position in the matter by saying that he was prepared to teach that the earth was either flat or round, according to the preference of a majority of his patrons.

The ministry was the profession that suffered most—and still suffers, though there has been great improvement—on account of not only ignorant but in many cases immoral men who claimed that they were "called to preach." In the earlier days of freedom almost every coloured man who learned to read would receive "a call to preach" within a few days after he began reading. At my home in West Virginia the process of being called to the ministry was a very interesting one. Usually the "call" came when the individual was sitting in church. Without warning the one called would fall upon the floor as if struck by a bullet, and would lie there for hours, speechless and motionless. Then the news would spread all through the neighbourhood that this individual had received a "call." If he were inclined to resist the summons, he would fall or be made to fall a second or third time. In the end he always yielded to the call. While I wanted an education badly, I confess that in my youth I had a fear that when I had learned to read and write well I would receive one of these "calls;" but, for some reason, my call never came.

When we add the number of wholly ignorant men who preached or "exhorted" to that of those who possessed something of an education, it can be seen at a glance that the supply of ministers was large. In fact, some time ago I knew a certain church that had a total membership of about two hundred, and eighteen of that number were ministers. But, I repeat, in many communities in the South the character of the ministry is being improved, and I believe that within the next two or three decades a very large proportion of the unworthy ones will have disappeared. The "calls" to preach, I am glad to say, are not nearly so numerous now as they were formerly, and the calls to some industrial occupation are growing more numerous. The improvement that has taken place in the character of the teachers is even more marked than in the case of the ministers.

During the whole of the Reconstruction period our people throughout the South looked to the Federal Government for everything, very much as a child looks to its mother. This was not unnatural. The central government gave them freedom, and the whole Nation had been enriched for more than two centuries by the labour of the Negro. Even as a youth, and later in manhood, I had the feeling that it was cruelly wrong in the central government, at the beginning of our freedom, to fail to make some provision for the general education of our people in addition to what the states might do, so that the people would be the better prepared for the duties of citizenship.

It is easy to find fault, to remark what might have been done, and perhaps, after all, and under all the circumstances, those in charge of the conduct of affairs did the only thing that could be done at the time. Still, as I look back now over the entire period of our freedom, I cannot help feeling that it would have been wiser if some plan could have been put in operation which would have made the possession of a certain amount of education or property, or both, a test for the exercise of the franchise, and a way provided by which this test should be made to apply honestly and squarely to both the white and black races.

Though I was but little more than a youth during the period of Reconstruction, I had the feeling that mistakes were being made, and that things could not remain in the condition that they were in then very long. I felt that the Reconstruction policy, so far as it related to my race, was in a large measure on a false foundation, was artificial and forced. In many cases it seemed to me that the ignorance of my race was being used as a tool with which to help white men into office, and that there was an element in the North which wanted to punish the Southern white men by forcing the Negro into positions over the heads of the Southern whites. I felt that the Negro would be the one to suffer for this in the end. Besides, the general political agitation drew the attention of our people away from the more fundamental matters of perfecting themselves in the industries at their doors and in securing property.

The temptations to enter political life were so alluring that I came very near yielding to them at one time, but I was kept from doing so by the feeling that I would be helping in a more substantial way by assisting in the laying of the foundation of the race through a generous education of the hand, head, and heart. I saw coloured men who were members of the state legislatures, and county officers, who, in some cases, could not read or write, and whose morals were as weak as their education. Not long ago, when passing through the streets of a certain city in the South, I heard some brick-masons calling out, from the top of a two-story brick building on which they were working, for the "Governor" to "hurry up and bring up some more bricks." Several times I heard the command, "Hurry up, Governor!" Hurry up, Governor!" My curiosity was aroused to such an extent that I made inquiry as to who the "Governor" was, and soon found that he was a coloured man who at one time had held the position of Lieutenant-Governor of his state.

But not all the coloured people who were in office during Reconstruction were unworthy of their positions, by any means. Some of them, like the late Senator B. K. Bruce, Governor Pinchback, and many others, were strong, upright, useful men. Neither were all the class designated as carpetbaggers dishonourable men. Some of them, like ex-Governor Bullock, of Georgia, were men of high character and usefulness.

Of course the coloured people, so largely without education, and wholly without experience in government, made tremendous mistakes, just as any people similarly situated would have done. Many of the Southern whites have a feeling that, if the Negro is permitted to exercise his political rights now to any degree, the mistakes of the Reconstruction period will repeat themselves. I do not think this would be true, because the Negro is a much stronger and wiser man than he was thirty-five years ago, and he is fast learning the lesson that he cannot afford to act in a manner that will alienate his Southern white neighbours from him. More and more I am convinced that the final solution of the political end of our race problem will be for each state that finds it necessary to change the law bearing upon the franchise to make the law apply with absolute honesty, and without opportunity for double dealing or evasion, to both races alike. Any other course my daily observation in the South convinces me, will be unjust to the Negro, unjust to the white man, and unfair to the rest of the states in the Union, and will be, like slavery, a sin that at some time we shall have to pay for.

In the fall of 1878, after having taught school in Malden for two years, and after I had succeeded in preparing several of the young men and women, besides my two brothers, to enter the Hampton Institute, I decided to spend some months in study at Washington, D.C. I remained there for eight months. I derived a great deal of benefit from the studies which I pursued, and I came into contact with some strong men and women. At the institution I attended there was no industrial training given to the students, and I had an opportunity of comparing the influence of an institution with no industrial training with that of one like the Hampton Institute, that emphasized the industries. At this school I found the students, in most cases, had more money, were better dressed, wore the latest style of all manner of clothing, and in some cases were more brilliant mentally. At Hampton it was a standing rule that, while the institution would be responsible for securing some one to pay the tuition for the students, the men and women themselves must provide for their own board, books, clothing, and room wholly by work, or partly by work and partly in cash. At the institution at which I now was, I found that a large proportion of the students by some means had their personal expenses paid for them. At Hampton the student was constantly making the effort through the industries to help himself, and that every effort was of immense value in character-building. The students at the other school seemed to be less self-dependent. They seemed to give more attention to mere outward appearances. In a word, they did not appear to me to be beginning at the bottom, on a real, solid foundation, to the extent that they were at Hampton. They knew more about Latin and Greek when they left school, but they seemed to know less about life and its conditions as they would meet it at their homes. Having lived for a number of years in the midst of comfortable surroundings, they were not as much inclined as the Hampton students to go into the country districts of the South, where there was little of comfort, to take up work for our people, and they were more inclined to yield to the temptation to become hotel waiters and Pullman-car porters as their life-work.

During the time I was a student in Washington the city was crowded with coloured people, many of whom had recently come from the South. A large proportion of these people had been drawn to Washington because they felt that they could lead a life of ease there. Others had secured minor government positions, and still another large class was there in the hope of securing Federal positions. A number of coloured men— some of them very strong and brilliant—were in the House of Representatives at that time, and one, the Hon. B. K. Bruce, was in the Senate. All this tended to make Washington an attractive place for members of the coloured race. Then, too, they knew that at all times they could have the protection of the law in the District of Columbia. The public schools in Washington for coloured people were better then than they were elsewhere. I took great interest in studying the life of our people there closely at that time. I found that while among them there was a large element of substantial, worthy citizens, there was also a superficiality about the life of a large class that greatly alarmed me. I saw young coloured men who were not earning more than four dollars a week spend two dollars or more for a buggy on Sunday to ride up and down Pennsylvania Avenue in, in order that they might try to convince the world that they were worth thousands. I saw other young men who received seventy-five or one hundred dollars per month from the Government, who were in debt at the end of every month. I saw men who but a few months previous were members of Congress, then without employment and in poverty. Among a large class there seemed to be a dependence upon the Government for every conceivable thing. The members of this class had little ambition to create a position for themselves, but wanted the Federal officials to create one for them. How many times I wished then, and have often wished since, that by some power of magic I might remove the great bulk of these people into the country districts and plant them upon the soil, upon the solid and never deceptive foundation of Mother Nature, where all nations and races that have ever succeeded have gotten their start,—a start that at first may be slow and toilsome, but one that nevertheless is real.

In Washington I saw girls whose mothers were earning their living by laundrying. These girls were taught by their mothers, in rather a crude way it is true, the industry of laundrying. Later, these girls entered the public schools and remained there perhaps six or eight years. When the public school course was finally finished, they wanted more costly dresses, more costly hats and shoes. In a word, while their wants had been increased, their ability to supply their wants had not been increased in the same degree. On the other hand, their six or eight years of book education had weaned them away from the occupation of their mothers. The result of this was in too many cases that the girls went to the bad. I often thought how much wiser it would have been to give these girls the same amount of mental training—and I favour any kind of training, whether in the languages or mathematics, that gives strength and culture to the mind—but at the same time to give them the most thorough training in the latest and best methods of laundrying and other kindred occupations.

CHAPTER VI
BLACK RACE AND RED RACE

During the year that I spent in Washington, and for some little time before this, there had been considerable agitation in the state of West Virginia over the question of moving the capital of the state from Wheeling to some other central point. As a result of this, the Legislature designated three cities to be voted upon by the citizens of the state as the permanent seat of government. Among these cities was Charleston, only five miles from Malden, my home. At the close of my school year in Washington I was very pleasantly surprised to receive, from a committee of white people in Charleston, an invitation to canvass the state in the interests of that city. This invitation I accepted, and spent nearly three months in speaking in various parts of the state. Charleston was successful in winning the prize, and is now the permanent seat of government.

The reputation that I made as a speaker during this campaign induced a number of persons to make an earnest effort to get me to enter political life, but I refused, still believing that I could find other service which would prove of more permanent value to my race. Even then I had a strong feeling that what our people most needed was to get a foundation in education, industry, and property, and for this I felt that they could better afford to strive than for political preferment. As for my individual self, it appeared to me to be reasonably certain that I could succeed in political life, but I had a feeling that it would be a rather selfish kind of success—individual success at the cost of failing to do my duty in assisting in laying a foundation for the masses.

At this period in the progress of our race a very large proportion of the young men who went to school or to college did so with the expressed determination to prepare themselves to be great lawyers, or Congressmen, and many of the women planned to become music teachers; but I had a reasonably fixed idea, even at that early period in my life, that there was need for something to be done to prepare the way for successful lawyers, Congressmen, and music teachers.

I felt that the conditions were a good deal like those of an old coloured man, during the days of slavery, who wanted to learn how to play on the guitar. In his desire to take guitar lessons he applied to one of his young masters to teach him; but the young man, not having much faith in the ability of the slave to master the guitar at his age, sought to discourage him by telling him: "Uncle Jake, I will give you guitar lessons; but, Jake, I will have to charge you three dollars for the first lesson, two dollars for the second lesson, and one dollar for the third lesson. But I will charge you only twenty-five cents for the last lesson."

Uncle Jake answered: "All right, boss, I hires you on dem terms. But, boss! I wants yer to be sure an' give me dat las' lesson first."

Soon after my work in connection with the removal of the capital was finished, I received an invitation which gave me great joy and which at the same time was a very pleasant surprise. This was a letter from General Armstrong, inviting me to return to Hampton at the next Commencement to deliver what was called the "post-graduate address." This was an honour which I had not dreamed of receiving. With much care I prepared the best address that I was capable of. I chose for my subject "The Force That Wins."

As I returned to Hampton for the purpose of delivering this address, I went over much of the same ground—now, however, covered entirely by railroad—that I had traversed nearly six years before, when I first sought entrance into Hampton Institute as a student. Now I was able to ride the whole distance in the train. I was constantly contrasting this with my first journey to Hampton. I think I may say, without seeming egotism, that it is seldom that five years have wrought such a change in the life and aspirations of an individual.

At Hampton I received a warm welcome from teachers and students. I found that during my absence from Hampton the institute each year had been getting closer to the real needs and conditions of our people; that the industrial teaching, as well as that of the academic department, had greatly improved. The plan of the school was not modelled after that of any other institution then in existence, but every improvement was made under the magnificent leadership of General Armstrong solely with the view of meeting and helping the needs of our people as they presented themselves at the time. Too often, it seems to me, in missionary and educational work among undeveloped races, people yield to the temptation of doing that which was done a hundred years before, or is being done in other communities a thousand miles away. The temptation often is to run each individual through a certain educational mould, regardless of the condition of the subject or the end to be accomplished. This was not so at Hampton Institute.

The address which I delivered on Commencement Day seems to have pleased every one, and many kind and encouraging words were spoken to me regarding it. Soon after my return to my home in West Virginia, where I had planned to continue teaching, I was again surprised to receive a letter from General Armstrong, asking me to return to Hampton partly as a teacher and partly to pursue some supplementary studies. This was in the summer of 1879. Soon after I began my first teaching in West Virginia I had picked out four of the brightest and most promising of my pupils, in addition to my two brothers, to whom I have already referred, and had given them special attention, with the view of having them go to Hampton. They had gone there, and in each case the teachers had found them so well prepared that they entered advanced classes. This fact, it seems, led to my being called back to Hampton as a teacher. One of the young men that I sent to Hampton in this way is now Dr. Samuel E. Courtney, a successful physician in Boston, and a member of the School Board of that city.

About this time the experiment was being tried for the first time, by General Armstrong, of educating Indians at Hampton. Few people then had any confidence in the ability of the Indians to receive education and to profit by it. General Armstrong was anxious to try the experiment systematically on a large scale. He secured from the reservations in the

Western states over one hundred wild and for the most part perfectly ignorant Indians, the greater proportion of whom were young men. The special work which the General desired me to do was to be a sort of "house father" to the Indian young men—that is, I was to live in the building with them and have the charge of their discipline, clothing, rooms, and so on. This was a very tempting offer, but I had become so much absorbed in my work in West Virginia that I dreaded to give it up. However, I tore myself away from it. I did not know how to refuse to perform any service that General Armstrong desired of me.

On going to Hampton, I took up my residence in a building with about seventy-five Indian youths. I was the only person in the building who was not a member of their race. At first I had a good deal of doubt about my ability to succeed. I knew that the average Indian felt himself above the white man, and, of course, he felt himself far above the Negro, largely on account of the fact of the Negro having submitted to slavery—a thing which the Indian would never do. The Indians, in the Indian Territory, owned a large number of slaves during the days of slavery. Aside from this, there was a general feeling that the attempt to educate and civilize the red men at Hampton would be a failure. All this made me proceed very cautiously, for I felt keenly the great responsibility. But I was determined to succeed. It was not long before I had the complete confidence of the Indians, and not only this, but I think I am safe in saying that I had their love and respect. I found that they were about like any other human beings; that they responded to kind treatment and resented ill-treatment. They were continually planning to do something that would add to my happiness and comfort. The things that they disliked most, I think, were to have their long hair cut, to give up wearing their blankets, and to cease smoking; but no white American ever thinks that any other race is wholly civilized until he wears the white man's clothes, eats the white man's food, speaks the white man's language, and professes the white man's religion.

When the difficulty of learning the English language was subtracted, I found that in the matter of learning trades and in mastering academic studies there was little difference between the coloured and Indian students. It was a constant delight to me to note the interest which the coloured students took in trying to help the Indians in every way possible. There were a few of the coloured students who felt that the Indians ought not to be admitted to Hampton, but these were in the minority. Whenever they were asked to do so, the Negro students gladly took the Indians as room-mates, in order that they might teach them to speak English and to acquire civilized habits.

I have often wondered if there was a white institution in this country whose students would have welcomed the incoming of more than a hundred companions of another race in the cordial way that these black students at Hampton welcomed the red ones. How often I have wanted to say to white students that they lift themselves up in proportion as they help to lift others, and the more unfortunate the race, and the lower in the scale of civilization, the more does one raise one's self by giving the assistance.

This reminds me of a conversation which I once had with the Hon. Frederick Douglass. At one time Mr. Douglass was travelling in the state of Pennsylvania, and was forced, on account of his colour, to ride in the baggage-car, in spite of the fact that he had paid the same price for his passage that the other passengers had paid. When some of the white passengers went into the baggage-car to console Mr. Douglass, and one of them said to him: "I am sorry, Mr. Douglass, that you have been degraded in this manner," Mr. Douglass straightened himself up on the box upon which he was sitting, and replied: "They cannot degrade Frederick Douglass. The soul that is within me no man can degrade. I am not the one that is being degraded on account of this treatment, but those who are inflicting it upon me."

In one part of our country, where the law demands the separation of the races on the railroad trains, I saw at one time a rather amusing instance which showed how difficult it sometimes is to know where the black begins and the white ends.

There was a man who was well known in his community as a Negro, but who was so white that even an expert would have hard work to classify him as a black man. This man was riding in the part of the train set aside for the coloured passengers. When the train conductor reached him, he showed at once that he was perplexed. If the man was a Negro, the conductor did not want to send him into the white people's coach; at the same time, if he was a white man, the conductor did not want to insult him by asking him if he was a Negro. The official looked him over carefully, examining his hair, eyes, nose, and hands, but still seemed puzzled. Finally, to solve the difficulty, he stooped over and peeped at the man's feet. When I saw the conductor examining the feet of the man in question, I said to myself, "That will settle it;" and so it did, for the trainman promptly decided that the passenger was a Negro, and let him remain where he was. I congratulated myself that my race was fortunate in not losing one of its members.

My experience has been that the time to test a true gentleman is to observe him when he is in contact with individuals of a race that is less fortunate than his own. This is illustrated in no better way than by observing the conduct of the old-school type of Southern gentleman when he is in contact with his former slaves or their descendants.

An example of what I mean is shown in a story told of George Washington, who, meeting a coloured man in the road once, who politely lifted his hat, lifted his own in return. Some of his white friends who saw the incident criticized Washington for his action. In reply to their criticism George Washington said: "Do you suppose that I am going to permit a poor, ignorant, coloured man to be more polite than I am?"

While I was in charge of the Indian boys at Hampton, I had one or two experiences which illustrate the curious workings of caste in America. One of the Indian boys was taken ill, and it became my duty to take him to Washington, deliver him over to the Secretary of the Interior, and get a receipt for him, in order that he might be returned to his Western reservation. At that time I was rather ignorant of the ways of the world. During my journey to Washington, on a steamboat, when the bell rang for dinner, I was careful to wait and not enter the dining room until after the greater part of the passengers had finished their meal. Then, with my charge, I went to the dining saloon. The man in charge politely informed me that the Indian could be served, but that I could not. I never could understand how he knew just where to draw the colour line, since the Indian and I were of about the same complexion. The steward, however, seemed to be an expert in this matter. I had been directed by the authorities at Hampton to stop at a certain hotel in Washington with my charge, but when I went to this hotel the clerk stated that he would be glad to receive the Indian into the house, but said that he could not accommodate me.

An illustration of something of this same feeling came under my observation afterward. I happened to find myself in a town in which so much excitement and indignation were being expressed that it seemed likely for a time that there would be a lynching. The occasion of the trouble was that a dark-skinned man had stopped at the local hotel. Investigation, however, developed the fact that this individual was a citizen of Morocco, and that while travelling in this country he spoke the English language. As soon as it was learned that he was not an American Negro, all the signs of indignation disappeared. The man who was the innocent cause of the excitement, though, found it prudent after that not to speak English.

At the end of my first year with the Indians there came another opening for me at Hampton, which, as I look back over my life now, seems to have come providentially, to help to prepare me for my work at Tuskegee later. General Armstrong had found out that there was quite a number of young coloured men and women who were intensely in earnest in wishing to get an education, but who were prevented from entering Hampton Institute because they were too poor to be able to pay any portion of the cost of their board, or even to supply themselves with books. He conceived the idea of starting a night-school in connection with the Institute, into which a limited number of the most promising of these young men and women would be received, on condition that they were to work for ten hours during the day, and attend school for two hours at night. They were to be paid something above the cost of their board for their work. The greater part of their earnings was to be reserved in the school's treasury as a fund to be drawn on to pay their board when they had spent one or two years in the night-school. In this way they would obtain a start in their books and a knowledge of some trade or industry, in addition to the other far-reaching benefits of the institution.

General Armstrong asked me to take charge of the night-school, and I did so. At the beginning of this school there were about twelve strong, earnest men and women who entered the class. During the day the greater part of the young men worked in the school's sawmill, and the young women worked in the laundry. The work was not easy in either place, but in all my teaching I never taught pupils who gave me such genuine satisfaction as these did. They were good students, and mastered their work thoroughly. They were so much in earnest that only the ringing of the retiring-bell would make them stop studying, and often they would urge me to continue the lessons after the usual hour for going to bed had come.

These students showed so much earnestness, both in their hard work during the day, as well as in their application to their studies at night, that I gave them the name of "The Plucky Class"—a name which soon grew popular and spread throughout the institution. After a student had been in the night-school long enough to prove what was in him, I gave him a printed certificate which read something like this:

"This is to certify that James Smith is a member of The Plucky Class of the Hampton Institute, and is in good and regular standing."

The students prized these certificates highly, and they added greatly to the popularity of the night-school. Within a few weeks this department had grown to such an extent that there were about twenty-five students in attendance. I have followed the course of many of these twenty-five men and women ever since then, and they are now holding important and useful positions in nearly every part of the South. The night-school at Hampton, which started with only twelve students, now numbers between three and four hundred, and is one of the permanent and most important features of the institution.

CHAPTER VII
EARLY DAYS AT TUSKEGEE

During the time that I had charge of the Indians and the night-school at Hampton, I pursued some studies myself, under the direction of the instructors there. One of these instructors was the Rev. Dr. H. B. Frissell, the present Principal of the Hampton Institute, General Armstrong's successor.

In May, 1881, near the close of my first year in teaching the night-school, in a way that I had not dared expect, the opportunity opened for me to begin my life-work. One night in the chapel, after the usual chapel exercises were over, General Armstrong referred to the fact that he had received a letter from some gentlemen in Alabama asking him to recommend some one to take charge of what was to be a normal school for the coloured people in the little town of Tuskegee in that state. These gentlemen seemed to take it for granted that no coloured man suitable for the position could be secured, and they were expecting the General to recommend a white man for the place. The next day General Armstrong sent for me to come to his office, and much to my surprise, asked me if I thought I could fill the position in Alabama. I told him that I would be willing to try. Accordingly, he wrote to the people who had applied to him for the information, that he did not know of any white man to suggest, but if they would be willing to take a coloured man, he had one whom he could recommend. In this letter he gave them my name.

Several days passed before anything more was heard about the matter. Some time afterward, one Sunday evening during the chapel exercises, a messenger came in and handed the General a telegram. At the end of the exercises he read the telegram to the school. In substance, these were its words: "Booker T. Washington will suit us. Send him at once."

There was a great deal of joy expressed among the students and teachers, and I received very hearty congratulations. I began to get ready at once to go to Tuskegee. I went by way of my old home in West Virginia, where I remained for several days, after which I proceeded to Tuskegee. I found Tuskegee to be a town of about two thousand inhabitants, nearly one-half of whom were coloured. It was in what was known as the Black Belt of the South. In the county in which Tuskegee is situated the coloured people outnumbered the whites by about three to one. In some of the adjoining and near-by counties the proportion was not far from six coloured persons to one white.

I have often been asked to define the term "Black Belt." So far as I can learn, the term was first used to designate a part of the country which was distinguished by the colour of the soil. The part of the country possessing this thick, dark, and naturally rich soil was, of course, the part of the South where the slaves were most profitable, and consequently they were taken there in the largest numbers. Later, and especially since the war, the term seems to be used wholly in a political sense—that is, to designate the counties where the black people outnumber the white.

Before going to Tuskegee I had expected to find there a building and all the necessary apparatus ready for me to begin teaching. To my disappointment, I found nothing of the kind. I did find, though, that which no costly building and apparatus can supply,—hundreds of hungry, earnest souls who wanted to secure knowledge.

Tuskegee seemed an ideal place for the school. It was in the midst of the great bulk of the Negro population, and was rather secluded, being five miles from the main line of railroad, with which it was connected by a short line. During the days of slavery, and since, the town had been a centre for the education of the white people. This was an added advantage, for the reason that I found the white people possessing a degree of culture and education that is not surpassed by many locations. While the coloured people were ignorant, they had not, as a rule, degraded and weakened their bodies by vices such as are common to the lower class of people in the large cities. In general, I found the relations between the two races pleasant. For example, the largest, and I think at that time the only hardware store in the town was owned and operated jointly by a coloured man and a white man. This co-partnership continued until the death of the white partner.

I found that about a year previous to my going to Tuskegee some of the coloured people who had heard something of the work of education being done at Hampton had applied to the state Legislature, through their representatives, for a small appropriation to be used in starting a normal school in Tuskegee. This request the Legislature had complied with to the extent of granting an annual appropriation of two thousand dollars. I soon learned, however, that this money could be used only for the payment of the salaries of the instructors, and that there was no provision for securing land, buildings, or apparatus. The task before me did not seem a very encouraging one. It seemed much like making bricks without straw. The coloured people were overjoyed, and were constantly offering their services in any way in which they could be of assistance in getting the school started.

My first task was to find a place in which to open the school. After looking the town over with some care, the most suitable place that could be secured seemed to be a rather dilapidated shanty near the coloured Methodist church, together with the church itself as a sort of assembly-room. Both the church and the shanty were in about as bad condition as was possible. I recall that during the first months of school that I taught in this building it was in such poor repair that, whenever it rained, one of the older students would very kindly leave his lessons and hold an umbrella over me while I heard the recitations of the others. I remember, also, that on more than one occasion my landlady held an umbrella over me while I ate breakfast.

At the time I went to Alabama the coloured people were taking considerable interest in politics, and they were very anxious that I should become one of them politically, in every respect. They seemed to have a little distrust of strangers in this regard. I recall that one man, who seemed to have been designated by the others to look after my political destiny, came to me on several occasions and said, with a good deal of earnestness: "We wants you to be sure to vote jes' like we votes. We can't read de newspapers very much, but we knows how to vote, an' we wants you to vote jes' like we votes." He added: "We watches de white man, and we keeps watching de white man till we finds out which way de white man's gwine to vote; an' when we finds out which way de white man's gwine to vote, den we votes 'xactly de other way. Den we knows we's right."

I am glad to add, however, that at the present time the disposition to vote against the white man merely because he is white is largely disappearing, and the race is learning to vote from principle, for what the voter considers to be for the best interests of both races.

I reached Tuskegee, as I have said, early in June, 1881. The first month I spent in finding accommodations for the school, and in travelling through Alabama, examining into the actual life of the people, especially in the country districts, and in getting the school advertised among the class of people that I wanted to have attend it. The most of my travelling was done over the country roads, with a mule and a cart or a mule and a buggy wagon for conveyance. I ate and slept with the people, in their little cabins. I saw their farms, their schools, their churches. Since, in the case of the most of these visits, there had been no notice given in advance that a stranger was expected, I had the advantage of seeing the real, everyday life of the people.

In the plantation districts I found that, as a rule, the whole family slept in one room, and that in addition to the immediate family there sometimes were relatives, or others not related to the family, who slept in the same room. On more than one occasion I went outside the house to get ready for bed, or to wait until the family had gone to bed. They usually contrived some kind of a place for me to sleep, either on the floor or in a special part of another's bed. Rarely was there any place provided in the cabin where one could bathe even the face and hands, but usually some provision was made for this outside the house, in the yard.

The common diet of the people was fat pork and corn bread. At times I have eaten in cabins where they had only corn bread and "black-eye peas" cooked in plain water. The people seemed to have no other idea than to live on this fat meat and corn bread,—the meat, and the meal of which the bread was made, having been bought at a high price at a store in town, notwithstanding the fact that the land all about the cabin homes could easily have been made to produce nearly every kind of garden vegetable that is raised anywhere in the country. Their one object seemed to be to plant nothing but cotton; and in many cases cotton was planted up to the very door of the cabin.

In these cabin homes I often found sewing machines which had been bought, or were being bought, on installments, frequently at a cost of as much as sixty dollars, or showy clocks for which the occupants of the cabins had paid twelve or fourteen dollars. I remember that on one occasion when I went into one of these cabins for dinner, when I sat down to the table for a meal with the four members of the family, I noticed that, while there were five of us at the table, there was but one fork for the five of us to use. Naturally there was an awkward pause on my part. In the opposite corner of that same cabin was an organ for which the people told me they were paying sixty dollars in monthly installments. One fork, and a sixty-dollar organ!

In most cases the sewing-machine was not used, the clocks were so worthless that they did not keep correct time—and if they had, in nine cases out of ten there would have been no one in the family who could have told the time of day—while the organ, of course, was rarely used for want of a person who could play upon it.

In the case to which I have referred, where the family sat down to the table for the meal at which I was their guest, I could see plainly that this was an awkward and unusual proceeding, and was done in my honour. In most cases, when the family got up in the morning, for example, the wife would put a piece of meat in a frying-pan and put a lump of dough in a "skillet," as they called it. These utensils would be placed on the fire, and in ten or fifteen minutes breakfast would be ready. Frequently the husband would take his bread and meat in his hand and start for the field, eating as he walked. The mother would sit down in a corner and eat her breakfast, perhaps from a plate and perhaps directly from the "skillet" or frying-pan, while the children would eat their portion of the bread and meat while running about the yard. At certain seasons of the year, when meat was scarce, it was rarely that the children who were not old enough or strong enough to work in the fields would have the luxury of meat.

The breakfast over, and with practically no attention given to the house, the whole family would, as a general thing, proceed to the cotton-field. Every child that was large enough to carry a hoe was put to work, and the baby – for usually there was at least one baby—would be laid down at the end of the cotton row, so that its mother could give it a certain amount of attention when she had finished chopping her row. The noon meal and the supper were taken in much the same way as the breakfast.

All the days of the family would be spent after much this same routine, except Saturday and Sunday. On Saturday the whole family would spend at least half a day, and often a whole day, in town. The idea in going to town was, I suppose, to do shopping, but all the shopping that the whole family had money for could have been attended to in ten minutes by one person. Still, the whole family remained in town for most of the day, spending the greater part of the time in standing on the streets, the women, too often, sitting about somewhere smoking or dipping snuff. Sunday was usually spent in going to some big meeting. With few exceptions, I found that the crops were mortgaged in the counties where I went, and that the most of the coloured farmers were in debt. The state had not been able to build schoolhouses in the country districts, and, as a rule, the schools were taught in churches or in log cabins. More than once, while on my journeys, I found that there was no provision made in the house used for school purposes for heating the building during the winter, and consequently a fire had to be built in the yard, and teacher and pupils passed in and out of the house as they got cold or warm. With few exceptions, I found the teachers in these country schools to be miserably poor in preparation for their work, and poor in moral character. The schools were in session from three to five months. There was practically no apparatus in the schoolhouses, except that occasionally there was a rough blackboard. I recall that one day I went into a schoolhouse—or rather into an abandoned log cabin that was being used as a schoolhouse—and found five pupils who were studying a lesson from one book. Two of these, on the front seat, were using the book between them; behind these were two others peeping over the shoulders of the first two, and behind the four was a fifth little fellow who was peeping over the shoulders of all four.

What I have said concerning the character of the schoolhouses and teachers will also apply quite accurately as a description of the church buildings and the ministers.

I met some very interesting characters during my travels. As illustrating the peculiar mental processes of the country people, I remember that I asked one coloured man, who was about sixty years old, to tell me something of his history. He said that he had been born in Virginia, and sold into Alabama in 1845. I asked him how many were sold at the same time. He said, "There were five of us; myself and brother and three mules."

In giving all these descriptions of what I saw during my month of travel in the country around Tuskegee, I wish my readers to keep in mind the fact that there were many encouraging exceptions to the conditions which I have described. I have stated in such plain words what I saw, mainly for the reason that later I want to emphasize the encouraging changes that have taken place in the community, not wholly by the work of the Tuskegee school, but by that of other institutions as well.

CHAPTER VIII
TEACHING SCHOOL IN A STABLE
AND A HEN HOUSE

I confess that what I saw during my month of travel and investigation left me with a very heavy heart. The work to be done in order to lift these people up seemed almost beyond accomplishing. I was only one person, and it seemed to me that the little effort which I could put forth could go such a short distance toward bringing about results. I wondered if I could accomplish anything, and if it were worth while for me to try.

Of one thing I felt more strongly convinced than ever, after spending this month in seeing the actual life of the coloured people, and that was that, in order to lift them up, something must be done more than merely to imitate New England education as it then existed. I saw more clearly than ever the wisdom of the system which General Armstrong had inaugurated at Hampton. To take the children of such people as I had been among for a month, and each day give them a few hours of mere book education, I felt would be almost a waste of time.

After consultation with the citizens of Tuskegee, I set July 4, 1881, as the day for the opening of the school in the little shanty and church which had been secured for its accommodation. The white people, as well as the coloured, were greatly interested in the starting of the new school, and the opening day was looked forward to with much earnest discussion. There were not a few white people in the vicinity of Tuskegee who looked with some disfavour upon the project. They questioned its value to the coloured people, and had a fear that it might result in bringing about trouble between the races. Some had the feeling that in proportion as the Negro received education, in the same proportion would his value decrease as an economic factor in the state. These people feared the result of education would be that the Negroes would leave the farms, and that it would be difficult to secure them for domestic service.

The white people who questioned the wisdom of starting this new school had in their minds pictures of what was called an educated Negro, with a high hat, imitation gold eye-glasses, a showy walking stick, kid gloves, fancy boots, and what not—in a word, a man who was determined to live by his wits. It was difficult for these people to see how education would produce any other kind of a coloured man.

In the midst of all the difficulties which I encountered in getting the little school started, and since then through a period of nineteen years, there are two men among all the many friends of the school in Tuskegee upon whom I have depended constantly for advice and guidance; and the success of the undertaking is largely due to these men, from whom I have never sought anything in vain. I mention them simply as types. One is a white man and an ex-slaveholder, Mr. George W. Campbell; the other is a black man and an ex-slave, Mr. Lewis Adams. These were the men who wrote to General Armstrong for a teacher.

Mr. Campbell is a merchant and banker, and had had little experience in dealing with matters pertaining to education. Mr. Adams was a mechanic, and had learned the trades of shoemaking, harness-making, and tin smithing during the days of slavery. He had never been to school a day in his life, but in some way he had learned to read and write while a slave. From the first, these two men saw clearly what my plan of education was, sympathized with me, and supported me in every effort. In the days which were darkest financially for the school, Mr. Campbell was never appealed to when he was not willing to extend all the aid in his power. I do not know two men, one an ex-slaveholder, one an ex-slave, whose advice and judgment I would feel more like following in everything which concerns the life and development of the school at Tuskegee than those of these two men.

I have always felt that Mr. Adams, in a large degree, derived his unusual power of mind from the training given his hands in the process of mastering well three trades during the days of slavery. If one goes to-day into any Southern town, and asks for the leading and most reliable coloured man in the community, I believe that in five cases out of ten he will be directed to a Negro who learned a trade during the days of slavery.

On the morning that the school opened, thirty students reported for admission. I was the only teacher. The students were about equally divided between the sexes. Most of them lived in Macon County, the county in which Tuskegee is situated, and of which it is the county-seat. A great many more students wanted to enter the school, but it had been decided to receive only those who were above fifteen years of age, and who had previously received some education. The greater part of the thirty were public-school teachers, and some of them were nearly forty years of age. With the teachers came some of their former pupils, and when they were examined it was amusing to note that in several cases the pupil entered a higher class than did his former teacher. It was also interesting to note how many big books some of them had studied, and how many high-sounding subjects some of them claimed to have mastered. The bigger the book and the longer the name of the subject, the prouder they felt of their accomplishment. Some had studied Latin, and one or two Greek. This they thought entitled them to special distinction.

In fact, one of the saddest things I saw during the month of travel which I have described was a young man, who had attended some high school, sitting down in a one-room cabin, with grease on his clothing, filth all around him, and weeds in the yard and garden, engaged in studying a French grammar.

The students who came first seemed to be fond of memorizing long and complicated, "rules" in grammar and mathematics, but had little thought or knowledge of applying these rules to the everyday affairs of their life. One subject which they liked to talk about, and tell me that they had mastered, in arithmetic, was "banking and discount," but I soon found out that neither they nor almost any one in the neighbourhood in which they lived had ever had a bank account. In registering the names of the students, I found that almost every one of them had one or more middle initials. When I asked what the "J" stood for, in the name of John J. Jones, it was explained to me that this was a part of his "entitles." Most of the students wanted to get an education because they thought it would enable them to earn more money as school-teachers.

Notwithstanding what I have said about them in these respects, I have never seen a more earnest and willing company of young men and women than these students were. They were all willing to learn the right thing as soon as it was shown them what was right. I was determined to start them off on a solid and thorough foundation, so far as their books were concerned. I soon learned that most of them had the merest smattering of the high-sounding things that they had studied. While they could locate the Desert of Sahara or the capital of China on an artificial globe, I found out that the girls could not locate the proper places for the knives and forks on an actual dinner-table, or the places on which the bread and meat should be set.

I had to summon a good deal of courage to take a student who had been studying cube root and "banking and discount," and explain to him that the wisest thing for him to do first was thoroughly to master the multiplication table.

The number of pupils increased each week, until by the end of the first month there were nearly fifty. Many of them, however, said that, as they could remain only for two or three months, they wanted to enter a high class and get a diploma the first year if possible.

At the end of the first six weeks a new and rare face entered the school as a co-teacher. This was Miss Olivia A. Davidson, who later became my wife. Miss Davidson was born in Ohio, and received her preparatory education in the public schools of that state. When little more than a girl, she heard of the need of teachers in the South. She went to the state of Mississippi and began teaching there. Later she taught in the city of Memphis. While teaching in Mississippi, one of her pupils became ill with smallpox. Everyone in the community was so frightened that no one would nurse the boy. Miss Davidson closed her school and remained by the bedside of the boy night and day until he recovered. While she was at her Ohio home on her vacation, the worst epidemic of yellow fever broke out in Memphis, Tenn., that perhaps has ever occurred in the South. When she heard of this, she at once telegraphed the Mayor of Memphis, offering her services as a yellow-fever nurse, although she had never had the disease.

Miss Davidson's experience in the South showed her that the people needed something more than mere book-learning. She heard of the Hampton system of education, and decided that this was what she wanted in order to prepare herself for better work in the South. The attention of Mrs. Mary Hemenway, of Boston, was attracted to her rare ability. Through Mrs. Hemenway's kindness and generosity, Miss Davidson, after graduating at Hampton, received an opportunity to complete a two years' course of training at the Massachusetts State Normal School at Framingham.

Before she went to Framingham, some one suggested to Miss Davidson that, since she was so very light in colour, she might find it more comfortable not to be known as a coloured woman in this school in Massachusetts. She at once replied that under no circumstances and for no considerations would she consent to deceive any one in regard to her racial identity.

Soon after her graduation from the Framingham institution, Miss Davidson came to Tuskegee, bringing into the school many valuable and fresh ideas as to the best methods of teaching, as well as a rare moral character and a life of unselfishness that I think has seldom been equalled. No single individual did more toward laying the foundations of the Tuskegee Institute so as to insure the successful work that has been done there than Olivia A. Davidson.

Miss Davidson and I began consulting as to the future of the school from the first. The students were making progress in learning books and in developing their minds; but it became apparent at once that, if we were to make any permanent impression upon those who had come to us for training, we must do something besides teach them mere books. The students had come from homes where they had had no opportunities for lessons which would teach them how to care for their bodies. With few exceptions, the homes in Tuskegee in which the students boarded were but little improvement upon those from which they had come. We wanted to teach the students how to bathe; how to care for their teeth and clothing. We wanted to teach them what to eat, and how to eat it properly, and how to care for their rooms. Aside from this, we wanted to give them such a practical knowledge of some one industry, together with the spirit of industry, thrift, and economy, that they would be sure of knowing how to make a living after they had left us. We wanted to teach them to study actual things instead of mere books alone.

We found that the most of our students came from the country districts, where agriculture in some form or other was the main dependence of the people. We learned that about eighty-five per cent of the coloured people in the Gulf states depended upon agriculture for their living. Since this was true, we wanted to be careful not to educate our students out of sympathy with agricultural life, so that they would be attracted from the country to the cities, and yield to the temptation of trying to live by their wits. We wanted to give them such an education as would fit a large proportion of them to be teachers, and at the same time cause them to return to the plantation districts and show the people there how to put new energy and new ideas into farming, as well as into the intellectual and moral and religious life of the people.

All these ideas and needs crowded themselves upon us with a seriousness that seemed well-nigh overwhelming. What were we to do? We had only the little old shanty and the abandoned church which the good coloured people of the town of Tuskegee had kindly loaned us for the accommodation of the classes. The number of students was increasing daily. The more we saw of them, and the more we travelled through the country districts, the more we saw that our efforts were reaching, to only a partial degree, the actual needs of the people whom we wanted to lift up through the medium of the students whom we should educate and send out as leaders.

The more we talked with the students, who were then coming to us from several parts of the state, the more we found that the chief ambition among a large proportion of them was to get an education so that they would not have to work any longer with their hands.

This is illustrated by a story told of a coloured man in Alabama, who, one hot day in July, while he was at work in a cotton-field, suddenly stopped, and, looking toward the skies, said: "O Lawd, de cotton am so grassy, de work am so hard, and the sun am so hot dat I b'lieve dis darky am called to preach!"

About three months after the opening of the school, and at the time when we were in the greatest anxiety about our work, there came into the market for sale an old and abandoned plantation which was situated about a mile from the town of Tuskegee. The mansion house—or "big house," as it would have been called—which had been occupied by the owners during slavery, had been burned. After making a careful examination of this place, it seemed to be just the location that we wanted in order to make our work effective and permanent.

But how were we to get it? The price asked for it was very little— only five hundred dollars – but we had no money, and we were strangers in the town and had no credit. The owner of the land agreed to let us occupy the place if we could make a payment of two hundred and fifty dollars down, with the understanding that the remaining two hundred and fifty dollars must be paid within a year. Although five hundred dollars was cheap for the land, it was a large sum when one did not have any part of it.

In the midst of the difficulty I summoned a great deal of courage and wrote to my friend General J. F. B. Marshall, the Treasurer of the Hampton Institute, putting the situation before him and beseeching him to lend me the two hundred and fifty dollars on my own personal responsibility. Within a few days a reply came to the effect that he had no authority to lend me money belonging to the Hampton Institute, but that he would gladly lend me the amount needed from his own personal funds.

I confess that the securing of this money in this way was a great surprise to me, as well as a source of gratification. Up to that time I never had had in my possession so much money as one hundred dollars at a time, and the loan which I had asked General Marshall for seemed a tremendously large sum to me. The fact of my being responsible for the repaying of such a large amount of money weighed very heavily upon me.

I lost no time in getting ready to move the school on to the new farm. At the time we occupied the place there were standing upon it a cabin, formerly used as the dining room, an old kitchen, a stable, and an old hen-house. Within a few weeks we had all of these structures in use. The stable was repaired and used as a recitation-room, and very presently the hen-house was utilized for the same purpose.

I recall that one morning, when I told an old coloured man who lived near, and who sometimes helped me, that our school had grown so large that it would be necessary for us to use the hen-house for school purposes, and that I wanted him to help me give it a thorough cleaning out the next day, he replied, in the most earnest manner: "What you mean, boss? You sholy ain't gwine clean out de hen-house in de *day*-time?"

Nearly all the work of getting the new location ready for school purposes was done by the students after school was over in the afternoon. As soon as we got the cabins in condition to be used, I determined to clear up some land so that we could plant a crop. When I explained my plan to the young men, I noticed that they did not seem to take to it very kindly. It was hard for them to see the connection between clearing land and an education. Besides, many of them had been school-teachers, and they questioned whether or not clearing land would be in keeping with their dignity. In order to relieve them from any embarrassment, each afternoon after school I took my axe and led the way to the woods. When they saw that I was not afraid or ashamed to work, they began to assist with more enthusiasm. We kept at the work each afternoon, until we had cleared about twenty acres and had planted a crop.

In the meantime Miss Davidson was devising plans to repay the loan. Her first effort was made by holding festivals, or "suppers." She made a personal canvass among the white and coloured families in the town of Tuskegee, and got them to agree to give something, like a cake, a chicken, bread, or pies, that could be sold at the festival. Of course the coloured people were glad to give anything that they could spare, but I want to add that Miss Davidson did not apply to a single white family, so far as I now remember, that failed to donate something; and in many ways the white families showed their interest in the school.

Several of these festivals were held, and quite a little sum of money was raised. A canvass was also made among the people of both races for direct gifts of money, and most of those applied to gave small sums. It was often pathetic to note the gifts of the older coloured people, most of whom had spent their best days in slavery. Sometimes they would give five cents, sometimes twenty-five cents. Sometimes the contribution was a quilt, or a quantity of sugarcane. I recall one old coloured woman, who was about seventy years of age, who came to see me when we were raising money to pay for the farm. She hobbled into the room where I was, leaning on a cane. She was clad in rags; but they were clean. She said: "Mr. Washin'ton, God knows I spent de bes' days of my life in slavery. God knows I's ignorant an' poor; but," she added, "I knows what you an' Miss Davidson is tryin' to do. I knows you is tryin' to make better men an' better women for de coloured race. I ain't got no money, but I wants you to take dese six eggs, what I's been savin' up, an' I wants you to put dese six eggs into de eddication of dese boys an' gals."

Since the work at Tuskegee started, it has been my privilege to receive many gifts for the benefit of the institution, but never any, I think, that touched me so deeply as this one.

CHAPTER IX
ANXIOUS DAYS AND SLEEPLESS NIGHTS

The coming of Christmas, that first year of our residence in Alabama, gave us an opportunity to get a farther insight into the real life of the people. The first thing that reminded us that Christmas had arrived was the "foreday" visits of scores of children rapping at our doors, asking for "Chris'mus gifts! Chris'mus gifts!" Between the hours of two o'clock and five o'clock in the morning I presume that we must have had a half-hundred such calls. This custom prevails throughout this portion of the South to-day.

During the days of slavery it was a custom quite generally observed throughout all the Southern states to give the coloured people a week of holiday at Christmas, or to allow the holiday to continue as long as the "yule log" lasted. The male members of the race, and often the female members, were expected to get drunk. We found that for a whole week the coloured people in and around Tuskegee dropped work the day before Christmas, and that it was difficult to get any one to perform any service from the time they stopped work until after the New Year. Persons who at other times did not use strong drink thought it quite the proper thing to indulge in it rather freely during the Christmas week. There was a widespread hilarity, and a free use of guns, pistols, and gunpowder generally. The sacredness of the season seemed to have been almost wholly lost sight of.

During this first Christmas vacation I went some distance from the town to visit the people on one of the large plantations. In their poverty and ignorance it was pathetic to see their attempts to get joy out of the season that in most parts of the country is so sacred and so dear to the heart. In one cabin I noticed that all that the five children had to remind them of the coming of Christ was a single bunch of firecrackers, which they had divided among them. In another cabin, where there were at least a half-dozen persons, they had only ten cents' worth of ginger-cakes, which had been bought in the store the day before. In another family they had only a few pieces of sugarcane. In still another cabin I found nothing but a new jug of cheap, mean whiskey, which the husband and wife were making free use of, notwithstanding the fact that the husband was one of the local ministers. In a few instances I found that the people had gotten hold of some bright-coloured cards that had been designed for advertising purposes, and were making the most of those. In other homes some member of the family had bought a new pistol. In the majority of cases there was nothing to be seen in the cabin to remind one of the coming of the Saviour, except that the people had ceased work in the fields and were lounging about their homes. At night, during Christmas week, they usually had what they called a "frolic," in some cabin on the plantation. This meant a kind of rough dance, where there was likely to be a good deal of whiskey used, and where there might be some shooting or cutting with razors.

While I was making this Christmas visit I met an old coloured man who was one of the numerous local preachers, who tried to convince me, from the experience Adam had in the Garden of Eden, that God had cursed all labour, and that, therefore, it was a sin for any man to work. For that reason this man sought to do as little work as possible. He seemed at that time to be supremely happy, because he was living, as he expressed it, through one week that was free of sin.

In the school we made a special effort to teach our students the meaning of Christmas, and to give them lessons in its proper observance. In this we have been successful to a degree that makes me feel safe in saying that the season now has a new meaning, not only through all that immediate region, but, in a measure, wherever our graduates have gone.

At the present time one of the most satisfactory features of the Christmas and Thanksgiving seasons at Tuskegee is the unselfish and beautiful way in which our graduates and students spend their time in administering to the comfort and happiness of others, especially the unfortunate. Not long ago some of our young men spent a holiday in rebuilding a cabin for a helpless coloured woman who is about seventy-five years old. At another time I remember that I made it known in chapel, one night, that a very poor student was suffering from cold, because he needed a coat. The next morning two coats were sent to my office for him.

I have referred to the disposition on the part of the white people in the town of Tuskegee and vicinity to help the school. From the first, I resolved to make the school a real part of the community in which it was located. I was determined that not one should have the feeling that it was a foreign institution, dropped down in the midst of the people, for which they had no responsibility and in which they had no interest. I noticed that the very fact that they had been asked to contribute toward the purchase of the land made them begin to feel as if it was going to be their school, to a large degree. I noted that just in proportion as we made the white people feel that the institution was a part of the life of the community, and that, while we wanted to make friends in Boston, for example, we also wanted to make white friends in Tuskegee, and that we wanted to make the school of real service to all the people, their attitude toward the school became favourable.

Perhaps I might add right here, what I hope to demonstrate later, that, so far as I know, the Tuskegee school at the present time has no warmer and more enthusiastic friends anywhere than it has among the white citizens of Tuskegee and throughout the state of Alabama and the entire South. From the first, I have advised our people in the South to make friends in every straightforward, manly way with their next-door neighbour, whether he be a black man or a white man. I have also advised them, where no principle is at stake, to consult the interests of their local communities, and to advise with their friends in regard to their voting.

For several months the work of securing the money with which to pay for the farm went on without ceasing. At the end of three months enough was secured to repay the loan of two hundred and fifty dollars to General Marshall, and within two months more we had secured the entire five hundred dollars and had received a deed of the one hundred acres of land. This gave us a great deal of satisfaction. It was not only a source of satisfaction to secure a permanent location for the school, but it was equally satisfactory to know that the greater part of the money with which it was paid for had been gotten from the white and coloured people in the town of Tuskegee. The most of this money was obtained by holding festivals and concerts, and from small individual donations

Our next effort was in the direction of increasing the cultivation of the land, so as to secure some return from it, and at the same time give the students training in agriculture. All the industries at Tuskegee have been started in natural and logical order, growing out of the needs of a community settlement. We began with farming, because we wanted something to eat.

Many of the students, also, were able to remain in school but a few weeks at a time, because they had so little money with which to pay their board. Thus another object which made it desirable to get an industrial system started was in order to make it available as a means of helping the students to earn money enough so that they might be able to remain in school during the nine months' session of the school year.

The first animal that the school came into possession of was an old blind horse given us by one of the white citizens of Tuskegee. Perhaps I may add here that at the present time the school owns over two hundred horses, colts, mules, cows, calves, and oxen, and about seven hundred hogs and pigs, as well as a large number of sheep and goats.

The school was constantly growing in numbers, so much so that, after we had got the farm paid for, the cultivation of the land begun, and the old cabins which we had found on the place somewhat repaired, we turned our attention toward providing a large, substantial building. After having given a good deal of thought to the subject, we finally had the plans drawn for a building that was estimated to cost about six thousand dollars. This seemed to us a tremendous sum, but we knew that the school must go backward or forward, and that our work would mean little unless we could get hold of the students in their home life.

One incident which occurred about this time gave me a great deal of satisfaction as well as surprise. When it became known in the town that we were discussing the plans for a new, large building, a Southern white man who was operating a sawmill not far from Tuskegee came to me and said that he would gladly put all the lumber necessary to erect the building on the grounds, with no other guarantee for payment than my word that it would be paid for when we secured some money. I told the man frankly that at the time we did not have in our hands one dollar of the money needed. Notwithstanding this, he insisted on being allowed to put the lumber on the grounds. After we had secured some portion of the money we permitted him to do this.

Miss Davidson again began the work of securing in various ways small contributions for the new building from the white and coloured people in and near Tuskegee. I think I never saw a community of people so happy over anything as were the coloured people over the prospect of this new building. One day, when we were holding a meeting to secure funds for its erection, an old, ante-bellum coloured man came a distance of twelve miles and brought in his ox-cart a large hog. When the meeting was in progress, he rose in the midst of the company and said that he had no money which he could give, but that he had raised two fine hogs, and that he had brought one of them as a contribution toward the expenses of the building. He closed his announcement by saying: "Any nigger that's got any love for his race, or any respect for himself, will bring a hog to the next meeting." Quite a number of men in the community also volunteered to give several days' work, each, toward the erection of the building.

After we had secured all the help that we could in Tuskegee, Miss Davidson decided to go North for the purpose of securing additional funds. For weeks she visited individuals and spoke in churches and before Sunday schools and other organizations. She found this work quite trying, and often embarrassing. The school was not known, but she was not long in winning her way into the confidence of the best people in the North.

The first gift from any Northern person was received from a New York lady whom Miss Davidson met on the boat that was bringing her North. They fell into a conversation, and the Northern lady became so much interested in the effort being made at Tuskegee that before they parted Miss Davidson was handed a check for fifty dollars. For some time before our marriage, and also after it, Miss Davidson kept up the work of securing money in the North and in the South by interesting people by personal visits and through correspondence. At the same time she kept in close touch with the work at Tuskegee, as lady principal and classroom teacher. In addition to this, she worked among the older people in and near Tuskegee, and taught a Sunday school class in the town. She was never very strong, but never seemed happy unless she was giving all of her strength to the cause which she loved. Often, at night, after spending the day in going from door to door trying to interest persons in the work at Tuskegee, she would be so exhausted that she could not undress herself. A lady upon whom she called, in Boston, afterward told me that at one time when Miss Davidson called to see her and sent up her card the lady was detained a little before she could see Miss Davidson, and when she entered the parlour she found Miss Davidson so exhausted that she had fallen asleep.

While putting up our first building, which was named Porter Hall, after Mr. A. H. Porter, of Brooklyn, N. Y., who gave a generous sum toward its erection, the need for money became acute. I had given one of our creditors a promise that upon a certain day he should be paid four hundred dollars. On the morning of that day we did not have a dollar. The mail arrived at the school at ten o'clock, and in this mail there was a check sent by Miss Davidson for exactly four hundred dollars. I could relate many instances of almost the same character. This four hundred dollars was given by two ladies in Boston. Two years later, when the work at Tuskegee had grown considerably, and when we were in the midst of a season when we were so much in need of money that the future looked doubtful and gloomy, the same two Boston ladies sent us six thousand dollars. Words cannot describe our surprise, or the encouragement that the gift brought to us. Perhaps I might add here that for fourteen years these same friends have sent us six thousand dollars each year.

As soon as the plans were drawn for the new building, the students began digging out the earth where the foundations were to be laid, working after the regular classes were over. They had not fully outgrown the idea that it was hardly the proper thing for them to use their hands, since they had come there, as one of them expressed it, "to be educated, and not to work." Gradually, though, I noted with satisfaction that a sentiment in favour of work was gaining ground. After a few weeks of hard work the foundations were ready, and a day was appointed for the laying of the corner-stone.

When it is considered that the laying of this corner-stone took place in the heart of the South, in the "Black Belt," in the centre of that part of our country that was most devoted to slavery; that at that time slavery had been abolished only about sixteen years; that only sixteen years before that no Negro could be taught from books without the teacher receiving the condemnation of the law or of public sentiment—when all this is considered, the scene that was witnessed on that spring day at Tuskegee was a remarkable one. I believe there are few places in the world where it could have taken place.

The principal address was delivered by the Hon. Waddy Thompson, the Superintendent of Education for the county. About the corner-stone were gathered the teachers, the students, their parents and friends, the county officials—who were white—and all the leading white men in that vicinity, together with many of the black men and women whom these same white people but a few years before had held a title to as property. The members of both races were anxious to exercise the privilege of placing under the corner-stone some memento.

Before the building was completed we passed through some very trying seasons. More than once our hearts were made to bleed, as it were, because bills were falling due that we did not have the money to meet. Perhaps no one who has not gone through the experience, month after month, of trying to erect buildings and provide equipment for a school when no one knew where the money was to come from, can properly appreciate the difficulties under which we laboured. During the first years at Tuskegee I recall that night after night I would roll and toss on my bed, without sleep, because of the anxiety and uncertainty which we were in regarding money. I knew that, in a large degree, we were trying an experiment – that of testing whether or not it was possible for Negroes to build up and control the affairs of a large educational institution. I knew that if we failed it would injure the whole race. I knew that the presumption was against us. I knew that in the case of white people beginning such an enterprise it would be taken for granted that they were going to succeed, but in our case I felt that people would be surprised if we succeeded. All this made a burden which pressed down on us, sometimes, it seemed, at the rate of a thousand pounds to the square inch.

In all our difficulties and anxieties, however, I never went to a white or a black person in the town of Tuskegee for any assistance that was in their power to render, without being helped according to their means. More than a dozen times, when bills figuring up into the hundreds of dollars were falling due, I applied to the white men of Tuskegee for small loans, often borrowing small amounts from as many as a half-dozen persons, to meet our obligations. One thing I was determined to do from the first, and that was to keep the credit of the school high; and this, I think I can say without boasting, we have done all through these years.

I shall always remember a bit of advice given me by Mr. George W. Campbell, the white man to whom I have referred as the one who induced General Armstrong to send me to Tuskegee. Soon after I entered upon the work Mr. Campbell said to me, in his fatherly way: "Washington, always remember that credit is capital."

At one time when we were in the greatest distress for money that we ever experienced, I placed the situation frankly before General Armstrong. Without hesitation he gave me his personal check for all the money which he had saved for his own use. This was not the only time that General Armstrong helped Tuskegee in this way. I do not think I have ever made this fact public before.

During the summer of 1882, at the end of the first year's work of the school, I was married to Miss Fannie N. Smith, of Malden, W. Va. We began keeping house in Tuskegee early in the fall. This made a home for our teachers, who now had been increased to four in number. My wife was also a graduate of the Hampton Institute. After earnest and constant work in the interests of the school, together with her house-keeping duties, my wife passed away in May, 1884. One child, Portia M. Washington, was born during our marriage.

From the first, my wife most earnestly devoted her thoughts and time to the work of the school, and was completely one with me in every interest and ambition. She passed away, however, before she had an opportunity of seeing what the school was designed to be.

CHAPTER X
A HARDER TASK THAN MAKING BRICKS
WITHOUT STRAW

From the very beginning, at Tuskegee, I was determined to have the students do not only the agricultural and domestic work, but to have them erect their own buildings. My plan was to have them, while performing this service, taught the latest and best methods of labour, so that the school would not only get the benefit of their efforts, but the students themselves would be taught to see not only utility in labour, but beauty and dignity; would be taught, in fact, how to lift labour up from mere drudgery and toil, and would learn to love work for its own sake. My plan was not to teach them to work in the old way, but to show them how to make the forces of nature – air, water, steam, electricity, horse-power—assist them in their labour.

At first many advised against the experiment of having the buildings erected by the labour of the students, but I was determined to stick to it. I told those who doubted the wisdom of the plan that I knew that our first buildings would not be so comfortable or so complete in their finish as buildings erected by the experienced hands of outside workmen, but that in the teaching of civilization, self-help, and self-reliance, the erection of the buildings by the students themselves would more than compensate for any lack of comfort or fine finish.

I further told those who doubted the wisdom of this plan, that the majority of our students came to us in poverty, from the cabins of the cotton, sugar, and rice plantations of the South, and that while I knew it would please the students very much to place them at once in finely constructed buildings, I felt that it would be following out a more natural process of development to teach them how to construct their own buildings. Mistakes I knew would be made, but these mistakes would teach us valuable lessons for the future.

During the now nineteen years' existence of the Tuskegee school, the plan of having the buildings erected by student labour has been adhered to. In this time forty buildings, counting small and large, have been built, and all except four are almost wholly the product of student labour. As an additional result, hundreds of men are now scattered throughout the South who received their knowledge of mechanics while being taught how to erect these buildings. Skill and knowledge are now handed down from one set of students to another in this way, until at the present time a building of any description or size can be constructed wholly by our instructors and students, from the drawing of the plans to the putting in of the electric fixtures, without going off the grounds for a single workman.

Not a few times, when a new student has been led into the temptation of marring the looks of some building by lead pencil marks or by the cuts of a jack-knife, I have heard an old student remind him: "Don't do that. That is our building. I helped put it up."

In the early days of the school I think my most trying experience was in the matter of brick making. As soon as we got the farm work reasonably well started, we directed our next efforts toward the industry of making bricks. We needed these for use in connection with the erection of our own buildings; but there was also another reason for establishing this industry. There was no brickyard in the town, and in addition to our own needs there was a demand for bricks in the general market.

I had always sympathized with the "Children of Israel," in their task of "making bricks without straw," but ours was the task of making bricks with no money and no experience.

In the first place, the work was hard and dirty, and it was difficult to get the students to help. When it came to brick making, their distaste for manual labour in connection with book education became especially manifest. It was not a pleasant task for one to stand in the mud-pit for hours, with the mud up to his knees. More than one man became disgusted and left the school.

We tried several locations before we opened up a pit that furnished brick clay. I had always supposed that brick making was very simple, but I soon found out by bitter experience that it required special skill and knowledge, particularly in the burning of the bricks. After a good deal of effort we moulded about twenty-five thousand bricks, and put them into a kiln to be burned. This kiln turned out to be a failure, because it was not properly constructed or properly burned. We began at once, however, on a second kiln. This, for some reason, also proved a failure. The failure of this kiln made it still more difficult to get the students to take any part in the work. Several of the teachers, however, who had been trained in the industries at Hampton, volunteered their services, and in some way we succeeded in getting a third kiln ready for burning. The burning of a kiln required about a week. Toward the latter part of the week, when it seemed as if we were going to have a good many thousand bricks in a few hours, in the middle of the night the kiln fell. For the third time we had failed.

The failure of this last kiln left me without a single dollar with which to make another experiment. Most of the teachers advised the abandoning of the effort to make bricks. In the midst of my troubles I thought of a watch which had come into my possession years before. I took this watch to the city of Montgomery, which was not far distant, and placed it in a pawn-shop. I secured cash upon it to the amount of fifteen dollars, with which to renew the brick making experiment. I returned to Tuskegee, and, with the help of the fifteen dollars, rallied our rather demoralized and discouraged forces and began a fourth attempt to make bricks. This time, I am glad to say, we were successful. Before I got hold of any money, the time-limit on my watch had expired, and I have never seen it since; but I have never regretted the loss of it.

Brick making has now become such an important industry at the school that last season our students manufactured twelve hundred thousand of first-class bricks, of a quality suitable to be sold in any market. Aside from this, scores of young men have mastered the brick making trade – both the making of bricks by hand and by machinery— and are now engaged in this industry in many parts of the South.

MAKING BRICKS WITHOUT STRAW

The making of these bricks taught me an important lesson in regard to the relations of the two races in the South. Many white people who had had no contact with the school, and perhaps no sympathy with it, came to us to buy bricks because they found out that ours were good bricks. They discovered that we were supplying a real want in the community. The making of these bricks caused many of the white residents of the neighbourhood to begin to feel that the education of the Negro was not making him worthless, but that in educating our students we were adding something to the wealth and comfort of the community. As the people of the neighbourhood came to us to buy bricks, we got acquainted with them; they traded with us and we with them. Our business interests became intermingled. We had something which they wanted; they had something which we wanted. This, in a large measure, helped to lay the foundation for the pleasant relations that have continued to exist between us and the white people in that section, and which now extend throughout the South.

Wherever one of our brick makers has gone in the South, we find that he has something to contribute to the well-being of the community into which he has gone; something that has made the community feel that, in a degree, it is indebted to him, and perhaps, to a certain extent, dependent upon him. In this way pleasant relations between the races have been stimulated.

My experience is that there is something in human nature which always makes an individual recognize and reward merit, no matter under what colour skin merit is found. I have found, too, that it is the visible, the tangible, that goes a long ways in softening prejudices. The actual sight of a first-class house that a Negro has built is ten times more potent than pages of discussion about a house that he ought to build, or perhaps could build.

The same principle of industrial education has been carried out in the building of our own wagons, carts, and buggies, from the first. We now own and use on our farm and about the school dozens of these vehicles, and every one of them has been built by the hands of the students. Aside from this, we help supply the local market with these vehicles. The supplying of them to the people in the community has had the same effect as the supplying of bricks, and the man who learns at Tuskegee to build and repair wagons and carts is regarded as a benefactor by both races in the community where he goes. The people with whom he lives and works are going to think twice before they part with such a man.

The individual who can do something that the world wants done will, in the end, make his way regardless of his race. One man may go into a community prepared to supply the people there with an analysis of Greek sentences. The community may not at that time be prepared for, or feel the need of, Greek analysis, but it may feel its need of bricks and houses and wagons. If the man can supply the need for those, then, it will lead eventually to a demand for the first product, and with the demand will come the ability to appreciate it and to profit by it.

About the time that we succeeded in burning our first kiln of bricks we began facing in an emphasized form the objection of the students to being taught to work. By this time it had gotten to be pretty well advertised throughout the state that every student who came to Tuskegee, no matter what his financial ability might be, must learn some industry. Quite a number of letters came from parents protesting against their children engaging in labour while they were in the school. Other parents came to the school to protest in person. Most of the new students brought a written or a verbal request from their parents to the effect that they wanted their children taught nothing but books. The more books, the larger they were, and the longer the titles printed upon them, the better pleased the students and their parents seemed to be.

I gave little heed to these protests, except that I lost no opportunity to go into as many parts of the state as I could, for the purpose of speaking to the parents, and showing them the value of industrial education. Besides, I talked to the students constantly on the subject. Notwithstanding the unpopularity of industrial work, the school continued to increase in numbers to such an extent that by the middle of the second year there was an attendance of about one hundred and fifty, representing almost all parts of the state of Alabama, and including a few from other states.

In the summer of 1882 Miss Davidson and I both went North and engaged in the work of raising funds for the completion of our new building. On my way North I stopped in New York to try to get a letter of recommendation from an officer of a missionary organization who had become somewhat acquainted with me a few years previous. This man not only refused to give me the letter, but advised me most earnestly to go back home at once, and not make an attempt to get money, for he was quite sure that I would never get more than enough to pay my travelling expenses. I thanked him for his advice, and proceeded on my journey.

The first place I went to in the North, was Northampton, Mass., where I spent nearly a half-day in looking for a coloured family with whom I could board, never dreaming that any hotel would admit me. I was greatly surprised when I found that I would have no trouble in being accommodated at a hotel.

We were successful in getting money enough so that on Thanksgiving Day of that year we held our first service in the chapel of Porter Hall, although the building was not completed.

In looking about for some one to preach the Thanksgiving sermon, I found one of the rarest men that it has ever been my privilege to know. This was the Rev. Robert C. Bedford, a white man from Wisconsin, who was then pastor of a little coloured Congregational church in Montgomery, Ala. Before going to Montgomery to look for some one to preach this sermon I had never heard of Mr. Bedford. He had never heard of me. He gladly consented to come to Tuskegee and hold the Thanksgiving service. It was the first service of the kind that the coloured people there had ever observed, and what a deep interest they manifested in it! The sight of the new building made it a day of Thanksgiving for them never to be forgotten.

Mr. Bedford consented to become one of the trustees of the school, and in that capacity, and as a worker for it, he has been connected with it for eighteen years. During this time he has borne the school upon his heart night and day, and is never so happy as when he is performing some service, no matter how humble, for it. He completely obliterates

98

himself in everything, and looks only for permission to serve where service is most disagreeable, and where others would not be attracted. In all my relations with him he has seemed to me to approach as nearly to the spirit of the Master as almost any man I ever met.

A little later there came into the service of the school another man, quite young at the time, and fresh from Hampton, without whose service the school never could have become what it is. This was Mr. Warren Logan, who now for seventeen years has been the treasurer of the Institute, and the acting principal during my absence. He has always shown a degree of unselfishness and an amount of business tact, coupled with a clear judgement, that has kept the school in good condition no matter how long I have been absent from it. During all the financial stress through which the school has passed, his patience and faith in our ultimate success have not left him.

As soon as our first building was near enough to completion so that we could occupy a portion of it—which was near the middle of the second year of the school—we opened a boarding department. Students had begun coming from quite a distance, and in such increasing numbers that we felt more and more that we were merely skimming over the surface, in that we were not getting hold of the students in their home life.

We had nothing but the students and their appetites with which to begin a boarding department. No provision had been made in the new building for a kitchen and dining room; but we discovered that by digging out a large amount of earth from under the building we could make a partially lighted basement room that could be used for a kitchen and dining room. Again I called on the students to volunteer for work, this time to assist in digging out the basement. This they did, and in a few weeks we had a place to cook and eat in, although it was very rough and uncomfortable. Any one seeing the place now would never believe that it was once used for a dining room.

The most serious problem, though, was to get the boarding department started off in running order, with nothing to do with in the way of furniture, and with no money with which to buy anything. The merchants in the town would let us have what food we wanted on credit. In fact, in those earlier years I was constantly embarrassed because people seemed to have more faith in me than I had in myself. It was pretty hard to cook, however, without stoves, and awkward to eat without dishes. At first the cooking was done out-of-doors, in the old-fashioned, primitive style, in pots and skillets placed over a fire. Some of the carpenters' benches that had been used in the construction of the building were utilized for tables. As for dishes, there were too few to make it worth while to spend time in describing them.

No one connected with the boarding department seemed to have any idea that meals must be served at certain fixed and regular hours, and this was a source of great worry. Everything was so out of joint and so inconvenient that I feel safe in saying that for the first two weeks something was wrong at every meal. Either the meat was not done or had been burnt, or the salt had been left out of the bread, or the tea had been forgotten.

Early one morning I was standing near the dining-room door listening to the complaints of the students. The complaints that morning were especially emphatic and numerous, because the whole breakfast had been a failure. One of the girls who had failed to get any breakfast came out and went to the well to draw some water to drink to take the place of the breakfast which she had not been able to get. When she reached the well, she found that the rope was broken and that she could get no water. She turned from the well and said, in the most discouraged tone, not knowing that I was where I could hear her, "We can't even get water to drink at this school." I think no one remark ever came so near discouraging me as that one.

At another time, when Mr. Bedford—whom I have already spoken of as one of our trustees, and a devoted friend of the institution—was visiting the school, he was given a bedroom immediately over the dining room. Early in the morning he was awakened by a rather animated discussion between two boys in the dining room below. The discussion was over the question as to whose turn it was to use the coffee-cup that morning. One boy won the case by proving that for three mornings he had not had an opportunity to use the cup at all.

But gradually, by patience and hard work, we brought order out of chaos, just as will be true of any problem if we stick to it with patience and wisdom and earnest effort.

As I look back now over that part of our struggle, I am glad that we had it. I am glad that we endured all those discomforts and inconveniences. I am glad that our students had to dig out the place for their kitchen and dining room. I am glad that our first boarding-place was in that dismal, ill-lighted, and damp basement. Had we started in a fine, attractive, convenient room, I fear we would have "lost our heads" and become "stuck up." It means a great deal, I think, to start off on a foundation which one has made for one's self.

When our old students return to Tuskegee now, as they often do, and go into our large, beautiful, well-ventilated, and well-lighted dining room, and see tempting, well-cooked food—largely grown by the students themselves—and see tables, neat tablecloths and napkins, and vases of flowers upon the tables, and hear singing birds, and note that each meal is served exactly upon the minute, with no disorder, and with almost no complaint coming from the hundreds that now fill our dining room, they, too, often say to me that they are glad that we started as we did, and built ourselves up year by year, by a slow and natural process of growth.

CHAPTER XI
MAKING THEIR BEDS BEFORE THEY COULD LIE ON THEM

A little later in the history of the school we had a visit from General J. F. B. Marshall, the Treasurer of the Hampton Institute, who had had faith enough to lend us the first two hundred and fifty dollars with which to make a payment down on the farm. He remained with us a week, and made a careful inspection of everything. He seemed well pleased with our progress, and wrote back interesting and encouraging reports to Hampton. A little later Miss Mary F. Mackie, the teacher who had given me the "sweeping" examination when I entered Hampton, came to see us, and still later General Armstrong himself came.

At the time of the visits of these Hampton friends the number of teachers at Tuskegee had increased considerably, and the most of the new teachers were graduates of the Hampton Institute. We gave our Hampton friends, especially General Armstrong, a cordial welcome. They were all surprised and pleased at the rapid progress that the school had made within so short a time. The coloured people from miles around came to the school to get a look at General Armstrong, about whom they had heard so much. The General was not only welcomed by the members of my own race, but by the Southern white people as well.

This first visit which General Armstrong made to Tuskegee gave me an opportunity to get an insight into his character such as I had not before had. I refer to his interest in the Southern white people. Before this I had had the thought that General Armstrong, having fought the Southern white man, rather cherished a feeling of bitterness toward the white South, and was interested in helping only the coloured man there.

But this visit convinced me that I did not know the greatness and generosity of the man. I soon learned, by his visits to the Southern white people, and from his conversations with them that he was as anxious about the prosperity and happiness of the white race as the black. He cherished no bitterness against the south, and was happy when an opportunity offered for manifesting his sympathy. In all my acquaintance with General Armstrong I never heard him speak, in public or in private, a single bitter word against the white man in the South. From his example in this respect I learned the lesson that great men cultivate love, and that only little men cherish a spirit of hatred. I learned that assistance given to the weak makes the one who gives it strong; and that oppression of the unfortunate makes one weak.

It is now long ago that I learned this lesson from General Armstrong, and resolved that I would permit no man, no matter what his colour might be, to narrow and degrade my soul by making me hate him. With God's help, I believe that I have completely rid myself of any ill feeling toward the Southern white man for any wrong that he may have inflicted upon my race. I am made to feel just as happy now when I am rendering service to Southern white men as when the service is rendered to a member of my own race. I pity from the bottom of my heart any individual who is so unfortunate as to get into the habit of holding race prejudice.

The more I consider the subject, the more strongly I am convinced that the most harmful effect of the practice to which the people in certain sections of the South have felt themselves compelled to resort, in order to get rid of the force of the Negroes' ballot, is not wholly in the wrong done to the Negro, but in the permanent injury to the morals of the white man the injury is permanent. I have noted time and time again that when an individual perjures himself in order to break the force of the black man's ballot, he soon learns to practise dishonesty in other relations of life, not only where the Negro is concerned, but equally so where a white man is concerned. The white man who begins by cheating a Negro usually ends by cheating a white man. The white man who begins to break the law by lynching a Negro soon yields to the temptation to lynch a white man. All this, it seems to me, makes it important that the whole Nation lend a hand in trying to lift the burden of ignorance from the South.

Another thing that is becoming more apparent each year in the development of education in the South is the influence of General Armstrong's idea of education; and this not upon the blacks alone, but upon the whites also. At the present time there is almost no Southern state that is not putting forth efforts in the direction of securing industrial education for its white boys and girls, and in most cases it is easy to trace the history of these efforts back to General Armstrong.

Soon after the opening of our humble boarding department students began coming to us in still larger numbers. For weeks we not only had to contend with the difficulty of providing board, with no money, but also with that of providing sleeping accommodations. For this purpose we rented a number of cabins near the school. These cabins were in a dilapidated condition, and during the winter months the students who occupied them necessarily suffered from the cold. We charged the students eight dollars a month—all they were able to pay—for their board. This included, besides board, room, fuel, and washing. We also gave the students credit on their board bills for all the work which they did for the school which was of any value to the institution. The cost of tuition, which was fifty dollars a year for each student, we had to secure then, as now, wherever we could.

This small charge in cash gave us no capital with which to start a boarding department. The weather during the second winter of our work was very cold. We were not able to provide enough bed-clothes to keep the students warm. In fact, for some time we were not able to provide, except in a few cases, bedsteads and mattresses of any kind. During the coldest nights I was so troubled about the discomfort of the students that I could not sleep myself. I recall that on several occasions I went in the middle of the night to the shanties occupied by the young men, for the purpose of comforting them. Often I found some of them sitting huddled around a fire, with the one blanket which we had been able to provide wrapped around them, trying in this way to keep warm. During the whole night some of them did not attempt to lie down. One morning, when the night previous had been unusually cold, I asked those of the students in the chapel who thought that they had been frostbitten during the night to raise their hands. Three hands went up. Notwithstanding these experiences, there was almost no complaining on the part of the students. They knew that we were doing the best that we could for them. They were happy in the privilege of being permitted to enjoy any kind of opportunity that would enable them to improve their condition. They were constantly asking what they might do to lighten the burdens of the teachers.

I have heard it stated more than once, both in the North and in the South, that coloured people would not obey and respect each other when one member of the race is placed in a position of authority over others. In regard to this general belief and these statements, I can say that during the nineteen years of my experience at Tuskegee I never, either by word or act, have been treated with disrespect by any student or officer connected with the institution. On the other hand, I am constantly embarrassed by the many acts of thoughtful kindness. The students do not seem to want to see me carry a large book or a satchel or any kind of a burden through the grounds. In such cases more than one always offers to relieve me. I almost never go out of my office when the rain is falling that some student does not come to my side with an umbrella and ask to be allowed to hold it over me.

While writing upon this subject, it is a pleasure for me to add that in all my contact with the white people of the South I have never received a single personal insult. The white people in and near Tuskegee, to an especial degree, seem to count it a privilege to show me all the respect within their power, and often go out of their way to do this.

Not very long ago I was making a journey between Dallas (Texas) and Houston. In some way it became known in advance that I was on the train. At nearly every station at which the train stopped, numbers of white people, including in most cases the officials of the town, came aboard and introduced themselves and thanked me heartily for the work that I was trying to do for the South.

On another occasion, when I was making a trip from Augusta, Georgia, to Atlanta, being rather tired from much travel, I rode in a

Pullman sleeper. When I went into the car, I found there two ladies from Boston whom I knew well. These good ladies were perfectly ignorant, it seems, of the customs of the South, and in the goodness of their hearts insisted that I take a seat with them in their section. After some hesitation I consented. I had been there but a few minutes when one of them, without my knowledge, ordered supper to be served to the three of us. This embarrassed me still further. The car was full of Southern white men, most of whom had their eyes on our party. When I found that supper had been ordered, I tried to contrive some excuse that would permit me to leave the section, but the ladies insisted that I must eat with them. I finally settled back in my seat with a sigh, and said to myself, "I am in for it now, sure."

To add further to the embarrassment of the situation, soon after the supper was placed on the table one of the ladies remembered that she had in her satchel a special kind of tea which she wished served, and as she said she felt quite sure the porter did not know how to brew it properly, she insisted upon getting up and preparing and serving it herself. At last the meal was over; and it seemed the longest one that I had ever eaten. When we were through, I decided to get myself out of the embarrassing situation and go into the smoking-room, where most of the men were by that time, to see how the land lay. In the meantime, however, it had become known in some way throughout the car who I was. When I went into the smoking-room I was never more surprised in my life than when each man, nearly every one of them a citizen of Georgia, came up and introduced himself to me and thanked me earnestly for the work that I was trying to do for the whole South. This was not flattery, because each one of these individuals knew that he had nothing to gain by trying to flatter me.

From the first I have sought to impress the students with the idea that Tuskegee is not my institution, or that of the officers, but that it is their institution, and that they have as much interest in it as any of the trustees or instructors. I have further sought to have them feel that I am at the institution as their friend and adviser, and not as their overseer. It has been my aim to have them speak with directness and frankness about anything that concerns the life of the school. Two or three times a year I ask the students to write me a letter criticizing or making complaints or suggestions about anything connected with the institution. When this is not done, I have them meet me in the chapel for a heart-to-heart talk about the conduct of the school. There are no meetings with our students that I enjoy more than these, and none are more helpful to me in planning for the future. These meetings, it seems to me, enable me to get at the very heart of all that concerns the school. Few things help an individual more than to place responsibility upon him, and to let him know that you trust him. When I have read of labour troubles between employers and employees, I have often thought that many strikes and similar disturbances might be avoided if the employers would cultivate the habit of getting nearer to their employees, of consulting and advising with them, and letting them feel that the interests of the two are the same. Every individual responds to confidence, and this is not more true of any race than of the Negroes. Let them once understand that you are unselfishly interested in them, and you can lead them to any extent.

It was my aim from the first at Tuskegee to not only have the buildings erected by the students themselves, but to have them make their own furniture as far as was possible. I now marvel at the patience of the students while sleeping upon the floor while waiting for some kind of a bedstead to be constructed, or at their sleeping without any kind of a mattress while waiting for something that looked like a mattress to be made.

In the early days we had very few students who had been used to handling carpenters' tools, and the bedsteads made by the students then were very rough and very weak. Not unfrequently when I went into the students' rooms in the morning I would find a least two bedsteads lying about on the floor. The problem of providing mattresses was a difficult one to solve. We finally mastered this, however, by getting some cheap cloth and sewing pieces of this together so as to make large bags. These bags we filled with the pine straw—or, as it is sometimes called, pine needles—which we secured from the forests near by. I am glad to say that the industry of mattress-making has grown steadily since then, and has been improved to such an extent that at the present time it is an important branch of the work which is taught systematically to a number of our girls, and that the mattresses that now come out of the mattress-shop at Tuskegee are about as good as those bought in the average store. For some time after the opening of the boarding department we had no chairs in the students' bedrooms or in the dining rooms. Instead of chairs we used stools which the students constructed by nailing together three pieces of rough board. As a rule, the furniture in the students' rooms during the early days of the school consisted of a bed, some stools, and sometimes a rough table made by the students. The plan of having the students make the furniture is still followed, but the number of pieces in a room has been increased, and the workmanship has so improved that little fault can be found with the articles now. One thing that I have always insisted upon at Tuskegee is that everywhere there should be absolute cleanliness. Over and over again the students were reminded in those first years—and are reminded now—that people would excuse us for our poverty, for our lack of comforts and conveniences, but that they would not excuse us for dirt.

Another thing that has been insisted upon at the school is the use of the tooth-brush. "The gospel of the tooth-brush," as General Armstrong used to call it, is a part of our creed at Tuskegee. No student is permitted to remain who does not keep and use a tooth-brush. Several times, in recent years, students have come to us who brought with them almost no other article except a tooth-brush. They had heard from the lips of older students about our insisting upon the use of this, and so, to make a good impression, they brought at least a tooth-brush with them. I remember that one morning, not long ago, I went with the lady principal on her usual morning tour of inspection of the girls' rooms. We found one room that contained three girls who had recently arrived at the school. When I asked them if they had tooth-brushes, one of the girls replied, pointing to a brush: "Yes, sir. That is our brush. We bought it together, yesterday." It did not take them long to learn a different lesson.

It has been interesting to note the effect that the use of the tooth-brush has had in bringing about a higher degree of civilization among the students. With few exceptions, I have noticed that, if we can get a student to the point where, when the first or second tooth-brush disappears, he of his own motion buys another, I have not been disappointed in the future of that individual. Absolute cleanliness of the body has been insisted upon from the first. The students have been taught to bathe as regularly as to take their meals. This lesson we began teaching before we had anything in the shape of a bath-house. Most of the students came from plantation districts, and often we had to teach them how to sleep at night; that is, whether between the two sheets—after we got to the point where we could provide them two sheets—or under both of them. Naturally I found it difficult to teach them to sleep between two sheets when we were able to supply but one. The importance of the use of the nightgown received the same attention.

For a long time one of the most difficult tasks was to teach the students that all the buttons were to be kept on their clothes, and that there must be no torn places and no grease-spots. This lesson, I am pleased to be able to say, has been so thoroughly learned and so faithfully handed down from year to year by one set of students to another that often at the present time, when the students march out of chapel in the evening and their dress is inspected, as it is every night, not one button is to be found missing.

CHAPTER XII
RAISING MONEY

When we opened our boarding department, we provided rooms in the attic of Porter Hall, our first building, for a number of girls. But the number of students, of both sexes, continued to increase. We could find rooms outside the school grounds for many of the young men, but the girls we did not care to expose in this way. Very soon the problem of providing more rooms for the girls, as well as a larger boarding department for all the students, grew serious. As a result, we finally decided to undertake the construction of a still larger building—a building that would contain rooms for the girls and boarding accommodations for all.

After having had a preliminary sketch of the needed building made, we found that it would cost about ten thousand dollars. We had no money whatever with which to begin; still we decided to give the needed building a name. We knew we could name it, even though we were in doubt about our ability to secure the means for its construction. We decided to call the proposed building Alabama Hall, in honour of the state in which we were labouring. Again Miss Davidson began making efforts to enlist the interest and help of the coloured and white people in and near Tuskegee. They responded willingly, in proportion to their means. The students, as in the case of our first building, Porter Hall, began digging out the dirt in order to allow of the laying of the foundations.

When we seemed at the end of our resources, so far as securing money was concerned, something occurred which showed the greatness of General Armstrong—something which proved how far he was above the ordinary individual. When we were in the midst of great anxiety as to where and how we were to get funds for the new building, I received a telegram from General Armstrong asking me if I could spend a month travelling with him through the North, and asking me, if I could do so, to come to Hampton at once. Of course I accepted General Armstrong's invitation, and went to Hampton immediately. On arriving there I found that the General had decided to take a quartette of singers through the North, and hold meetings for a month in important cities, at which meetings he and I were to speak. Imagine my surprise when the General told me, further, that these meetings were to be held, not in the interests of Hampton, but in the interests of Tuskegee, and that the Hampton Institute was to be responsible for all the expenses.

Although he never told me so in so many words, I found out that General Armstrong took this method of introducing me to the people of the North, as well as for the sake of securing some immediate funds to be used in the erection of Alabama Hall. A weak and narrow man would have reasoned that all the money which came to Tuskegee in this way would be just so much taken from the Hampton Institute; but none of these selfish or short-sighted feelings ever entered the breast of General Armstrong. He was too big to be little, too good to be mean. He knew that the people in the North who gave money gave it for the purpose of helping the whole cause of Negro civilization, and not merely for the advancement of any one school. The General knew, too, that the way to strengthen Hampton was to make it a centre of unselfish power in the working out of the whole Southern problem.

In regard to the addresses which I was to make in the North, I recall just one piece of advice which the General gave me. He said: "Give them an idea for every word." I think it would be hard to improve upon this advice; and it might be made to apply to all public speaking. From that time to the present I have always tried to keep his advice in mind.

Meetings were held in New York, Brooklyn, Boston, Philadelphia, and other large cities, and at all of these meetings General Armstrong pleaded, together with myself, for help, not for Hampton, but for Tuskegee. At these meetings an especial effort was made to secure help for the building of Alabama Hall, as well as to introduce the school to the attention of the general public. In both these respects the meetings proved successful.

After that kindly introduction I began going North alone to secure funds. During the last fifteen years I have been compelled to spend a large proportion of my time away from the school, in an effort to secure money to provide for the growing needs of the institution. In my efforts to get funds I have had some experiences that may be of interest to my readers. Time and time again I have been asked, by people who are trying to secure money for philanthropic purposes, what rule or rules I followed to secure the interest and help of people who were able to contribute money to worthy objects. As far as the science of what is called begging can be reduced to rules, I would say that I have had but two rules. First, always to do my whole duty regarding making our work known to individuals and organizations; and, second, not to worry about the results. This second rule has been the hardest for me to live up to. When bills are on the eve of falling due, with not a dollar in hand with which to meet them, it is pretty difficult to learn not to worry, although I think I am learning more and more each year that all worry simply consumes, and to no purpose, just so much physical and mental strength that might otherwise be given to effective work. After considerable experience in coming into contact with wealthy and noted men, I have observed that those who have accomplished the greatest results are those who "keep under the body"; are those who never grow excited or lose self-control, but are always calm, self-possessed, patient, and polite. I think that President William McKinley is the best example of a man of this class that I have ever seen.

In order to be successful in any kind of undertaking, I think the main thing is for one to grow to the point where he completely forgets himself; that is, to lose himself in a great cause. In proportion as one loses himself in this way, in the same degree does he get the highest happiness out of his work.

My experience in getting money for Tuskegee has taught me to have no patience with those people who are always condemning the rich because they are rich, and because they do not give more to objects of charity. In the first place, those who are guilty of such sweeping criticisms do not know how many people would be made poor, and how much suffering would result, if wealthy people were to part all at once with any large proportion of their wealth in a way to disorganize and cripple great business enterprises. Then very few persons have any idea of the large number of applications for help that rich people are constantly being flooded with. I know wealthy people who receive as many as twenty calls a day for help. More than once, when I have gone into the offices of rich men, I have found half a dozen persons waiting to see them and all come for the same purpose, that of securing money. And all these calls in person, to say nothing of the applications received through the mails. Very few people have any idea of the amount of money given away by persons who never permit their names to be known. I have often heard persons condemned for not giving away money, who, to my own knowledge, were giving away thousands of dollars every year so quietly that the world knew nothing about it.

As an example of this, there are two ladies in New York, whose names rarely appear in print, but who, in a quiet way, have given us the means with which to erect three large and important buildings during the last eight years. Besides the gift of these buildings, they have made other generous donations to the school. And they not only help Tuskegee, but they are constantly seeking opportunities to help other worthy causes.

Although it has been my privilege to be the medium through which a good many hundred thousand dollars have been received for the work at Tuskegee, I have always avoided what the world calls "begging." I often tell people that I have never "begged" any money, and that I am not a "beggar." My experience and observation have convinced me that persistent asking outright for money from the rich does not, as a rule, secure help. I have usually proceeded on the principle that persons who possess sense enough to earn money have sense enough to know how to give it away, and that the mere making known of the facts regarding Tuskegee, and especially the facts regarding the work of the graduates, has been more effective than outright begging. I think that the presentation of facts, on a high, dignified plane, is all the begging that most rich people care for.

While the work of going from door to door and from office to office is hard, disagreeable, and costly in bodily strength, yet it has some compensations. Such work gives one a rare opportunity to study human nature. It also has its compensations in giving one an opportunity to meet some of the best people in the world—to be more correct, I think I should say *the best* people in the world. When one takes a broad survey of the country, he will find that the most useful and influential people in it are those who take the deepest interest in institutions that exist for the purpose of making the world better.

At one time, when I was in Boston, I called at the door of a rather wealthy lady, and was admitted to the vestibule and sent up my card. While I was waiting for an answer, her husband came in, and asked me in the most abrupt manner what I wanted. When I tried to explain the object of my call, he became still more ungentlemanly in his words and manner, and finally grew so excited that I left the house without waiting for a reply from the lady. A few blocks from that house I called to see a gentleman who received me in the most cordial manner. He wrote me his check for a generous sum, and then, before I had had an opportunity to thank him, said: "I am so grateful to you, Mr. Washington, for giving me the opportunity to help a good cause. It is a privilege to have a share in it. We in Boston are constantly indebted to you for doing *our* work." My experience in securing money convinces me that the first type of man is growing more rare all the time, and the latter type is increasing; that is, that, more and more, rich people are coming to regard men and women who apply to them for help for worthy objects, not as beggars, but as agents for doing their work.

In the city of Boston I have rarely called upon an individual for funds that I have not been thanked for calling usually before I could get an opportunity to thank the donor for the money. In that city the donors seem to feel, in a large degree, that an honour is being conferred upon them in their being permitted to give. Nowhere else have I met with, in so large a measure, this fine and Christlike spirit as in the city of Boston, although there are many notable instances of it outside that city. I repeat my belief that the world is growing in the direction of giving. I repeat that the main rule by which I have been guided in collecting money is to do my full duty in regard to giving people who have money an opportunity to help.

In the early years of the Tuskegee school I walked the streets or travelled country roads in the North for days and days without receiving a dollar. Often it has happened, when during the week I had been disappointed in not getting a cent from the very individuals from whom I most expected help, and when I was almost broken down and discouraged, that generous help has come from some one who I had had little idea would give at all.

I recall that on one occasion I obtained information that led me to believe that a gentleman who lived about two miles out in the country from Stamford, Conn., might become interested in our efforts at Tuskegee if our conditions and needs were presented to him. On an unusually cold and stormy day I walked the two miles to see him. After some difficulty I succeeded in securing an interview with him. He listened with some degree of interest to what I had to say, but did not give me anything. I could not help having the feeling that, in a measure, the three hours that I had spent in seeing him had been thrown away. Still, I had followed my usual rule of doing my duty. If I had not seen him, I should have felt unhappy over neglect of duty.

Two years after this visit a letter came to Tuskegee from this man, which read like this: "Enclosed I send you a New York draft for ten thousand dollars, to be used in furtherance of your work. I had placed this sum in my will for your school, but deem it wiser to give it to you while I live. I recall with pleasure your visit to me two years ago."

I can hardly imagine any occurrence which could have given me more genuine satisfaction than the receipt of this draft. It was by far the largest single donation which up to that time the school had ever received. It came at a time when an unusually long period had passed since we had received any money. We were in great distress because of lack of funds, and the nervous strain was tremendous. It is difficult for me to think of any situation that is more trying on the nerves than that of conducting a large institution, with heavy financial obligations to meet, without knowing where the money is to come from to meet these obligations from month to month.

In our case I felt a double responsibility, and this made the anxiety all the more intense. If the institution had been officered by white persons, and had failed, it would have injured the cause of Negro education; but I knew that the failure of our institution, officered by Negroes, would not only mean the loss of a school, but would cause people, in a large degree, to lose faith in the ability of the entire race. The receipt of this draft for ten thousand dollars, under all these circumstances, partially lifted a burden that had been pressing down upon me for days.

From the beginning of our work to the present I have always had the feeling, and lose no opportunity to impress our teachers with the same idea, that the school will always be supported in proportion as the inside of the institution is kept clean and pure and wholesome.

The first time I ever saw the late Collis P. Huntington, the great railroad man, he gave me two dollars for our school. The last time I saw him, which was a few months before he died, he gave me fifty thousand dollars toward our endowment fund. Between these two gifts there were others of generous proportions which came every year from both Mr. and Mrs. Huntington.

Some people may say that it was Tuskegee's good luck that brought to us this gift of fifty thousand dollars. No, it was not luck. It was hard work. Nothing ever comes to one, that is worth having, except as a result of hard work. When Mr. Huntington gave me the first two dollars, I did not blame him for not giving me more, but made up my mind that I was going to convince him by tangible results that we were worthy of larger gifts. For a dozen years I made a strong effort to convince Mr. Huntington of the value of our work. I noted that just in proportion as the usefulness of the school grew, his donations increased. Never did I meet an individual who took a more kindly and sympathetic interest in our school than did Mr. Huntington. He not only gave money to us, but took time in which to advise me, as a father would a son, about the general conduct of the school.

More than once I have found myself in some pretty tight places while collecting money in the North. The following incident I have never related but once before, for the reason that I feared that people would not believe it. One morning I found myself in Providence, Rhode Island, without a cent of money with which to buy breakfast. In crossing the street to see a lady from whom I hoped to get some money, I found a bright new twenty-five-cent piece in the middle of the streetcar track. I not only had this twenty-five cents for my breakfast, but within a few minutes I had a donation from the lady on whom I had started to call.

At one of our Commencements I was bold enough to invite the Rev. E. Winchester Donald, D. D., rector of Trinity Church, Boston, to preach the Commencement sermon. As we then had no room large enough to accommodate all who would be present, the place of meeting was under a large, improvised arbour, built partly of brush and partly of rough boards. Soon after Dr. Donald had begun speaking, the rain came down in torrents, and he had to stop, while some one held an umbrella over him.

The boldness of what I had done never dawned upon me until I saw the picture made by the rector of Trinity Church standing before that large audience under an old umbrella, waiting for the rain to cease so that he could go on with his address.

It was not very long before the rain ceased and Dr. Donald finished his sermon; and an excellent sermon it was, too, in spite of the weather. After he had gone to his room, and had gotten the wet threads of his clothes dry, Dr. Donald ventured the remark that a large chapel at Tuskegee would not be out of place. The next day a letter came from two ladies who were then travelling in Italy, saying that they had decided to give us the money for such a chapel as we needed.

A short time ago we received twenty thousand dollars from Mr. Andrew Carnegie, to be used for the purpose of erecting a new library building. Our first library and reading-room were in a corner of a shanty, and the whole thing occupied a space about five by twelve feet. It required ten years of work before I was able to secure Mr. Carnegie's interest and help. The first time I saw him, ten years ago, he seemed to take but little interest in our school, but I was determined to show him that we were worthy of his help. After ten years of hard work I wrote him a letter reading as follows:

BOOKER T. WASHINGTON

December 15, 1900.
Mr. Andrew Carnegie,
5 W. Fifty-first St., New York.

Dear Sir: Complying with the request which you made of me when I saw you at your residence a few days ago, I now submit in writing an appeal for a library building for our institution.

We have 1100 students, 86 officers and instructors, together with their families, and about 200 coloured people living near the school, all of whom would make use of the library building.

We have over 12,000 books, periodicals, etc., gifts from our friends, but we have not suitable place for them, and we have no suitable reading-room.

Our graduates go to work in every section of the South, and whatever knowledge might be obtained in the library would serve to assist in the elevation of the whole Negro race.

Such a building as we need could be erected for about $20,000. All of the work for the building, such as brickmaking, brick-masonry, carpentry, blacksmithing, etc., would be done by the students. The money which you would give would not only supply the building, but the erection of the building would give a large number of students an opportunity to learn the building trades, and the students would use the money paid to them to keep themselves in school. I do not believe that a similar amount of money often could be made go so far in uplifting a whole race.

If you wish further information, I shall be glad to furnish it.
Yours truly,
Booker T. Washington, Principal.

The next mail brought back the following reply: "I will be very glad to pay the bills for the library building as they are incurred, to the extent of twenty thousand dollars, and I am glad of this opportunity to show the interest I have in your noble work."

I have found that strict business methods go a long way in securing the interest of rich people. It has been my constant aim at Tuskegee to carry out, in our financial and other operations, such business methods as would be approved of by any New York banking house.

I have spoken of several large gifts to the school; but by far the greater proportion of the money that has built up the institution has come in the form of small donations from persons of moderate means.

It is upon these small gifts, which carry with them the interest of hundreds of donors, that any philanthropic work must depend largely for its support. In my efforts to get money I have often been surprised at the patience and deep interest of the ministers, who are besieged one very hand and at all hours of the day for help. If no other consideration had convinced me of the value of the Christian life, the Christlike work which the Church of all denominations in America has done during the last thirty-five years for the elevation of the black man would have made me a Christian. In a large degree it has been the pennies, the nickels, and the dimes which have come from the Sunday-schools, the Christian Endeavour societies, and the missionary societies, as well as from the church proper, that have helped to elevate the Negro at so rapid a rate.

This speaking of small gifts reminds me to say that very few Tuskegee graduates fail to send us an annual contribution. These contributions range from twenty-five cents up to ten dollars.

Soon after beginning our third year's work we were surprised to receive money from three special sources, and up to the present time we have continued to receive help from them. First, the State Legislature of Alabama increased its annual appropriation from two thousand dollars to three thousand dollars; I might add that still later it increased this sum to four thousand five hundred dollars a year. The effort to secure this increase was led by the Hon. M. F. Foster, the member of the Legislature from Tuskegee. Second, we received one thousand dollars from the John F. Slater Fund. Our work seemed to please the trustees of this fund, as they soon began increasing their annual grant. This has been added to from time to time until at present we receive eleven thousand dollars annually from this Fund. The other help to which I have referred came in the shape of an allowance from the Peabody Fund. This was at first five hundred dollars, but it has since been increased to fifteen hundred dollars.

The effort to secure help from the Slater and Peabody Funds brought me into contact with two rare men—men who have had much to do in shaping the policy for the education of the Negro. I refer to the Hon. J.

L. M. Curry, of Washington, who is the general agent for these two funds, and Mr. Morris K. Jesup, of New York. Dr. Curry is a native of the South, an ex-Confederate soldier, yet I do not believe there is any man in the country who is more deeply interested in the highest welfare of the Negro than Dr. Curry, or one who is more free from race prejudice. He enjoys the unique distinction of possessing to an equal degree the confidence of the black man and the Southern white man. I shall never forget the first time I met him. It was in Richmond, Va., where he was then living. I had heard much about him. When I first went into his presence, trembling because of my youth and inexperience, he took me by the hand so cordially, and spoke such encouraging words, and gave me such helpful advice regarding the proper course to pursue, that I came to know him then, as I have known him ever since, as a high example of one who is constantly and unselfishly at work for the betterment of humanity.

Mr. Morris K. Jesup, the treasurer of the Slater Fund, I refer to because I know of no man of wealth and large and complicated business responsibilities who gives not only money but his time and thought to the subject of the proper method of elevating the Negro to the extent that is true of Mr. Jesup. It is very largely through his effort and influence that during the last few years the subject of industrial education has assumed the importance that it has, and been placed on its present footing.

CHAPTER XIII
TWO THOUSAND MILES FOR A
FIVE-MINUTE SPEECH

Soon after the opening of our boarding department, quite a number of students who evidently were worthy, but who were so poor that they did not have any money to pay even the small charges at the school, began applying for admission. This class was composed of both men and women. It was a great trial to refuse admission to these applicants, and in 1884 we established a night-school to accommodate a few of them.

The night school was organized on a plan similar to the one which I had helped to establish at Hampton. At first it was composed of about a dozen students. They were admitted to the night-school only when they had no money with which to pay any part of their board in the regular day-school. It was further required that they must work for ten hours during the day at some trade or industry, and study academic branches for two hours during the evening. This was the requirement for the first one or two years of their stay. They were to be paid something above the cost of their board, with the understanding that all of their earnings, except a very small part, were to be reserved in the school's treasury, to be used for paying their board in the regular day-school after they had entered that department. The night-school, started in this manner, has grown until there are at present four hundred and fifty-seven students enrolled in it alone.

There could hardly be a more severe test of a student's worth than this branch of the Institute's work. It is largely because it furnishes such a good opportunity to test the backbone of a student that I place such high value upon our night-school. Any one who is willing to work ten hours a day at the brick-yard, or in the laundry, through one or two years, in order that he or she may have the privilege of studying academic branches for two hours in the evening, has enough bottom to warrant being further educated.

After the student has left the night-school he enters the day-school, where he takes academic branches four days in a week, and works at his trade two days. Besides this he usually works at his trade during the three summer months. As a rule, after a student has succeeded in going through the night-school test, he finds a way to finish the regular course in industrial and academic training. No student, no matter how much money he may be able to command, is permitted to go through school without doing manual labour. In fact, the industrial work is now as popular as the academic branches. Some of the most successful men and women who have graduated from the institution obtained their start in the night-school.

While a great deal of stress is laid upon the industrial side of the work at Tuskegee, we do not neglect or overlook in any degree the religious and spiritual side. The school is strictly undenominational, but it is thoroughly Christian, and the spiritual training of the students is not neglected. Our preaching service, prayer-meetings, Sunday-school, Christian Endeavour Society, Young Men's Christian Association, and various missionary organizations, testify to this.

In 1885, Miss Olivia Davidson, to whom I have already referred as being largely responsible for the success of the school during its early history, and I were married. During our married life she continued to divide her time and strength between our home and the work of the school. She not only continued to work in the school at Tuskegee, but also kept up her habit of going North to secure funds. In 1889 she died, after four years of happy married life and eight years of hard and happy work for the school. She literally wore herself out in her never ceasing efforts in behalf of the work that she so dearly loved. During our married life there were born to us two bright, beautiful boys, Baker Taliaferro and Ernest Davidson. The older of these, Baker, has already mastered the brickmaker's trade at Tuskegee.

BOOKER T. WASHINGTON

I have often been asked how I began the practice of public speaking. In answer I would say that I never planned to give any large part of my life to speaking in public. I have always had more of an ambition to *do* things than merely to talk *about* doing them. It seems that when I went North with General Armstrong to speak at the series of public meetings to which I have referred, the President of the National Educational Association, the Hon. Thomas W. Bicknell, was present at one of those meetings and heard me speak. A few days afterward he sent me an invitation to deliver an address at the next meeting of the Educational Association. This meeting was to be held in Madison, Wis. I accepted the invitation. This was, in a sense, the beginning of my public-speaking career.

On the evening that I spoke before the Association there must have been not far from four thousand persons present. Without my knowing it, there were a large number of people present from Alabama, and some from the town of Tuskegee. These white people afterward frankly told me that they went to this meeting expecting to hear the South roundly abused, but were pleasantly surprised to find that there was no word of abuse in my address. On the contrary, the South was given credit for all the praiseworthy things that it had done. A white lady who was a teacher in a college in Tuskegee wrote back to the local paper that she was gratified, as well as surprised, to note the credit which I gave the white people of Tuskegee for their help in getting the school started. This address at Madison was the first that I had delivered that in any large measure dealt with the general problem of the races. Those who heard it seemed to be pleased with what I said and with the general position that I took.

When I first came to Tuskegee, I determined that I would make it my home, that I would take as much pride in the right actions of the people of the town as any white man could do, and that I would, at the same time, deplore the wrong-doing of the people as much as any white man. I determined never to say anything in a public address in the North that I would not be willing to say in the South. I early learned that it is a hard matter to convert an individual by abusing him, and that this is more often accomplished by giving credit for all the praiseworthy actions performed than by calling attention alone to all the evil done.

TWO THOUSAND MILES FOR A FIVE-MINUTE SPEECH

While pursuing this policy I have not failed, at the proper time and in the proper manner, to call attention, in no uncertain terms, to the wrongs which any part of the South has been guilty of. I have found that there is a large element in the South that is quick to respond to straightforward, honest criticism of any wrong policy. As a rule, the place to criticize the South, when criticism is necessary, is in the South —not in Boston. A Boston man who came to Alabama to criticize Boston would not effect so much good, I think, as one who had his word of criticism to say in Boston.

In this address at Madison I took the ground that the policy to be pursued with reference to the races was, by every honourable means, to bring them together and to encourage the cultivation of friendly relations, instead of doing that which would embitter. I further contended that, in relation to his vote, the Negro should more and more consider the interests of the community in which he lived, rather than seek alone to please some one who lived a thousand miles away from him and from his interests.

In this address I said that the whole future of the Negro rested largely upon the question as to whether or not he should make himself, through his skill, intelligence, and character, of such undeniable value to the community in which he lived that the community could not dispense with his presence. I said that any individual who learned to do something better than anybody else—learned to do a common thing in an uncommon manner—had solved his problem regardless of the colour of his skin, and that in proportion as the Negro learned to produce what other people wanted and must have, in the same proportion would he be respected.

I spoke of an instance where one of our graduates had produced two hundred and sixty-six bushels of sweet potatoes from an acre of ground, in a community where the average production had been only forty-nine bushels to the acre. He had been able to do this by reason of his knowledge of the chemistry of the soil and by his knowledge of improved methods of agriculture. The white farmers in the neighbour-hood respected him, and came to him for ideas regarding the raising of

126

sweet potatoes. These white farmers honoured and respected him because he, by his skill and knowledge, had added something to the wealth and the comfort of the community in which he lived. I explained that my theory of education for the Negro would not, for example, confine him for all time to farm life—to the production of the best and the most sweet potatoes—but that, if he succeeded in this line of industry, he could lay the foundations upon which his children and grandchildren could grow to higher and more important things in life.

Such, in brief, were some of the views I advocated in this first address dealing with the broad question of the relation of the two races, and since that time I have not found any reason for changing my views on any important point.

In my early life I used to cherish a feeling of ill will toward any one who spoke in bitter terms against the Negro, or who advocated measures that tended to oppress the black man or take from him opportunities for growth in the most complete manner. Now, whenever I hear any one advocating measures that are meant to curtail the development of another, I pity the individual who would do this. I know that the one who makes this mistake does so because of his own lack of opportunity for the highest kind of growth. I pity him because I know that he is trying to stop the progress of the world, and because I know that in time the development and the ceaseless advance of humanity will make him ashamed of his weak and narrow position. One might as well try to stop the progress of a mighty railroad train by throwing his body across the track, as to try to stop the growth of the world in the direction of giving mankind more intelligence, more culture, more skill, more liberty, and in the direction of extending more sympathy and more brotherly kindness.

The address which I delivered at Madison, before the National Educational Association, gave me a rather wide introduction in the North, and soon after that opportunities began offering themselves for me to address audiences there.

I was anxious, however, that the way might also be opened for me to speak directly to a representative Southern white audience. A partial opportunity of this kind, one that seemed to me might serve as an entering wedge, presented itself in 1893, when the international meeting of Christian Workers was held at Atlanta, Ga. When this invitation came to me, I had engagements in Boston that seemed to make it impossible for me to speak in Atlanta. Still, after looking over my list of dates and places carefully, I found that I could take a train from Boston that would get me into Atlanta about thirty minutes before my address was to be delivered, and that I could remain in that city about sixty minutes before taking another train for Boston. My invitation to speak in Atlanta stipulated that I was to confine my address to five minutes. The question, then, was whether or not I could put enough into a five-minute address to make it worth while for me to make such a trip.

I knew that the audience would be largely composed of the most influential class of white men and women, and that it would be a rare opportunity for me to let them know what we were trying to do at Tuskegee, as well as to speak to them about the relations of the races. So I decided to make the trip. I spoke for five minutes to an audience of two thousand people, composed mostly of Southern and Northern whites. What I said seemed to be received with favour and enthusiasm. The Atlanta papers of the next day commented in friendly terms on my address, and a good deal was said about it in different parts of the county. I felt that I had in some degree accomplished my object—that of getting a hearing from the dominant class of the South.

The demands made upon me for public addresses continued to increase, coming in about equal numbers from my own people and from Northern whites. I gave as much time to these addresses as I could spare from the immediate work at Tuskegee. Most of the addresses in the North were made for the direct purpose of getting funds with which to support the school. Those delivered before the coloured people had for their main object the impressing upon them of the importance of industrial and technical education in addition to academic and religious training.

I now come to that one of the incidents in my life which seems to have excited the greatest amount of interest, and which perhaps went further than anything else in giving me a reputation that in a sense might be called National. I refer to the address which I delivered at the opening of the Atlanta Cotton States and International Exposition, at Atlanta, Ga., September 18, 1895.

So much has been said and written about this incident, and so many questions have been asked me concerning the address, that perhaps I may be excused for taking up the matter with some detail. The five-minute address in Atlanta, which I came from Boston to deliver, was possibly the prime cause for an opportunity being given me to make the second address there. In the spring of 1895 I received a telegram from prominent citizens in Atlanta asking me to accompany a committee from that city to Washington for the purpose of appearing before a committee of Congress in the interest of securing Government help for the Exposition. The committee was composed of about twenty-five of the most prominent and most influential white men of Georgia. All the members of this committee were white men except Bishop Grant, Bishop Gaines, and myself. The Mayor and several other city and state officials spoke before the committee. They were followed by the two coloured bishops. My name was the last on the list of speakers. I had never before appeared before such a committee, nor had I ever delivered any address in the capital of the Nation. I had many misgivings as to what I ought to say, and as to the impression that my address would make. While I cannot recall in detail what I said, I remember that I tried to impress upon the committee, with all the earnestness and plainness of any language that I could command, that if Congress wanted to do something which would assist in ridding the South of the race question and making friends between the two races, it should, in every proper way, encourage the material and intellectual growth of both races. I said that the Atlanta Exposition would present an opportunity for both races to show what advance they had made since freedom, and would at the same time afford encouragement to them to make still greater progress.

I tried to emphasize the fact that while the Negro should not be deprived by unfair means of the franchise, political agitation alone would not save him, and that back of the ballot he must have property, industry, skill, economy, intelligence, and character, and that no race without these elements could permanently succeed. I said that in granting the appropriation Congress could do something that would prove to be of real and lasting value to both races, and that it was the first great opportunity of the kind that had been presented since the close of the Civil War.

I spoke for fifteen or twenty minutes, and was surprised at the close of my address to receive the hearty congratulations of the Georgia committee and of the members of Congress who were present. The Committee was unanimous in making a favourable report, and in a few days the bill passed Congress. With the passing of this bill the success of the Atlanta Exposition was assured.

Soon after this trip to Washington the directors of the Exposition decided that it would be a fitting recognition of the coloured race to erect a large and attractive building which should be devoted wholly to showing the progress of the Negro since freedom. It was further decided to have the building designed and erected wholly by Negro mechanics. This plan was carried out. In design, beauty, and general finish the Negro Building was equal to the others on the grounds.

After it was decided to have a separate Negro exhibit, the question arose as to who should take charge of it. The officials of the Exposition were anxious that I should assume this responsibility, but I declined to do so, on the plea that the work at Tuskegee at that time demanded my time and strength. Largely at my suggestion, Mr. I. Garland Penn, of Lynchburg, Va., was selected to be at the head of the Negro department. I gave him all the aid that I could. The Negro exhibit, as a whole, was large and creditable. The two exhibits in this department which attracted the greatest amount of attention were those from the Hampton Institute and the Tuskegee Institute. The people who seemed to be the most surprised, as well as pleased, at what they saw in the Negro Building were the Southern white people.

As the day for the opening of the Exposition drew near, the Board of Directors began preparing the programme for the opening exercises. In the discussion from day to day of the various features of this programme, the question came up as to the advisability of putting a member of the Negro race on for one of the opening addresses, since the Negroes had been asked to take such a prominent part in the Exposition. It was argued, further, that such recognition would mark the good feeling prevailing between the two races. Of course there were those who were opposed to any such recognition of the rights of the Negro, but the Board of Directors, composed of men who represented the best and most progressive element in the South, had their way, and voted to invite a black man to speak on the opening day. The next thing was to decide upon the person who was thus to represent the Negro race. After the question had been canvassed for several days, the directors voted unanimously to ask me to deliver one of the opening-day addresses, and in a few days after that I received the official invitation.

The receiving of this invitation brought to me a sense of responsibility that it would be hard for any one not placed in my position to appreciate. What were my feelings when this invitation came to me? I remembered that I had been a slave; that my early years had been spent in the lowest depths of poverty and ignorance, and that I had had little opportunity to prepare me for such a responsibility as this. It was only a few years before that time that any white man in the audience might have claimed me as his slave; and it was easily possible that some of my former owners might be present to hear me speak.

I knew, too, that this was the first time in the entire history of the Negro that a member of my race had been asked to speak from the same platform with white Southern men and women on any important National occasion. I was asked now to speak to an audience composed of the wealth and culture of the white South, the representatives of my former masters. I knew, too, that while the greater part of my audience would be composed of Southern people, yet there would be present a large number of Northern whites, as well as a great many men and women of my own race.

I was determined to say nothing that I did not feel from the bottom of my heart to be true and right. When the invitation came to me, there was not one word of intimation as to what I should say or as to what I should omit. In this I felt that the Board of Directors had paid a tribute to me. They knew that by one sentence I could have blasted, in a large degree, the success of the Exposition. I was also painfully conscious of the fact that, while I must be true to my own race in my utterances, I had it in my power to make such an ill-timed address as would result in preventing any similar invitation being extended to a black man again for years to come. I was equally determined to be true to the North, as well as to the best element of the white South, in what I had to say.

The papers, North and South, had taken up the discussion of my coming speech, and as the time for it drew near this discussion became more and more widespread. Not a few of the Southern white papers were unfriendly to the idea of my speaking. From my own race I received many suggestions as to what I ought to say. I prepared myself as best I could for the address, but as the eighteenth of September drew nearer, the heavier my heart became, and the more I feared that my effort would prove a failure and a disappointment.

The invitation had come at a time when I was very busy with my school work, as it was the beginning of our school year. After preparing my address, I went through it, as I usually do with all those utterances which I consider particularly important, with Mrs. Washington, and she approved of what I intended to say. On the sixteenth of September, the day before I was to start for Atlanta, so many of the Tuskegee teachers expressed a desire to hear my address that I consented to read it to them in a body. When I had done so, and had heard their criticisms and comments, I felt somewhat relieved, since they seemed to think well of what I had to say.

On the morning of September 17, together with Mrs. Washington and my three children, I started for Atlanta. I felt a good deal as I suppose a man feels when he is on his way to the gallows. In passing through the town of Tuskegee I met a white farmer who lived some distance out in the country. In a jesting manner this man said: "Washington, you have spoken before the Northern white people, the Negroes in the South, and to us country white people in the South; but in Atlanta, tomorrow, you will have before you the Northern whites, the Southern whites, and the Negroes all together. I am afraid that you have got yourself into a tight place." This farmer diagnosed the situation correctly, but his frank words did not add anything to my comfort.

In the course of the journey from Tuskegee to Atlanta both coloured and white people came to the train to point me out, and discussed with perfect freedom, in my hearing, what was going to take place the next day. We were met by a committee in Atlanta. Almost the first thing that I heard when I got off the train in that city was an expression something like this, from an old coloured man near by: "Dat's de man of my race what's gwine to make a speech at de Exposition tomorrow. I'se sho' gwine to hear him."

Atlanta was literally packed, at the time, with people from all parts of this country, and with representatives of foreign governments, as well as with military and civic organizations. The afternoon papers had forecasts of the next day's proceedings in flaring headlines. All this tended to add to my burden. I did not sleep much that night. The next morning, before day, I went carefully over what I intended to say. I also kneeled down and asked God's blessing upon my effort. Right here, perhaps, I ought to add that I make it a rule never to go before an audience, on any occasion, without asking the blessing of God upon what I want to say.

I always make it a rule to make especial preparation for each separate address. No two audiences are exactly alike. It is my aim to reach and talk to the heart of each individual audience, taking it into my confidence very much as I would a person. When I am speaking to an audience, I care little for how what I am saying is going to sound in the newspapers, or to another audience, or to an individual. At the time, the audience before me absorbs all my sympathy, thought, and energy.

Early in the morning a committee called to escort me to my place in the procession which was to march to the Exposition grounds. In this procession were prominent coloured citizens in carriages, as well as several Negro military organizations. I noted that the Exposition officials seemed to go out of their way to see that all of the coloured people in the procession were properly placed and properly treated. The procession was about three hours in reaching the Exposition grounds, and during all of this time the sun was shining down upon us disagreeably hot. When we reached the grounds, the heat, together with my nervous anxiety, made me feel as if I were about ready to collapse, and to feel that my address was not going to be a success. When I entered the audience-room, I found it packed with humanity from bottom to top, and there were thousands outside who could not get in.

The room was very large, and well suited to public speaking. When I entered the room, there were vigorous cheers from the coloured portion of the audience, and faint cheers from some of the white people. I had been told, while I had been in Atlanta, that while many white people were going to be present to hear me speak, simply out of curiosity, and that others who would be present would be in full sympathy with me, there was a still larger element of the audience which would consist of those who were going to be present for the purpose of hearing me make a fool of myself, or, at least, of hearing me say some foolish thing, so that they could say to the officials who had invited me to speak, "I told you so!"

One of the trustees of the Tuskegee Institute, as well as my personal friend, Mr. William H. Baldwin, Jr. was at the time General Manager of the Southern Railroad, and happened to be in Atlanta on that day. He was so nervous about the kind of reception that I would have, and the effect that my speech would produce, that he could not persuade himself to go into the building, but walked back and forth in the grounds outside until the opening exercises were over.

CHAPTER XIV
THE ATLANTA EXPOSITION ADDRESS

The Atlanta Exposition, at which I had been asked to make an address as a representative of the Negro race, as stated in the last chapter, was opened with a short address from Governor Bullock. After other interesting exercises, including an invocation from Bishop Nelson, of Georgia, a dedicatory ode by Albert Howell, Jr., and addresses by the President of the Exposition and Mrs. Joseph Thompson, the President of the Woman's Board, Governor Bullock introduced me with the words, "We have with us to-day a representative of Negro enterprise and Negro civilization."

When I arose to speak, there was considerable cheering, especially from the coloured people. As I remember it now, the thing that was uppermost in my mind was the desire to say something that would cement the friendship of the races and bring about hearty cooperation between them. So far as my outward surroundings were concerned, the only thing that I recall distinctly now is that when I got up, I saw thousands of eyes looking intently into my face. The following is the address which I delivered:

MR. PRESIDENT AND
GENTLEMEN OF THE BOARD OF DIRECTORS AND CITIZENS:

One-third of the population of the South is of the Negro race. No enterprise seeking the material, civil, or moral welfare of this section can disregard this element of our population and reach the highest success. I but convey to you, Mr. President and Directors, the sentiment of the masses of my race when I say that in no way have the value and manhood of the American Negro been more fittingly and generously recognized than by the managers of this magnificent Exposition at every stage of its progress. It is a recognition that will do more to cement the friendship of the two races than any occurrence since the dawn of our freedom.

Not only this, but the opportunity here afforded will awaken among us a new era of industrial progress. Ignorant and inexperienced, it is not strange that in the first years of our new life we began at the top instead of at the bottom; that a seat in Congress or the state legislature was more sought than real estate or industrial skill; that the political convention or stump speaking had more attractions than starting a dairy farm or truck garden.

A ship lost at sea for many days suddenly sighted a friendly vessel. From the mast of the unfortunate vessel was seen a signal, "Water, water; we die of thirst!" The answer from the friendly vessel at once came back, "Cast down your bucket where you are." A second time the signal, "Water, water; send us water!" ran up from the distressed vessel, and was answered, "Cast down your bucket where you are." And a third and fourth signal for water was answered, "Cast down your bucket where you are." The captain of the distressed vessel, at last heeding the injunction, cast down his bucket, and it came up full of fresh, sparkling water from the mouth of the Amazon River. To those of my race who depend on bettering their condition in a foreign land or who underestimate the importance of cultivating friendly relations with the Southern white man, who is their next-door neighbour, I would say: "Cast down your bucket where you are"—cast it down in making friends in every manly way of the people of all races by whom we are surrounded.

Cast it down in agriculture, mechanics, in commerce, in domestic service, and in the professions. And in this connection it is well to bear in mind that whatever other sins the South may be called to bear, when it comes to business, pure and simple, it is in the South that the Negro is given a man's chance in the commercial world, and in nothing is this Exposition more eloquent than in emphasizing this chance. Our greatest danger is that in the great leap from slavery to freedom we may overlook the fact that the masses of us are to live by the productions of our hands, and fail to keep in mind that we shall prosper in proportion as we learn to dignify and glorify common labour and put brains and skill into the common occupations of life; shall prosper in proportion as we learn to draw the line between the superficial and the substantial, the ornamental gewgaws of life and the useful. No race can prosper till it learns that there is as much dignity in tilling a field as in writing a poem. It is at the bottom of life we must begin, and not at the top. Nor should we permit our grievances to overshadow our opportunities.

To those of the white race who look to the incoming of those of foreign birth and strange tongue and habits for the prosperity of the South, were I permitted I would repeat what I say to my own race, "Cast down your bucket where you are." Cast it down among the eight millions of Negroes whose habits you know, whose fidelity and love you have tested in days when to have proved treacherous meant the ruin of your firesides. Cast down your bucket among these people who have, without strikes and labour wars, tilled your fields, cleared your forests, builded your railroads and cities, and brought forth treasures from the bowels of the earth, and helped make possible this magnificent representation of the progress of the South. Casting down your bucket among my people, helping and encouraging them as you are doing on these grounds, and to education of head, hand, and heart, you will find that they will buy your surplus land, make blossom the waste places in your fields, and run your factories. While doing this, you can be sure in the future, as in the past, that you and your families will be surrounded by the most patient, faithful, law-abiding, and unresentful people that the world has seen. As we have proved our loyalty to you in the past, in nursing your children, watching by the sick-bed of your mothers and fathers, and often following them with tear-dimmed eyes to their graves, so in the future, in our humble way, we shall stand by you with a devotion that no foreigner can approach, ready to lay down our lives, if need be in defence of yours, interlacing our industrial, commercial, civil, and religious life with yours in a way that shall make the interests of both races one. In all things that are purely social we can be as separate as the fingers, yet one as the hand in all things essential to mutual progress.

There is no defence or security for any of us except in the highest intelligence and development of all. If anywhere there are efforts tending to curtail the fullest growth of the Negro, let these efforts be turned into stimulating, encouraging, and making him the most useful and intelligent citizen. Effort or means so invested will pay a thousand per cent interest. These efforts will be twice blessed—"blessing him that gives and him that takes."

There is no escape through law of man or God from the inevitable:

The laws of changeless justice bind

Oppressor with oppressed;

And close as sin and suffering joined

We march to fate abreast.

Nearly sixteen millions of hands will aid you in pulling the load upward, or they will pull against you the load downward. We shall constitute one-third and more of the ignorance and crime of the South, or one-third its intelligence and progress; we shall contribute one-third to the business and industrial prosperity of the South, or we shall prove a veritable body of death, stagnating, depressing, retarding every effort to advance the body politic.

Gentlemen of the Exposition, as we present to you our humble effort at an exhibition of our progress, you must not expect overmuch. Starting thirty years ago with ownership here and there in a few quilts and pumpkins and chickens (gathered from miscellaneous sources), remember the path that has led from these to the inventions and production of agricultural implements, buggies, steam-engines, newspapers, books, statuary, carving, paintings, the management of drug-stores and banks, has not been trodden without contact with thorns and thistles. While we take pride in what we exhibit as a result of our independent efforts, we do not for a moment forget that our part in this exhibition would fall far short of your expectations but for the constant help that has come to our educational life, not only from the Southern states, but especially from Northern philanthropists, who have made their gifts a constant stream of blessing and encouragement.

The wisest among my race understand that the agitation of questions of social equality is the extremist folly, and that progress in the enjoyment of all the privileges that will come to us must be the result of severe and constant struggle rather than of artificial forcing. No race that has anything to contribute to the markets of the world is long in any degree ostracized. It is important and right that all privileges of the law be ours, but it is vastly more important that we be prepared for the exercises of these privileges. The opportunity to earn a dollar in a factory just now is worth infinitely more than the opportunity to spend a dollar in an opera-house.

In conclusion, may I repeat that nothing in thirty years has given us more hope and encouragement, and drawn us so near to you of the white race, as this opportunity offered by the Exposition; and here bending, as it were, over the altar that represents the results of the struggles of your race and mine, both starting practically empty-handed three decades ago, I pledge that in your effort to work out the great and intricate problem which God has laid at the doors of the South, you shall have at all times the patient, sympathetic help of my race; only let this be constantly in mind, that, while from representations in these buildings of the product of field, of forest, of mine, of factory, letters, and art, much good will come, yet far above and beyond material benefits will be that higher good, that, let us pray God, will come, in a blotting out of sectional differences and racial animosities and suspicions, in a determination to administer absolute justice, in a willing obedience among all classes to the mandates of law. This, this, coupled with our material prosperity, will bring into our beloved South a new heaven and a new earth.

The first thing that I remember, after I had finished speaking, was that Governor Bullock rushed across the platform and took me by the hand, and that others did the same. I received so many and such hearty congratulations that I found it difficult to get out of the building. I did not appreciate to any degree, however, the impression which my address seemed to have made, until the next morning, when I went into the business part of the city. As soon as I was recognized, I was surprised to find myself pointed out and surrounded by a crowd of men who wished to shake hands with me. This was kept up on every street on to which I went, to an extent which embarrassed me so much that I went back to my boarding-place. The next morning I returned to Tuskegee. At the station in Atlanta, and at almost all of the stations at which the train stopped between that city and Tuskegee, I found a crowd of people anxious to shake hands with me.

The papers in all part of the United States published the address in full, and for months afterward there were complimentary editorial references to it. Mr. Clark Howell, the editor of the Atlanta *Constitution*, telegraphed to a New York paper, among other words, the following, "I do not exaggerate when I say that Professor Booker T. Washington's address yesterday was one of the most notable speeches, both as to character and as to the warmth of its reception, ever delivered to a Southern audience. The address was a revelation. The whole speech is a platform upon which blacks and whites can stand with full justice to each other."

The Boston *Transcript* said editorially: "The speech of Booker T. Washington at the Atlanta Exposition, this week, seems to have dwarfed all the other proceedings and the Exposition itself. The sensation that it has caused in the press has never been equalled."

I very soon began receiving all kinds of propositions from lecture bureaus, and editors of magazines and papers, to take the lecture platform, and to write articles. One lecture bureau offered me fifty thousand dollars, or two hundred dollars a night and expenses, if I would place my services at its disposal for a given period. To all these communications I replied that my life-work was at Tuskegee; and that whenever I spoke it must be in the interests of the Tuskegee school and my race, and that I would enter into no arrangements that seemed to place a mere commercial value upon my services.

Some days after its delivery I sent a copy of my address to the President of the United States, the Hon. Grover Cleveland. I received from him the following autograph reply:

October 6, 1895
GRAY GABLES, BUZZARD'S BAY, MASS.,
BOOKER T. WASHINGTON, ESQ.:

MY DEAR SIR: I thank you for sending me a copy of your address delivered at the Atlanta Exposition.

I thank you with much enthusiasm for making the address. I have read it with intense interest, and I think the Exposition would be fully justified if it did not do more than furnish the opportunity for its delivery. Your words cannot fail to delight and encourage all who wish well for your race; and if our coloured fellow-citizens do not from your utterances gather new hope and form new determinations to gain every valuable advantage offered them by their citizenship, it will be strange indeed.

Yours very truly,
GROVER CLEVELAND

THE ATLANTA EXPOSITION ADDRESS

Later I met Mr. Cleveland, for the first time, when, as president, he visited the Atlanta Exposition. At the request of myself and others he consented to spend an hour in the Negro Building, for the purpose of inspecting the Negro exhibit and of giving the coloured people in attendance an opportunity to shake hands with him. As soon as I met Mr. Cleveland I became impressed with his simplicity, greatness, and rugged honesty. I have met him many times since then, both at public functions and at his private residence in Princeton, and the more I see of him the more I admire him. When he visited the Negro Building in Atlanta he seemed to give himself up wholly, for that hour, to the coloured people. He seemed to be as careful to shake hands with some old coloured "auntie" clad partially in rags, and to take as much pleasure in doing so, as if he were greeting some millionaire. Many of the coloured people took advantage of the occasion to get him to write his name in a book or on a slip of paper. He was as careful and patient in doing this as if he were putting his signature to some great state document.

Mr. Cleveland has not only shown his friendship for me in many personal ways, but has always consented to do anything I have asked of him for our school. This he has done, whether it was to make a personal donation or to use his influence in securing the donations of others. Judging from my personal acquaintance with Mr. Cleveland, I do not believe that he is conscious of possessing any colour prejudice. He is too great for that. In my contact with people I find that, as a rule, it is only the little, narrow people who live for themselves, who never read good books, who do not travel, who never open up their souls in a way to permit them to come into contact with other souls—with the great outside world. No man whose vision is bounded by colour can come into contact with what is highest and best in the world. In meeting men, in many places, I have found that the happiest people are those who do the most for others; the most miserable are those who do the least. I have also found that few things, if any, are capable of making one so blind and narrow as race prejudice. I often say to our students, in the course of my talks to them on Sunday evenings in the chapel, that the longer I live and the more experience I have of the world, the more

I am convinced that, after all, the one thing that is most worth living for—and dying for, if need be—is the opportunity of making some one else more happy and more useful.

The coloured people and the coloured newspapers at first seemed to be greatly pleased with the character of my Atlanta address, as well as with its reception. But after the first burst of enthusiasm began to die away, and the coloured people began reading the speech in cold type, some of them seemed to feel that they had been hypnotized. They seemed to feel that I had been too liberal in my remarks toward the Southern whites, and that I had not spoken out strongly enough for what they termed the "rights" of the race. For a while there was a reaction, so far as a certain element of my own race was concerned, but later these reactionary ones seemed to have been won over to my way of believing and acting.

While speaking of changes in public sentiment, I recall that about ten years after the school at Tuskegee was established, I had an experience that I shall never forget. Dr. Lyman Abbott, then the pastor of Plymouth Church, and also editor of the *Outlook* (then the *Christian Union*), asked me to write a letter for his paper giving my opinion of the exact condition, mental and moral, of the coloured ministers in the South, as based upon my observations. I wrote the letter, giving the exact facts as I conceived them to be. The picture painted was a rather black one—or, since I am black, shall I say "white"? It could not be otherwise with a race but a few years out of slavery, a race which had not had time or opportunity to produce a competent ministry.

What I said soon reached every Negro minister in the country, I think, and the letters of condemnation which I received from them were not few. I think that for a year after the publication of this article every association and every conference or religious body of any kind, of my race, that met, did not fail before adjourning to pass a resolution condemning me, or calling upon me to retract or modify what I had said. Many of these organizations went so far in their resolutions as to advise parents to cease sending their children to Tuskegee. One association even appointed a "missionary" whose duty it was to warn the people against sending their children to Tuskegee. This missionary had a son in the school, and I noticed that, whatever the "missionary" might have said or done with regard to others, he was careful not to take his son away from the institution. Many of the coloured papers, especially those that were the organs of religious bodies, joined in the general chorus of condemnation or demands for retraction.

During the whole time of the excitement, and through all the criticism, I did not utter a word of explanation or retraction. I knew that I was right, and that time and the sober second thought of the people would vindicate me. It was not long before the bishops and other church leaders began to make a careful investigation of the conditions of the ministry, and they found out that I was right. In fact, the oldest and most influential bishop in one branch of the Methodist Church said that my words were far too mild. Very soon public sentiment began making itself felt, in demanding a purifying of the ministry. While this is not yet complete by any means, I think I may say, without egotism, and I have been told by many of our most influential ministers, that my words had much to do with starting a demand for the placing of a higher type of men in the pulpit. I have had the satisfaction of having many who once condemned me thank me heartily for my frank words.

The change of the attitude of the Negro ministry, so far as regards myself, is so complete that at the present time I have no warmer friends among any class than I have among the clergymen. The improvement in the character and life of the Negro ministries one of the most gratifying evidences of the progress of the race. My experience with them, as well as other events in my life, convince me that the thing to do, when one feels sure that he has said or done the right thing, and is condemned, is to stand still and keep quiet. If he is right, time will show it.

In the midst of the discussion which was going on concerning my Atlanta speech, I received the letter which I give below, from Dr. Gilman, the President of Johns Hopkins University, who had been made chairman of the judges of award in connection with the Atlanta Exposition:

BOOKER T. WASHINGTON

JOHNS HOPKINS UNIVERSITY, BALTIMORE,
PRESIDENT'S OFFICE, SEPTEMBER 30,1895

DEAR MR. WASHINGTON: Would it be agreeable to you to be one of the Judges of Award in the Department of Education at Atlanta? If so, I shall be glad to place your name upon the list. A line by telegraph will be welcomed.

Yours very truly,
D. C. GILMAN.

I think I was even more surprised to receive this invitation than I had been to receive the invitation to speak at the opening of the Exposition. It was to be a part of my duty, as one of the jurors, to pass not only upon the exhibits of the coloured schools, but also upon those of the white schools. I accepted the position, and spent a month in Atlanta in performance of the duties which it entailed. The board of jurors was a large one, consisting in all of sixty members. It was about equally divided between Southern white people and Northern white people. Among them were college presidents, leading scientists and men of letters, and specialists in many subjects. When the group of jurors to which I was assigned met for organization, Mr. Thomas Nelson Page, who was one of the number, moved that I be made secretary of that division, and the motion was unanimously adopted. Nearly half of our division were Southern people. In performing my duties in the inspection of the exhibits of white schools I was in every case treated with respect, and at the close of our labours I parted from my associates with regrets.

I am often asked to express myself more freely than I do upon the political condition and the political future of my race. These recollections of my experience in Atlanta give me the opportunity to do so briefly. My own belief is, although I have never before said so in so many words, that the time will come when the Negro in the South will be accorded all the political rights which his ability, character, and material possessions entitle him to. I think, though, that the opportunity to freely exercise such political rights will not come in any large degree through outside or artificial forcing, but will be accorded to the Negro by the Southern white people themselves, and that they will protect

143

him in the exercise of those rights. Just as soon as the South gets over the old feeling that it is being forced by "foreigners," or "aliens," to do something which it does not want to do, I believe that the change in the direction that I have indicated is going to begin. In fact, there are indications that it is already beginning in a slight degree.

Let me illustrate my meaning. Suppose that some months before the opening of the Atlanta Exposition there had been a general demand from the press and public platform outside the South that a Negro be given a place on the opening programme, and that a Negro be placed upon the board of jurors of award. Would any such recognition of the race have taken place? I do not think so. The Atlanta officials went as far as they did because they felt it to be a pleasure, as well as a duty, to reward what they considered merit in the Negro race. Say what we will, there is something in human nature which we cannot blot out, which makes one man, in the end, recognize and reward merit in another, regardless of colour or race.

I believe it is the duty of the Negro—as the greater part of the race is already doing—to deport himself modestly in regard to political claims, depending upon the slow but sure influences that proceed from the possession of property, intelligence, and high character for the full recognition of his political rights. I think that the according of the full exercise of political rights is going to be a matter of natural, slow growth, not an over-night, gourd-vine affair. I do not believe that the Negro should cease voting, for a man cannot learn the exercise of self-government by ceasing to vote, any more than a boy can learn to swim by keeping out of the water, but I do believe that in his voting he should more and more be influenced by those of intelligence and character who are his next-door neighbours.

I know coloured men who, through the encouragement, help, and advice of Southern white people, have accumulated thousands of dollars' worth of property, but who, at the same time, would never think of going to those same persons for advice concerning the casting of their ballots. This, it seems to me, is unwise and unreasonable, and should cease. In saying this I do not mean that the Negro should truckle, or not vote from principle, for the instant he ceases to vote from principle he loses the confidence and respect of the Southern white man even.

I do not believe that any state should make a law that permits an ignorant and poverty-stricken white man to vote, and prevents a black man in the same condition from voting. Such a law is not only unjust, but it will react, as all unjust laws do, in time; for the effect of such a law is to encourage the Negro to secure education and property, and at the same time it encourages the white man to remain ignorance and poverty. I believe that in time, through the operation of intelligence and friendly race relations, all cheating at the ballot-box in the South will cease. It will become apparent that the white man who begins by cheating a Negro out of his ballot soon learns to cheat a white man out of his, and that the man who does this ends his career of dishonesty by the theft of property or by some equally serious crime. In my opinion, the time will come when the South will encourage all of its citizens to vote. It will see that it pays better, from every standpoint, to have healthy, vigorous life than to have that political stagnation which always results when one-half of the population has no share and no interest in the Government.

As a rule, I believe in universal, free suffrage, but I believe that in the South we are confronted with peculiar conditions that justify the protection of the ballot in many of the states, for a while at least, either by an educational test, a property test, or by both combined; but whatever tests are required, they should be made to apply with equal and exact justice to both races.

CHAPTER XV
THE SECRET OF SUCCESS IN PUBLIC SPEAKING

As to how my address at Atlanta was received by the audience in the exposition building, I think I prefer to let Mr. James Creelman, the noted war correspondent, tell. Mr. Creelman was present, and telegraphed the following account to the *New York World:*

ATLANTA, SEPTEMBER 18.

While President Cleveland was waiting at Gray Gables to-day, to send the electric spark that started the machinery of the Atlanta Exposition, a Negro Moses stood before a great audience of white people and delivered an oration that marks a new epoch in the history of the South; and a body of Negro troops marched in a procession with the citizen soldiery of Georgia and Louisiana. The whole city is thrilling to-night with a realization of the extraordinary significance of these two unprecedented events. Nothing has happened since Henry Grady's immortal speech before the New England society in New York that indicates so profoundly the spirit of the New South, except, perhaps the opening of the Exposition itself.

When Professor Booker T. Washington, Principal of an industrial school for coloured people in Tuskegee, Ala. stood on the platform of the Auditorium, with the sun shining over the heads of his auditors into his eyes, and with his whole face lit up with the fire of prophecy, Clark Howell, the successor of Henry Grady, said to me, "That man's speech is the beginning of a moral revolution in America."

It is the first time that a Negro has made a speech in the South on any important occasion before an audience composed of white men and women. It electrified the audience, and the response was as if it had come from the throat of a whirlwind.

Mrs. Thompson had hardly taken her seat when all eyes were turned on a tall tawny Negro sitting in the front row of the platform. It was Professor Booker T. Washington, President of the Tuskegee (Alabama) Normal and Industrial Institute, who must rank from this time forth as the foremost man of his race in America. Gilmore's Band played the "Star-Spangled Banner," and the audience cheered. The tune changed to "Dixie" and the audience roared with shrill "hi-yis." Again the music changed, this time to "Yankee Doodle," and the clamour lessened.

THE SECRET OF SUCCESS IN PUBLIC SPEAKING

All this time the eyes of the thousands present looked straight at the Negro orator. A strange thing was to happen. A black man was to speak for his people, with none to interrupt him. As Professor Washington strode to the edge of the state, the low, descending sun shot fiery rays through the windows into his face. A great shout greeted him. He turned his head to avoid the blinding light, and moved about the platform for relief. Then he turned his wonderful countenance to the sun without a blink of the eyelids, and began to talk.

There was a remarkable figure; tall, bony, straight as a Sioux chief, high forehead, straight nose, heavy jaws, and strong, determined mouth, with big white teeth, piercing eyes, and a commanding manner. The sinews stood out on his bronzed neck, and his muscular right arm swung high in the air, with a lead-pencil grasped in the clinched brown fist. His big feet were planted squarely, with the heels together and the toes turned out. His voice rang out clear and true, and he paused impressively as he made each point. Within ten minutes the multitude was in an uproar of enthusiasm—handkerchiefs were waved, canes were flourished, hats were tossed in the air. The fairest women of Georgia stood up and cheered. It was as if the orator had bewitched them.

And when he held his dusky hand high above his head, with the fingers stretched wide apart, and said to the white people of the South on behalf of his race, "In all things that are purely social we can be as separate as the fingers, yet one as the hand in all things essential to mutual progress," the great wave of sound dashed itself against the walls, and the whole audience was on its feet in a delirium of applause, and I thought at that moment of the night when Henry Grady stood among the curling wreaths of tobacco-smoke in Delmonico's banquet-hall and said, "I am a Cavalier among Roundheads."

I have heard the great orators of many countries, but not even Gladstone himself could have pleaded a cause with more consummate power than did this angular Negro, standing in a nimbus of sunshine, surrounded by the men who once fought to keep his race in bondage. The roar might swell ever so high, but the expression of his earnest face never changed.

A ragged, ebony giant, squatted on the floor in one of the aisles, watched the orator with burning eyes and tremendous face until the supreme burst of applause came, and then the tears ran down his face. Most of the negroes in the audience were crying, perhaps without knowing just why.

At the close of the speech Governor Bullock rushed across the stage and seized the orator's hand. Another shout greeted this demonstration, and for a few minutes the two men stood facing each other, hand in hand.

So far as I could spare the time from the immediate work at Tuskegee, after my Atlanta address, I accepted some of the invitations to speak in public which came to me, especially those that would take me into territory where I thought it would pay to plead the cause of my race, but I always did this with the understanding that I was to be free to talk about my life-work and the needs of my people. I also had it understood that I was not to speak in the capacity of a professional lecturer, or for mere commercial gain.

In my efforts on the public platform I never have been able to understand why people come to hear me speak. This question I never can rid myself of. Time and time again, as I have stood in the street in front of a building and have seen men and women passing in large numbers into the audience-room where I was to speak, I have felt ashamed that I should be the cause of people—as it seemed to me—wasting a valuable hour of time. Some years ago I was to deliver an address before a literary society in Madison, Wis. An hour before the time set for me to speak, a fierce snow-storm began, and continued for several hours. I made up my mind that there would be no audience, and that I should not have to speak, but, as a matter of duty, I went to the church, and found it packed with people. The surprise gave me a shock that I did not recover from during the whole evening.

People often ask me if I feel nervous before speaking, or else they suggest that, since I speak so often, they suppose that I get used to it. In answer to this question I have to say that I always suffer intensely from nervousness before speaking. More than once, just before I was to make an important address, this nervous strain has been so great that I have resolved never again to speak in public. I not only feel nervous before speaking, but after I have finished I usually feel a sense of regret, because it seems to me as if I had left out of my address the main thing and the best thing that I had meant to say.

There is a great compensation, though, for this preliminary nervous suffering, that comes to me after I have been speaking for about ten minutes, and have come to feel that I have really mastered my audience, and that we have gotten into full and complete sympathy with each other. It seems to me that there is rarely such a combination of mental and physical delight in any effort as that which comes to a public speaker when he feels that he has a great audience completely within his control. There is a thread of sympathy and oneness that connects a public speaker with his audience, that is just as strong as though it was something tangible and visible. If in an audience of a thousand people there is one person who is not in sympathy with my views, or is inclined to be doubtful, cold, or critical, I can pick him out. When I have found him I usually go straight at him, and it is a great satisfaction to watch the process of his thawing out. I find that the most effective medicine for such individuals is administered at first in the form of a story, although I never tell an anecdote simply for the sake of telling one. That kind of thing, I think, is empty and hollow, and an audience soon finds it out.

I believe that one always does himself and his audience an injustice when he speaks merely for the sake of speaking. I do not believe that one should speak unless, deep down in his heart, he feels convinced that he has a message to deliver. When one feels, from the bottom of his feet to the top of his head, that he has something to say that is going to help some individual or some cause, then let him say it; and in delivering his message I do not believe that many of the artificial rules of elocution can, under such circumstances, help him very much. Although there are certain things, such as pauses, breathing, and pitch of voice, that are very important, none of these can take the place of *soul* in an address. When I have an address to deliver, I like to forget all about the rules for the proper use of the English language, and all about rhetoric and that sort of thing, and I like to make the audience forget all about these things, too.

Nothing tends to throw me off my balance so quickly, when I am speaking, as to have some one leave the room. To prevent this, I make up my mind, as a rule, that I will try to make my address so interesting, will try to state so many interesting facts one after another, that no one can leave. The average audience, I have come to believe, wants facts rather than generalities or sermonizing. Most people, I think, are able to draw proper conclusions if they are given the facts in an interesting form on which to base them.

As to the kind of audience that I like best to talk to, I would put at the top of the list an organization of strong, wide-awake, business men, such, for example, as is found in Boston, New York, Chicago, and Buffalo. I have found no other audience so quick to see a point, and so responsive. Within the last few years I have had the privilege of speaking before most of the leading organizations of this kind in the large cities of the United

States. The best time to get hold of an organization of business men is after a good dinner, although I think that one of the worst instruments of torture that was ever invented is the custom which makes it necessary for a speaker to sit through a fourteen-course dinner, every minute of the time feeling sure that his speech is going to prove a dismal failure and disappointment.

I rarely take part in one of these long dinners that I do not wish that I could put myself back in the little cabin where I was a slave boy, and again go through the experience there—one that I shall never forget—of getting molasses to eat once a week from the "big house." Our usual diet on the plantation was corn bread and pork, but on Sunday morning my mother was permitted to bring down a little molasses from the "big house" for her three children, and when it was received how I did wish that every day was Sunday! I would get my tin plate and hold it up for the sweet morsel, but I would always shut my eyes while the molasses was being poured out into the plate, with the hope that when I opened them I would be surprised to see how much I had got. When I opened my eyes I would tip the plate in one direction and another, so as to make the molasses spread all over it, in the full belief that there would be more of it and that it would last longer if spread out in this way. So strong are my childish impressions of those Sunday morning feasts that it would be pretty hard for any one to convince me that there is not more molasses on a plate when it is spread all over the plate than when it occupies a little corner—if there is a corner in a plate. At any rate, I have never believed in "cornering" syrup. My share of the syrup was usually about two tablespoonfuls, and those two spoonfuls of molasses were much more enjoyable to me than is a fourteen-course dinner after which I am to speak.

Next to a company of business men, I prefer to speak to an audience of Southern people, of either race, together or taken separately. Their enthusiasm and responsiveness are a constant delight. The "amens" and "dat's de truf" that come spontaneously from the coloured individuals are calculated to spur any speaker on to his best efforts. I think that next in order of preference I would place a college audience. It has been my privilege to deliver addresses at many of our leading colleges, including Harvard,

Yale, Williams, Amherst, Fisk University, the University of Pennsylvania, Wellesley, the University of Michigan, Trinity College in North Carolina, and many others.

It has been a matter of deep interest to me to note the number of people who have come to shake hands with me after an address, who say that this is the first time they have ever called a Negro "Mister."

When speaking directly in the interests of the Tuskegee Institute, I usually arrange, some time in advance, a series of meetings in important centres. This takes me before churches, Sunday-schools, Christian Endeavour Societies, and men's and women's clubs. When doing this I sometimes speak before as many as four organizations in a single day.

Three years ago, at the suggestion of Mr. Morris K. Jesup, of New York, and Dr. J. L. M. Curry, the general agent of the fund, the trustees of the John F. Slater Fund voted a sum of money to be used in paying the expenses of Mrs. Washington and myself while holding a series of meetings among the coloured people in the large centres of Negro population, especially in the large cities of the ex-slaveholding states. Each year during the last three years we have devoted some weeks to this work. The plan that we have followed has been for me to speak in the morning to the ministers, teachers, and professional men. In the afternoon Mrs. Washington would speak to the women alone, and in the evening I spoke to a large mass-meeting. In almost every case the meetings have been attended not only by the coloured people in large numbers, but by the white people. In Chattanooga, Tenn., for example, there was present at the mass-meeting an audience of not less than three thousand persons, and I was informed that eight hundred of these were white. I have done no work that I really enjoyed more than this, or that I think has accomplished more good.

These meetings have given Mrs. Washington and myself an opportunity to get first-hand, accurate information as to the real condition of the race, by seeing the people in their homes, their churches, their Sunday-schools, and their places of work, as well as in the prisons and dens of crime. These meetings also gave us an opportunity to see the relations that exist between the races. I never feel so hopeful about the race as I do after being engaged in a series of these meetings. I know that on such occasions there is much that comes to the surface that is superficial and deceptive, but I have had experience enough not to be deceived by mere signs and fleeting enthusiasms. I have taken pains to go to the bottom of things and get facts, in a cold, business-like manner.

I have seen the statement made lately, by one who claims to know what he is talking about, that, taking the whole Negro race into account, ninety per cent of the Negro women are not virtuous. There never was a baser falsehood uttered concerning a race, or a statement made that was less capable of being proved by actual facts.

No one can come into contact with the race for twenty years, as I have done in the heart of the South, without being convinced that the race is constantly making slow but sure progress materially, educationally, and morally. One might take up the life of the worst element in New York City, for example, and prove almost anything he wanted to prove concerning the white man, but all will agree that this is not a fair test.

Early in the year 1897 I received a letter inviting me to deliver an address at the dedication of the Robert Gould Shaw monument in Boston. I accepted the invitation. It is not necessary for me, I am sure, to explain who Robert Gould Shaw was, and what he did. The monument to his memory stands near the head of Boston Common, facing the State House. It is counted to be the most perfect piece of art of the kind to be found in the country.

The exercises connected with the dedication were held in Music Hall, in Boston, and the great hall was packed from top to bottom with one of the most distinguished audiences that ever assembled in the city. Among those present there were more persons representing the famous old anti-slavery element than it is likely will ever be brought together in the country again. The late Hon. Roger Wolcott, then Governor of Massachusetts, was the presiding officer, and on the platform with him were many other officials and hundreds of distinguished men. A report of the meeting which appeared in the Boston *Transcript* will describe it better than any words of mine could do:

THE SECRET OF SUCCESS IN PUBLIC SPEAKING

The core and kernel of yesterday's great noon meeting in honour of the Brotherhood of Man, in Music Hall, was the superb address of the Negro President of Tuskegee. "Booker T. Washington received his Harvard A. M. Last June, the first of his race," said Governor Wolcott, "to receive an honorary degree from the oldest university in the land, and this for the wise leadership of his people." When Mr. Washington rose in the flag-filled, enthusiasm-warmed, patriotic, and glowing atmosphere of Music Hall, people felt keenly that here was the civic justification of the old abolition spirit of Massachusetts; in his person the proof of her ancient and indomitable faith; in his strong thought and rich oratory, the crown and glory of the old war days of suffering and strife. The scene was full of historic beauty and deep significance. "Cold" Boston was alive with the fire that is always hot in her heart for righteousness and truth. Rows and rows of people who are seldom seen at any public function, whole families of those who are certain to be out of town on a holiday, crowded the place to overflowing. The city was at her birthright *fete* in the persons of hundreds of her best citizens, men and women whose names and lives stand for the virtues that make for honourable civic pride.ˆ

Battle-music had filled the air. Ovation after ovation, applause warm and prolonged, had greeted the officers and friends of Colonel Shaw, the sculptor, St. Gaudens, the memorial Committee, the Governor and his staff, and the Negro soldiers of the Fifty-fourth Massachusetts as they came upon the platform or entered the hall. Colonel Henry Lee, of Governor Andrews's old staff, had made a noble, simple presentation speech for the committee, paying tribute to Mr. John M. Forbes, in whose stead he served. Governor Wolcott had made his short, memorable speech, saying, "Fort Wagner marked an epoch in the history of a race, and called it into manhood." Mayor Quincy had received the monument for the city of Boston. The story of Colonel Shaw and his black regiment had been told in gallant words, and then, after the singing of *Mine eyes have seen the glory Of the coming of the Lord,* Booker Washington arose. It was, of course, just the moment for him. The multitude, shaken out if its usual symphony-concert calm, quivered with an excitement that was not suppressed. A dozen times it had sprung to its feet to cheer and wave and hurrah, as one person. When this man of culture and voice and power, as well as a dark skin, began, and uttered the names of Stearns and of Andrew, feeling began to mount. You could see tears glisten in the eyes of soldiers and civilians. When the orator turned to the coloured soldiers on the platform, to the colour-bearer of Fort Wagner, who smilingly bore still the flag he had never lowered even when wounded, and said, "To you, to the scarred and scattered remnants of the Fifty-fourth, who, with empty sleeve and wanting leg, have honoured this occasion with your presence, to you, your commander is not dead. Though Boston erected no monument and history recorded no story, in you and in the loyal race which you represent, Robert Gould Shaw would have a monument which time could not wear away," then came the climax of the emotion of the day and the hour. It was Roger Wolcott, as well as the Governor of Massachusetts, the individual representative of the people's sympathy as well as the chief magistrate, who had sprung first to his feet and cried, "Three cheers to Booker T. Washington!"

Among those on the platform was Sergeant William H. Carney, of New Bedford, Mass., the brave coloured officer who was the colour-bearer at Fort Wagner and held the American flag. In spite of the fact that a large part of his regiment was killed, he escaped, and exclaimed, after the battle was over, "The old flag never touched the ground."

This flag Sergeant Carney held in his hands as he sat on the platform, and when I turned to address the survivors of the coloured regiment who were present, and referred to Sergeant Carney, he rose, as if by instinct, and raised the flag. It has been my privilege to witness a good many satisfactory and rather sensational demonstrations in connection with some of my public addresses, but in dramatic effect I have never seen or experienced anything which equalled this. For a number of minutes the audience seemed to entirely lose control of itself.

In the general rejoicing throughout the country which followed the close of the Spanish-American war, peace celebrations were arranged in several of the large cities. I was asked by President William R. Harper, of the University of Chicago, who was chairman of the committee of invitations for the celebration to be held in the city of Chicago, to deliver one of the addresses at the celebration there. I accepted the invitation, and delivered two addresses there during the Jubilee week. The first of these, and the principal one, was given in the Auditorium, on the evening of Sunday, October 16. This was the largest audience that I have ever addressed, in any part of the country; and besides speaking in the main Auditorium, I also addressed, that same evening, two overflow audiences in other parts of the city.

It was said that there were sixteen thousand persons in the Auditorium, and it seemed to me as if there were as many more on the outside trying to get in. It was impossible for any one to get near the entrance without the aid of a policeman. President William McKinley attended this meeting, as did also the members of his Cabinet, many foreign ministers, and a large number of army and navy officers, many of whom had distinguished themselves in the war which had just closed. The speakers, besides myself, on Sunday evening, were Rabbi Emil G. Hirsch, Father Thomas P. Hodnett, and Dr. John H. Barrows.

THE SECRET OF SUCCESS IN PUBLIC SPEAKING

The Chicago *Times-Herald*, in describing the meeting, said of my address:

He pictured the Negro choosing slavery rather than extinction; recalled Crispus Attucks shedding his blood at the beginning of the American Revolution, that white Americans might be free, while black Americans remained in slavery; rehearsed the conduct of the Negroes with Jackson at New Orleans; drew a vivid and pathetic picture of the Southern slaves protecting and supporting the families of their masters while the latter were fighting to perpetuate black slavery; recounted the bravery of coloured troops at Port Hudson and Forts Wagner and Pillow, and praised the heroism of the black regiments that stormed El Caney and Santiago to give freedom to the enslaved people of Cuba, forgetting, for the time being, the unjust discrimination that law and custom make against them in their own country.

In all of these things, the speaker declared, his race had chosen the better part. And then he made his eloquent appeal to the consciences of the white Americans: "When you have gotten the full story of the heroic conduct of the Negro in the Spanish-American war, have heard it from the lips of Northern soldier and Southern soldier, from ex-abolitionist and ex-masters, then decide within yourselves whether a race that is thus willing to die for its country should not be given the highest opportunity to live for its country."

The part of the speech which seemed to arouse the wildest and most sensational enthusiasm was that in which I thanked the President for his recognition of the Negro in his appointments during the Spanish-American war. The President was sitting in a box at the right of the stage. When I addressed him I turned toward the box, and as I finished the sentence thanking him for his generosity, the whole audience rose and cheered again and again, waving handkerchiefs and hats and canes, until the President arose in the box and bowed his acknowledgments. At that the enthusiasm broke out again, and the demonstration was almost indescribable.

One portion of my address at Chicago seemed to have been misunderstood by the Southern press, and some of the Southern papers took occasion to criticize me rather strongly. These criticisms continued for several weeks, until I finally received a letter from the editor of the *Age-Herald*, published in Birmingham, Ala., asking me if I would say just what I meant by this part of my address. I replied to him in a letter which seemed to satisfy my critics. In this letter I said that I had made it a rule never to say before a

Northern audience anything that I would not say before an audience in the South. I said that I did not think it was necessary for me to go into extended explanations; if my seventeen years of work in the heart of the South had not been explanation enough, I did not see how words could explain. I said that I made the same plea that I had made in my address at Atlanta, for the blotting out of race prejudice in "commercial and civil relations." I said that what it termed social recognition was a question which I never discussed, and then I quoted from my Atlanta address what I had said there in regard to that subject.

In meeting crowds of people at public gatherings, there is one type of individual that I dread. I mean the crank. I have become so accustomed to these people now that I can pick them out at a distance when I see them elbowing their way up to me. The average crank has a long beard, poorly cared for, a lean, narrow face, and wears a black coat. The front of his vest and coat are slick with grease, and his trousers bag at the knees.

In Chicago, after I had spoken at a meeting, I met one of these fellows. They usually have some process for curing all of the ills of the world at once. This Chicago specimen had a patent process by which he said Indian corn could be kept through a period of three or four years, and he felt sure that if the Negro race in the South would, as a whole, adopt his process, it would settle the whole race question. It mattered nothing that I tried to convince him that our present problem was to teach the Negroes how to produce enough corn to last them through one year. Another Chicago crank had a scheme by which he wanted me to join him in an effort to close up all the National banks in the country. If that was done, he felt sure it would put the Negro on his feet.

The number of people who stand ready to consume one's time, to no purpose, is almost countless. At one time I spoke before a large audience in Boston in the evening. The next morning I was awakened by having a card brought to my room, and with it a message that someone was anxious to see me. Thinking that it must be something very important, I dressed hastily and went down. When I reached the hotel office I found a blank and innocent-looking individual waiting for me, who coolly remarked: "I heard you talk at a meeting last night.

I rather like your talk, and so I came in this morning to hear you talk some more."

I am often asked how it is possible for me to superintend the work at Tuskegee and at the same time be so much away from the school. In partial answer to this I would say that I think I have learned, in some degree at least, to disregard the old maxim which says, "Do not get others to do that which you can do yourself." My motto, on the other hand, is, "Do not do that which others can do as well."

One of the most encouraging signs in connection with the Tuskegee school is found in the fact that the organization is so thorough that the daily work of the school is not dependent upon the presence of any one individual. The whole executive force, including instructors and clerks, now numbers eighty-six. This force is so organized and subdivided that the machinery of the school goes on day by day like clockwork. Most of our teachers have been connected with the institution for a number of years, and are as much interested in it as I am. In my absence, Mr. Warren Logan, the treasurer, who has been at the school seventeen years, is the executive. He is efficiently supported by Mrs. Washington, and by my faithful secretary, Mr. Emmett J. Scott, who handles the bulk of my correspondence and keeps me in daily touch with the life of the school, and who also keeps me informed of whatever takes place in the South that concerns the race. I owe more to this tact, wisdom, and hard work than I can describe.

The main executive work of the school, whether I am at Tuskegee or not, centres in what we call the executive council. This council meets twice a week, and is composed of the nine persons who are at the head of the nine departments of the school. For example: Mrs. B. K. Bruce, the Lady Principal, the widow of the late ex-senator Bruce, is a member of the council, and represents in it all that pertains to the life of the girls at the school. In addition to the executive council there is a financial committee of six, that meets every week and decides upon the expenditures for the week. Once a month, and sometimes oftener, there is a general meeting of all the instructors. Aside from these there are innumerable smaller meetings, such as that of the instructors in the

Phelps Hall Bible Training School, or of the instructors in the agricultural department.

In order that I may keep in constant touch with the life of the institution, I have a system of reports so arranged that a record of the school's work reaches me every day in the year, no matter in what part of the country I am. I know by these reports even what students are excused from school, and why they are excused—whether for reasons of ill health or otherwise. Through the medium of these reports I know each day what the income of the school in money is; I know how many gallons of milk and how many pounds of butter come from the dairy; what the bill of fare for the teachers and students is; whether a certain kind of meat was boiled or baked, and whether certain vegetables served in the dining room were bought from a store or procured from our own farm. Human nature I find to be very much the same the world over, and it is sometimes not hard to yield to the temptation to go to a barrel of rice that has come from the store – with the grain all prepared to go into the pot—rather than to take the time and trouble to go to the field and dig and wash one's own sweet potatoes, which might be prepared in a manner to take the place of the rice.

I am often asked how, in the midst of so much work, a large part of which is before the public, I can find time for any rest or recreation, and what kind of recreation or sports I am fond of. This is rather a difficult question to answer. I have a strong feeling that every individual owes it to himself, and to the cause which he is serving, to keep a vigorous, healthy body, with the nerves steady and strong, prepared for great efforts and prepared for disappointments and trying positions. As far as I can, I make it a rule to plan for each day's work—not merely to go through with the same routine of daily duties, but to get rid of the routine works as early in the day as possible, and then to enter upon some new or advance work. I make it a rule to clear my desk every day, before leaving my office, of all correspondence and memoranda, so that on the morrow I can begin a *new* day of work. I make it a rule never to let my work drive me, but to so master it, and keep it in such complete control, and to keep so far ahead of it, that I will be the master instead of the servant. There is a physical and mental and spiritual enjoyment that comes from a consciousness of being the absolute master of one's work, in all its details, that is very satisfactory and inspiring. My experience teaches me that, if one learns to follow this plan, he gets a freshness of body and vigour of mind out of work that goes a long way toward keeping him strong and healthy. I believe that when one can grow to the point where he loves his work, this gives him a kind of strength that is most valuable.

When I begin my work in the morning, I expect to have a successful and pleasant day of it, but at the same time I prepare myself for unpleasant and unexpected hard places. I prepare myself to hear that one of our school buildings is on fire, or has burned, or that some disagreeable accident has occurred, or that some one has abused me in a public address or printed article, for something that I have done or omitted to do, or for something that he had heard that I had said— probably something that I had never thought of saying.

In nineteen years of continuous work I have taken but one vacation. That was two years ago, when some of my friends put the money into my hands and forced Mrs. Washington and myself to spend three months in Europe. I have said that I believe it is the duty of every one to keep his body in good condition. I try to look after the little ills, with the idea that if I take care of the little ills the big ones will not come. When I find myself unable to sleep well, I know that something is wrong. If I find any part of my system the least weak, and not performing its duty, I consult a good physician. The ability to sleep well, at any time and in any place, I find of great advantage. I have so trained myself that I can lie down for a nap of fifteen or twenty minutes, and get up refreshed in body and mind.

I have said that I make it a rule to finish up each day's work before leaving it. There is, perhaps, one exception to this. When I have an unusually difficult question to decide—one that appeals strongly to the emotions—I find it a safe rule to sleep over it for a night, or to wait until I have had an opportunity to talk it over with my wife and friends.

As to my reading; the most time I get for solid reading is when I am on the cars. Newspapers are to me a constant source of delight and recreation. The only trouble is that I read too many of them. Fiction I care little for. Frequently I have to almost force myself to read a novel that is on every one's lips. The kind of reading that I have the greatest fondness for is biography. I like to be sure that I am reading about a real man or a real thing. I think I do not go too far when I say that I have read nearly every book and magazine article that has been written about Abraham Lincoln. In literature he is my patron saint.

Out of the twelve months in a year I suppose that, on an average, I spend six months away from Tuskegee. While my being absent from the school so much unquestionably has its disadvantages, yet there are at the same time some compensations. The change of work brings a certain kind of rest. I enjoy a ride of a long distance on the cars, when I am permitted to ride where I can be comfortable. I get rest on the cars, except when the inevitable individual who seems to be on every train approaches me with the now familiar phrase: "Isn't this Booker Washington? I want to introduce myself to you." Absence from the school enables me to lose sight of the unimportant details of the work, and study it in a broader and more comprehensive manner than I could do on the grounds. This absence also brings me into contact with the best work being done in educational lines, and into contact with the best educators in the land.

But, after all this is said, the time when I get the most solid rest and recreation is when I can be at Tuskegee, and, after our evening meal is over, can sit down, as is our custom, with my wife and Portia and Baker and Davidson, my three children, and read a story, or each take turns in telling a story. To me there is nothing on earth equal to that, although what is nearly equal to it is to go with them for an hour or more, as we like to do on Sunday afternoons, into the woods, where we can live for a while near the heart of nature, where no one can disturb or vex us, surrounded by pure air, the trees, the shrubbery, the flowers, and the sweet fragrance that springs from a hundred plants, enjoying the chirp of the crickets and the songs of the birds. This is solid rest.

My garden, also, what little time I can be at Tuskegee, is another source of rest and enjoyment. Somehow I like, as often as possible, to touch nature, not something that is artificial or an imitation, but the real thing. When I can leave my office in time so that I can spend thirty or forty minutes in spading the ground, in planting seeds, in digging about the plants, I feel that I am coming into contact with something that is giving me strength for the many duties and hard places that await me out in the big world. I pity the man or woman who has never learned to enjoy nature and to get strength and inspiration out of it.

Aside from the large number of fowls and animals kept by the school, I keep individually a number of pigs and fowls of the best grades, and in raising these I take a great deal of pleasure. I think the pig is my favourite animal. Few things are more satisfactory to me than a high-grade Berkshire or Poland China pig.

Games I care little for. I have never seen a game of football. In cards I do not know one card from another. A game of old-fashioned marbles with my two boys, once in a while, is all I care for in this direction. I suppose I would care for games now if I had had any time in my youth to give to them, but that was not possible.

CHAPTER XVI
EUROPE

In 1893 I was married to Miss Margaret James Murray, a native of Mississippi, and a graduate of Fisk University, in Nashville, Tenn., who had come to Tuskegee as a teacher several years before, and at the time we were married was filling the position of Lady Principal. Not only is Mrs. Washington completely one with me in the work directly connected with the school, relieving me of many burdens and perplexities, but aside from her work on the school grounds, she carries on a mothers' meeting in the town of Tuskegee, and a plantation work among the women, children, and men who live in a settlement connected with a large plantation about eight miles from Tuskegee. Both the mothers' meeting and the plantation work are carried on, not only with a view to helping those who are directly reached, but also for the purpose of furnishing object-lessons in these two kinds of work that may be followed by our students when they go out into the world for their own life-work.

Aside from these two enterprises, Mrs. Washington is also largely responsible for a woman's club at the school which brings together, twice a month, the women who live on the school grounds and those who live near, for the discussion of some important topic. She is also the President of what is known as the Federation of Southern Coloured Women's Clubs, and is Chairman of the Executive Committee of the National Federation of Coloured Women's Clubs.

Portia, the oldest of my three children, has learned dressmaking. She has unusual ability in instrumental music. Aside from her studies at Tuskegee, she has already begun to teach there.

Baker Taliaferro is my next oldest child. Young as he is, he has already nearly mastered the brickmason's trade. He began working at this trade when he was quite small, dividing his time between this and class work; and he has developed great skill in the trade and a fondness for it. He says that he is going to be an architect and brickmason. One of the most satisfactory letters that I have ever received from any one came to me from Baker last summer. When I left home for the summer, I told him that he must work at his trade half of each day, and that the other half of the day he could spend as he pleased. When I had been away from home two weeks, I received the following letter from him:

Tuskegee, Alabama

My dear Papa: Before you left home you told me to work at my trade half of each day. I like my work so much that I want to work at my trade all day. Besides, I want to earn all the money I can, so that when I go to another school I shall have money to pay my expenses.

Your son,
Baker

My youngest child, Ernest Davidson Washington, says that he is going to be a physician. In addition to going to school, where he studies books and has manual training, he regularly spends a portion of his time in the office of our resident physician, and has already learned to do many of the duties which pertain to a doctor's office.

The thing in my life which brings me the keenest regret is that my work in connection with public affairs keeps me for so much of the time away from my family, where, of all places in the world, I delight to be. I always envy the individual whose life-work is so laid that he can spend his evenings at home. I have sometimes thought that people who have this rare privilege do not appreciate it as they should. It is such a rest and relief to get away from crowds of people, and handshaking, and travelling, and get home, even if it be for but a very brief while.

Another thing at Tuskegee out of which I get a great deal of pleasure and satisfaction is in the meeting with our students, and teachers, and their families, in the chapel for devotional exercises every evening at half-past eight, the last thing before retiring for the night. It is an inspiring sight when one stands on the platform there and sees before him eleven or twelve hundred earnest young men and women; and one cannot but feel that it is a privilege to help to guide them to a higher and more useful life.

In the spring of 1899 there came to me what I might describe as almost the greatest surprise of my life. Some good ladies in Boston arranged a public meeting in the interests of Tuskegee, to be held in the Hollis Street Theatre. This meeting was attended by large numbers of the best people of Boston, of both races. Bishop Lawrence presided. In addition to an address made by myself, Mr. Paul Lawrence Dunbar read from his poems, and Dr. W. E.B. DuBois read an original sketch.

Some of those who attended this meeting noticed that I seemed unusually tired, and some little time after the close of the meeting, one of the ladies who had been interested in it asked me in a casual way if I had ever been to Europe. I replied that I never had. She asked me if I had ever thought of going, and I told her no; that it was something entirely beyond me. This conversation soon passed out of my mind, but a few days afterward I was informed that some friends in Boston, including Mr. Francis J. Garrison, had raised a sum of money sufficient to pay all the expenses of Mrs. Washington and myself during a three or four months' trip to Europe. It was added with emphasis that we *must* go. A year previous to this Mr. Garrison had attempted to get me to promise to go to Europe for a summer's rest, with the understanding that he would be responsible for raising the money among his friends for the expenses of the trip. At that time such a journey seemed so entirely foreign to anything that I should ever be able to undertake that I confess I did not give the matter very serious attention; but later Mr. Garrison joined his efforts to those of the ladies whom I have mentioned, and when their plans were made known to me Mr. Garrison not only had the route mapped out, but had, I believe, selected the steamer upon which we were to sail.

The whole thing was so sudden and so unexpected that I was

completely taken off my feet. I had been at work steadily for eighteen years in connection with Tuskegee, and I had never thought of anything else but ending my life in that way. Each day the school seemed to depend upon me more largely for its daily expenses, and I told these Boston friends that, while I thanked them sincerely for their thoughtfulness and generosity, I could not go to Europe, for the reason that the school could not live financially while I was absent. They then informed me that Mr. Henry L. Higginson, and some other good friends who I know do not want their names made public, were then raising a sum of money which would be sufficient to keep the school in operation while I was away. At this point I was compelled to surrender. Every avenue of escape had been closed.

Deep down in my heart the whole thing seemed more like a dream than like reality, and for a long time it was difficult for me to make myself believe that I was actually going to Europe. I had been born and largely reared in the lowest depths of slavery, ignorance, and poverty. In my childhood I had suffered for want of a place to sleep, for lack of food, clothing, and shelter. I had not had the privilege of sitting down to a dining-table until I was quite well grown. Luxuries had always seemed to me to be something meant for white people, not for my race. I had always regarded Europe, and London, and Paris, much as I regard heaven. And now could it be that I was actually going to Europe? Such thoughts as these were constantly with me.

Two other thoughts troubled me a good deal. I feared that people who heard that Mrs. Washington and I were going to Europe might not know all the circumstances, and might get the idea that we had become, as some might say, "stuck up," and were trying to "show off." I recalled that from my youth I had heard it said that too often, when people of my race reached any degree of success, they were inclined to unduly exalt themselves; to try and ape the wealthy, and in so doing to lose their heads. The fear that people might think this of us haunted me a good deal. Then, too, I could not see how my conscience would permit me to spare the time from my work and be happy. It seemed mean and selfish in me to be taking a vacation while others were at work and while there was so much that needed to be done. From the time I could remember, I had always been at work, and I did not see how I could spend three or four months in doing nothing. The fact was that I did not know how to take a vacation.

Mrs. Washington had much the same difficulty in getting away, but she was anxious to go because she thought that I needed the rest. There were many important National questions bearing upon the life of the race which were being agitated at that time, and this made it all the harder for us to decide to go. We finally gave our Boston friends our promise that we would go, and then they insisted that the date of our departure be set as soon as possible. So we decided upon May 10. My good friend Mr. Garrison kindly took charge of all the details necessary for the success of the trip, and he, as well as other friends, gave us a great number of letters of introduction to people in France and England, and made other arrangements for our comfort and convenience abroad. Good-bys were said at Tuskegee, and we were in New York May 9, ready to sail the next day. Our daughter Portia, who was then studying in South Framingham, Mass., came to New York to see us off. Mr. Scott, my secretary, came with me to New York, in order that I might clear up the last bit of business before I left. Other friends also came to New York to see us off. Just before we went on board the steamer another pleasant surprise came to us in the form of a letter from two generous ladies, stating that they had decided to give us the money with which to erect a new building to be used in properly housing all our industries for girls at Tuskegee.

We were to sail on the *Friesland*, of the Red Star Line, and a beautiful vessel she was. We went on board just before noon, the hour of sailing. I had never before been on board a large ocean steamer, and the feeling which took possession of me when I found myself there is rather hard to describe. It was a feeling, I think, of awe mingled with delight. We were agreeably surprised to find that the captain, as well as several of the other officers, not only knew who we were, but was expecting us and gave us a pleasant greeting. There were several passengers whom we knew, including Senator Sewell, of New Jersey, and Edward Marshall, the newspaper correspondent. I had just a little fear that we would not be treated civilly by some of the passengers. This fear was based upon what I had heard other people of my race, who had crossed the ocean, say about unpleasant experiences in crossing the ocean in American vessels. But in our case, from the captain down to the most humble servant, we were treated with the greatest kindness. Nor was this kindness confined to those who were connected with the steamer; it was shown by all the passengers also. There were not a few Southern men and women on board, and they were as cordial as those from other parts of the country.

As soon as the last good-bys were said, and the steamer had cut loose from the wharf, the load of care, anxiety, and responsibility which I had carried for eighteen years began to lift itself from my shoulders at the rate, it seemed to me, of a pound a minute. It was the first time in all those years that I had felt, even in a measure, free from care; and my feeling of relief it is hard to describe on paper. Added to this was the delightful anticipation of being in Europe soon. It all seemed more like a dream than like a reality.

Mr. Garrison had thoughtfully arranged to have us have one of the most comfortable rooms on the ship. The second or third day out I began to sleep, and I think that I slept at the rate of fifteen hours a day during the remainder of the ten days' passage. Then it was that I began to understand how tired I really was. These long sleeps I kept up for a month after we landed on the other side. It was such an unusual feeling to wake up in the morning and realize that I had no engagements; did not have to take a train at a certain hour; did not have an appointment to meet some one, or to make an address, at a certain hour. How different all this was from some of the experiences that I have been through when travelling, when I have sometimes slept in three different beds in a single night!

When Sunday came, the captain invited me to conduct the religious services, but, not being a minister, I declined. The passengers, however, began making requests that I deliver an address to them in the dining-saloon some time during the voyage, and this I consented to do. Senator

Sewell presided at this meeting. After ten days of delightful weather, during which I was not seasick for a day, we landed at the interesting old city of Antwerp, in Belgium.

The next day after we landed happened to be one of those number-less holidays which the people of those countries are in the habit of observing. It was a bright, beautiful day. Our room in the hotel faced the main public square, and the sights there—the people coming in from the country with all kinds of beautiful flowers to sell, the women coming in with their dogs drawing large, brightly polished cans filled with milk, the people streaming into the cathedral—filled me with a sense of newness that I had never before experienced.

After spending some time in Antwerp, we were invited to go with a party of a half-dozen persons on a trip through Holland. This party included Edward Marshall and some American artists who had come over on the same steamer with us. We accepted the invitation, and enjoyed the trip greatly. I think it was all the more interesting and instructive because we went for most of the way on one of the slow, old-fashioned canal-boats. This gave us an opportunity of seeing and studying the real life of the people in the country districts. We went in this way as far as Rotterdam, and later went to The Hague, where the Peace Conference was then in session, and where we were kindly received by the American representatives.

The thing that impressed itself most on me in Holland was the thoroughness of the agriculture and the excellence of the Holstein cattle. I never knew, before visiting Holland, how much it was possible for people to get out of a small plot of ground. It seemed to me that absolutely no land was wasted. It was worth a trip to Holland, too, just to get a sight of three or four hundred fine Holstein cows grazing in one of those intensely green fields.

From Holland we went to Belgium, and made a hasty trip through that country, stopping at Brussels, where we visited the battlefield of Waterloo. From Belgium we went direct to Paris, where we found that Mr. Theodore Stanton, the son of Mrs. Elizabeth Cady Stanton, had kindly provided accommodations for us. We had barely got settled in

Paris before an invitation came to me from the University Club of Paris to be its guest at a banquet which was soon to be given. The other guests were ex-President Benjamin Harrison and Archbishop Ireland, who were in Paris at the time. The American Ambassador, General Horace Porter, presided at the banquet. My address on this occasion seemed to give satisfaction to those who heard it. General Harrison kindly devoted a large portion of his remarks at dinner to myself and to the influence of the work at Tuskegee on the American race question. After my address at this banquet other invitations came to me, but I declined the most of them, knowing that if I accepted them all, the object of my visit would be defeated. I did, however, consent to deliver an address in the American chapel the following Sunday morning, and at this meeting General Harrison, General Porter, and other distinguished Americans were present.

Later we received a formal call from the American Ambassador, and were invited to attend a reception at this residence. At this reception we met many Americans, among them Justices Fuller and Harlan, of the United States Supreme Court. During our entire stay of a month in Paris, both the American Ambassador and his wife, as well as several other Americans, were very kind to us.

While in Paris we saw a good deal of the now rather famous American Negro painter, Mr. Henry O. Tanner, whom we had formerly known in America. It was very satisfactory to find how well known Mr. Tanner was in the field of art, and to note the high standing which all classes accorded to him. When we told some Americans that we were going to the Luxembourg Palace to see a painting by an American Negro, it was hard to convince them that a Negro had been thus honoured. I do not believe that they were really convinced of the fact until they saw the picture for themselves. My acquaintance with Mr. Tanner reinforced in my mind the truth which I am constantly trying to impress upon our students at Tuskegee—and on our people throughout the country, as far as I can reach them with my voice—that any man, regardless of colour, will be recognized and rewarded just in proportion as he learns to do something well—learns to do it better than someone else—however humble the thing may be. As I have said, I believe that my race will succeed in proportion as it learns to do a common thing in an uncommon manner; learns to do a thing so thoroughly that no one can improve upon what it has done; learns to make its services of indispensable value. This was the spirit that inspired me in my first effort at Hampton, when I was given the opportunity to sweep and dust that schoolroom. In a degree I felt that my whole future life depended upon the thoroughness with which I cleaned that room, and I was determined to do it so well that no one could find any fault with the job. Few people ever stopped, I found, when looking at his pictures, to inquire whether Mr. Tanner was a Negro painter, a French painter, or a German painter. They simply knew that he was able to produce something which the world wanted—a great painting—and the matter of his colour did not enter into their minds. When a Negro girl learns to cook, to wash dishes, to sew, to write a book, or a Negro boy learns to groom horses, or to grow sweet potatoes, or to produce butter, or to build a house, or to be able to practise medicine, as well or better than some one else, they will be rewarded regardless of race or colour. In the long run, the world is going to have the best, and any difference in race, religion, or previous history will not long keep the world from what it wants.

I think that the whole future of my race hinges on the question as to whether or not it can make itself of such indispensable value that the people in the town and the state where we reside will fell that our presence is necessary to the happiness and well-being of the community. No man who continues to add something to the material, intellectual, and moral well-being of the place in which he lives is long left without proper reward. This is a great human law which cannot be permanently nullified.

The love of pleasure and excitement which seems in large measure to possess the French people impressed itself upon me. I think they are more noted in this respect than is true of the people of my own race. In point of morality and moral earnestness I do not believe that the French are ahead of my own race in America. Severe competition and the great stress of life have led them to learn to do things more thoroughly and to exercise greater economy; but time, I think, will bring my race to the same point. In the matter of truth and high honour I do not believe that the average Frenchman is ahead of the American Negro; while so far as mercy and kindness to dumb animals to, I believe my race is far ahead. In fact, when I left France, I had more faith in the future of the black man in America than I had ever possessed.

From Paris we went to London, and reached there early in July, just about the height of the London social season. Parliament was in session, and there was a great deal of gaiety. Mr. Garrison and other friends had provided us with a large number of letters of introduction, and they had also sent letters to other persons in different parts of the United Kingdom, apprising these people of our coming. Very soon after reaching London we were flooded with invitations to attend all manner of social functions, and a great many invitations came to me asking that I deliver public addresses. The most of these invitations I declined, for the reason that I wanted to rest. Neither were we able to accept more than a small proportion of the other invitations. The Rev. Dr. Brooke Herford and Mrs. Herford, whom I had known in Boston, consulted with the American Ambassador, the Hon. Joseph Choate, and arranged for me to speak at a public meeting that was largely attended. There were many distinguished persons present, among them several members of Parliament, including Mr. James Bryce, who spoke at the meeting. What the American Ambassador said in introducing me, as well as a synopsis of what I said, was widely published in England and in the American papers at the time. Dr. and Mrs. Herford gave Mrs. Washington and myself a reception, at which we had the privilege of meeting some of the best people in England. Throughout our stay in London Ambassador Choate was most kind and attentive to us. At the Ambassador's reception I met, for the first time, Mark Twain.

We were the guests several times of Mrs. T. Fisher Unwin, the daughter of the English statesman, Richard Cobden. It seemed as if both Mr. and Mrs. Unwin could not do enough for our comfort and happiness. Later, for nearly a week, we were the guests of the daughter of John Bright, now Mrs. Clark, of Street, England. Both Mr. and Mrs. Clark, with their daughter, visited us at Tuskegee the next year. In Birmingham, England, we were the

guests for several days of Mr. Joseph Sturge, whose father was a great aboli-
tionist and friend of Whittier and Garrison. It was a great privilege to meet
throughout England those who had known and honoured the late William
Lloyd Garrison, the Hon. Frederick Douglass, and other abolitionists. The
English abolitionists with whom we came in contact never seemed to tire of
talking about these two Americans. Before going to England I had had no
proper conception of the deep interest displayed by the abolitionists of
England in the cause of freedom, nor did I realize the amount of substantial
help given by them.

In Bristol, England, both Mrs. Washington and I spoke at the Women's
Liberal Club. I was also the principal speaker at the Commencement
exercises of the Royal College for the Blind. These exercises were held in the
Crystal Palace, and the presiding officer was the late Duke of Westminster,
who was said to be, I believe, the richest man in England, if not in the
world. The Duke, as well as his wife and their daughter, seemed to be pleased
with what I said, and thanked me heartily. Through the kindness of Lady
Aberdeen, my wife and I were enabled to go with a party of those who were
attending the International Congress of Women, then in session in
London, to see Queen Victoria, at Windsor Castle, where, afterward, we
were all the guests of her Majesty at tea. In our party was Miss Susan B.
Anthony, and I was deeply impressed with the fact that one did not often
get an opportunity to see, during the same hour, two women so remarkable
in different ways as Susan B. Anthony and Queen Victoria.

In the House of Commons, which we visited several times, we met Sir
Henry M. Stanley. I talked with him about Africa and its relation to the
American Negro, and after my interview with him I became more
convinced than ever that there was no hope of the American Negro's
improving his condition by emigrating to Africa.

On various occasions Mrs. Washington and I were the guests of Englishmen in their country homes, where, I think, one sees the Englishman
at his best. In one thing, at least, I feel sure that the English are ahead of
Americans, and that is, that they have learned how to get more out of life.
The home life of the English seems to me to be about as perfect as anything
can be. Everything moves like clockwork. I was impressed, too, with the

deference that the servants show to their "masters" and "mistresses,"—terms which I suppose would not be tolerated in America. The English servant expects, as a rule, to be nothing but a servant, and so he perfects himself in the art to a degree that no class of servants in America has yet reached. In our country the servant expects to become, in a few years, a "master" himself. Which system is preferable? I will not venture an answer.

Another thing that impressed itself upon me throughout England was the high regard that all classes have for law and order, and the ease and thoroughness with which everything is done. The Englishmen, I found, took plenty of time for eating, as for everything else. I am not sure if, in the long run, they do not accomplish as much or more than rushing, nervous Americans do.

My visit to England gave me a higher regard for the nobility than I had had. I had no idea that they were so generally loved and respected by the masses, nor had I any correct conception of how much time and money they spent in works of philanthropy, and how much real heart they put into this work. My impression had been that they merely spent money freely and had a "good time."

It was hard for me to get accustomed to speaking to English audiences. The average Englishman is so serious, and is so tremendously in earnest about everything, that when I told a story that would have made an American audience roar with laughter, the Englishmen simply looked me straight in the face without even cracking a smile.

When the Englishman takes you into his heart and friendship, he binds you there as with cords of steel, and I do not believe that there are many other friendships that are so lasting or so satisfactory. Perhaps I can illustrate this point in no better way than by relating the following incident. Mrs. Washington and I were invited to attend a reception given by the Duke and Duchess of Sutherland, at Stafford House—said to be the finest house in London; I may add that I believe the Duchess of Sutherland is said to be the most beautiful woman in England. There must have been at least three hundred persons at this reception. Twice during the evening the Duchess sought us out for a conversation, and she asked me to write her when we got home, and tell her more about the work at Tuskegee. This I did. When

Christmas came we were surprised and delighted to receive her photograph with her autograph on it. The correspondence has continued, and we now feel that in the Duchess of Sutherland we have one of our warmest friends.

After three months in Europe we sailed from Southampton in the steamship *St. Louis.* On this steamer there was a fine library that had been presented to the ship by the citizens of St. Louis, Mo. In this library I found a life of Frederick Douglass, which I began reading. I became especially interested in Mr. Douglass's description of the way he was treated on shipboard during his first or second visit to England. In this description he told how he was not permitted to enter the cabin, but had to confine himself to the deck of the ship. A few minutes after I had finished reading this description I was waited on by a committee of ladies and gentlemen with the request that I deliver an address at a concert which was to be given the following evening. And yet there are people who are bold enough to say that race feeling in America is not growing less intense! At this concert the Hon. Benjamin B. Odell, Jr., the present governor of New York, presided. I was never given a more cordial hearing anywhere. A large proportion of the passengers were Southern people. After the concert some of the passengers proposed that a subscription be raised to help the work at Tuskegee, and the money to support several scholarships was the result.

While we were in Paris I was very pleasantly surprised to receive the following invitation from the citizens of West Virginia and of the city near which I had spent my boyhood days:

CHARLESTON, W. VA., MAY 16, 1899.
PROFESSOR BOOKER T. WASHINGTON, PARIS, FRANCE:

DEAR SIR: Many of the best citizens of West Virginia have united in liberal expressions of admiration and praise of your worth and work, and desire that on your return from Europe you should favour them with your presence and with the inspiration of your words. We most sincerely indorse this move, and on behalf of the citizens of Charleston extend to you our most cordial invitation to have you come to us, that we may honour you who have done so much by your life and work to honour us.

We are, Very truly yours,
THE COMMON COUNCIL OF THE CITY OF CHARLESTON,
BY W. HERMAN SMITH, MAYOR

This invitation from the City Council of Charleston was accompanied by the following:

PROFESSOR BOOKER T. WASHINGTON,
PARIS, FRANCE:

DEAR SIR: We, the citizens of Charleston and West Virginia, desire to express our pride in you and the splendid career that you have thus far accomplished, and ask that we be permitted to show our pride and interest in a substantial way.

Your recent visit to your old home in our midst awoke within us the keenest regret that we were not permitted to hear you and render some substantial aid to your work, before you left for Europe.

In view of the foregoing, we earnestly invite you to share the hospitality of our city upon your return from Europe, and give us the opportunity to hear you and put ourselves in touch with your work in a way that will be most gratifying to yourself, and that we may receive the inspiration of your words and presence.

An early reply to this invitation, with an indication of the time you may reach our city, will greatly oblige,

> Yours very respectfully,
> The Charleston *Daily Gazette*, The *Daily Mail-Tribune*, G. W. Atkinson, Governor; E.L.Boggs, Secretary to Governor; Wm. M. O. Dawson, Secretary of State; L. M. La Follette, Auditor; J. R. Trotter, Superintendent of Schools; E. W. Wilson, ex-Governor; W. A. MacCorkle, ex-Governor; John Q. Dickinson, President Kanawha Valley Bank; L. Prichard, President Charleston National Bank; Geo. S. Couch, President Kanawha National Bank; Ed. Reid, Cashier Kanawha National Bank; Geo. S. Laidley, Superintendent City Schools; L. E. McWhorter, President Board of Education; Chas. K. Payne, wholesale merchant; and many others.

This invitation, coming as it did from the City Council, the state officers, and all the substantial citizens of both races of the community where I had spent my boyhood, and from which I had gone a few years before, unknown, in poverty and ignorance, in quest of an education, not only surprised me, but almost unmanned me. I could not understand what I had done to deserve it all.

I accepted the invitation, and at the appointed day was met at the railway station at Charleston by a committee headed by ex-Governor W. A. MacCorkle, and composed of men of both races. The public reception was held in the Opera-House at Charleston. The Governor of the state, the Hon. George W. Atkinson, presided, and an address of welcome was made by ex-Governor MacCorkle. A prominent part in the reception was taken by the coloured citizens. The Opera-House was filled with citizens of both races, and among the white people were many for whom I had worked when a boy. The next day Governor and Mrs. Atkinson gave me a public reception at the State House, which was attended by all classes.

Not long after this the coloured people in Atlanta, Georgia, gave me a reception at which the Governor of the state presided, and a similar reception was given me in New Orleans, which was presided over by the Mayor of the city. Invitations came from many other places which I was not able to accept.

CHAPTER XVII
LAST WORDS

Before going to Europe some events came into my life which were great surprises to me. In fact, my whole life has largely been one of surprises. I believe that any man's life will be filled with constant, unexpected encouragements of this kind if he makes up his mind to do his level best each day of his life—that is, tries to make each day reach as nearly as possible the high-water mark of pure, unselfish, useful living. I pity the man, black or white, who has never experienced the joy and satisfaction that come to one by reason of an effort to assist in making some one else more useful and more happy.

Six months before he died, and nearly a year after he had been stricken with paralysis, General Armstrong expressed a wish to visit Tuskegee again before he passed away. Notwithstanding the fact that he had lost the use of his limbs to such an extent that he was practically helpless, his wish was gratified, and he was brought to Tuskegee. The owners of the Tuskegee Railroad, white men living in the town, offered to run a special train, without cost, out to the main station—Chehaw, five miles away—to meet him. He arrived on the school grounds about nine o'clock in the evening. Some one had suggested that we give the General a "pine-knot torchlight reception." This plan was carried out, and the moment that his carriage entered the school grounds he began passing between two lines of lighted and waving "fat pine" wood knots held by over a thousand students and teachers. The whole thing was so novel and surprising that the General was completely overcome with happiness. He remained a guest in my home for nearly two months, and, although almost wholly without the use of voice or limb, he spent nearly every hour in devising ways and means to help the South. Time and time again he said to me, during this visit, that it was not only the duty of the country to assist in elevating the Negro of the South, but the poor white man as well. At the end of his visit I resolved anew to devote myself more earnestly than ever to the cause which was so near his heart. I said that if a man in his condition was willing to think, work, and act, I should not be wanting in furthering in every possible way the wish of his heart.

The death of General Armstrong, a few weeks later, gave me the privilege of getting acquainted with one of the finest, most unselfish, and most attractive men that I have ever come in contact with. I refer to the Rev. Dr. Hollis B. Frissell, now the Principal of the Hampton Institute, and General Armstrong's successor. Under the clear, strong, and almost perfect leadership of Dr. Frissell, Hampton has had a career of prosperity and usefulness that is all that the General could have wished for. It seems to be the constant effort of Dr. Frissell to hide his own great personality behind that of General Armstrong—to make himself of "no reputation" for the sake of the cause.

More than once I have been asked what was the greatest surprise that ever came to me. I have little hesitation in answering that question. It was the following letter, which came to me one Sunday morning when I was sitting on the veranda of my home at Tuskegee, surrounded by my wife and three children:

HARVARD UNIVERSITY,
CAMBRIDGE, MAY 28, 1896
PRESIDENT BOOKER T. WASHINGTON,

MY DEAR SIR: Harvard University desires to confer on you at the approaching Commencement an honorary degree; but it is our custom to confer degrees only on gentlemen who are present. Our Commencement occurs this year on June 24, and your presence would be desirable from about noon till about five o'clock in the afternoon. Would it be possible for you to be in Cambridge on that day?

Believe me, with great regard,
Very truly yours,
CHARLES W. ELIOT.

180

This was a recognition that had never in the slightest manner entered into my mind, and it was hard for me to realize that I was to be honoured by a degree from the oldest and most renowned university in America. As I sat upon my veranda, with this letter in my hand, tears came into my eyes. My whole former life—my life as a slave on the plantation, my work in the coal-mine, the times when I was without food and clothing, when I made my bed under a sidewalk, my struggles for an education, the trying days I had had at Tuskegee, days when I did not know where to turn for a dollar to continue the work there, the ostracism and sometimes oppression of my race, all this passed before me and nearly overcame me.

I had never sought or cared for what the world calls fame. I have always looked upon fame as something to be used in accomplishing good. I have often said to my friends that if I can use whatever prominence may have come to me as an instrument with which to do good, I am content to have it. I care for it only as a means to be used for doing good, just as wealth may be used. The more I come into contact with wealthy people, the more I believe that they are growing in the direction of looking upon their money simply as an instrument which God has placed in their hand for doing good with. I never go to the office of Mr. John D. Rockefeller, who more than once has been generous to Tuskegee, without being reminded of this. The close, careful, and intimate investigation that he always makes in order to be sure that every dollar that he gives will do the most good—an investigation that is just as searching as if he were investing money in a business enterprise—convinces me that the growth in this direction is most encouraging.

At nine o'clock, on the morning of June 24, I met President Eliot, the Board of Overseers of Harvard University, and the other guests, at the designated place on the university grounds, for the purpose of being escorted to Sanders Theatre, where the Commencement exercises were to be held and degrees conferred. Among others invited to be present for the purpose of receiving a degree at this time were General Nelson A. Miles, Dr. Bell, the inventor of the Bell telephone, Bishop Vincent, and the Rev. Minot J. Savage. We were placed in line immediately behind the President and the Board of Overseers, and directly afterward the Governor of Massachusetts, escorted by the Lancers, arrived and took his place in the line of march by the side of President Eliot. In the line there were also various other officers and professors, clad in cap and gown. In this order we marched to Sanders Theatre, where, after the usual commencement exercises, came the conferring of the honorary degrees. This, it seems, is always considered the most interesting feature at Harvard. It is not known, until the individuals appear, upon whom the honorary degrees are to be conferred, and those receiving these honours are cheered by the students and others in proportion to their popularity. During the conferring of the degrees excitement and enthusiasm are at the highest pitch.

When my name was called, I rose, and President Eliot, in beautiful and strong English, conferred upon me the degree of Master of Arts. After these exercises were over, those who had received honorary degrees were invited to lunch with the President. After the lunch we were formed in line again, and were escorted by the Marshal of the day, who that year happened to be Bishop William Lawrence, through the grounds, where, at different points, those who had been honoured were called by name and received the Harvard yell. This march ended at Memorial Hall, where the alumni dinner was served. To see over a thousand strong men, representing all that is best in State, Church, business, and education, with the glow and enthusiasm of college loyalty and college pride,—which has, I think, a peculiar Harvard flavour,—is a sight that does not easily fade from memory.

Among the speakers after dinner were President Eliot, Governor Roger Wolcott, General Miles, Dr. Minot J. Savage, the Hon. Henry Cabot Lodge, and myself. When I was called upon, I said, among other things:

It would in some measure relieve my embarrassment if I could, even in a slight degree, feel myself worthy of the great honour which you do me to-day. Why you have called me from the Black Belt of the South, from among my humble people, to share in the honours of this occasion, is not for me to explain; and yet it may not be inappropriate for me to suggest that it seems to me that one of the most vital questions that touch our American life is how to bring the strong, wealthy, and learned into helpful touch with the poorest, most ignorant, and humblest, and at the same time make one appreciate the vitalizing, strengthening influence of the other. How shall we make the mansions on yon Beacon Street feel and see the need of the spirits in the lowliest cabin in Alabama cotton-fields or Louisiana sugar-bottoms? This problem Harvard University is solving, not by bringing itself down, but by bring the masses up.

If my life in the past has meant anything in the lifting up of my people and the bringing about of better relations between your race and mine, I assure you from this day it will mean doubly more. In the economy of God there is but one standard by which an individual can succeed—there is but one for a race. This country demands that every race shall measure itself by the American standard. By it a race must rise or fall, succeed or fail, and in the last analysis mere sentiment counts for little. During the next half-century and more, my race must continue passing through the severe American crucible. We are to be tested in our patience, our forbearance, our perseverance, our power to endure wrong, to withstand temptations, to economize, to acquire and use skill; in our ability to compete, to succeed in commerce, to disregard the superficial for the real, the appearance for the substance, to be great and yet small, learned and yet simple, high and yet the servant of all.

As this was the first time that a New England university had conferred an honorary degree upon a Negro, it was the occasion of much newspaper comment throughout the country. A correspondent of a New York paper said:

When the name of Booker T. Washington was called, and he arose to acknowledge and accept, there was such an outburst of applause as greeted no other name except that of the popular soldier patriot, General Miles. The applause was not studied and stiff, sympathetic and condoling; it was enthusiasm and admiration. Every part of the audience from pit to gallery joined in, and a glow covered the cheeks of those around me, proving sincere appreciation of the rising struggle of an ex-slave and the work he has accomplished for his race.

A Boston paper said, editorially:

In conferring the honorary degree of Master of Arts upon the Principal of Tuskegee Institute, Harvard University has honoured itself as well as the object of this distinction. The work which Professor Booker T. Washington has accomplished for the education, good citizenship, and popular enlightenment in his chosen field of labour in the South entitles him to rank with our national benefactors. The university which can claim him on its list of sons, whether in regular course or *honoris causa*, may be proud.

It has been mentioned that Mr. Washington is the first of his race to receive an honorary degree from a New England university. This, in itself, is a distinction. But the degree was not conferred because Mr. Washington is a coloured man, or because he was born in slavery, but because he has shown, by his work for the elevation of the people of the Black Belt of the South, a genius and a broad humanity which count for greatness in any man, whether his skin be white or black.

Another Boston paper said:

It is Harvard which, first among New England colleges, confers an honorary degree upon a black man. No one who has followed the history of Tuskegee and its work can fail to admire the courage, persistence, and splendid common sense of Booker T. Washington. Well may Harvard honour the ex-slave, the value of whose services, alike to his race and country, only the future can estimate.

The correspondent of the New York *Times* wrote:

All the speeches were enthusiastically received, but the coloured man carried off the oratorical honours, and the applause which broke out when he had finished was vociferous and long-continued.

Soon after I began work at Tuskegee I formed a resolution, in the secret of my heart, that I would try to build up a school that would be of so much service to the country that the President of the United States would one day come to see it. This was, I confess, rather a bold resolution, and for a number of years I kept it hidden in my own thoughts, not daring to share it with any one.

In November, 1897, I made the first move in this direction, and that was in securing a visit from a member of President McKinley's Cabinet, the Hon. James Wilson, Secretary of Agriculture. He came to deliver an address at the formal opening of the Slater-Armstrong Agricultural Building, our first large building to be used for the purpose of giving training to our students in agriculture and kindred branches.

In the fall of 1898 I heard that President McKinley was likely to visit Atlanta, Georgia, for the purpose of taking part in the Peace Jubilee exercises to be held there to commemorate the successful close of the Spanish-American war. At this time I had been hard at work, together with our teachers, for eighteen years, trying to build up a school that we thought would be of service to the Nation, and I determined to make a direct effort to secure a visit from the President and his Cabinet. I went to Washington, and I was not long in the city before I found my way to the White House. When I got there I found the waiting rooms full of people, and my heart began to sink, for I feared there would not be much chance of my seeing the President that day, if at all. But at any rate, I got an opportunity to see Mr. J. Addison Porter, the secretary to the President, and explained to him my mission. Mr. Porter kindly sent my card directly to the President, and in a few minutes word came from Mr. McKinley that he would see me.

How any man can see so many people of all kinds, with all kinds of errands, and do so much hard work, and still keep himself calm, patient, and fresh for each visitor in the way that President McKinley does, I cannot understand. When I saw the President he kindly thanked me for the work which we were doing at Tuskegee for the interests of the country. I then told him briefly, the object of my visit. I impressed upon him the fact that a visit from the Chief Executive of the Nation would not only encourage our students and teachers, but would help the entire race. He seemed interested, but did not make a promise to go to Tuskegee, for the reason that his plans about going to Atlanta were not then fully made; but he asked me to call the matter to his attention a few weeks later.

By the middle of the following month the President had definitely decided to attend the Peace Jubilee at Atlanta. I went to Washington again and saw him, with a view of getting him to extend his trip to Tuskegee. On this second visit Mr. Charles W. Hare, a prominent white citizen of Tuskegee, kindly volunteered to accompany me, to reinforce my invitation with one from the white people of Tuskegee and the vicinity.

Just previous to my going to Washington the second time, the country had been excited, and the coloured people greatly depressed, because of several severe race riots which had occurred at different points in the South. As soon as I saw the President, I perceived that his heart was greatly burdened by reason of these race disturbances. Although there were many people waiting to see him, he detained me for some time, discussing the condition and prospects of the race. He remarked several times that he was determined to show his interest and faith in the race, not merely in words, but by acts. When I told him that I thought that at that time scarcely anything would go farther in giving hope and encouragement to the race than the fact that the President of the Nation would be willing to travel one hundred and forty miles out of his way to spend a day at a Negro institution, he seemed deeply impressed.

While I was with the President, a white citizen of Atlanta, a Democrat and an ex-slaveholder, came into the room, and the President asked his opinion as to the wisdom of his going to Tuskegee. Without hesitation the Atlanta man replied that it was the proper thing for him to do. This opinion was reinforced by that friend of the race, Dr. J. L. M. Curry. The President promised that he would visit our school on the 16th of December.

When it became known that the President was going to visit our school, the white citizens of the town of Tuskegee—a mile distant from the school—were as much pleased as were our students and teachers. The white people of the town, including both men and women, began arranging to decorate the town, and to form themselves into committees for the purpose of cooperating with the officers of our school in order that the distinguished visitor might have a fitting reception. I think I never realized before this how much the white people of Tuskegee and vicinity thought of our institution. During the days when we were preparing for the President's reception, dozens of these people came to me and said that, while they did not want to push themselves into prominence, if there was anything they could do to help, or to relieve me personally, I had but to intimate it and they would be only too glad to assist. In fact, the thing that touched me almost as deeply as the visit of the President itself was the deep pride which all classes of citizens in Alabama seemed to take in our work.

The morning of December 16th brought to the little city of Tuskegee such a crowd as it had never seen before. With the President came Mrs. McKinley and all of the Cabinet officers but one; and most of them brought their wives or some members of their families. Several prominent generals came, including General Shafter and General Joseph Wheeler, who were recently returned from the Spanish-American war. There was also a host of newspaper correspondents. The Alabama Legislature was in session at Montgomery at this time. This body passed a resolution to adjourn for the purpose of visiting Tuskegee. Just before the arrival of the President's party the Legislature arrived, headed by the governor and other state officials.

The citizens of Tuskegee had decorated the town from the station to the school in a generous manner. In order to economize in the matter of time, we arranged to have the whole school pass in review before the President. Each student carried a stalk of sugar-cane with some open bolls of cotton fastened to the end of it. Following the students the work of all departments of the school passed in review, displayed on "floats" drawn by horses, mules, and oxen. On these floats we tried to exhibit not only the present work of the school, but to show the contrasts between the old methods of doing things and the new. As an example, we showed the old method of dairying in contrast with the improved methods, the old methods of tilling the soil in contrast with the new, the old methods of cooking and housekeeping in contrast with the new. These floats consumed an hour and a half of time in passing.

In his address in our large, new chapel, which the students had recently completed, the President said, among other things:

To meet you under such pleasant auspices and to have the opportunity of a personal observation of your work is indeed most gratifying. The Tuskegee Normal and Industrial Institute is ideal in its conception, and has already a large and growing reputation in the country, and is not unknown abroad. I congratulate all who are associated in this undertaking for the good work which it is doing in the education of its students to lead lives of honour and usefulness, thus exalting the race for which it was established.

Nowhere, I think, could a more delightful location have been chosen for this unique educational experiment, which has attracted the attention and won the support even of conservative philanthropists in all sections of the country.

To speak of Tuskegee without paying special tribute to Booker T. Washington's genius and perseverance would be impossible. The inception of this noble enterprise was his, and he deserves high credit for it. His was the enthusiasm and enterprise which made its steady progress possible and established in the institution its present high standard of accomplishment. He has won a worthy reputation as one of the great leaders of his race, widely known and much respected at home and abroad as an accomplished educator, a great orator, and a true philanthropist.

LAST WORDS

The Hon. John D. Long, the Secretary of the Navy, said in part:

I cannot make a speech to-day. My heart is too full—full of hope, admiration , and pride for my countrymen of both sections and both colours. I am filled with gratitude and admiration for your work, and from this time forward I shall have absolute confidence in your progress and in the solution of the problem in which you are engaged.

The problem, I say, has been solved. A picture has been presented to-day which should be put upon canvas with the pictures of Washington and Lincoln, and transmitted to future time and generations—a picture which the press of the country should spread broadcast over the land, a most dramatic picture, and that picture is this: The President of the United States standing on this platform; on one side the Governor of Alabama, on the other, completing the trinity, a representative of a race only a few years ago in bondage, the coloured President of the Tuskegee Normal and Industrial Institute.

God bless the president under whose majesty such a scene as that is presented to the American people. God bless the state of Alabama, which is showing that it can deal with this problem for itself. God bless the orator, philanthropist, and disciple of the Great Master—who, if he were on earth, would be doing the same work—Booker T. Washington.

Postmaster General Smith closed the address which he made with these words:

We have witnessed many spectacles within the last few days. We have seen the magnificent grandeur and the magnificent achievements of one of the great metropolitan cities of the South. We have seen heroes of the war pass by in procession. We have seen floral parades. But I am sure my colleagues will agree with me in saying that we have witnessed no spectacle more impressive and more encouraging, more inspiring for our future, than that which we have witnessed here this morning.

Some days after the President returned to Washington I received the letter which follows:

Executive Mansion, Washington, Dec. 23, 1899.

DEAR SIR: By this mail I take pleasure in sending you engrossed copies of the souvenir of the visit of the President to your institution. These sheets bear the autographs of the President and the members of the Cabinet who accompanied him on the trip. Let me take this opportunity of congratulating you most heartily and sincerely upon the great success of the exercises provided for and entertainment furnished us under your auspices during our visit to Tuskegee. Every feature of the programme was perfectly executed and was viewed or participated in with the heartiest satisfaction by every visitor present. The unique exhibition which you gave of your pupils engaged in their industrial vocations was not only artistic but thoroughly impressive. The tribute paid by the President and his

Cabinet to your work was none too high, and forms a most encouraging augury, I think, for the future prosperity of your institution. I cannot close without assuring you that the modesty shown by yourself in the exercises was most favourably commented upon by all the members of our party.

With best wishes for the continued advance of your most useful and patriotic undertaking, kind personal regards, and the compliments of the season, believe me, always,

Very sincerely yours,
JOHN ADDISON PORTER,
Secretary to the President.

TO PRESIDENT BOOKER T. WASHINGTON,
Tuskegee Normal and Industrial
Institute, Tuskegee, Ala.

Twenty years have now passed since I made the first humble effort at Tuskegee, in a broken-down shanty and an old hen-house, without owning a dollar's worth of property, and with but one teacher and thirty students. At the present time the institution owns twenty-three hundred acres of land, over seven hundred of which are under cultivation each year, entirely by student labour. There are now upon the grounds, counting large and small, forty buildings; and all except four of these have been almost wholly erected by the labour of our students. While the students are at work upon the land and in erecting buildings, they are taught, by competent instructors, the latest methods of agriculture and the trades connected with building.

There are in constant operation at the school, in connection with thorough academic and religious training, twenty-eight industrial departments. All of these teach industries at which our men and women can find immediate employment as soon as they leave the institution. The only difficulty now is that the demand for our graduates from both white and black people in the South is so great that we cannot supply more than one-half the persons for whom applications come to us. Neither have we the buildings nor the money for current expenses to enable us to admit to the school more than one-half the young men and women who apply to us for admission.

In our industrial teaching we keep three things in mind: first, that the student shall be so educated that he shall be enabled to meet conditions as they exist *now*, in the part of the South where he lives—in a word, to be able to do the thing which the world wants done; second, that every student who graduates from the school shall have enough skill, coupled with intelligence and moral character, to enable him to make a living for himself and others; third, to send every graduate out feeling and knowing that labour is dignified and beautiful—to make each one love labour instead of trying to escape it. In addition to the agricultural training which we give to young men, and the training given to our girls in all the usual domestic employments, we now train a number of girls in agriculture each year. These girls are taught gardening, fruit-growing, dairying, bee-culture, and poultry-raising.

While the institution is in no sense denominational, we have a department known as the Phelps Hall Bible Training School, in which a number of students are prepared for the ministry and other forms of Christian work, especially work in the country districts. What is equally important, each one of these students works half of each day at some industry, in order to get skill and the love of work, so that when he goes out from the institution he is prepared to set the people with whom he goes to labour a proper example in the matter of industry.

The value of our property is now over $300,000. If we add to this our endowment fund, which at present is $215,000, the value of the total property is now nearly half a million dollars. Aside from the need for more buildings and for money for current expenses, the endowment fund should be increased to at least $500,000. The annual current expenses are now about $80,000. The greater part of this I collect each year by going from door to door and from house to house. All of our property is free from mortgage, and is deeded to an undenominational board of trustees who have the control of the institution.

From thirty students the number has grown to eleven hundred, coming from twenty-seven states and territories, from Africa, Cuba, Porto Rico, Jamaica, and other foreign countries. In our departments there are eighty-six officers and instructors; and if we add the families of our instructors, we have a constant population upon our grounds of not far from fourteen hundred people.

I have often been asked how we keep so large a body of people together, and at the same time keep them out of mischief. There are two answers: that the men and women who come to us for an education are in earnest; and that everybody is kept busy. The following outline of our daily work will testify to this:

5 A.M., rising bell; 5:50 A.M., warning breakfast bell; 6 A.M., breakfast bell; 6:20 A.M., breakfast over; 6:20 to 6:50 A.M., rooms are cleaned; 6:50, work bell; 7:30, morning study hour; 8:20, morning school bell; 8:25, inspection of young men's toilet in ranks; 8:40, devotional exercises in chapel; 8:55, "five minutes with the daily news;" 9 A.M., class work begins; 12, class work closes; 12:15 P.M., dinner; 1 P.M., work bell; 1:30 P.M., class work begins; 3:30 P.M., class work ends; 5:30 P.M., bell to "knock off" work; 6 P.M., supper; 7:10 P.M., evening prayers; 7:30 P.M., evening study hours; 8:45 P.M., evening study hour closes; 9:20 P.M., warning retiring bell; 9:30 P.M., retiring bell.

We try to keep constantly in mind the fact that the worth of the school is to be judged by its graduates. Counting those who have finished the full course, together with those who have taken enough training to enable them to do reasonably good work, we can safely say that at least three thousand men and women from Tuskegee are now at work in different parts of the South; men and women who, by their own example or by direct effort are showing the masses of our race how to improve their material, educational, and moral and religious life. What is equally important, they are exhibiting a degree of common sense and self-control which is causing better relations to exist between the races, and is causing the Southern white man to learn to believe in the value of educating the men and women of my race. Aside from this, there is the influence that is constantly being exerted through the mothers' meeting and the plantation work conducted by Mrs. Washington.

Wherever our graduates go, the changes which soon begin to appear in the buying of land, improving homes, saving money, in education, and in high moral character are remarkable. Whole communities are fast being revolutionized through the instrumentality of these men and women.

Ten years ago I organized at Tuskegee the first Negro Conference. This is an annual gathering which now brings to the school eight or nine hundred representative men and women of the race, who come to spend a day in finding out what the actual industrial, mental, and moral conditions of the people are, and in forming plans for improvement. Out from this central Negro Conference at Tuskegee have grown numerous state and local conferences which are doing the same kind of work. As a result of the influence of these gatherings, one delegate reported at the last annual meeting that ten families in his community had bought and paid for homes. On the day following the annual Negro Conference, there is held the "Workers' Conference." This is composed of officers and teachers who are engaged in educational work in the larger institutions in the South. The Negro Conference furnished a rare opportunity for these workers to study the real condition of the rank and file of the people.

In the summer of 1900, with the assistance of such prominent coloured men as Mr. T. Thomas Fortune, who has always upheld my hands in every effort, I organized the National Negro Business League, which held its first meeting in Boston, and brought together for the first time a large number of the coloured men who are engaged in various lines of trade or business in different parts of the United States. Thirty states were represented at our first meeting. Out of this national meeting grew state and local business leagues.

In addition to looking after the executive side of the work at Tuskegee, and raising the greater part of the money for the support of the school, I cannot seem to escape the duty of answering at least a part of the calls which come to me unsought to address Southern white audiences and audiences of my own race, as well as frequent gatherings in the North. As to how much of my time is spent in this way, the following clipping from a Buffalo (N.Y.) paper will tell. This has reference to an occasion when I spoke before the National Educational Association in that city.

BOOKER T. WASHINGTON

Booker T. Washington, the foremost educator among the coloured people of the world, was a very busy man from the time he arrived in the city the other night from the West and registered at the Iroquois. He had hardly removed the stains of travel when it was time to partake of supper. Then he held a public levee in the parlours of the Iroquois until eight o'clock. During that time he was greeted by over two hundred eminent teachers and educators from all parts of the United States. Shortly after eight o'clock he was driven in a carriage to Music Hall, and in one hour and a half he made two ringing addresses, to as many as five thousand people, on Negro education. Then Mr. Washington was taken in charge by a delegation of coloured citizens, headed by the Rev. Mr. Watkins, and hustled off to a small informal reception, arranged in honour of the visitor by the people of his race.

Nor can I, in addition to making these addresses, escape the duty of calling the attention of the South and of the country in general, through the medium of the press, to matters that pertain to the interests of both races. This, for example, I have done in regard to the evil habit of lynching. When the Louisiana State Constitutional Convention was in session, I wrote an open letter to that body pleading for justice for the race. In all such efforts I have received warm and hearty support from the Southern newspapers, as well as from those in all other parts of the country.

Despite superficial and temporary signs which might lead one to entertain a contrary opinion, there was never a time when I felt more helpful for the race than I do at the present. The great human law that in the end recognizes and rewards merit is everlasting and universal. The outside world does not know, neither can it appreciate, the struggle that is constantly going on in the hearts of both the Southern white people and their former slaves to free themselves from racial prejudice; and while both races are thus struggling they should have the sympathy, the support, and the forbearance of the rest of the world.

As I write the closing words of this autobiography I find myself— not by design—in the city of Richmond, Virginia: the city which only a few decades ago was the capital of the Southern Confederacy, and where, about twenty-five years ago, because of my poverty I slept night after night under a sidewalk.

This time I am in Richmond as the guest of the coloured people of the city; and came at their request to deliver an address last night to

193

both races in the Academy of Music, the largest and finest audience room in the city. This was the first time that the coloured people had ever been permitted to use this hall. The day before I came, the City Council passed a vote to attend the meeting in a body to hear me speak. The state Legislature, including the House of Delegates and the Senate, also passed a unanimous vote to attend in a body. In the presence of hundreds of coloured people, many distinguished white citizens, the City Council, the state Legislature, and state officials, I delivered my message, which was one of hope and cheer; and from the bottom of my heart I thanked both races for this welcome back to the state that gave me birth.

BOOKER T. WASHINGTON
TUSKEGEE NORMAL AND INDUSTRIAL INSTITUTE,
TUSKEGEE, ALABAMA

Selections From:

CHARACTER BUILDING
By
BOOKER T. WASHINGTON

Addresses delivered on Sunday evenings to
the students of Tuskegee Institute

TWO SIDES OF LIFE

There are quite a number of divisions into which life can be divided, but for the purposes of this evening I am going to speak of two; the bright side of life and the dark side.

In thought, in talk, in action, I think you will find that you can separate life into these two divisions—the dark side and the bright side, the discouraging side and the encouraging side. You will find, too, that there are two classes of people, just as there are two divisions of the subject. There is one class that is schooling itself, and constantly training itself, to look upon the dark side of life; and there is another class, made up of people who are, consciously or unconsciously, constantly training themselves to look upon the bright side of life.

Now it is not wise to go too far in either direction. The person who schools himself to see the dark side of life is likely to make a mistake, and the person who schools himself to look only upon the bright side of life, forgetting all else, also is apt to make a mistake.

Notwithstanding this, I think I am right in saying that the persons who accomplish most in this world, those to whom on account of their helpfulness the world looks most for service—those who are most useful in every way—are those who are constantly seeing and appreciating the bright side as well as the dark side of life.

You will sometimes find two persons who get up in the morning, perhaps a morning that is overcast with shadows—a damp, wet, rainy, uninviting morning—and one of these persons will speak of the morning as being gloomy, will speak of the mud-puddles about the house, of the rain, and of all of the disagreeable features. The second person, the one who has schooled himself to see the brighter side of life, the beautiful things in life, will speak of the beauties that are in the rain drops, and the freshness of the newly bathed flowers, shrubs and trees. Notwithstanding the gloomy and generally disconsolate appearance of things, he will find something attractive in the scene out of doors, and will discover something in the gloomy morning that will cheer him.

Suppose that you see these same two persons eat their breakfast. Perhaps they will find out that the rolls are bad, but that the coffee is excellent. If the rolls are poor, it is a great deal better in such a case to get into the habit—a habit that you will find pays from every standpoint—of being able to forget how unpalatable they are, and to let your thoughts dwell upon the good and satisfactory coffee. Call the attention of your near neighbour at the table to the excellence of the coffee. What is the result of that kind of schooling? You will grow up to be an individual whom people will like to see coming near them—an individual to whom people will go for encouragement when the hours are dark, and when everything seems to be discouraging.

In just the same way, when you go into the class-rooms to recite your lessons, do not dwell upon any mistakes that you may think you see the teacher make, or upon any weakness in the presentation of the lesson. All teachers make mistakes sometimes, and you may depend upon it that it is an excellent teacher and a person of fine character who, when he or she has made a mistake, says frankly and plainly, "I have made a mistake," or "I don't know." It takes a very good and a very bright teacher to say, "I don't know." No teacher knows everything about every subject. A good teacher will say frankly and clearly, "I don't know. I cannot answer that question."

Let me tell you, right here, too, that when you go out from here to become teachers yourselves—as a large proportion of you will go—whenever you get to a point where a student asks you a question which you are not able to answer, or asks you something about a subject on which you are not well informed, you will find it better to say frankly and honestly, "I am unable to answer your question." Your students will

198

respect you a great deal more for your frankness and honesty. Education is not what a person is able to hold in his head, so much as it is what a person is able to find. I believe it was Daniel Webster who said that the truly educated man was not the one who had all knowledge in his head, but the one who knew where to look for information upon any subject upon which at any time he might want information. Each individual who wishes to succeed must get that kind of discipline. He must get such training that he will know where to go and get facts, rather than try to train himself to hold all facts in his head.

I want you to go out from this institution so trained and so developed that you will be constantly looking for the bright, encouraging and beautiful things in life. It is the weak individual, as a rule, who is constantly calling attention to the other side—to the dark and discouraging things of life. When you go into your class-rooms, I repeat, try to forget and overlook any weak points that you may think you see. Remember, and dwell upon, the consideration that has been given to the lesson, the faithfulness with which it was prepared, and the earnestness with which it is presented. Try to recall and to remember every good thing and every encouraging thing which has come under your observation, whether it has been in the class-room, or in the shop, or in the field. No matter where you are, seize hold on the encouraging things with which you come in contact.

In connection with the personality of their teachers, it is very unfortunate for students to form a habit of continually finding fault, of criticizing, of seeing nothing but what the student may think are weak points. Try to get into a frame of mind where you will be constantly seeing and calling attention to the strong and beautiful things which you observe in the life and work of your teachers. Grow into the habit of talking about the bright side of life. When you meet a fellow student, a teacher, or anybody, or when you write letters home, get into the habit of calling attention to the bright things of life that you have seen, the things that are beautiful, the things that are charming. Just in proportion as you do this, you will find that you will not only influence yourself in the right direction, but that you will also influence others that way. It is a very bad habit to get into, that of being continually moody and discouraged, and of making the atmosphere uncomfortable for everybody who comes within ten feet of you. There are some people who are so constantly looking on the dark side of life that they cannot see anything but that side. Everything that comes from their mouths is unpleasant, about this thing and that thing, and they make the whole atmosphere around them unpleasant for themselves and for everybody with whom they come in contact. Such persons are surely undesirable. Why, I have seen people coming up the road who caused me to feel like wanting to cross over on to the other side of the way so as not to meet them. I didn't want to hear their tales of misery and woe. I had heard those tales so many times that I didn't want to get into the atmosphere of the people who told them.

It is often very easy to influence others in the wrong direction, and to grow into such a moody fault-finding disposition that one not only is miserable and unhappy himself, but makes every one with whom he comes in contact miserable and unhappy. The persons who live constantly in a fault-finding atmosphere, who see only the dark side of life, become negative characters. They are the people who never go forward. They never suggest a line of activity. They live simply on the negative side of life. Now, as students, you cannot afford to grow in that way. We want to send each one of you out from here, not as a negative force, but as a strong, positive, helpful force in the world. You will not accomplish the task which we expect of you if you go with a moody, discouraged, fault-finding disposition. To do the most that lies in you, you must go with a heart and head full of hope and faith in the world, believing that there is work for you to do, believing that you are the person to accomplish that work, and the one who is going to accomplish it.

In nine cases out of ten, the person who cultivates the habit of looking on the dark side of life is the little person, the miserable person, the one who is weak in mind, heart and purpose. On the other hand, the person who cultivates the habit of looking on the bright side of life, and who calls attention to the beautiful and encouraging things in life is, in nine cases out of ten, the strong individual, the one to whom the world goes for intelligent advice and support. I am trying to get you to see, as students, the best things in life. Do not be satisfied with second-hand or third-hand things in life. Do not be satisfied until you have put yourselves into that atmosphere where you can seize and hold on to the very highest and most beautiful things that can be got out of life.

CALLING THINGS BY
THEIR RIGHT NAMES

A few evenings ago I talked with you about the importance of learning to be simple, humble and child-like before going out into the world.
You should remain in school until you get to the point where you feel
that you do not know anything, where you feel that you are willing to
learn from any one who can teach you.

Unfortunately there are many things here in the South which tend
to lead away from this simplicity to which I have referred. There is a
great inclination to make things appear what they are not. For example:
take the schools. There is a great tendency to call schools by names
which do not belong to them, and which do not correctly represent
that which in reality exists. You will find the habit growing more prevalent every year, I fear, of calling a school a university, or a college, or an
academy, or a high-school. In fact we seldom hear of a plain, common,
public or graded school.

We do ourselves no good when we yield to that temptation. If a
school is a public school, call it one; but do not think that we gain
anything by calling a little country school, with two or three rooms and
one or two teachers, where some of the students are studying the alphabet, a university. And still this is too often done throughout the South,
as you know. No respect or confidence is gained by the practice, but, on
the contrary, sensible people get disgusted with such false pretences.
When you go out into the world and meet with such cases as this, try to
make the people see that it is a great deal better to call their small public
school by a name which truly represents it, than to call it a high-school

or an academy. I do not by any means intend to say that schools do not have the right to aspire to become high-schools and colleges. What I mean to say is that it is hurtful to the race to get into the habit of calling every little institution of learning that is opened, a college or a university. It weakens us and prevents us from getting a solid, sure foundation.

Again, we make the same mistake when we call every preacher or person who stands in a pulpit to read from it, "Doctor," whether or not that degree has been conferred upon him. Sensible people get tired of that kind of thing. The degree of Doctor of Divinity was once held in the highest esteem, and was conferred only upon those ministers who had really become entitled to it because of some original research or other work of high scholarship. Among highly educated people this rule holds still. But to-day, especially in the South, many a little institution that opens its doors and calls itself a college or a university, is beginning to confer degrees, and make doctors of divinity of persons who are unworthy of degrees. And sometimes, should these persons fail to get an institution to confer a degree on them, they confer it on themselves! The habit is getting to be so common that in little towns the ministers are calling themselves Doctors. One pastor will meet another and say, "Good morning, Doctor," and the other, wishing to be as polite as his friend, will say, "How are you, Doctor?" and so it goes on, until both begin to believe they really are Doctors. Now this practice is not only ridiculous, but it is very hurtful to us as a race, and it should be discouraged.

Much the same criticism may be made of many of those who teach. A person who teaches a little country school, perhaps in a brush arbour, is called "Professor." Every person who leads a string band is called "Professor," I was in a small town not long ago, and I heard the people speaking of some one as "the professor." I was anxious to know who the professor was. So I waited a few minutes, and finally the professor came up, and I recognized him as a member of one of our preparatory classes. Now, don't suffer the world to put you in this silly, ridiculous position. If people attempt to call you "Professor," or by any other title that is not yours, tell them that you are not a professor, that you are a simple mister. That is a good enough title for any one. We have the same right to become professors as any other people, when we occupy positions which entitle us to that name, but we drag that title, which ought to be a badge of scholarship, down into the mud and mire when we allow it to be misapplied.

We carry a similar kind of deception into our school work when, in the essays which we read and the orations which we deliver, we simply rehearse matter a great deal of which has been copied from some one else. Go into almost any church where there is one of the doctors of divinity to whom I have referred, and you will hear sermons copied out of books and pamphlets. The essays, the orations, the sermons that are not the productions of the people who pretend to write them, all come from this false foundation.

Then there is another error to which I wish to call your attention. In many parts of the South, especially in the cities and towns, there are excellent public schools, well equipped in every way with apparatus and material, and provided with good, competent teachers, but in some cases these schools are crippled by reason of the fact that there are little denominational schools which deprive the public schools of their rightful attendance. If the school can't be in the church of some particular denomination, it must be near it. In the average town there may be the denominational school of the African Methodist Episcopal church, of the Zion church, of the Baptist church, of the Wesleyan Methodist church, and so on, all in different parts of the town. Instead of supporting one public school, provided at the expense of the town or city, there exists this little, narrow denomination spirit, which is robbing these innocent children of their education. We want to say to such people as these, people who are content so to deprive their children, and have them taught by some second-rate teacher, that they are wrong. We want you to let the people know that the great public-school system of America is the nation's greatest glory, and that we do not help matters when we attempt to tear down the public school. Of course it is the right and the duty of every denomination to erect its own theological seminaries and its colleges, where the special tenets of that denomination are taught to those who

are preparing for its pulpit; but no one has a right to let this denominational spirit defeat the work of a public school to which all should be
free to go.

I have in mind a place where the coloured people have an excellent
school, equal to that of the whites. I went through the building and
found it supplied with improved apparatus and capable teachers, and
saw that first-class work was done there. Later, I was taken about a mile
outside the city, where there was a school with an incapable teacher, and
some sixty or seventy pupils being poorly taught. Here was a third-rate
teacher in a third-rate building, poor work, and the children suffering
for lack of proper instruction. Why? Simply because the people wanted
a school of their own denomination in that part of the city.

Now you want to cultivate courage, and see to it that you are brave
enough to condemn these wrongs and to show the people the mistakes
which they make in these matters.

I mention all these things because they hinder us from getting a
solid foundation. They hinder us, further, in that in many cases they
prevent us from getting the right power of leadership in teaching, in the
work of the ministry, and in many other respects. Wherever you go,
then, make up your minds that you are going to make your influence
felt in favour of better prepared teachers and preachers—in better preparation of all those who stand for leaders of the people. Just in proportion
as you set you lives right in this matter, will the masses of the race be
inclined to follow you.

THE CULTIVATION OF STABLE HABITS

I am going to speak with you a few minutes this evening upon the matter of stability. I want you to understand when you start out in school, that no individual can accomplish anything unless he means to stick to what he undertakes. No matter how many possessions he may have, no matter how much he may have in this or that direction, no matter how much learning or skill of hand he may possess, an individual cannot succeed unless, at the same time, he possesses that quality which will enable him to stick to what he undertakes. In a word he is not to be jumping from this thing to that thing.

That is the reason why so many ministers fail. They preach awhile, and then jump to something else. They do not stick to one thing. It is the same with many lawyers and doctors. They do not stick to what they undertake. Many business men fail for the same reason. When an individual gets a reputation—no matter what he has undertaken— of not having the quality of sticking to a thing until he succeeds in reaching the end, that reputation nullifies the influence for good of the better traits of his character in every direction. It is said of him that he is unstable.

I want you to begin your school life with the idea that you are going to stick to whatever you undertake until you have completed it. I take it for granted that all of you have come here with that idea in mind; that before you came here you sat down and talked the matter over with your father and mother, read over the circulars giving information about the school, and then deliberately decided that this institution was the one whose course of study you wished to complete. I take it for granted that you have come here with that end in view, and I want to say to you now, that you will injure yourselves, your parents, and the institution—and you will hurt your own reputation—unless, after having come here with the determination to succeed, you remain here for that purpose, and remain for the full time, until you receive your diploma. I hope every individual here, every young man and woman at the school, is here with the determination that he or she will not give up the struggle until the object aimed at has been attained.

You are at a stage now, when, if you begin jumping about here and there, if you begin in this course of study and then go to that course of study, you will very likely be jumping about from one thing to another all your life. You must make up your minds, after coming here, to do well whatever you undertake. This is a good rule not only to begin your school life with, but also to begin your later life with.

Perhaps I was never more interested than I was last evening in Montgomery, while standing on one of the streets there for an hour. I seldom stand on any street for an hour, but last night I did stand on that street for an hour, in front of a large, beautiful store that is owned by Mr. J.W. Adams, and watched the notice taken of the display of millinery made in his store windows by two girls that finished their academic and industrial courses at this school—Miss Jemmie Pierce and Miss Lydia Robinson. The first Monday in October is always the day in Montgomery for what they call the millinery openings; on that day the stores which handle such goods all make a great display of ladies; hats and bonnets. It was surprising and interesting to note how these two girls had entered a great city like Montgomery and had taken entire charge of the millinery department in a large store. Hundreds of people stopped to comment favourably upon the taste that was displayed in the decoration of those windows.

Now, all this work was done by two Tuskegee graduates. And the complimentary remarks that were made came not only from coloured people but from white people as well. No one could tell from the windows of that store whether it was a coloured or white establishment.

Many of the white ladies who were standing there did not know that they were standing in front of a store that was owned by a black man. It had none of the usual earmarks about it. Usually when you go into coloured establishments you see grease on the doors or on the counters; or you see this sign or that sign that this is a coloured man's establishment. Those of you here who are gong to go into business after you leave school do not want to have any such earmarks about your establishments. Such a store as that of Mr. Adams is the kind of a store to have.

Now, these two young women have made a reputation for themselves. They went into the millinery division while they were here, and they remained until they graduated. One of them, I believe had not finished in the millinery department when she received her academic diploma, and so she came back last year and took a post-graduate course in millinery. It is interesting and encouraging to see these two young women succeeding in their work, and it all comes from their determination to succeed, and because they had sense enough to finish what they had undertaken.

That is the lesson that you all want to learn. If you do not learn it now, in a large degree you will be failures in life. You want to be like these young women. You want to fight it out. Now if you mean to get your diploma, you are going to have a hard time. Some of you are going to be without shoes, without a hat, without proper clothing of any kind. You will get discouraged because you have not as nice a dress or as nice a hat as this person or that person. I would not give a snap of my finger for a person who would give up for that. The thing for you to do is to fight it out. Get something in your head, and don't worry about what you can get to put on it. The clothes will come afterward.

You are going to be greatly discouraged sometimes, but if you will heed the lesson of fighting out what you have undertaken, that same disposition will follow you all through your life, and you will get a reputation, because people will say of you that there is a person who sticks to whatever he or she undertakes. One of the saddest things in life is to see an individual who has grown to old age, with no profession, with no calling whatever from which he is sure of getting an independent living. It is sad to see such individuals without money, without homes, in their old age, simply because they did not learn the lesson of saving money and getting for themselves a beautiful home when they ought to have done this. And so, all through life, we can point to many people who have not learned this lesson—that for whatever they undertake they must pay the price which the world asks of them if they would succeed. If we are going to succeed we must pay the price for what we get; and he who accomplishes the most, accomplishes it in a humble and straightforward way, by sticking to what he has undertaken. He who does this finds in the end that he has achieved a tremendous success.

EDUCATION THAT EDUCATES*

Perhaps I am safe in saying that during the last ten days you have not given much systematic effort to book study in the usual sense. When interruptions come such as we have just had, taking you away from your regular routine work and study, and the preparation of routine lessons is interrupted, the first thought to some may be that this time is lost, in so far as it relates to education in the ordinary sense; that it is so much time taken away from that part of one's life that should be devoted to acquiring education. I suppose that during the last few days the questions have come to many of you: "What are we gaining? What are we getting from the irregularity that has characterized the school grounds within the last week, that will in any degree compensate for the amount of book study that we have lost?"

To my mind I do not believe that you have lost anything by the interruption. On the other hand, I am convinced that you have got the best kind of education. I do not mean to say that we can depend upon it for all time to come for systematic training of the mind, but so far as real education, so far as development of the mind and heart and body are concerned, I do not believe that a single student has lost anything by the irregularity of the last week or more.

You have gained in this respect: in preparing for the reception and entertainment of the President of the United States and his Cabinet, and the distinguished persons who accompanied the party, you have had to do an amount of original thinking which you, perhaps, have

---

*This talk was given soon after the visit of President McKinley to Tuskegee Institute in the fall of 1898.

never had to do before in your lives. You have been compelled to think; you have been compelled to put more than your bodily strength into what you have been doing. You could not have made the magnificent exhibition of our work which you have made if you had not been compelled to do original thinking and execution. Most of you never saw such an exhibition before; I never did. Those of you who had to construct floats that would illustrate our agricultural work and our mechanical and academic work, had to put a certain amount of original thought into the planning of these floats, in order to make them show the work to the best advantage; and two-thirds of you—yes, practically all of you—had never seen anything of the kind before. For this reason it was a matter that had to be thought out by you and planned out by you, and then put into visible shape.

Now compare that kind of education with the mere committing to memory of certain rules, or something which some one else thought out and executed a thousand years ago perhaps—and that is what a large part of our education really is. Education in the usual sense of the word is the mere committing to memory of something which has been known before us. Now during the last ten days we have had to solve problems of our own, not problems and puzzles that some one else originated for us. I do not believe that there is a person connected with the institution who is not stronger in mind, who is not more self-confident and self-reliant, so far as the qualities related to what he is able to do with his mind or his hands, than he was ten or twelve days ago. There is the benefit that came to all of us. It put us to thinking and planning; it brought us in to contact with things that are out of the ordinary; and there is no education that surpasses this. I see more and more every year that the world is to be brought to the study of men and of things, rather than to the study of mere books. You will find more and more as the years go by, that people will gradually lay aside books, and study the nature of man in a way they have never done as yet. I tell you, then, that in this interruption of the regular school work you have not lost anything;—you have gained; you have had your minds awakened, your faculties strengthened, and your hands guided.

I do not wish to speak of this matter egotistically, but it is true that I have heard a great many persons from elsewhere mention the pleasure which they have received in meeting Tuskegee students, because when they come in contact with a student who has been here, they are impressed with the fact that he or she does not seem to be dead or sleepy. They say that when they meet a Tuskegee boy or girl they find a person who has had contact with real life. The education that you have been getting during the last few days, you will find, as the years go by, has been of a kind that will serve you in good stead all through your lives.

Just in proportion as we learn to execute something, to put our education into tangible form—as we have been doing during the last few days—in just the same proportion will we find ourselves of value as individuals and as a race. Those people who came here to visit us knew perfectly well that we could commit to memory certain lines of poetry, they knew we were able to solve certain problems in algebra and geometry, they understood that we could learn certain rules in chemistry and agriculture; but what interested them most was to see us put into visible form the results of our education. Just in proportion as an individual is able to do that, he is of value to the world. That is the object of the work which we are trying to do here. We are trying to turn out men and women who are able to do something that the world wants done, that the world needs to have done. Just in proportion as you can comply with that demand you will find that there is a place for you—there is going to be standing room. We are going to train you so that when you get to that place, if you fail in it, the failure will not be our fault.

It is a great satisfaction to have connected with a race men and women who are able to do something, not merely to talk about doing it, not merely to theorize about doing it, but actually to do something that makes the world better to live in, something that enhances the comforts and conveniences of life. I had a good example of this last week. I wanted something done in my office which required a practical knowledge of electricity. It was a great satisfaction when I called upon one of the teachers, to have him do the work in a careful, praiseworthy manner. It is very well to talk or lecture about electricity, but it is better to be able to do something of value with one's knowledge of electricity.

And so, as you go on, increasing your ability to do things of value, you will find that the problem which often now-a-days looks more and more difficult of solution will gradually become easier. One of the Cabinet members who were here a few days ago said, after witnessing the exhibition which you made here, that the islands which this country had taken into its possession during the recent war are soon going to require the service of every man and woman we can turn out from this institution. You will find it true, not only in this country but in other countries, that the demand will be more and more for people who can do something. Just in proportion as we can, as a race, get the reputation which I spoke to you about a few days ago, you will find there will be places for us. Regardless of colour or condition, the world is going to give the places of trust and remuneration to the men and women who can do a certain thing as well as anybody else or better. This is the whole problem. Shall we prepare ourselves to do something as well as anybody else or better? Just in proportion as we do this, you will find that nothing under the sun will keep us back.

INDIVIDUAL RESPONSIBILITY

I have referred in a general way, before this, when I have been speaking to you, to the fact that each one of you ought to feel an interest in whatever task is set you to do here over and above the mere bearing which that task has on your own life. I wish to speak more specifically tonight on the subject—on what I may term the importance of your feeling a sense of personal responsibility not only for the successful performance of every task set you, but for the successful outcome of every worthy undertaking with which you come in contact.

You ought to realize that your actions will not affect yourselves alone. In this age it is almost impossible for a man to live for himself alone. On every side our lives touch those of others; their lives touch ours. Even if it were possible to live otherwise, few would wish to. A narrow life, a selfish life, is almost sure to be not only unprofitable but unhappy. The happy people and the successful people are those who go out of their way to reach and influence for good as many persons as they can. In order to do this, though, in order best to fit one's self to live this kind of life, it is important that certain habits be acquired; and an essential one of these is the habit of realizing one's responsibility to others.

Your actions will affect other people in one way or another, and you will be responsible for the result. You ought always to remember this, and govern yourselves accordingly. Suppose it is the matter of the recitation of a lesson, for instance. Some one may say: "It is nobody's business but my own if I fail in a recitation. Nobody will suffer but me." This is not so. Indirectly you injure your teacher also, for while a conscientious, hard-working teacher ought not to be blamed for the failures of pupils who do not learn simply because they do not want to, or are too lazy to try, it is generally the case that a teacher's reputation gains or loses as his or her class averages high or low. And each failure in recitation, for whatever cause, brings down the average. Then, too, you are having an influence upon your classmates, even if it be unconscious. There is hardly ever a student who is not observed by some one at some time as an example. "There is such a boy," some other student says to himself. "He has failed in class every so many times, and still he gets along. It can't make much difference if I fail once." And as a result he neglects his duty, and does fail.

The same thing is true of work in the industrial departments. Too many students try to see how easily they can get through the day, or the work period, and yet not get into trouble. Or even if they take more interest than this they care for their work only for the sake of what they can get out of it for themselves, either as pay, or as instruction which will enable them to work for pay at some later time. Now there ought to be a higher impulse behind your efforts than that. Each student ought to feel that he or she has a personal responsibility to do each task in the very best manner possible. You owe this not only to your fellow-students, your teachers, the school, and the people who support the institution, but owe it to yourselves because it is right and honest, because nothing less than this is right and honest, and because you never can be really successful and really happy until you do study and work and live in this way.

I have been led to speak specifically on this subject to-night on account of two occurrences here which have come to my notice. One of these illustrates the failure on the part of students to feel this sense of responsibility to which I have referred. The other affords an illustration of the possession by a student of a feeling of personal interest and personal responsibility which has been very gratifying and encouraging. The first incident, I may say, occurred some months ago. It is possible that the students who were concerned in it may not be here now or, if they are, that it would not happen again. I certainly hope not.

A gentleman who had been visiting here was to go away. He left word at the office of his wish, saying that he planned to leave town on the five o'clock train in the afternoon. A boy was sent from the office early in the afternoon with a note to the barn ordering a carriage to take this gentleman and his luggage to the station. Half-past four came, and the man had his luggage brought down to the door of the building in which he had been staying, so as to be ready when the team came. But no team came. The visitor finally became so anxious that he walked over to the barn himself. Just as he reached the barn he met the man who was in charge there, with the note in his hand. The note had only just that moment reached this man, and of course no carriage had been sent because the first person who felt that he had any responsibility in the matter had only just learned that a carriage was wanted. The boy who had brought the note had given it to another boy, and he to someone else, and he, perhaps, to someone else. At any rate it had been delayed because no one had taken enough interest in the errand to see that whatever business the note referred to received proper attention. This occurred, as I have said, several months ago, before the local train here went over to Chehaw to meet all of the trains. It happened that this particular passenger was going north, and it was possible by driving to Chehaw for him to get there in time to take the north-bound train. If he had been going the other way, though, towards Montgomery, he would have lost the train entirely, and, as chanced to be the case, would have been unable to keep a very important engagement. As it was, he was obliged to ride to Chehaw in a carriage, and the time of a man and team, which otherwise would have been saved, was required to take him there.

Now when such a thing as this happens, no amount of saying, "I am sorry," by the person or persons to blame, will help the matter any. It is too late to help it then. The thing to do is to feel some responsibility in seeing that things are done right yourself. Take enough interest in whatever you are engaged in to see that it is going to come out in the end just as nearly right, just as nearly perfect, as anything you can do will go towards making it right or perfect. And if the task or errand passes out of your hands before it is completed, do not feel that your responsibility in the matter ends until you have impressed it upon the minds and heart of the person to whom you turn over the further performance of the duty.

The world is looking for men and women who can tell one why they can do this thing or that thing, how a certain difficulty was surmounted or a certain obstacle removed. But the world has little patience with the man or woman who takes no real interest in the performance of a duty, or who runs against a snag and gets discouraged, and then simply tells why he did not do a thing, and gives excuses instead of results. Opportunities never come a second time, nor do they wait for our leisure. The years come to us but once, and they come then only to pass swiftly on, bearing the ineffaceable record we have put upon them. If we wish to make them beautiful years or profitable years, we must do it moment by moment as they glide before us.

The other case to which I have referred is pleasanter to speak about. One day this spring, after it had got late enough in the season so that it was not as a general thing necessary to have fires to heat our buildings, a student passing Phelps Hall noticed that there was a volume of black smoke pouring out of one of the chimneys there. Some boys might not have noticed the smoke at all; others would have said that it came from the chimney; still others would have said that it was none of their business anyway, and would have gone along. This boy was different. He noticed the smoke, and although he saw, or thought he saw that it came from the chimney, and if so was probably no sign of harm, he felt that any smoke at all there at that time was an unusual thing that it ought to be investigated for fear it might mean danger to the building. He was not satisfied until he had gone into the building and had inspected every floor clear up to the attic, to see that the chimney and the building were not in danger. As it happened, the janitor had built a fire in the basement for some reason, so that the young man's anxiety fortunately was unfounded, but I am heartily glad he had such an anxiety, and that he could not rest until he found out whether there was any foundation for it or not. I shall feel that all of our buildings are safe for his being here, and when he graduates and goes away I hope he will leave many others here who will have the same sense of personal responsibility which he had. Let me tell you, here and now, that unless you young men and young women come to have this characteristic, your lives are going to fall far short of the best and noblest achievement possible.

We frequently hear the word "lucky" used with reference to a man's life. Two boys start out in the world at the same time, having the same amount of education. When twenty years have passed, we find one of them wealthy and independent; we find him a successful professional man with an assured reputation, or perhaps at the head of a large commercial establishment employing many men, or perhaps a farmer owning and cultivating hundreds of acres of land. We find the second boy, grown now to be a man, working for perhaps a dollar or a dollar and a half a day, and living from hand to mouth in a rented house. When we remember that the boys started out in life equal-handed, we may be tempted to remark that the first boy has been fortunate, that fortune has smiled upon him; and that the second has been unfortunate. There is no such nonsense as that. When the first boy saw a thing that he knew he ought to do, he did it; and he kept rising from one position to another until he became independent. The second boy was an eye-servant who was afraid that he would do more than he was paid to do—he was afraid that he would give fifty cents' worth of labour for twenty-five cents. He watched the clock, for fear that he would work one minute past twelve o'clock at noon and past six o'clock at night. He did not feel that he had any responsibility to look out for his employer's interests. The first boy did a dollar's worth of work for fifty cents. He was always ready to be at the store before time; and then, when the bell rang to stop work, he would go to his employer and ask him if there was not something more that ought to be done that night before he went home. It was this quality in the first boy that made him valuable and caused him to rise. Why should we call him "fortunate" or "lucky?" I think it would be much more suitable to say of him: "He is responsible."

INFLUENCING BY EXAMPLE

A few evenings ago, while in Cincinnati, I was very pleasantly surprised after speaking at a large meeting to be invited by a company of young coloured men to attend for a few minutes a reception at their club room. I expected, when I went to the place designated, to find a number of young men who, perhaps, had hired a room and fitted it up for the purpose of gratifying their own selfish pleasures. I found that this was not the case. Instead, I found fifteen young men whose ages ranged from eighteen to twenty years, who had banded themselves together in a club known as the "Winona Club," for the purpose of improving themselves, and further, for the purpose, so far as possible, of getting hold of other young coloured men in the city who were inclined in the wrong direction. I found a room beautifully fitted up, with a carpet on the floor, with beautiful pictures upon the walls, with books and pictures in their little library, and with fifteen of the brightest, most honest, and cleanest looking young men that it has been my pleasure to meet for a long time.

It was a very pleasant surprise to find these young men, especially in the midst of the temptations of a Northern city, in the midst of evil surroundings, banded together for influencing others in the right direction.

These young men came together, and at their first meeting said that they were going to band themselves together for the purpose of improving themselves and helping others. They said that the first article in their constitution should be to the effect that there should be no gambling in that club; that there must be no strong drink allowed in that club, and that there should be nothing there that was not in keeping with the life of a true and high-minded gentleman.

I repeat that it was very pleasant and encouraging for me to find such work as this going on in Cincinnati. What was equally gratifying, and surprising, was that at the close of the reception they presented me with a neat sum of money which they had collected, and asked that this money be used to defray the expenses of some student at the school here.

Now the point I especially want to make tonight is this: all of you must bear in mind the fact that you are not only to keep yourselves clean, and pure, and sober, and true, in every respect, but you owe a constant responsibility to yourself to see that you exert a helpful influence on others also.

A large proportion of you are to go from here into great cities. Some of you will go into such cities as Montgomery, and some, perhaps, will go into the cities of the North—although I hope that the most of you will see your way clear to remain in the South. I believe that you will do better to remain in the country districts than to go into the cities. I believe that you will find it to your advantage in every way to try to live in a small town, or in a country district, rather than in a city. I believe that we are at our best in country life—in agricultural life—and too often at our worst in city life. Now when you go out into the world for yourselves, you must remember in the first place that you cannot hold yourselves up unless you keep engaged and out of idleness. No idle person is ever safe, whether he be rich or poor. Make up your minds, whether you are to live in the city or in the country, that you are going to be constantly employed.

In a rich and prosperous country like America there is absolutely no excuse for persons living in idleness. I have little patience with persons who go around whining that they cannot find anything to do. Especially is this true in the South. Where the soil is cheap there is little or no excuse for any man or woman going about complaining that he or she cannot find work. You cannot set proper examples unless you, yourself, are constantly employed. See to it, then, whether you live in a city, a town, or in a country district, that you are constantly employed when you are not engaged in the proper kind of recreation, or in rest. Unless you do this you will find that you will go down as thousands of our young men have gone down—as thousands of our young men are constantly going down—who yield to the temptations which beset them.

Refrain from staking your earnings upon games of chance. See to it that you pass by those things which tend to your degradation. Teach this to others. Teach those with whom you come in contact that they cannot lead strong, moral lives unless they keep away from the gambling table. See to it that you regulate your life properly; that you regulate your hours of sleep. Have the proper kinds of recreation. Quite a number of our young men in the cities stay up until twelve, one and two o'clock each night. Sometimes they are at a dance, and sometimes at the gambling table, or in some brothel, or drinking in some saloon. As a result they go late to their work, and in a short time you hear them complaining about having lost their positions. They will tell you that they have lost their jobs on account of race prejudice, or because their former employers are not going to hire coloured help any longer. But you will find, if you learn the real circumstances, that it is much more likely they have lost their jobs because they were not punctual, or on account of carelessness.

Then, too, you will find that you will go down if you yield to the temptation of indulging in strong drink. That is a thing that is carrying a great many of our young men down. I do not say that all of our men are of this class, or that all of them yield to temptations, because I can go into many of the large cities and find just such men as those in Cincinnati to whom I have referred. You cannot hope to succeed if you keep bad company. As far as possible try to form the habit of spending your nights at home. There is nothing worse for a young man or young woman than to get into the habit of thinking that he or she must spend every night on the street or in some public place.

I want you, as you go out from this institution, whether you are graduates or not, whether you have been here one year or four years

—to go out with the idea that you must set a high example for every one in your community. You must remember that the people are watching you every day. If you yield to the temptation of strong drink, of going into bad company, others will do the same thing. They will shape their lives after yours. You must so shape your lives that the hundreds and thousands of those who are looking to you for guidance may profit by your example.

UNIMPROVED OPPORTUNITIES

Several of the things which I shall say to you to-night may not sound very agreeable or encouraging to many of you, yet I think you will agree with me that they are facts that cannot be denied.

We must recognize the fact, in the first place, that our condition as a race is, in a large measure, different from the condition of the white race by which we are surrounded; that our capacity is very largely different from that of the people of the white race. I know we like to say the opposite. It sounds well in compositions, does well in rhetoric, and makes a splendid essay, for us to make the opposite assertion. It does very well in a newspaper article, but when we come down to hard facts we must acknowledge that our condition and capacity are not equal to those of the majority of the white people with whom we come in daily contact.

Of course that does not sound very well; but to say that we are equal to the whites is to say that slavery was no disadvantage to us. That is the logic of it. To illustrate. Suppose a person has been confined in a sick room, deprived of the use of his faculties, the use of his body and senses, and that he comes out and is placed by the side of a man who has been healthy in body and mind. Are these two persons in the same condition? Are they equal in capacity? Is the young animal of a week old, although he has all the characteristics that his mother has, as strong as she? With proper development he will be, in time, as strong as she, but it is unreasonable to say that he is as strong at present. And so, I think, this is all that we can say of ourselves—with proper development our condition and capacity will be the same as those of the people of any other race.

Now, the fact that our capacity as a people is different, and that the conditions which we must meet are different, makes it reasonable for us to believe that, when the question of education is considered, we shall find that different education methods are desirable for us from those which would be appropriate to the needs of a people whose capacity and conditions are different from ours. What we most need, in my opinion, for the next few generations, is such an education as will help us most effectually to conquer the forces of nature;—I mean in the general sense of supplying food, clothing, homes, and a substantial provision for the future.

Do not think that I mean by this that I do not believe in every individual getting all the education he or she can get,—for I do. But since for some years to come, at least, it must of necessity be impossible for all of our young people to get all the education possible, or even all they may want to get, I believe they should apply their energies to getting such a training as will be best fitted to supply their immediate needs.

In Scotland, for instance, where higher education has been within reach of the people for many years, and where the people have reached a high degree of civilization, it is not out of place for the young people to give their time and attention to the study of metaphysics and of law and the other professions. Of course I do not mean to say that we shall not have lawyers and metaphysicians and other professional men after a while, but I do mean to say that I think the efforts of a large majority of us should be devoted to securing the material necessities of life.

When you speak to the average person about labor—industrial work, especially—he seems to get the idea at once that you are opposed to his head being educated—that you simply wish to put him to work. Anybody that knows anything about industrial education knows that it teaches a person just the opposite—how not to work. It teaches him to make water work for him,—air, steam, all the forces of nature. That is what is meant by industrial education.

Let us make an illustration. Yesterday I was over in the creamery and became greatly interested in the process of separating the cream. The only energy spent was that required to turn a crank. The apparatus had been so constructed as to utilize natural forces. Now compare the old process of butter-making with the new. Before, you had to go through a long process of drudgery before the cream could be separated from the milk, and then another long process before the cream could be turned into butter, and then, even after churning three or four hours at a time, you got only a small portion of butter. Now what we mean by giving you an industrial education is to teach you so to put brains into your work that if your work is butter-making, you can make butter simply by standing at a machine and turning a crank.

If you are studying chemistry, be sure you get all you can out of the course here, and then go to a higher school somewhere else. Become as proficient in the science as you can. When you have done this, do not sit down and wait for the world to honour you because you know a great deal about chemistry—you will be disappointed if you do—but if you wish to make the best use of your knowledge of chemistry, come back here to the South and use it in making this poor soil rich, and in making good butter where the farmers have made poor butter before. Used in this way you will find that your knowledge of chemistry will cause others to honour you.

During the last thirty years we, as a race, have let some golden opportunities slip from us, and partly, I fear, because we have not had enough plain talk in the direction I am following with you to-night. If you ever have an opportunity to go into any of the large cities of the North you will be able to see for yourselves what I mean. I remember that the first time I went North—and it was not so very many years ago—it was not an uncommon thing to see the barber shops in the hands of coloured men. I know coloured men who in that way could have become comfortably rich. You cannot find to-day in the city of New York or Boston a first-class barber shop in the hands of coloured men. That opportunity is gone, and something is wrong that it is so. Coming nearer home; go to Montgomery, Memphis, New Orleans, and you will find that the barber shops are gradually slipping away from the hands of the coloured men, and they are going back into dark streets and opening little holes. These opportunities have slipped from us largely because we have not learned to dignify labour. The coloured man puts a dirty little chair and a pair of razors into a dirtier looking hole, while the white man opens his shop on one of the principal streets, or in connection with some fashionable hotel, fits it up luxuriously with carpets, handsome mirrors and other attractive furniture, and calls the place a "tonsorial parlour." The proprietor sits at his desk and takes the cash. He has transformed what we call drudgery into a paying business.

Still another instance. You can remember that only a few years ago one of the best paying positions that a large number of coloured men filled was that of doing whitewashing. A few years ago it would not have been hard to see coloured men in Boston, Philadelphia or Washington carrying a whitewash tub and a long pole into somebody's house to do a job of whitewashing. You go into the North to-day, and you will find very few coloured men at that work. White men learned that they could dignify that branch of labour, and they began to study it in schools. They gained a knowledge of chemistry which would enable them to understand the mixing of the necessary ingredients; they learned decorating and frescoing; and now they call themselves "house decorators." Now that job is gone, perhaps to come no more; for now that these men have elevated this work, and introduced more intelligent skill into it, do you suppose any one is going to allow some old man with a pole and a bucket to come into the house?

Then there is the field occupied by the cooks. You know that all over the South we have held—and still hold to a large extent—the matter of cooking in our hands. Wherever there was any cooking to be done, a coloured man or a coloured woman did it. But while we still have something of a monopoly of this work, it is a fact that even this is slipping away from us. People do not wish always to eat fried meat, and bread that is made almost wholly of water and salt. They get tired of such food, and they desire a person to cook for them who will put brains into the work. To meet this demand white people have transformed what was once the menial occupation of cooking into a profession; they have gone to school and studied how to elevate this work, and if we can judge by the almost total absence of coloured cooks in the North, we are led to believe that they have learned how. Even here in the South coloured cooks are gradually disappearing, and unless they exert them-selves they will go entirely. They have disappeared in the North because they have not kept pace with the demand for the most improved methods of cooking, and because they have not realized that the world is moving forward rapidly in the march of civilization. A few days ago, when in Chicago, I noticed in one of the fashionable restaurants a fine-looking man, well dressed, who seemed to be the proprietor. I asked who he was, and was told that he was the "chef," as he is called—the head cook. Of course I was surprised to see a man dressed so stylishly and presenting such an air of culture, filling the place of chief cook in a restaurant, but I remembered then, more forcibly than ever, that cooking had been transformed into a profession—into dignified labour.

Still another opportunity is going, and we laugh when we mention it, although it is really no laughing matter. When we think of what we might have done to elevate it in the same way that white persons have elevated it, we realize that it was an opportunity after all. I refer to the opportunity which was in boot-blacking. Of course, here in the South, we have that yet, to a large extent, because the competition here is not quite so sharp as in the North. In too many Southern towns and cities, if you wish your shoes blacked, you wait until you meet a boy with a box slung over his shoulder. When he begins to polish your shoes you will very likely see that he uses a much-worn shoe brush, or, worse still, a scrubbing brush, and unless you watch him closely there is a chance that he will polish your shoes with stove polish. But if you go into a Northern city you will find that such a boy as this does not stand a chance of making a living. White boys and even men have opened shops which they have fitted up with carpets, pictures, mirrors, and comfort-able chairs, and sometimes their brushes are even run by electricity. They have the latest newspapers always within reach for their patrons to read while their work is being done, and they grow rich. The man who owns and runs such a place as that is not called a "boot-black;" he is called the proprietor of such and such a "Shoe-blacking Emporium." And that chance is gone to come no more. Now there are many coloured men who understand about electricity, but where is the coloured man who would apply his knowledge of that science to running brushes in a boot-black stand?

In the South it was a common thing when anybody was taken ill to notify the old mammy nurse. We had a monopoly of the nursing business for many years, and up to a short time ago it was the common opinion that nobody could nurse but one of those old black mammies. But this idea is being dissipated. In the North, when a person gets ill, he does not think of sending for any one but a professional nurse, one who has received a diploma from some nurse-training school, or a certificate of proficiency from some reputable institution.

I hope you have understood me in what I have been trying to say of these little things. They all tend to show that if we are to keep pace with the progress of civilization, we must pay attention to the small things as well as the larger and more important things in life. They go to prove that we must put brains into what we do. If education means anything at all, it means putting brains into the common affairs of life and making something of them. That is just what we are seeking to tell to the world through the work of this institution.

There are many opportunities all about us where we can use our education. You very rarely see a man idle who knows all about house-building, who knows how to draw plans, to test the strength of materials that enter into the making of a first-class house. Did you ever see such a man out of a job? Did you ever see such a man as that writing letters to this place and that place applying for work? People are wanted all over the world who can do work well. Men and women are wanted who understand the preparation and supplying of food—I don't mean in the small menial sense—but people who know all about it. Even in this there is a great opportunity. A few days ago I met a woman who had spent years in this country and in Europe studying the subject of food economics in all its details. I learned that this person is in constant demand by institutions of learning and other establishments where the preparation and the serving of food are important features. She spends a few months at each institution. She is wanted everywhere, because she has applied her education to one of the most important necessities of life.

And so you will find it all through life—those persons who are going to be constantly sought after, constantly in demand, are those who make the best use of their opportunities, who work unceasingly to become proficient in whatever they attempt to do. Always be sure that you have something out of which you can make a living, and then you will not only be independent, but you will be in a much better position to help your fellow-men.

I have spoken about these matters at this length because I believe them to be the foundation of our future success. We often hear a man spoken of as having moral character. A man cannot have moral character unless he has something to wear, and something to eat three hundred and sixty-five days in a year. He cannot have any religion either. You will find at the bottom of much crime the fact that the criminals have not had the common necessities of life supplied them. Men must have some of the comforts and conveniences—certainly the necessities of life—supplied them before they can be morally or religiously what they ought to be.

LAST WORDS

We have come to the close of another school year. Some of you will go out from among us now, not to return. Others will go home for the summer vacation and return at the end of that for the next school year.

As you go out, there is one thing that I want to especially caution you about. Don't go home and feel that you are better than the rest of the folks in your neighbourhood because you have been away at school. Don't go home and feel ashamed of your parents because you think they don't know as much as you think you know. Don't think that you are too good to help them. It would be better for you not to have any education, than for you to go home and feel ashamed of your parents, or not want to help them.

Let me tell you of one of the most encouraging and most helpful things that I have known of in connection with the life of our students after they leave this institution. I was in a Southern city, and going about among the homes of the people of our race. Among these homes I noticed one which was so neat looking that it was conspicuous. I asked the person who was with me, "How is it that this house is in such good condition, looks so much better than some of the others in the neighbourhood?" "It is like this," said the man who was accompanying me. "The people who live there have a son whom they sent to your school, at considerable self-denial to themselves. This young man came home from school a few weeks ago. For some time after he came back he did not have work to keep him busy, and so he employed his spare time in fixing up his parents' home. He fixed the roof and chimney, put new palings in the fence where they were needed and did such things as that. Then he got a stock of paint and painted the house thoroughly, two coats, outside and in. That is why the place looks so neat."

Such testimony as that is very helpful. It shows that the students carry out from here the spirit which we try to inculcate.

Another thing. Go home and lead a simple life. Don't give the impression that you think education means superficiality and dress.

Be polite; to white and coloured people, both. It is possible for you, by paying heed to this, to do a great deal toward securing and preserving pleasant relations between the people of both races in the South. Try to have your manners in this respect so good that people will notice them and ask where you have been, at what school you learned to be so polite. You will find that politeness counts for a great deal, not only in helping you to get work, but in helping you to keep it.

Don't be ashamed to go to church and Sunday school, to the Young Men's Christian Association and the Christian Endeavour Society. Show that education has only deepened your interest in such things. Have no going backward. Be clean, in your person, your language and in your thoughts.

It seems appropriate during these closing days of the school year to re-emphasize, if possible, that for which the institution stands. We want to have every student get what we have—in our egotism, perhaps—called the "Tuskegee spirit;" that is, to get hold of the spirit of the institution, get hold of that for which it stands; and then spread that spirit just as widely as possible, and plant it just as deeply as it is possible to plant it.

In addition to the members of our graduating class, we have each year a large number of students who go out to spend their vacations. Some of these will return at the close of vacation, but some, for various reasons, will not return. Whether you go out as graduates, whether you go out to return or not to return, it is important that all of you get hold of the "Tuskegee spirit;" the spirit of giving yourselves, in order that you may help lift up others. In no matter how small a degree it may be, see that you are assisting some one else.

Now, after a number of years' experience, the institution feels that it has reached a point where it can, with some degree of authority, give advice as to the best way in which you can spend your life.

In the first place, as to your location—the place where you shall work. I very much hope that the larger part of the students who go out from Tuskegee will choose the country districts for their place of work, rather than the large cities. For one thing, you will find that the larger places are much better supplied with workers and helpers than is true of the towns, and especially of the country districts. The cities are better supplied with churches and schools, with everything that tends to uplift people; and they are at the same time much more prolific of those agencies which tend to pull people down. Notwithstanding this latter fact, the greater portion, by far, of those who need help live in the country districts. I think a census report will show that eighty per cent of our people are to be found in the country and small towns. I advise you, then, to go into the country and the towns, rather than into the cities.

Then, as to the manner of work. You must make up your minds in the first place, as I have said before, that you are going to make some sacrifice, that you are going to live your lives in an unselfish way, in order that you may help some one. Go out with a spirit that will not allow you to become discouraged when you have opposition, when you meet with obstacles to be overcome. You must go with a determination that you are going to succeed in whatever undertaking you have entered upon.

I do not attempt to give you specific advice as to the kind of work you shall do, but I should say that in a general way I believe that you can accomplish more good—and perhaps this will hold good for the next fifty years here in the South—by taking a country school for your nucleus. Take a three months school, and gradually impress upon the people of the community the need of having a longer school. Get them to add one month to three months, and then another month, until they get to the point where they will have six, seven or eight months of school in a year. Then get them to where they will see the importance of building a decent school-house—getting out of the one-room log cabin school-house—and of having suitable apparatus for instruction.

LAST WORDS

There are two things you must fix your mind on: the building of a suitable school-house and the arousing in the people, at the same time, a spirit that will make them support your efforts. In order to do this you must go into the country with the idea of staying there for some time at least. Plant yourself in the community, and by economical living, year by year, manage to buy land for yourself, on which to build a nice and comfortable home. You will find that the longer you stay there the more the people will give you their confidence, and the more they will respect and love you.

I find that many of our graduates have done excellent work by having a farm in connection with their schools. This is true, also, of many who did not remain here to graduate. I have in mind such a man. He has been teaching school in one of the counties of this State for seven or eight years. He has lengthened the school year to eight months. He has a nice cottage with four rooms in it, and a beautiful farm of forty acres. This man is carrying out the "Tuskegee idea."

There will be some of you who can spend your life to better advantage by devoting it to farming than to any other industry. I speak of farming particularly, because I believe that to be the great foundation upon which we must build for the future. I believe that we are coming to the point where we are going to be recognized for our worth in the proportion that we secure an agricultural foundation. Throughout the South we can give ourselves in a free, open way to getting hold of property and building homes, in a way that we cannot do in any other industry. In farming, as in teaching, no matter where you go, remember to go with the "Tuskegee spirit."

I want the boys to go out and do as Mr. N.E. Henry is doing; I want the girls to go out and do as Miss Anna Davis and Miss Lizzie Wright are doing. I want you to go out into the country districts and build up schools. I would not advise you to be too ambitious at first. Be willing to begin with a small salary and work your way up gradually. I have in mind one young man who began teaching school for five dollars a month; another who began teaching in the open air under a tree.

Then, too, I want you to go out in a spirit of liberality toward the white people with whom you come in contact. That is an important matter. When I say this I do not mean that you shall go lowering your manhood or your dignity. Go in a manly way, in a straightforward and honourable way, and then you will show the white people that you are not of a belittling race, that the prejudice which so many people possess cannot come among you and those with whom you work. If you can extend a helping hand to a white person, feel just as happy in doing so as in helping a black person.

In the sight of God there is no colour line, and we want to cultivate a spirit that will make us forget that there is such a line anywhere. We want to be larger and broader than the people who would oppress us on account of our colour.

No one ever loses anything by being a gentleman or a lady. No person ever lost anything by being broad. Remember that if we are kind and useful, if we are moral, if we go out and practise these traits, no matter what people say about us, they cannot pull us down. But, on the other hand, if we are without the spirit of usefulness, if we are without morality, without liberality, without economy and property, without all those qualities which go to make a people and a nation great and strong, no matter what we may say about ourselves and what other people may say about us, we are losing ground. Nobody can give us those qualities merely by praising us and talking well about us; and when we possess them, nobody can take them from us by speaking ill of us.

THE HERITAGE SERIES

Candace Press

Candace Press, Inc., 2215 29th Street S.E., Suite B8, Grand Rapids, Michigan 49508

Religion and Sexuality

Other Books of Related Interest:

Opposing Viewpoints Series

Reproductive Technologies

Current Controversies Series

The Abortion Controversy

Homosexuality

"Congress shall make no law ... abridging the freedom of speech, or of the press."

First Amendment to the U.S. Constitution

The basic foundation of our democracy is the First Amendment guarantee of freedom of expression. The Opposing Viewpoints series is dedicated to the concept of this basic freedom and the idea that it is more important to practice it than to enshrine it.

OPPOSING
VIEWPOINTS®
SERIES

| Religion and Sexuality

Kevin Hillstrom, Book Editor

GREENHAVEN PRESS

An imprint of Thomson Gale, a part of The Thomson Corporation

THOMSON

GALE

Detroit • New York • San Francisco • New Haven, Conn. • Waterville, Maine • London

Christine Nasso, *Publisher*
Elizabeth Des Chenes, *Managing Editor*

© 2008 The Gale Group.

Star logo is a trademark and Gale and Greenhaven Press are registered trademarks used herein under license.

For more information, contact:
Greenhaven Press
27500 Drake Rd.
Farmington Hills, MI 48331-3535
Or you can visit our Internet site at http://www.gale.com

ALL RIGHTS RESERVED
No part of this work covered by the copyright hereon may be reproduced or used in any form or by any means—graphic, electronic, or mechanical, including photocopying, record-ing, taping, Web distribution, or information storage retrieval systems—without the written permission of the publisher.

Articles in Greenhaven Press anthologies are often edited for length to meet page require-ments. In addition, original titles of these works are changed to clearly present the main thesis and to explicitly indicate the author's opinion. Every effort is made to ensure that Greenhaven Press accurately reflects the original intent of the authors. Every effort has been made to trace the owners of copyrighted material.

Cover photograph reproduced by permission of Justin Sullivan/Getty Images.

LIBRARY OF CONGRESS CATALOGING-IN-PUBLICATION DATA

Religion and sexuality / Kevin Hillstrom, book editor.
     p. cm. -- Opposing Viewpoints
Includes bibliographical references and index.
ISBN-13: 978-0-7377-3749-3 (hardcover)
ISBN-13: 978-0-7377-3750-9 (pbk.)
ISBN-10: 0-7377-3750-6
1. Sex--Religious aspects. 2. Homosexuality--Religious aspects. 3. Birth control--Religious aspects. 4. Religious leaders--Sexual behavior. I. Hillstrom, Kevin, 1963-
HQ63.R45 2008
205'.66--dc22
                                                                   2007025661

ISBN-10: 0-7377-3749-2
ISBN-10: 0-7377-3749-2

Printed in the United States of America
10 9 8 7 6 5 4 3 2 1

Contents

Chapter 3: Is a Belief in God Incompatible with Reproductive Rights?

Chapter 4: What Issues of Sexuality Surround Religious Leaders?

Why Consider Opposing Viewpoints?

"The only way in which a human being can make some approach to knowing the whole of a subject is by hearing what can be said about it by persons of every variety of opinion and studying all modes in which it can be looked at by every character of mind. No wise man ever acquired his wisdom in any mode but this."

John Stuart Mill

In our media-intensive culture it is not difficult to find differing opinions. Thousands of newspapers and magazines and dozens of radio and television talk shows resound with differing points of view. The difficulty lies in deciding which opinion to agree with and which "experts" seem the most credible. The more inundated we become with differing opinions and claims, the more essential it is to hone critical reading and thinking skills to evaluate these ideas. Opposing Viewpoints books address this problem directly by presenting stimulating debates that can be used to enhance and teach these skills. The varied opinions contained in each book examine many different aspects of a single issue. While examining these conveniently edited opposing views, readers can develop critical thinking skills such as the ability to compare and contrast authors' credibility, facts, argumentation styles, use of persuasive techniques, and other stylistic tools. In short, the Opposing Viewpoints series is an ideal way to attain the higher-level thinking and reading skills so essential in a culture of diverse and contradictory opinions.

In addition to providing a tool for critical thinking, Opposing Viewpoints books challenge readers to question their own strongly held opinions and assumptions. Most people form their opinions on the basis of upbringing; peer pressure; and personal, cultural, or professional bias. By reading carefully balanced opposing views, readers must directly confront new ideas as well as the opinions of those with whom they disagree. This is not to simplistically argue that everyone who reads opposing views will—or should—change his or her opinion. Instead, the series enhances readers' understanding of their own views by encouraging confrontation with opposing ideas. Careful examination of others' views can lead to the readers' understanding of the logical inconsistencies in their own opinions, perspective on why they hold an opinion, and consideration of the possibility that their opinion requires further evaluation.

Evaluating Other Opinions

To ensure that this type of examination occurs, Opposing Viewpoints books present all types of opinions. Prominent spokespeople on different sides of each issue as well as well-known professionals from many disciplines challenge the reader. An additional goal of the series is to provide a forum for other, less-known, or even unpopular viewpoints. The opinion of an ordinary person who has had to make the decision to cut off life support from a terminally ill relative, for example, may be just as valuable and provide just as much insight as a medical ethicist's professional opinion. The editors have two additional purposes in including these less-known views. One, the editors encourage readers to respect others' opinions—even when not enhanced by professional credibility. It is only by reading or listening to and objectively evaluating others' ideas that one can determine whether they are worthy of consideration. Two, the inclusion of such viewpoints encourages the important critical thinking skill of objectively evaluating an author's credentials and bias. This evaluation will illuminate an author's reasons for taking a particular stance on an issue and will aid in readers' evaluation of the author's ideas.

It is our hope that these books will give readers a deeper understanding of the issues debated and an appreciation of the complexity of even seemingly simple issues when good and honest people disagree. This awareness is particularly important in a democratic society such as ours in which people enter into public debate to determine the common good. Those with whom one disagrees should not be regarded as enemies but rather as people whose views deserve careful examination and may shed light on one's own.

Thomas Jefferson once said that "difference of opinion leads to inquiry, and inquiry to truth." Jefferson, a broadly educated man, argued that "if a nation expects to be ignorant and free . . . it expects what never was and never will be." As individuals and as a nation, it is imperative that we consider the opinions of others and examine them with skill and discernment. The Opposing Viewpoints series is intended to help readers achieve this goal.

David L. Bender and Bruno Leone,
Founders

Introduction

> "Sexual intimacy within God's bound-
> aries of a loving, committed marriage
> can provide tremendous joy and fun; it
> can celebrate intimacy and love; it can
> bring the blessing of children; and it can
> create and sustain the mysterious and
> sacred oneness of marriage. But if you
> let it burn outside of God's boundaries,
> it becomes a self-serving act that can
> and will destroy careers, marriages, chil-
> dren, reputations, and even life itself. . . .
> When sexual release is pursued outside
> of the one-man, one-woman sexual cel-
> ebration of marriage, then the sacred-
> ness of sex is violated. The very heart of
> this holy union is broken."
>
> —Tim A. Gardner,
> Christian counselor
> Sacred Sex

> "We have many voices today . . . insisting
> that theology deal more seriously with
> actual human sexual experience. . . . My
> hope is that out of these struggles in
> sexual theology, an ethic might increas-
> ingly emerge that will have several
> marks. It will be strongly sex-affirming,
> understanding sexual pleasure as a
> moral good rooted in the sacred value of
> our sensuality and erotic power, and not
> needing justification by procreative pos-
> sibility. It will be grounded in respect for
> our own and others' bodily integrity . . .

It will celebrate fidelity in our commitments without legalistic prescription as to the precise forms such fidelity must make. It will be an ethic whose principles apply equally and without double standards to persons of both genders, of all colors, ages, bodily conditions, and sexual orientations."

—James Nelson,
Theologian
Body Theology

Major world religions, including Islam, Judaism, Buddhism, Hinduism, and Christianity, provide ethical guidelines and tenets about human sexuality and sexual behavior. Many of these guidelines can be found in the leading holy books of these religions, such as the Qur'an, the Torah, and the New Testament. But even among devoted adherents to these religions, deep tensions and differences exist when it comes to the issue of sex. People of the same faith consult the same holy scriptures for guidance about sexual practice and sexual morality, only to reach remarkably different conclusions about how they and other members of society should behave. For example, some people interpret their holy texts literally because they believe that the authors were directly inspired by God. Others approach these same texts with the conviction that the authors of these books expressed current religious beliefs and tenets and did not intend to provide a literal account of events.

Theologians, religious leaders, and laity also differ in what they *emphasize* when they study their holy texts for guidance or inspiration. For example, Christian opponents of homosexuality and same-sex marriage often quote Biblical passages such as Leviticus 18:22, which states that "You shall not lie with a man as with a woman; it is an abomination" punishable by execution. By contrast, liberal Christians (as well as nonbelievers who are supportive of gay rights) emphasize biblical scriptures that advocate inclusion, love, and acceptance. They also seize on other scriptural passages about sexuality that are often ignored by others, such as Deuteronomy 22:13–21, which commands that if a new bride is discovered to not be a virgin, she should be immediately stoned to death.

Each side of the heated debates over homosexuality and gay rights thus enters the fray with plenty of scriptural argument to support its position. But the resulting clamor can make it difficult to establish even a fragile dialogue, let alone find common spiritual ground.

This hotly debated issue is but one of several located at the intersection of American attitudes about religion and sexuality that are discussed in the following chapters: How Do Religious Beliefs Shape Sexual Behavior? Should Homosexuality Be Condemned on Religious Grounds? Is a Belief in God Incompatible with Reproductive Rights? and What Issues of Sexuality Surround Religious Leaders? The widely divergent answers to these questions found in the pages that follow provide evidence of the deep divisions that run through American society on the subjects of sex and religion. Many of these views appear to be fixed and unchangeable, but at a minimum this presentation encourages people to critically examine their assumptions and beliefs—and perhaps it will help people on various sides of these issues to gain a greater understanding of deeply held beliefs that run counter to their own.

OPPOSING
VIEWPOINTS®
SERIES

CHAPTER 1

How Do Religious Beliefs
Shape Sexual Behavior?

Chapter Preface

Advocates and opponents of sexual activity outside of traditional marriage truly do see the world differently. As a result, the various positions seek to establish their own definitions of the issues—and stakes—involved when people engage in premarital sex. Proponents of premarital sex insist that as long as one's sexual partner is treated with respect and precautions are taken to address concerns about sexually transmitted diseases and unintended pregnancy, engaging in sex outside of marriage is morally defensible. In fact, many people who engage in premarital sex claim that their sexual activities reflect their determination to fully experience all that life has to offer, including exploring emotional intimacy with others and savoring the gift of bodily pleasure bestowed by God.

Opposition to sexual activity outside of traditional marriage is based in part on concerns about AIDS and other sexually transmitted diseases as well as unplanned pregnancies. But a great deal of the criticism of premarital sex is grounded in religious convictions. According to these critics, Bible teachings clearly stipulate that sex outside of marriage is, by definition, a moral wrong. People who hold this view believe that sexually active single people use rationalizations about their motivations as a way to excuse morally reprehensible behavior. Advocates of abstinence assert that the only sexual activity sanctioned by God occurs within marriage.

Few observers believe that the philosophical chasm between these two camps will be bridged any time soon. But both sides agree that religious beliefs are frequently the single most decisive factors in determining to which position a person will ultimately adhere. Studies indicate, for example, that teens from actively religious families and with friends who regularly attend religious services tend to have sex at later ages compared to teens whose parents and friends do not have strong religious beliefs. As the viewpoints in this chapter indicate, the two sides have profoundly different perspectives on what lessons this information holds for U.S. society as a whole.

> "I wanted someone to explain to me that I could be a faithful Christian and blithely continue having premarital sex. But in the end, I was never able to square sex outside of marriage with the Christian story about God, redemption, and human bodies."

Sex Is Intended for Traditional Marriage

Lauren F. Winner

In this viewpoint, Lauren F. Winner, a Christian essayist, author, and former book editor for Beliefnet, *explains why she believes that God intends for sex only to be practiced within the institution of marriage. She acknowledges that modern American culture is drenched with messages that encourage sexual permissiveness, but she claims that the Book of Genesis and the New Testament epistles of the apostle Paul make it clear God intended people to engage in sex only within marriage.*

Lauren F. Winner, *Real Sex: The Naked Truth About Chastity*. Ada, MI: Brazos Press, 2005, pp. 29–31, 32–34, 35–39, 40, 41–42. Copyright © 2005 by Lauren F. Winner. Reproduced by permission.

As you read, consider the following questions:

1. How does Winner use the story of Adam and Eve to make her point that even though human bodies are good, "it does not follow that everything bodies do is good"?

2. According to the author, how is sex outside marriage similar to Walt Disney's Wilderness Lodge Resort?

3. What is the name of the poem found in Hebrew scripture that is cited by the author as the "perfect expression" of sexuality as intended by God?

The bottom line is this: God created sex for marriage, and within a Christian moral vocabulary, it is impossible to defend sex outside of marriage. To more liberal readers, schooled on a generation of Christian ethics written in the wake of the sexual revolution, this may sound like old-fashioned hooey, but it is the simple, if sometimes difficult, truth.

For several years, I tried and tried to find a way to wiggle out of the church's traditional teaching that God requires chastity outside of marriage, and I failed. I read all the classics of 1970s Christian sexual ethics, all the appealing and comforting books that insisted that Christians must avoid not sex outside of marriage, but rather exploitative sex, or sex where you run the risk of getting hurt. These books suggest that it is not marriage per se, but rather the intent or state of mind of the people involved, that determines whether or not sex is good and appropriate; if a man and woman love each other, if they are committed to each other, or, for Pete's sake, if they are just honest with each other about their fling being a no-strings-attached, one-night stand, then sex between them is just fine. After all, as long as our 1970s man and woman care about each other, making love will be meaningful. In fact, sex might even liberate them, or facilitate their personal development.

Searching for Answers

Well. I tried to find these books persuasive. I wanted to find them persuasive. I wanted someone to explain to me that I could be a faithful Christian and blithely continue having premarital sex. But in the end, I was never able to square sex outside of marriage with the Christian story about God, redemption, and human bodies.

It wasn't just the liberal, supposedly liberating, books that left me cold. I didn't find many of the more conservative bromides all that persuasive either—the easy proof-texting that purports to draw a coherent sexual ethic from a few verses of Paul. To be sure, scripture has plenty to teach us about how rightly to order our sexual lives, but, as the church, we need to ask whether the starting point for a scriptural witness on sex is the isolated quotation of "thou shalt not," or whether a scriptural ethic of sex begins instead with the totality of the Bible, the narrative of God's redeeming love and humanity's attempt to reflect that through our institutions and practices. If our aim is to construct a rule book, perhaps the cut-and-paste approach to scripture is adequate: as the bumper sticker wisdom goes, *Jesus* (or in this case, Paul) *said it, I do it.* But if we see scripture not merely as a code of behavior but as a map of God's reality, and if we take seriously the pastoral task of helping unmarried Christians live chastely, the church needs not merely to recite decontextualized Bible verses, but to ground our ethic in the faithful living of the fullness of the gospel. As ethicist Thomas E. Breidenthal once put it, "We must do more than invoke the will of God if we wish to recover a viable Christian sexual morality. . . . Even if God's will is obvious, it cannot provide a rationale for any moral code until we are able to say, clearly and simply, how God's command speaks to us, how and why it addresses us not only as a demand but as good news.". . .

God's Vision of Sexuality

God made us with bodies; that is how we begin to know that He cares how we order our sexual lives. There is—and we will walk through it here—evidence aplenty from both scripture and tradition about how God intends sex, about where sex belongs and where it is disordered, about when sex is righteous and when it is sinful. But the starting point is this: God created us with bodies; God Himself incarnated in a human body; Jesus was raised again from the dead with a body; and one day we too will be resurrected with our bodies. That is the beginning of any Christian ethic—any moral theology—of how human beings in bodies interact with other bodies.

Sexuality touches every area of human life; even something as simple as a kiss can have social consequences (after The Kiss, you go from being the girl next door to being his girlfriend) and emotional consequences (you hadn't realized you liked him *that way* until then). Kisses can play on our psychological and spiritual registers. But sexuality, even mere kissing, is also, unavoidably, bodily. After all, we define a kiss by body parts: a kiss happens when lips meet a cheek or a hand, or when two sets of lips rub up against each other. Kissing can make our bodies tingle. And kisses can be slobbery; like other sexual deeds, they are messy in their embodiment.

So an investigation of God's vision for human sexuality would begin with God's vision for human bodies. And that investigation can be less simple than it seems. The Christian story, at its core, has very positive things to say about bodies, but throughout its history the church has sometimes equivocated. We Christians get embarrassed about our bodies. We are not always sure that God likes them very much. We are not sure whether bodies are good or bad; it follows that we are not sure whether sex is good or bad.

The Christian view of bodies—that is, God's view of bodies—cannot be abstracted from the biblical account of creation. God created people with bodies, and God declared that

23

they were good. It is sometimes hard for us modern-day Christians to grasp that central fact. Bodies are not simply pieces of furniture to decorate or display; they are not trappings about which we have conflicted feelings ("body images" that we need to revamp or retool); they are not objects to be dieted away, made to conform to popular standards, or made to perform unthinkable athletic feats with the help of drugs; they are neither tools for scoring points nor burdens to be overcome. They are simply good. A second-century Syrian Christian text, "The Odes of Solomon," can remind us of this basic truth. The speaker in the poem is God, and He is talking about human beings:

> I fashioned their members, and my own breasts I prepared for them,
>
> That they might drink my holy milk and live by it.
>
> I am pleased by them,
>
> And am not ashamed by them.
>
> For my workmanship are they,
>
> And the strength of my thoughts.

Sexual Desire and Sin

God's creation, including human bodies, is good, but it does not follow that everything bodies do is good. The next act of the Christian story is the fall—Adam and Eve disobey God and a great gulf grows between them and Him, a gulf signified by their being pushed out of the Garden. Indeed, it is interesting to note that sin entered the world through the bodily act of eating, and the consequences of the fall were telegraphed on human bodies—Adam would toil in physical labor, Eve would feel pain in childbirth and would desire her husband (a desire that can be understood as physical, emotional, and

God Can Not Be Removed from the Bedroom

Those who have chosen the full-libertarian agenda that God and ethics have nothing to do with the bedroom or reproduction have some tough questions to face. Are there any moral constraints at all on sexual or reproductive freedom? Is nothing morally required of us in matters of this quite significant part of human experience? Is one's "heart's desire" the trump card for all our decisions? One wonders what might be the source of the massive repression of compunction in priests who abused children, of teachers who seduced their students, of parents who violated their own. Surely such horrors have taken place for ages. But have they been done with such absence of guilt? And what of sex itself? Do the astounding profits in pornography, the mounting rates of sexually transmitted diseases, the images of pop and hip-hop music videos or the edgy offerings of the television and fashion industries offer any vision of sex that is even remotely connected to love, commitment or children?

John F. Kavanaugh, "Of Human Life," America,
vol. 194, no. 18, May 22, 2006.

spiritual), and both would die. Still, it would be an error to conclude that in a fallen world, everything bodies do is bad. Sexual desire is not, in itself, a wicked thing. Rather, in the fall, our sexual desires were disordered, and one task of Christian ethics is to help us rightly order them.

Genesis is only the starting point for understanding God's vision of the body. . . .

The most important—and also perhaps the most complex—figure in the articulation of a distinctively Christian understanding of the body is the apostle Paul. In his New Testament epistles, Paul meditates at length upon bodies. Paul is concerned with human bodies—what they are made of, what they are good for, and how Christians should inhabit them. He also uses the body as a theological metaphor that captures the essence of the Pauline understanding of the gospel. As Anglican theologian John A. T. Robinson eloquently put it, "The concept of the body forms the keystone of Paul's theology. . . . It is from the body of sin and death that we are delivered; it is through the body of Christ on the Cross that we are saved; it is into His body the Church that we are incorporated; it is by His body in the Eucharist that this Community is sustained; it is in our body that its new life is to be manifested; it is to a resurrection of this body to the likeness of His glorious body that we are destined." As Robinson notes, Paul encompasses almost all of the basics of Christian theology—humanity, sin, incarnation, atonement, ecclesiology, sacramentality, eschatology—in the single image of the body.

Christ and the Church

Paul assumes that his readers value and care for their own physical bodies. Indeed, when trying to explain to the Ephesians how much Christ loves the church, Paul draws an analogy between Christ's love and each person's love for his own body: "No one ever hated his own body; on the contrary, he keeps it nourished and warm, and that is how Christ treats the church, because it is his body, of which we are living parts." Paul takes for granted that bodies are good things, to be nourished and loved. He assumes his readers share his perspective and can begin to see that Christ tends to them just as carefully as they tend to their own bodies.

But Paul does not assume that bodies are morally neutral. He understands that bodies are the sites of longings and temptations, of desires that can sometimes trump reason and rectitude, of powers and passions that can be glorious but can also be dangerous. Bodies, Paul knows, are complicated. Though they were created good, their parts and impulses, their desires and leanings were corrupted in the fall, just as human emotions and human intellect were corrupted. It is hard for us moderns to hold Paul's two truths in tension. We want things to be clear-cut, yes or no, either/or. Bodies can be exploited; they can be destructive and dangerous. At the same time, bodies are good, as all of God's creation is good; and rightly ordered by a Christian moral vision, bodies are tools God uses for His glory. [religious historian Wayne] Meeks has captured the nuances of Paul's take on bodies. In Meeks's phrase, Paul insists that "what is done 'in the body' is morally significant"; however, Paul also maintains that "the human predicament is the result not of the limitations of physical existence, but of sin."

Bodies are central to the Christian story. Creation inaugurates bodies that are good, but the consequences of the fall are written on our bodies—our bodies will sweat as we labor in the fields, our bodies will hurt as we bear children, and, most centrally, our bodies will die. If the fall is written on the body, salvation happens in the body too. The kingdom of God is transmitted through Jesus's body and is sustained in Christ's Body, the church. Through the bodily suffering of Christ on the cross and the bodily resurrection of Christ from the dead, we are saved. Bodies are not just mirrors in which we see the consequence of the fall; they are also, in one theologian's phrase, "where God has chosen to find us in our fallenness." Bodies are who we are and where we live; they are not just things God created us with, but means of knowing Him and abiding with Him.

Sex and Genesis

Just as scripture's vision of bodies begins in Genesis, scripture's story about sex also begins in Genesis. God's vision for humanity is established in the Garden of Eden, and the uniqueness and one-ness of the marriage relationship between Adam and Eve is inaugurated in Genesis 1–2. In the first chapters of

Genesis, we learn that God created a relationship between Adam and Eve. This relationship is the context in which sex is first understood. In a graphic speech, Adam speaks of his and Eve's becoming one flesh. One-fleshness both is and is not metaphor. It captures an all-encompassing, overarching oneness—when they marry, husband and wife enter an institution that points them toward familial, domestic, emotional, and spiritual unity. But the one flesh of which Adam speaks is also overtly sexual, suggesting sexual intercourse, the only physical state other than pregnancy where it is hard to tell where one person's body stops and the other's starts.

This is why it is hard to discuss Christian sexual ethics abstracted from Christian social and marital ethics. When it comes to sex, one cannot leave out marriage. The *no* to sex outside marriage seems arbitrary and cruel apart from the Creator's *yes* to sex within marriage. Indeed, one can say that in Christianity's vocabulary the only real sex is the sex that happens in a marriage; the faux sex that goes on outside marriage is not really sex at all. The physical coming together that happens between two people who are not married is only a distorted imitation of sex, as Walt Disney's Wilderness Lodge Resort is only a simulation of real wilderness. The danger is that when we spend too much time in the simulations, we lose the capacity to distinguish between the ersatz and the real.

Even though we are fallen, we remain part of God's original creation. We were created in particular ways, with particular longings and desires and impulses. Those desires have become distorted in the fall, but they are still here within us, shaping our wants and our actions and our thoughts and our wishes. This is nowhere clearer than in human sexuality. The impulse for relationship with which God created humanity animates us—and powerful sexual desire is still with us, too. But one has only to flip through the pages of *Men's Health* or even glance at the nightly news to see that in contemporary society, men and women express sexual longings in all sorts of ways that are out of sync with God's vision of marital sex.

The Bible has something to say about all of this. The Bible understands what happened in the fall; and all the laws that biblical writers, from Moses to Paul, articulate are efforts to protect and perpetuate the ordering of things that was established in the Garden of Eden. The Mosaic laws about family relationships and sexual practices—even the faintly embarrassing and seemingly self-evident rules about avoiding incest and bestiality—do protective work, pointing to, guarding, and returning God's people to the created order, the world as God meant it to be. (Song of Songs, the erotic love poem found in Hebrew scripture, is the perfect expression of what this sexuality, restored by law and grace, looks like. It features a lover proclaiming to his beloved, "You are stately as a palm tree, and your breasts are like its clusters. . . . I will climb the palm tree and lay hold of its branches." The beloved responds with an invitation to "go out . . . into the vineyards, and see whether the vines have budded.")

Guidance from the Apostle Paul

Paul, in his often-quoted words about sexual behavior, is doing the same work as Mosaic law. He is thinking about sexuality in the context of the order of creation. In other words, Paul may be tweaking the specifics of Mosaic law, but in the grand scheme, he is not innovating. He is, like the leaders of the Old Testament, articulating boundaries and regulations that protect God's original intent that sex be expressed in marriage. . . .

Paul sometimes gets a reputation as a killjoy, a first-century prude who's concerned above all else with regulating people's sexual behavior. Abstracted from his larger vision of helping people live into God's ideals for creation, Paul's vision of human sexuality does indeed seem like a list of arbitrary rules. But Paul is not writing in a vacuum. He uses the literary technique of repetition to direct the reader's attention back to Genesis. In the middle of his first letter to the Corinthians, right after enjoining the Corinthians not to sleep with prostitutes and right before instructing the unmarried that it is better to marry than to burn, Paul quotes Genesis 2:24: "The two shall become one flesh." Paul's quotation is something of shorthand—it tells the reader to flip back to the second chapter of Genesis to find both the basis for and the elaboration of Paul's words on sexuality. . . .

This is not just a lesson in reading. It is also a pastoral point. Consider, as an example, the recent experience of my friend Kara, a campus minister in Illinois. Recently a student came to her, on fire for the Lord, and said, "I want to follow and serve Jesus, and the one thing I really want to know is, how far can I go with my boyfriend?" One could, I suppose, answer that question simply by pointing to a few verses from Paul, but a more complete, and perhaps more compelling, instruction is to begin with the picture of intended reality that is laid out in Genesis. Kara realized that answering her student's question required first answering a host of larger questions: *Who created us, and for what ends? What is God's creational intent?* and *What are we made for?*

I'll hazard a guess about Kara's student. When she's sitting on the sofa in a dark den with her boyfriend, random verses from Paul may not do much work. However, if this student's community helps form in her an understanding that she is God's creature, made for God's best purposes, she may indeed think very differently—even righteously—about sex, and bodies, and the context in which those bodies are to touch and be touched.

God and Creational Law

Our bodies and how we inhabit them point to the order of creation. God made us for sex within marriage; this is what the Reformed tradition would call a creational law. To see the biblical witness as an attempt to direct us to the created order, to God's rule of creation, is not to appeal to self-interest in a therapeutic or false way. It is rather to recognize the true goodness of God's creation; things as they were in the Garden of Eden are things at their most nourishing, they are things as they are meant to be. This is what Paul is saying when he speaks to the Corinthians: *Don't you know that when you give your body to a prostitute, you are uniting yourself to her?* To ask that question is to speak the wisdom of Proverbs in the idiom of law. It is a law that invites us into the created order of marital sex; a law that rightly orders our created desires for sexual pleasure and sexual connectedness; a law, in short, that cares for us and protects us, written by a Lawgiver who understands that life outside of God's created intent destroys us. By contrast, life lived inside the contours of God's law humanizes us and makes us beautiful. It makes us creatures living well in the created order. It gives us the opportunity to become who we are meant to be.

> *"Americans are forging a new sexual ethic for themselves. In typical American fashion, this new development is neither ideologically nor theologically driven. It is a response based on practicality and the civil guarantees of rights and liberties that most now just take for granted."*

Sex Is Morally Permissible Outside Traditional Marriage

Balfour Brickner

Some religious leaders and people of faith believe that sexual activity outside traditional marriage can be spiritually fulfilling, and they argue that religious restrictions on adult sexual activity outside marriage are unrealistic and prudish given the ways in which American culture and society have changed over the past few decades. The following viewpoint, written by Balfour Brickner, the senior rabbi emeritus at the Stephen Wise Free Synagogue in New York City, reflects this belief that a healthier "sexual ethic" is emerging in the United States.

Balfour Brickner, "The Death of the Nuclear Family: Towards a New Sexual Ethic in America," *Conscience*, vol. 25, Summer 2004, pp. 41–44. Copyright 2004, Catholics for a Free Choice. All rights reserved. Reproduced by permission.

As you read, consider the following questions:

1. What is the author's opinion of conservative religious organizations such as Focus on the Family, Concerned Women of America, and the Family Research Council?

2. How does the author feel about television shows such as *Sex and the City* that have considerable sexual content?

3. Who does the author compare to Constantine's legionnaires, who "carried [Christianity] to the world on . . . spear points"?

It is a truth that most of us know.

Politicians avoid discussing it publicly lest when they do they sound less honest than usual. The American population is pitifully hypocritical with it. Clergy, seeing it, offer neither wisdom, guidance nor leadership. Against it, the religious right conducts a fearsome but losing battle, while the broad extent of it is revealed by the mushrooming rash of gay marriages now flooding court houses across America.

What is this truth?

The nuclear family as we once knew it has crumbled. In its place a new understanding of family is emerging. That mythic television family of yesteryear, the happily married monogamous wife and husband, two drug-free children and a dog, living in a three-bedroom, two-bath house on a 100' x 100' plot in a cookie-cutter suburban development somewhere, hardly exists anywhere anymore. In fact, the reality is radically different.

Modern Trends

The most recent US census reveals that the marriage rate is declining precipitously, only 24 percent of households are made up of a married couple and children, and in some age cohorts as many as half of all marriages will end up in divorce. More people than ever before live together in permanent relationships without legal sanction. The number of unmarried couple households rose from 500,000 in 1970 to 5 million in 2004. More children are being born to or adopted—without social or religious stigma—by couples in such arrangements. It is almost the norm for gay and straight couples to live together unmarried and more widowed or divorced older folk find new partners and cohabit without marriage. A veritable epidemic of gay marriages has erupted across the land creating gay families that raise children in familial settings where, much to the dismay of braying religious fundamentalists, the kids are doing just fine with two mommies or two daddies. According to the 2000 census, 594,000 households in the United States were headed by same-sex partners, a figure considered by some experts to be conservative. Of those, about 33 percent of lesbian couples reported having children aged 18 or under, while 22 percent of male couples did.

Even the opprobrium of adultery has lost its moral and legal sting. In most of our nation's courts, adultery is no longer used as grounds for divorce. Its practice is so common that most of us just shrug on learning that our friends, neighbors or business associates are, or have been, involved in some "affair." After all, everyone knows that adulterous relationships are conducted regularly in the highest of professional, governmental and even clerical circles. So what?

The Conservative Viewpoint

Conservatives and religious fundamentalists represented by organizations like Focus on the Family, Concerned Women of America and the Family Research Council see these patterns as catastrophic, and do all in their power to reverse the trend. One can understand their desperation. After all, science, technology, philosophy, even Biblical studies, enlightened as they continue to be by archeology, have shattered their world at every level. They would like to see things return to some status quo ante where their world was secure, when folks believed the sun revolved around the earth, when there was no Hubble telescope to penetrate space to tell us that indeed our cosmos is 14 billion years old, not one created in six days, or when we could not prove that life evolved from lower to higher forms of being. The present situation, certainly the teaching of evolution in the schools, and the exposure of the young to "humanistic ideas," challenges the credibility of their faith at every level.

Bruised by these changes, angered by the hostility of what became a largely post-Christian era, many, mostly Christian traditionalists at first, sought solace by retreating into an otherworldly version of an earlier Christian identity. This movement became the fundamentalist stream of American Christianity that today [2004] dominates our nation's political life. They are frightened by, and infuriated with, contemporary social behavior, especially America's changed sexual attitudes and practices. While forgiving their own religious leaders their highly publicized sexual excesses, they cannot tolerate what they believe the rest of us are up to. They see such behavior as hastening the decline, if not the destruction, of all social structures. Little wonder they rail so vehemently against what they consider libertine sexual behavior among adolescents as well as between unmarried adults. To them, the use of, or teaching of birth control, family planning, a woman's right to abortion, etc. merely spreads the contagion. Such behavior, they are convinced, hastens the end of civilization.

But, since world catastrophe [the apocalypse] is a part of their theology anyway, one wonders why the deterioration of the family should worry them so much. Since in their view it is speeding the coming of the end of life as we know it, and the end is to be welcomed as a necessary precursor to the great Parousia [second coming of Jesus Christ] and subsequent rapture upwards into the heavenly future, why not welcome the destruction of the family brought on, as they claim, by libertines, liberals, humanists, "eastern elites" and other troubling types? Instead of cursing us as a form of the devil incarnate, (which they do) they should welcome us as doing their God's work. They don't. Perhaps there is an unresolved lacunae [gap] in their theological system?

A New Sexual Ethic

For those of us whose sociological views are not shaped by either religious or secular fundamentalism, America's changes in sexual attitudes and behavior do not represent a cataclysmic decline in morality. They do mean that our society is beginning to understand, accept and express sex and sexuality in more honest terms, stripped of the hypocrisy which characterized so much of our past behavior. We no longer see the need to decry sex publicly, while privately gorging ourselves on it. It means we are beginning to give a totally new definition to the word "family," one that is not dependent on a legal sanction, even as we recognize that the ideals conveyed by words like "love," "commitment" and "responsibility" continue to hold as much psychological power as any legal document ever did. People still want and seek family and all it ideally represents, including a home—that secure anchoring place which [American poet] Robert Frost once described as the place where, when you go there, they have to take you in.

Americans are forging a new sexual ethic for themselves. In typical American fashion, this new development is neither ideologically nor theologically driven. It is a response based on practicality and the civil guarantees of rights and liberties which most now just take for granted. Rarely do I officiate at a wedding nowadays where the bride and groom have separate addresses prior to the ceremony. Working couples find it too expensive to live separately. Older couples cohabit without the benefit of marriage for many reasons, some quite practical: threatened loss of Social Security for one of the two, disrupt-

"SOMEWHERE LiKE SODOM AND GOMORRAH, BUT WiTHOUT THE GUiLT!"

"Somewhere like Sodom and Gomorrah, but without the guilt!" cartoon by Dan Rosandich. CartoonStock.com.

ing inheritance arrangements for family members. The reasons are legion and legitimate.

Modern Women and Sexual Ethics

Most women now work. Their economic and social independence is handmaid to their freedom. Sexual freedom, greatly strengthened by the easy availability of effective birth control, is an undisputed corollary of their won and civilly protected status. This does not signal licentiousness or a casting off of personal behavioral standards. It is a long-delayed equity and women rightfully demand that the world see, understand and respect complete female emancipation at all levels of life.

This new status is remarkable for its honesty, its candor, its explicit demand for equal sexual pleasure and for its ability to take sex seriously while viewing it with a certain knowing humor and openness. Ours is the age of "Cosmo culture"

37

where in the pages of that magazine [*Cosmopolitan*] one can read of various techniques women can employ to bring them and their partners to simultaneously shared moments of exquisite physical pleasure. The mechanics of sex are taught openly, in print, on television, easily available for all to learn. Hopefully when that is achieved, the next step, understanding the mystique of sexuality, will be fully developed and enjoyed. We have turned a corner in our attitude toward human sexuality. *Playboy*, Larry Flynt [publisher of *Hustler*] and the comedian Lenny Bruce may have seemed outrageous in their time, but it took their excesses and the challenges they provoked in our courts to shatter the Comstockian [after Anthony Comstock, U.S. Postal Inspector known for censoring material] and puritanical restrictions that inhibited our culture's progress. People need to feel good—not guilty—about their sexuality and the new sexual age in which we are living. Publications like *Cosmopolitan*, TV shows like "Sex and the City" and "The L Word" and some of our more creative writers for film and stage are taking us there. But in all of this, one major social structure seems to be missing: America's religious institutions. The instrument that is supposed to give us our spiritual and moral base is absent. It is fair to ask: Are our religious establishments part of the problem or part of the solution?

The Question of Gay Clergy

The Methodist church's conflict over whether or not to allow "outed" lesbians to serve as clergy and the Episcopal church's response to the consecration as bishop of an openly gay priest are moments of light in an otherwise "wine dark" religious sea. In both of these instances, those who prevailed fought for the right of their clergy to serve. If only they were not noteworthy moments because of their uniqueness. It is depressing to see institutions that profess to see God's spirit in everyone allow their slavish adherence to archaic, doctrinal dogma drive people from one another and from some God they teach as the ultimate exemplar of love and understanding. A decade from now they will look back on this struggle and feel shame and humiliating embarrassment. They will wonder how we let such bigoted ignorance out of its cell.

Those in the Methodist communion who would have denied ordination to a professed lesbian minister, and the substantial minority within the American Episcopal church and its worldwide Anglican communion who oppose the consecration of a gay bishop base their opposition to accepting their clergy's homosexuality on a text found in the Hebrew Bible where in the 22nd verse of the 18th chapter of the book of Leviticus it states: "You shall not lie with a male as with a woman; it is an abomination."

Amazing that they choose to be governed by this demand, and risk splitting their already-weakened churches, while failing totally to observe the command in Deuteronomy 24 to stone all adulterers. Perhaps they fear too great a diminishment of their ranks were they too closely to observe that commandment? Moreover, one cannot help observing that the same texts which condemn homosexuality also condemn the eating of shellfish, yet nowadays it is hard to find a conservative churchman campaigning against the eating of shrimp, half a dozen oysters on the half shell or a boiled lobster. The faithful do have a tendency to conveniently pick and choose their commandments, don't they? Even more amazing is the realization that no such condemnation of homosexuality can be found in the basic four gospels of the New Testament, the texts most Christians, and certainly traditionalists, elevate to a position of authority transcending that of the Hebrew Bible, which they believe the New Testament supercedes.

Rejection Without Biblical Merit

An exclusion of homosexuals from all aspects of church life, including the highest calling of priestly leadership, cannot be validated from the four gospels or from the Hebrew Bible. One rabbinic scholar wisely reminds us that the Torah teaches that every human being is created in the image of divinity. Its entire leitmotif [recurring theme] is one that urges compassion and empathy for the stranger in our midst, reminding us that Jews were once oppressed strangers in the land of Egypt and from that experience should know the heart of the stranger (the torture of alienation to which they are subjected). The Hebrew Bible is full of sex and it is always presented in positive terms.

"Let your fountain be blessed, and rejoice in the wife of your youth, a lovely deer, a graceful doe. May her breasts satisfy you all times, may you be intoxicated always by her love" Proverbs 5:18–19. If that doesn't persuade you, turn to The Song of Songs 7:6–9.

This major thrust of biblical intent certainly trumps any single statement any where in scripture that might condemn homosexual behavior as "an abomination." Moreover, if it is true that *all* (italics mine) humans are created in the divine image, do not those who oppose granting gays their full rights negate the truth of biblical sentiment by urging us to treat gays differently from others? Or would they argue that gays are not either fully human or fully divine? Medical science would testify that they are fully human, albeit perhaps created with a different genetic arrangement—and doesn't that in some ways describe all of us? As to full divinity? One wonders what special gifts are possessed by opponents of full rights for homosexuals that enable them to discern the nature and the will of divinity.

Why are all but the right wing religious institutions so impotent in this arena. It cannot be because their bible teaches that sexuality is some negative, terrible hurtful business. No text in the four synoptic gospels deals negatively with sex. Other New Testament materials such as Romans and Corinthians may, but they are of a different qualitative category. So why the silence? Is it because those who speak for the church feel they have nothing to say? Is it because their clergy leadership is afraid of polarizing the membership of their institution at a time when those memberships are becoming increasingly conservative?

In the 1960s and 1970s organized religion played a critical role in the civil rights struggle, and later in the antiwar movement. Today it seems to have either failed to understand the seriousness of America's sexual revolution or it has turned away from its historic prophetic mandate. For whatever reasons, our religious bodies are not part of the solution to America's struggle to achieve full sexual freedom for all of its citizens.

Gay Rights and Christianity

Historians tell us that Christianity was carried to the world on the spear points of Constantine's legionnaires. Without that compelling persuasive force, Christianity might have languished for centuries as just another cult or faith in the ancient world, competing with all others for people's hearts and minds. Today [2004], the new battle is for full sexual freedom. It is being carried forward by a most unlikely band of foot soldiers: gays demanding their civil rights. Less than a decade ago, gays legitimately feared that in many parts of this country public exposure might cost them their lives. They no longer fear public opinion. They are demanding that the social and civil engines of our society confirm the rights they correctly believe are theirs by constitutional guarantee. Anger has replaced fear. Organized massive presence has replaced closeted isolation and the population of this vast country is slowly being forced to understand and accept the legitimacy of their demands. The trend toward total acceptance of homosexuality is irreversibly underway in America. It may take longer in some areas of our country than in others but the outcome is inevitable. No one could have foreseen the speed with which this has all happened. Perhaps it took the crucifixion of a gay young man [Matthew Shepard, murdered in 1998] on the barbed wire of a rural fence in Wyoming to further the goal. Perhaps it was the bludgeoning to death of a gay soldier [Barry Winchell, murdered in 1999] in a US Army barracks that helped attitudes change. Possibly it was gays demanding the right to march under their own banner in a St. Patrick's Day parade, or their own Gay Pride Week marches that helped change people's attitudes.

Probably it was a cumulation of all such incidents, each somewhat minuscule, but combined they became an irresistible force, given even greater focus by a president's pandering effort to define who is eligible for civil marriage by proposing to amend the US Constitution. [George W. Bush urged in 2004 an amendment defining marriage solely as the union between a man and a woman.] This action, initiated in an election year to mollify [soothe] a right-wing constituency on which the present administration heavily depends for electoral and financial support, has done more to galvanize the gay community and those who support it than perhaps any other single event since the 1980 shooting attack by a disgruntled former police officer at the Ramrod, a New York City gay bar.

Confronting Hypocrisies

We are slowly coming to terms with our own hypocrisies. Whereas in 1991, 71 percent of Americans said gay sex was always wrong, by 2002 that number had fallen to 53 percent with 32 percent saying that gay sex was not wrong at all. It is when the word "marriage" is introduced into the equation that toleration levels decline. For some reason(s) our citizenry, while increasingly supportive of extending legal rights to gays and their partners, including same-sex unions, balk when the issue of marriage is raised. Marriage, at least as a paradigm, seems to be the one issue about which Americans continue to care deeply. Allowing marriage for gays somehow seems to attack those religious foundations of our lives we would like to uphold in an ideal world, even though most do little to give them practical expression in their daily behavior. There is an element of hypocrisy here, but it is alright. We need occasionally to grant ourselves our slight idiosyncrasies. No society can be expected always to measure up to the plumb line of strict consistency on all social matters. Other societies may be more honest in their approach to sanctifying gay coupling. We, however, are still a young, somewhat adolescent society, struggling to emerge from the influence of Calvinist orthodoxies. Perhaps the debate over gay marriage should not be fought on religious grounds, but it is. While we seem able to tolerate gay civil unions, marriage strikes at the heart of approval. It is easier to tolerate than it is to approve. And the prospect of gay marriage threatens people with a government stamp of approval on homosexuality. Americans are not yet ready to go that far.

One psychoanalyst, Dr. Peter Wolson observed:

> The prospect of gay marriage ... strikes at the traditional nuclear anchor of American life and powerful childhood forces, it challenges the basic black and white stereotypes we grew up with and once that black and white is challenged, it brings us all into this crazy zone of existential uncertainty. (*New York Times*, August 10, 2003)

What is existentially threatening today will soon become non-threatening reality. We learned to accept integration. We have learned to live with adultery, and with couples living together extramaritally. We have even learned to accept female equality. We will soon get used to the idea of gay marriage.

Sex has changed in America. There is no going back.

> *"When it comes to sexual morality, many of us revel in relativism, also known as 'tolerance.' We no longer hide the fact that we live together and love together outside of marriage or that we have a sexual relationship with a person of the same sex."*

Attitudes About Sexuality Have Become Healthier Since the 1960s

Don Lattin

This viewpoint asserts that American sexual ethics have improved and attitudes toward sexuality have become healthier since the 1960s, when the "sexual revolution" first emerged. According to author Don Lattin, who was religion writer for the San Francisco Chronicle *for two decades, evolving ideas about sexual morality and ethics have made many Americans happier and more spiritually fulfilled. He acknowledges that sexual activity that takes place outside some ethical boundaries is immoral, but he argues that conservative religious conceptions of sexual ethics and morality are deeply flawed and should be dismissed.*

Don Lattin, "The Immoral Majority: Finding Sexual Ethics in the Godless Masses," *San Francisco Chronicle*, October 19, 2003, p. CM12. Copyright © 2003 Hearst Communications, Inc. Republished with permission of *San Francisco Chronicle*, conveyed through Copyright Clearance Center, Inc.

As you read, consider the following questions:

1. Who does the author refer to as "cafeteria Catholics"?
2. What is the author's perspective on the 1950s and its alleged emphasis on "traditional family values"?
3. How does Lattin use the life and teachings of Jesus to support his arguments about sexual morality?

For the past few years, I've talked to lots of "unchurched" Gen Xers and their Baby Boomer parents for a new book titled *Following Our Bliss—How the Spiritual Ideals of the Sixties Shape Our Lives Today*. Among the questions we explore are how one lives an ethical life outside the Judeo-Christian mainstream. What are your guideposts if you don't want your rules etched in stone and placed in the Supreme Court building in Montgomery, Ala.? [reference to Alabama Chief Justice Roy Moore's display of Ten Commandments in state building; monument removed, 2003] How do former fundamentalists decide what is right or wrong if they no longer fear God nor follow all 10 of the Ten Commandments? How do lapsed Catholics make moral decisions about sexuality without turning to the catechism of the Roman Catholic Church?

"The motivation for living an ethical life is not just intellectual or someone frightening you. It can be based emotionally on your sense of compassion and empathy. That's where soul and spirit come together," said Thomas Moore, a free-thinking Catholic and author of *Care of the Soul*, one of the mega-selling spirituality books of the 1990s.

"That's very important in an ethical life. You realize that we're all in this together. We live in a diverse world and need to have empathy for people with diverse views and lifestyles. The church has tried to use fear, but it doesn't work."

Moore and I were talking about how people can be Catholic without obeying the edicts of the pope or their Catholic bishop. Back in the 1950s, when he was entering adolescence, Moore left home to begin the years of study required for ordination as a Roman Catholic priest in a religious order. Thirteen years later, just six months before he was to take his final vows, Moore opted out of the clerical life. It was 1967, and Moore was 26.

Today [2003], Thomas Moore, writer, has influenced far more American Catholics than he would have as Thomas Moore, priest. "I'm still a monk at heart and the writing of these books is my spiritual practice," said Moore, who has two children. "It's not just a job. I realize how much of my Catholicism is involved in my life, but it's not the Catholicism that the church advocates. I don't care if I follow all the rules, but I have the spirit of it. In my own way, I do practice the faith. My Catholicism is part of my nature. It's part of me. It's a cultural thing and it makes no sense to me to disown it. So the alternative is to redefine it."

Spiritual seekers of my generation—those of us who profess to be into "spirituality, but not religion"—are notorious for this personalized approach to finding faith and making moral decisions. If we are Catholic, we are "cafeteria Catholics," picking and choosing our spiritual and ethical nourishment from the Roman menu. We stand accused of moral relativism in our ethics and philosophy—believing that right and wrong and good and bad change with time and circumstance.

Not that long ago, sex between two men or two women was considered immoral, unnatural or at least unspeakable by the civic and spiritual establishment. Today, we have openly gay members of Congress, the Board of Supervisors and the Episcopal House of Bishops.

When it comes to sexual morality, many of us revel in relativism, also known as "tolerance." We no longer hide the fact that we live together and love together outside of marriage, or that we have a sexual relationship with a person of the same sex.

Since the sexual revolution of the '60s and '70s, Jewish and Christian denominations have struggled with the culture's conflicting concepts of sexual morality. And the debate shows no signs of abating. Earlier this year, conservatives in the worldwide Anglican communion threatened schism when the Episcopal bishops of the United States ordained an openly gay bishop. That was just weeks after the Vatican declared that civil recognition of gay unions was a "legalization of evil." At their big summer church conventions, mainline Protestant denominations like the Presbyterian Church USA argue about gay rights and morality of homosexual unions on an annual basis.

Meanwhile, millions of younger Americans—the ones who are actually having most of the sex—could care less what Episcopal bishops, Vatican officials or Presbyterian delegates think about all this. But that does not mean their sexuality isn't connected to their spirituality or their sense of right and wrong. . . .

Rebecca Ann Parker is an ordained Methodist minister and president of Starr King School of Ministry, a Unitarian-Universalist seminary and member of the Graduate Theological Union consortium on Berkeley's "Holy Hill."

We're sitting in her office talking about sex. She is a short woman, with an easy smile and gray hair cut in a short and simple style. Parker and I were both born in 1953, smack dab in the middle of the Baby Boom years, and we both came of age in the middle of the sexual revolution.

"I was just coming of age in the early 1970s and remember the sexual freedom of the time. There was a sense that old boundaries were oppressive and destroying the life spirit. In a lot of ways that was true. The old boundaries were not healthy, but not having any values was also unhealthy. It wasn't that good for women, it wasn't that good for children, and maybe it wasn't that good for men either.

"In the last 30 years [between 1970 and 2000] we've been reconstructing an understanding of right relationship, or ethical boundaries," she said. "You had the women's movement

Sexuality and Sacredness

Historically, the Catholic church has laid down sexual laws that reflect a certain imperial attitude: Have as many children as possible in order to spread Catholicism far and wide. Protestant teaching emphasized that sex should be dour, painful, and an assigned duty of marriage. It was definitely not something one talked about. As Christians we have a lot of bad history to overcome. Maybe we should add "sex is good, sex is holy" to our daily prayers. . . .

Too much of the church's teaching on sex has been about rules and regulations. That approach won't work any more. Read the story of Jacob and Laban in Genesis. Jacob starts out as a "righteous man"—a rule-follower—but in his 20 years of sexual intrigue with Laban over Rachel and Leah, Jacob breaks all the rules. It is in this crucible of sin, however, that God transforms Jacob into a "baal teshuva"—a man of mercy.

This is what God intends—a life-shaping narrative that allows sex, sexuality, and sensuality to be part of the sacred and complex interplay of light and shadow across the human heart. In recovering a sacred, respectful sexuality we make our bodies a fit dwelling place for God. It may not get as much press as sin, but it's a good definition of church.

Rose Marie Berger, "Managing the Erotic Life,"
Sojourners, vol. 31, no. 3, May–June 2002.

deeply divided over pornography, or S&M [sadomasochism-gaining sexual pleasure by inflicting pain on another person]. OK. Let's say 'Sex is good' rather than 'Sex is bad.' I'm for that. But that kind of either/or is not an adequate way of parsing the problem. It's more complex than that. Even when you say sexuality is good, you have to ask 'When is it good?' Sex is this wonderful thing, but it's a little like fire. It can warm you, or it can burn you."

Then I asked Parker about sexual ethics—about the widespread disagreement in America today about what kind of sex is "good" and what kind of sex is "bad." What's the connection between our attitudes about monogamy, homosexuality and our religious tradition?

"There is a connection between monotheism and monogamy. Being faithful to the one true God. You have images of idolatry and apostasy being articulated as adultery or sexual licentiousness. Your right relationship to God is monogamous. You have one God like you have no other loves. Then you've got the notion of God creating male and female to be right with God. Those are the orders of creation. So to follow God's orders is to be heterosexual. Actually, the Bible itself has many more complicated human sexual behaviors than that. But for those of us born in the '50s, the ethics of that era were monogamous heterosexuality was right, and sex outside of marriage was wrong. If you were a Catholic, you also had the idea that sex for pleasure was wrong. What evolved from the 1950s was the idea that, 'Well, maybe sexuality is good.' Then the idea that sexual diversity was good."

OK. So far, so good. But on what do you base a sexual ethic if you don't base it on God, the Bible or religious tradition?

"I would base it on what's good for children," Parker replied. "I think it's good for children to have adults who are committed to them without question."

It's hard to argue against parents being totally committed to their children—but here goes:

Today, the family has been raised up as the most sacred and sovereign unit of society. Many of the families profiled in "Following Our Bliss" paid less attention to the kids than the children wanted, but the neglect was mostly benign, the byproduct of social idealism or a life a bit too centered on self-improvement. One of the themes running through my interviews with people born into the spiritual counterculture of

49

the '60s was this feeling that their parents were not there for them. It didn't matter that they were worshiping strange gods, following some messianic prophet or living promiscuous lives. It wasn't that Mom and Dad were out saving the world, or spreading Krishna consciousness, but simply that they were not available to the family. Many of these parents were more concerned about changing the world than raising their families.

Looking back on it, many of these adult children of the '60s retain some resentment about not being the center of their parents' universe. But those who inherited Mom and Dad's social idealism also see that there was a lot in the world that needed to be changed, and there still is. . . .

Sixties-bashing is facile [easy, simplistic]. In the 1990s, those titillating times were subject to endless sniping by the talking heads of television, apostles of the ordinary and other neo-conservative pundits [experts]. For many Christian commentators, the '60s became a metaphor for the Fall From Grace. It was more convenient to blame drug addiction, poverty, teen pregnancy and the breakdown of the family on a past period of permissiveness. It was also a good political strategy. Criticizing the excesses of the '60s shifts attention away from the recent undoing of the vital social gains of the decade. It was easier to preach a narrow and regressive sexual morality than to look at other forces threatening poor and middle-class families in the late 20th century—like the desperate shortage of affordable housing and the grinding necessity for both parents to hold jobs.

Our appraisal of the '60s flows from our ideas about the '50s—and many of those ideas are wrong. Sixties bashers claim America's moral, religious and familial life reached shining heights in the '50s, then collapsed into a cacophony of selfishness and sin. America's "Greatest Generation," we are told, saved the world in the '40s, then moved to the suburbs and set us on the path of peace and prosperity. In this fantasy, all began to unravel in the '60s, when a rebellious generation tore society apart and couldn't put it back together again. Our most grievous loss was said to be "traditional family values," three words that became the political battle cry of reactionary, post-'60s politics and religion.

In reality, there wasn't much about the faith and families of the '50s that were "traditional." If anything, the '50s was the aberrant decade, not the '60s and '70s. The post-World War II era saw an abnormal emphasis on piety, patriotism and the nuclear family. In fact, the decade was just a blip on the long-term charts of public piety. Our religious "revival" had more to do with demographics and politics than the hand of God. The Baby Boomers reached their Sunday-school years. This is when many families traditionally—and often temporarily—reconnect with church or synagogue.

Enough about "the greatest generation." It had its greatness, to be sure, but it is also the generation that built Japanese internment camps, saluted McCarthyism and mostly turned its face away from racism and anti-Semitism. Many of the problems we blame on the '60s—child abuse, domestic violence, substance abuse—were no less prevalent in the '50s. We just didn't talk about it then. It was much easier to hide all that behind the walls of our now-separate homes out in the suburbs. . . .

Powerful spirits moved the religious revolution of the '60s: idealism, innovation, empowerment and the search for authentic experience. They remain the hallmarks of the era. There was a thirst for authenticity, for telling it like it is. There was a turning away from materialism, greed and old roles. Many of us replayed Dustin Hoffman's role in the 1967 film "The Graduate," searching for our own life and our own set of values. Benjamin was right. You don't have to go into plastics. You can follow your bliss. There was a feeling of hope in the '60s that's hard for young people to imagine today.

Yet conservative evangelicals look at the signs of the times in San Francisco and tell us all signs point straight to hell. We are the mecca of alternative lifestyles, and as the Bay Area goes, so goes the nation. Take, for example, the following paragraph from a recent book by sociologist Alan Wolfe called *Moral Freedom: The Search for Virtue in a World of Choice*. Wolfe surveys the populations in places like Tipton, Iowa, and San Antonio, Texas, and comes to San Francisco only to find the counterpoint to all that is right and true in America.

"The most notorious events of the dreaded 1960s—the Free Speech Movement, violent resistance against the military draft, the rise of the Black Panthers, and the drug and music scene with its ground zero at Haight-Ashbury—happened either in San Francisco or across the bay in Berkeley and Oakland," Wolfe writes. "In the next decade Castro Street would become the main street of gay America, not only a direct confrontation with traditional American morality but also, by the end of the 1970s, a disease that seemed to vindicate the wrath of God. With a climate and scenic beauty too good to be true, San Francisco came to represent a repudiation of the self-discipline and delayed gratification that once constituted the core of both capitalist and Christian virtue. Political and theological conservatives therefore find in San Francisco everything that goes wrong when people believe that they can somehow live without obedience to firm rules of moral authority, handed down by tradition, tested by centuries of experience, and inscribed in the great moral and religious texts of the West."

And you thought we were just having a good time.

Don't get me wrong. Being a child of the '60s was not easy. Divorce is hard on families, and from 1960 to the mid-1980s, the divorce rate tripled and the number of children in one-parent homes doubled. Meanwhile, the percentage of teenage mothers who were unwed jumped from 15 percent to 61 percent. None of those are healthy trends, but it's too easy to blame the bogeymen of the counterculture and '60s permissiveness. Most people who divorce remarry and form new and extended kinship networks. Back in the '50s, pregnant girls got married, but they produced a lot of unhappy marriages and unloved children. Bad marriages are not necessarily better than good single-parent homes.

The leaders of today's Christian Right [in 2003] respond to the 1960s and women's liberation with fire-and-brimstone rhetoric. Pat Robertson, the televangelist and former GOP presidential candidate, proclaimed in a fund-raising letter in the 1990s that feminism was inspiring women to "leave their husbands, kill their children, practice witchcraft, destroy capitalism and become lesbians."

It's hard to decide which part of Robertson's rant is most shocking, especially from a man who claims to be a follower of Jesus, but let's just consider the parts about leaving husbands and destroying capitalism. According to the Bible, Jesus said his true disciple must reject his earthly life to follow the Master—he must "hate his own father and mother and wife and children and brothers and sisters." As for capitalism, the Savior advises the rich man to "sell what you own, and give the money to the poor, and you will have treasure in heaven; then come follow me." So much for capitalism and family values.

So what would Jesus do? What would he find good and bad about the spiritual legacy of the '60s? Search the Bible for clues about the Savior's worries about sex, wine and celebration, and you won't find much. And the Nazarene does not appear to have been a great advocate of traditional religion or traditional families. He inveighed against the accumulation of wealth and talked instead about voluntary simplicity, peace, justice, love and communal living. He was much more interested in saving the world than raising a family. Sound familiar?

Then, and now, we need to watch out for those who use sexual morality and "traditional family values" as smoke screens for selfishness. Sexual ethics and family values are important, but no more important than social ethics. It's time for us to stop buying into the reaction against San Francisco and the '60s, and find our way back to what was best about that time and this place.

| "Since [the 1960s] sexual freedom has proliferated, to the point where many people treat sexual conduct as though it were outside the scope of moral judgment altogether."

Attitudes About Sexuality Have Worsened Since the 1960s

Roger Scruton

Modern Americans have redefined sexual morality so that they can indulge in selfish and destructive sexual behavior without guilt, claims Roger Scruton in the following viewpoint. He believes that this practice first emerged in the 1960s and that it now looms as a serious threat to traditional marriage, upon which rests "the future of society." Roger Scruton is a British businessman, publisher, composer, and author whose credits include more than 30 books, including novels and works on philosophy and on political and cultural commentary.

As you read, consider the following questions:

1. According to the author, what is the fundamental difference between erotic and pornographic materials?

Roger Scruton, "The Moral Birds and Bees: Sex and Marriage, Properly Understood," *National Review*, vol. 55, September 15, 2003. Copyright © 2003 by National Review, Inc., 215 Lexington Avenue, New York, NY 10016. Reproduced by permission.-

2. What is Scruton's perspective on the issue of gay marriage?

3. According to Scruton, how have Americans avoided charges that they are hypocrites when it comes to issues of sexual behavior and morality?

In the England of the Forties, when my parents were courting, terms like "moral," "decent," and "clean living" applied primarily to sexual behavior. Immorality meant sleeping around (and how innocent the word "sleeping" now sounds!); indecency meant unsolicited advances; dirtiness meant whatever put the sexual object before the loving subject. Sexual morality issued from two firm and seemingly immovable premises: that the sexual act is innocent only when sanctified by marriage, and that marriage is a commitment between man and woman, to share their life, fortunes, and family, for better and for worse, until death do them part.

The Sixties put paid to that vision. Since then sexual freedom has proliferated, to the point where many people treat sexual conduct as though it were outside the scope of moral judgment altogether. It really doesn't matter, it is often said, what people do together, provided they freely enjoy it. Sure, pedophilia is wrong. But that is because real consent requires maturity; anything that adults agree to do in private is morally unimpeachable.

Now you can take that line and still believe in marriage, as a uniquely valuable institution with a distinctive place in the scheme of things. You may recognize that children need families, and that families depend on marriage as their binding principle. You may recognize this, and still believe that there is nothing wrong with extra-marital affairs, or intra-marital promiscuity (i.e., orgies, swapping). However, you would also have to believe that marital love can endure without sexual fidelity, that jealousy can be refined away from sexual love and eventually discarded, that marriages can dispense with the

Sex Always Affects Relationships

Our culture tells us that sex need not be taken seriously. A man has an affair and says, "It's nothing personal. It was just sex." College kids practice "hooking up" and say, "It's no big deal. It's just sex." People immerse themselves in pornography and visit strip clubs and say, "Hey, no one was harmed. It's entertainment." The truth is, there is no such thing as sex in a vacuum. Sex always affects relationships, it always affects you, and it always affects your mate. When sexual release is pursued outside of the one-man-one-woman sexual celebration of marriage, then the sacredness of sex is violated. The very heart of this holy union is broken. Sex always has tremendous consequences, either for incredible good or devastating harm.

Tim A. Gardner, "Sex's Mission: Why God Created Sexual Boundaries," Marriage Partnership, *vol. 19, issue 2, Summer 2002.*

kind of existential commitment whereby husband and wife consecrate their lives to each other. You would have to believe that sexual pleasure can be treated as an adjunct to our personal emotions, something that can be tasted in any circumstances and regardless of moral and personal ties. In short you would have to believe that human beings are quite different from those creatures described in our art and literature, for whom sexual desire has taken the form of erotic love and in whom erotic love has generally aspired to marriage.

Discarding Considerations of Sexual Morality

Many people do believe all that. Persuaded by the "research" reports of the Kinsey Institute, by Margaret Mead's fabricated account of sex in Samoa, by the Reich-Fromm-Norman O. Brown liberationist orthodoxy, and by latter-day antinomians [believers that faith alone can bring salvation] like Michel Foucault, they have come to assume that the attempts to distinguish right from wrong in sexual conduct, to separate legitimate from illegitimate sexual relations, and to surround the sexual act itself with an ethic of "pollution and taboo" (as the early anthropologists described it) are both unnecessary and oppressive. The only correct response to the problem posed by human sexuality, they believe, is to recognize that it is not a problem. It is we who choose, in Foucault's idiom to "problematize" the sexual act, and we do so in order to fortify hierarchical and oppressive relations that do us no conceivable good. By discarding sexual morality we free ourselves from our "mind forg'd manacles," [from English poet William Blake] so as to enjoy the harmless pleasures that the spoilsports have for so long taken pleasure in spoiling.

According to the gurus of sexual liberation, the real purpose of sex is not to express love or to generate children (which is another way of expressing love) but to obtain pleasurable sensations. Sexual initiation, according to their view of things, means learning to overcome guilt and shame, to put aside our hesitations, and to enjoy what is described in their literature (which is rapidly becoming the literature of "sex education" in our schools) as "good sex." This can occur with any partner of either sex, and requires no institutional preparation and no social endorsement.

That picture leaves out of consideration the phenomenon that distinguishes us from the other animals, and that also generates the need for a sexual morality, namely desire. Sexual desire is not a desire for sensations. It is a desire for a person: and I mean a person, not his or her body, conceived as an object in the physical world, but the person conceived as an incarnate subject, in whom the light of self-consciousness shines and who confronts me eye to eye and I to I. True desire is also a kind of petition: It demands reciprocity, mutuality, and a shared surrender. It is therefore compromising, jealous, and also threatening. No pursuit of a mere sensation could be compromising, jealous, or threatening in this way. Here lies the distinction between the erotic and the pornographic. Erotic literature is about wanting another person; pornography is about wanting sex.

The interpersonal nature of desire explains why unwanted advances are forbidden by the one to whom they might be addressed, and why they may be experienced as a kind of contamination. It explains why rape is so grave a crime: for rape is an invasion of the victim's freedom, and a dragging of the subject into the world of things. If you describe desire in the terms used by the advocates of liberation, the outrage and pollution of rape become impossible to explain. In fact, just about everything in human sexual behavior becomes impossible to explain. Which is why our society is now so confused about sex. We advocate a neutral, scientific view of sex, as a kind of pleasurable sensation in the private parts (which are rapidly ceasing to be private). And by teaching this view of things to children, we encourage them to a premature and depersonalized interest in their own sexuality. In effect we are endorsing in our heads a view of sex that we know in our hearts to be evil. For at some level we all recognize what our behavior denies, that true "sex education" consists not in permitting pleasure but in forbidding it, by fostering shame. And as our society loses its sense of shame, we begin to fear for our children, becoming hysterical at the thought of all those pedophiles out there—who are really the pedophiles in here, the very people who are eliciting in their children a depersonalized interest in sex.

Morality and Sexual Desire

Traditional morality did not exist to prevent sexual pleasure, but to assist in the growth of sexual desire, as an individualizing bond between people. Shame was the barrier behind which erotic energy accumulated, to the point where it could overflow as desire. Marriage was seen as the institutional expression of desire, rather than a way of restricting or denying it. The first purpose of marriage was to consecrate the union of the partners, to make holy and inviolable what would otherwise be a merely secular contract of cohabitation. Such was the view of marriage that arose in medieval Europe, and that is enshrined in our own literature of love. Nor have other civilizations really disagreed, despite all the varied customs that distinguish them. Islamic, Chinese, Japanese, and Hindu cultures have all concurred in representing sexual desire as an existential bond rather than a fleeting appetite, to be hedged round with shame and hesitation until socially endorsed and ceremonially accepted.

As with all moral sentiments, however, this one concerning the connection between desire and marriage has both a subjective meaning and a social role. Its subjective meaning lies in the exaltation and ennobling of our sexual urges, which are lifted from the realm of appetite and reconstituted as rational commitments. Its social role is to facilitate the sacrifices on which the next generation depends. Marriage is not merely a tie between man and woman; it is the principal forum in which social capital is passed on. By tying sexual fulfillment to the bearing of children, marriage offers a double guarantee of a stable home: the guarantee that comes from erotic love, and the guarantee that comes from the shared love of offspring. It offers children durable affection, a secure territory, moral examples, and moral discipline.

This is all so obvious as barely to deserve mention. As James Q. Wilson has shown, being born to an unmarried mother is by far the most significant factor disposing children to a life of crime—more significant than IQ, race, culture, or education. All of us therefore have a deep and lasting interest in marriage, as the only known way to reproduce the moral order. We have an interest in ensuring that this institution is not trivialized or abused, not reduced to a Disneyland carica-

How Do Religious Beliefs Shape Sexual Behavior?

ture or deprived of its privileged place in the scheme of things—which is, socially speaking, that of a link between generations.

The Nature of Marriage

Marriage in a religious society is a religious event: not a contract between mortals but a vow before the gods. Such a marriage raises the bond between husband and wife from the secular to the sacred sphere, so that whoever breaks the bond commits an act of sacrilege. Civil marriage (as introduced in modern times by the French revolutionaries) has gradually displaced the religious institution, so that marriage is now conducted by the civil authorities, and the change in status is not ontological [concerning the nature of being], like the change from secular to sacred, but legal. In effect marriage has become a contract and has gradually assumed the provisional and temporary character of all merely secular arrangements. This was not the intention of those who invented civil marriage. In taking over and secularizing the institution of marriage the state was hoping to confer fiscal privileges and legal guarantees that would substitute for religious sanctions, and so help to make our commitments durable. It did this from the belief that marriage is vital to the future of society. The state in effect lent its aid to traditional sexual morality, by privileging faithful union between man and wife. And it did so for the very good reason that the future of society depends on this kind of union.

Now, however, the marriage contract is being enlarged to accommodate the permissive morality. Marriage is ceasing to be a sacrificial union of lovers, in which future generations have a stake, and becoming a transitory agreement between people living now. It is from this perspective that we should view the controversy over gay marriage.

This is not really a controversy about the rights, freedoms, and life-chances of homosexuals. It is a controversy about the

61

institution of marriage itself. Can marriage retain its privileged place in our moral thinking when so effectively severed from the process of social reproduction? Already the secularization of marriage has led to easy divorce, serial polygamy, and growing insecurity among children. But marriage in its fundamental meaning is a form of lifelong commitment, in which absent generations have a stake. If marriage can be celebrated between homosexual partners, then it will cease entirely to be anything more than a contract of cohabitation, and the legal and fiscal privileges attached to it will seem both unjustified and dangerous, so many openings to litigation. Lovers' quarrels, exalted into marital disputes, will be endowed with an intransigent bitterness, while transient crushes will be foisted on friends and colleagues as institutional facts. In effect, marriage, as the institution through which society offers its endorsement and support to the raising of children, will have ceased to exist.

The demand to make institutions conform to our desires, rather than our desires to institutions, is one of the great American failings. Thanks to their Puritan heritage, Americans regard hypocrisy as a serious vice, and sin as so lamentable a condition that it must be avoided at all costs. If the only way to avoid sin is to redefine your sins as innocent pastimes, that is what Americans will do. Elsewhere in the world people have learned to extol marriage as the only innocent sexual relation, while nevertheless failing to live up to it. The important thing for normal un-Americans is to keep up appearances, to acknowledge one's own sinfulness, and to be prepared, when the crunch comes, to give up your lover for your spouse. [French author François] La Rochefoucauld famously described hypocrisy as the tribute that vice pays to virtue. In the sexual mores of today's America [in 2003], however, hypocrisy is regarded as the only genuine sin. Which is why, in America, sexual virtue gets no tributes at all.

> *"I had to go to Him when I was lonely.*
> *If I could be faithful to God during*
> *those times, I know I can be faithful to*
> *my husband."*

Religion Promotes Abstinence Until Marriage

Pamela Toussaint

At age 36, abstinence champion (and former Miss Black California) Lakita Garth kissed her long-time boyfriend for the first time—on their wedding day. In the following viewpoint, Garth discusses how her relationship with God enabled her to stay true to her vow of abstinence until marriage. She also encourages other young women to better appreciate the value of sexual purity, both to themselves and their future husbands. In addition, she comments on the ways in which many Christian congregations are struggling to deal with the topic of abstinence outside of marriage.

As you read, consider the following questions:

1. What perspective on sex outside of marriage did Garth's family have?

Pamela Toussaint, "The 36-Year-Old Virgin, How Abstinence Champion Lakita Garth Kept the Faith During the Long Years Before Her Wedding Night—and Beyond," *Today's Christian*, vol. 44, March–April 2006, pp. 20–23. Reproduced by permission of the author.

2. What scriptural passage did Garth embrace at age 17?

3. What term does the author use to describe people of faith who attempt to convert "nonbelieving" people they are dating to Christianity?

Last summer, 36-year-old Lakita Garth kissed her boyfriend of two years for the very first time—at the altar after they said, "I do."

She and her Mr. Right (literally—her husband's name is Jeffrey Wright) met at a health conference through a mutual friend. "I decided to preach to him, and surprisingly, he didn't go away!" laughs Lakita. When Jeff, a successful Christian publisher in Chicago, was able to spar with her considerable knowledge of biblical doctrine, she became even more intrigued. "I wanted a man who could rise to the challenge, someone I could follow," says Lakita, who was a virgin when she married. "I think women don't have high enough standards. Guys want a challenge, to respect you and to see that you're different. As soon as you start putting out, you lose all of that."

A brainy former beauty queen (she was 1995's Miss Black California), Lakita travels the nation telling "the naked truth" about sexual compromise. She has spoken at countless youth functions, been featured on MTV, and was a regular guest on Bill Maher's *Politically Incorrect*. One of her upcoming books on abstinence until marriage is titled *Give Him the Finger*.

Over two decades, Lakita had many opportunities to compromise her moral standard. However, amid the considerable societal pressure most single adults experience, she was able to stay sexually pure. Her training began early.

It Takes a Family

"In my family, if you had sex outside of marriage, someone got married, or someone got shot!" Lakita recalls with a laugh. Born and raised in a rough part of San Bernardino, Califor-

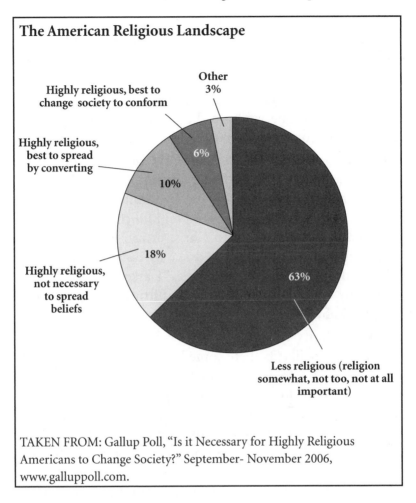

The American Religious Landscape

Other
3%

Highly religious, best to
change society to conform

Highly religious,
best to spread
by converting

6%

10%

18%

63%

Highly religious,
not necessary
to spread
beliefs

Less religious (religion
somewhat, not too, not at all
important)

TAKEN FROM: Gallup Poll, "Is it Necessary for Highly Religious
Americans to Change Society?" September- November 2006,
www.galluppoll.com.

nia, she jokes that her widowed mother slept with two men
every night—Smith and Wesson!

She claims that her "best forms of contraception" were her
four protective brothers. "Growing up, I was taught that rights
and responsibility went hand in hand," she says. "Today,
everyone's demanding rights but no one's talking about responsibility."

The strength of Lakita's extended family played a huge role
in shaping her strong resolve to stay pure, and to make her
life count for Christ. Raised in a then-segregated Alabama, her

uncles and cousins called Dr. Martin Luther King a family friend and frequent guest. "I come from a line of Christians that believe your faith must impact the culture. It has to go farther than your personal relationship with Christ." Self-control, self-discipline, and delayed gratification were staples in Lakita's upbringing, and are the key points she uses when teaching abstinence today [2006].

Despite her strong faith, Lakita did not grow up in the church—she admits that as a child she simply refused to go. "I thought church was where all the hypocrites were," she remembers, though her mother was a faithful churchgoer. Lakita finally made a commitment to Christ at age 17, and says she decided right then that she would live by Isaiah 54:5: "For thy Maker is thine husband". She recalls, "I asked myself, 'If God is really my Husband, then why am I flirting with some guy?' God even knows what I'm thinking!"

Lakita admits there were times when she asked herself other things too, like, Is there something wrong with me 'cause I don't have a boyfriend? Fortunately, her young mind wasn't given much room to explore that question—much of her free time was filled with sports or "cracking the books," and TV was usually off limits in the Garth home. In the long years of single adulthood, Lakita learned how to be comforted by God when she felt alone. "I had to go to Him when I was lonely," she says. "If I could be faithful to God during those times, I know I can be faithful to my husband."

Building Biblical Boundaries

Lakita's ministry is often to teenagers, but she finds Christian adult audiences even more challenging to address on issues of sexual purity. "Christian adults are the most clueless," she notes bluntly. "Many have never heard from the pulpit that sex before marriage is wrong," she says, citing how often singles have come up after her talks and told her so. "The Church needs to start preaching it, and then living it. We need to start equipping folks."

The 2004 Census Bureau's Current Population Survey reports that there are more people in the 30–34 age range who have never been married than there have been since 1970. That means it's likely that there are a greater number of older singles in our churches than we've seen in a long time. But are adult Sunday-school programs, or even church singles ministries, really meeting the needs of older singles? The answers vary, but many church programs seem to be heavy on events, but light on the biblically based teaching relevant to the issues single 30- and 40-somethings face.

Lakita warns single Christian women against "missionary dating," or trying to convert unbelievers while you get emotionally, and too-often physically, entangled. "You can't be the key to his spiritual maturity," she says. Lakita always realized that, because of her strong convictions to be holy, her dating pool would be smaller—which was okay with her. "To be single was to be undistracted in my devotion to God," she says.

When Lakita's relationship with Jeff became serious, they developed boundaries—which she notes many mature singles don't do—and stuck to them. The key to making it work? "The boundaries have to be backed by conviction." She emphasizes that her friendship and business relationship with Jeff was the foundation upon which romantic love blossomed in its proper time.

A Celibate Celebrity

Lakita's testimony of bold sexual purity has garnered much attention, in and out of Christian circles. As a single, she was featured in *Essence* magazine, and last year she shared her just-married bliss with the ladies of ABC's *The View* and readers of *People*. Now, almost a year into married life, she still says, "I'm so glad I waited. Everything is new and exciting. It's like going on a rollercoaster for the very first time!"

Her final word to singles: "Keep your options open." God's perfect mate for you may not look or sound like your "fantasy mate."

> *"Like every human capacity, sexuality is understood as a gift from God and is therefore a legitimate good, provided that it is exercised in faithful acceptance of a divine purpose."*

Religion Encourages Sexuality

Jonathan A. Stein

The following viewpoint asserts that human sexuality is a glorious gift from God that should be treasured, both as a deeply spiritual activity and as a way to experience physical pleasure. According to the author, Judaism teaches that sexual activity is an important path to self-fulfillment, provided that it is explored in a faithful relationship and with an "awareness of God's presence." The author of this viewpoint, Jonathan A. Stein, is a rabbi at Temple Shaaray Tefila in New York City.

As you read, consider the following questions:

1. What is the author's definition of a *Mitzvah*?

2. According to the author, how does Judaism view feelings of lust and sexual fantasies?

Jonathan A. Stein, "Mitzvah: A Liberal Jewish Look at Human Sexuality," *American Sexuality Magazine*, vol. 3, 2004. © National Sexuality Resource Center. Reproduced by permission.

3. Which of the ten proposed elements of liberal Jewish sexual values set forth by the author refer most directly to the importance of sexual pleasure and gratification?

Given the almost 4,000 years of Jewish history since Abraham, "Liberal Judaism," generally understood as one of the attempts to reconcile Jewish tradition and modernity, is a relatively new phenomenon. . . .

Sexuality, on the other hand, is as old as humanity, and is one of the issues that all religions address. Judaism is no exception. From Biblical times until today, Jews have had a lot to say on this subject. Recognizing the importance of trying to articulate an appropriate and relevant approach to sexual behavior in an increasingly sexualized American society, the three liberal Jewish movements . . . have grappled with this subject in recent years.

Traditional Attitude Toward Sexuality

All the movements within Judaism regard appropriate sexual behavior as a *mitzvah*, a sacred human activity potentially imbued with holiness (*kedushah* in Hebrew). Jewish tradition generally views human sexuality as inherently positive and joyous. Like every human capacity, sexuality is understood as a gift from God and is therefore a legitimate good, provided that it is exercised in faithful acceptance of a divine purpose and in reverent awareness of God's presence. Human sexual behavior is understood as both the means to procreation, the fulfillment of the *Torah's* first *mitzvah*, "Be fruitful and multiply. . ." and, in the right context, a way to experience physical delight and pleasure. . . .

In recent decades we have increasingly come to recognize that sexual behavior is always imbued with significance, be that significance physical, moral, emotional, spiritual, or psychological. Human sexual behavior has potential consequences for our self-image and for our relationships with other people.

In our age, irresponsible sexual behavior can too easily lead to disease and death. Judaism teaches that human sexuality reaches its heights in a faithful, covenantal relationship undergirded by a deep emotional commitment, as the ultimate expression of the most intimate of human bonds between two loving people and as a deeply spiritual, not merely physical, activity. If our sexuality is expected to reach its potential for personal fulfillment and moral content, its expression can never be casual.

Because of the many risks that are involved in human sexual behavior, Judaism has historically imposed discipline upon this area of life, setting boundaries and limits that are intended to safeguard both the people involved, and human sexuality itself, from abuse. Judaism has set these limits within the framework of the *mitzvot*. Our tradition's way of thinking about life is distinguished from other religious systems, in part, by the notion of *mitzvah*. In general, the *mitzvot* is a system of ethical and ritual demands based upon the performance of proper behaviors; proper feelings and intentions are not the primary goal. "Our tradition has generally refused to collapse the moral distinction between harboring impious thoughts and feelings and doing irresponsible deeds. One of the marks of moral dignity is the demonstrated capacity to control one's sexual urges." For example, Jewish thought has refused to blur the distinction between (the apparently normal and universal human) feelings of lust and the transformation of lust into specific sexual activity that might be considered immoral. Sexual fantasies, while perhaps not ideal, are not, in and of themselves, considered sinful unless they are acted upon.

Because our tradition is fundamentally oriented toward proper behavior, Judaism has historically deemed it appropriate and even necessary to evaluate human actions. Judaism is not a value free system of thought. Thus sexual conduct, along

Because we treat "sex" as dirty, we associate it with fear and shame, and silence effective sexual education. Public opinion polls consistently demonstrate that Americans want "comprehensive" sexual education—which integrates abstinence education with information on preventing pregnancy and sexually transmitted diseases. At the same time, these polls suggest public confusion about how to achieve sexual literacy. Unfortunately, public opinion is constantly manipulated through misinformation, and sexual conservatives have successfully created moral panics around issues dealing with sexuality.

Our goal is to raise sexual wellness in the United States by promoting sexual literacy. Sexual literacy is an attitude of openness and the desire to learn about sexuality throughout life. Sexually literate people do not mistake packaged sex for genuine sexuality. We need to get back to the basics of better public knowledge and understanding to increase our happiness and enjoyment in life. Sexual literacy is a key to social progress.

Gilbert Herdt, "A Message from NSRC Director Gilbert Herdt," National Sexuality Resource Center, www.nsrc.sfsu.edu.

with all other behaviors, have been subject to critical evaluation and sometimes harsh judgment.

Liberal Jewish Sexual Values

At the same time, Judaism holds out a number of ideals that undergird the foundation of Judaism's understanding of moral sexual behavior. Among these values are the following:

1. *B'tzelem Elohim* ("in the image of God"). This fundamental Jewish idea is first articulated in Genesis 1:27, "And God created Adam in the divine image . . . male

and female . . ." *B'tzelem Elohim* underscores the inherent dignity of every person and requires us to value one's self and one's sexual partner and to be sensitive to his/her needs. This moral principle demands consent and mutuality in sexual relationships.

2. *Emet* ("truth"). Authentic and ethical human relationships should be grounded in both truth and honesty. Both partners in an intimate relationship should strive to communicate lovingly and candidly. However, honesty that is destructive of the relationship may lack the quality of *rachamim*, mercy. In addition, falsehood that manipulates is sinful.

3. *Brivut* ("health"). Jewish tradition teaches us to rejoice in, and to maximize, our physical, emotional, and spiritual health. Adults of all ages and of all physical and mental capabilities can develop expressions of their sexuality that are both responsible and joyful. The abuse of human sexuality can be destructive to our emotional, spiritual, and physical health.

4. *Mishpat* ("justice"). Judaism insists that it is our duty to reach out and care for others, to treat all of those created in the image of God with respect and dignity, to strive to create equality and justice wherever people are treated unfairly, to help meet the needs of the less fortunate, and to engage in *tikkun olam*, the repair of God's creation. We strive to be sensitive to any abuse of power and victimization of other human beings. All forms of sexual harassment, incest, child molestation, and rape violate the value of *mishpat*. Our pursuit of *mishpat* inspires us to eradicate prejudice, inequality, and discrimination based upon gender or sexual orientation.

5. *Mishpachah* ("family"). The family is a cornerstone of human society and of Jewish life as well. The Torah, through the first *mitzvah* (Genesis 1:28), *p'ru u'rvu*, "be

fruitful and multiply," emphasizes the obligation of bringing children into the world through the institution of the family. In our age, the traditional notion of family is in the process of being redefined. Family also has multiple meanings in an age of increasingly complex biotechnology and choice. The importance of family, whether biologically or relationally based, remains the foundation of meaningful human existence.

6. *Tz'niyut* ("modesty"). The classic *Iggeret HaKodesh*, "The Holy Letter," sets forth the Jewish view that The Holy One did not create anything that is not beautiful and potentially good. The human body in itself is never to be considered an object of shame or embarrassment. Instead, ". . . it is the manner and context in which it (i.e., the body) is utilized, the ends to which it is used, which determine condemnation or praise." Our behavior should never reduce the human body to an object. Dress, language, and behavior should reflect respect for modesty and privacy. As Jews we acknowledge and celebrate the differences between public, private, and holy time, as well as the differences between public, private, and holy places.

7. *Brit* ("covenantal relationship"). For sexual expression in human relationships to reach the fullness of its potential, it should be grounded in fidelity and the intention of permanence. This grounding mirrors the historic Jewish ideal of the relationship between God and the people of Israel, with its mutual responsibilities and its assumption of constancy. A sexual relationship is covenantal when it is stable and enduring and includes mutual esteem, trust, and faithfulness.

8. *Simchah* ("joy"). As a powerful force in human life, sexuality has the potential to bring about physical closeness and pleasure, emotional intimacy and communica-

tion, as well as sexual pleasure and orgasm. Judaism teaches that procreation is not the sole purpose of sexual intimacy; it rejoices in the gratification that sexuality can bring to us. Judaism insists that the joy of human sexual activity should be experienced only in healthy and responsible human relationships.

9. *Ahavah* ("love"). The *mitzvah* from Leviticus 19:18, "You shall love your neighbor as yourself; I am Adonai," serves as an essential maxim of all human relationships. The Hebrew term *Ahavah* is used to describe the ideal relationship between God and humanity, as well as between people. The Jewish marriage ceremony speaks of "*Ahavah v'achavah, shalom v'reiyut*," "love and affection, wholeness and friendship" as ideals that undergird holy relationships. For Jews *Ahavah* is not only a feeling or emotion, but more importantly the concrete behaviors we display toward God and our fellow humans. *Ahavah* implies self esteem, the internal conviction that each of us should appear worthy in our own eyes. *Ahavah* forbids any abuse or violence in sexuality or any aspect of human relationships. *Ahavah* should be expressed through behavior that displays care, support, and empathy.

10. *K'dushah* ("holiness"). This value comes from the root meaning of the Hebrew word *K D Sh*, "distinct from all other, unique, set apart for an elevated purpose." The Torah instructs us: "You shall be holy, for I, Adonai your God, am holy" (Leviticus 19:2). Holiness is not a state of being; rather it is a continuing process of human striving for increasingly higher levels of moral living. In a liberal Jewish context, a relationship may attain a measure of *kedushah* when both partners voluntarily set themselves apart exclusively for each other, thereby finding unique emotional, sexual, and spiritual intimacy. . . .

A liberal Jewish approach to human sexuality reflects the self-consciousness of liberal Judaism generally: the attempt to synthesize a grounding in Jewish tradition with an awareness of the insights of modernity. Because sexuality is such a potent force in human life, this endeavor is particularly difficult. It requires a delicate balance that holds most dear the value of human life. That God has entrusted us with this trial should give us the confidence that we can, indeed, meet the challenge with wisdom and good judgment.

Periodical Bibliography

The following articles have been selected to supplement the diverse views presented in this chapter.

Paul R. Abramson and Steven D. Pinkerton — "Sexual Illiteracy: Why Johnny Can't Make Love," *American Sexuality Magazine*, vol. 3, no. 4, 2007, nsrc.sfsu.edu.

Jane Andrews — "My Daughter's Secret," *Today's Christian*, November–December 2004.

Lilian Calles Barger — "What I Learned from *Sex and the City*: Seeking a Spirituality of the Body," *Sojourners*, August 2004.

Rose Marie Berger — "Managing the Erotic Life," *Sojourners*, May–June 2002.

Scott La Counte — "TV Hook Ups: Television Tells Us Over and Over that Sex Is Fun, but That's Only Part of the Story," *Campus Life's Ignite Your Faith*, March–April 2006.

Daniel C. Maguire — "Sex and the Sacred," *Cross Currents*, Fall 2004.

Rosemary Radford Ruether — "Sexual Illiteracy," *Conscience*, Summer 2003.

Alexa Joy Sherman — "Looking for Love? Uh-Uh" *O, The Oprah Magazine*, October 2004.

Tim Stafford — "Let's Talk Sex: What Christian Books on the Topic Are, and Are Not, Communicating," *Christianity Today*, June 2004.

Arthur Waskow — "Eden and Ethics for a Grown-Up Society: How the Song of Songs Can Give Us a New Sexual Ethic for the 21st Century," *Conscience*, Winter 2005.

OPPOSING
VIEWPOINTS®
SERIES

CHAPTER 2

Should Homosexuality Be Condemned on Religious Grounds?

Chapter Preface

In February 2004 more than 4,000 same-sex couples went to city hall in San Francisco, California, and obtained marriage licenses—despite a state ban on gay marriage. Three months after the rush on marriage licenses in San Francisco, which was officially sanctioned and actively encouraged by city mayor Gavin Newsom, hundreds of same-sex couples in Massachusetts began getting married after the U.S. Supreme Court refused to block state legislation giving formal recognition to gay marriage.

These two events triggered an uproar across the nation. In some households and communities, the response was extremely negative: These people saw proof in the events in San Francisco and Massachusetts that the United States had lost its moral bearings and turned its back on God and the Bible. By contrast, the news that some gay American couples were finally securing legal recognition of their unions prompted rejoicing among homosexuals and supportive others who saw these events as just.

The political fallout from these developments came swiftly. During the summer and fall of 2004, eleven states added anti-gay marriage ballot initiatives and referendums to their ballots for the November 2004 election. In every one of these cases, the anti-gay marriage initiative was passed by voters. Moreover, many political observers believe that the intensifying debate over gay marriage motivated conservative voters to go to the polls in such great numbers that they provided the winning margin in President George W. Bush's narrow re-election victory over Democratic nominee John Kerry.

As the following viewpoints indicate, the strong emotions surrounding the issue of gay marriage are unlikely to subside any time soon—and finding common ground on this issue may be difficult. Proponents continue to frame the issue as one of basic fairness and fundamental civil rights, and they increasingly use scripture and the example of Jesus to support their arguments. Opponents, meanwhile, continue to characterize gay marriage as a threat to traditional marriage and an abomination before God, also using scripture in their arguments.

> *"How do you even reason with people who believe that, when something bad happens to [gays], it's God's wrath, but when something bad happens to [straight people], it's God's pop quiz?"*

Religious Opposition to Gay Marriage Is Based on Homophobia

Dan Savage

Many gay and lesbian Americans are convinced that opposition to homosexuality and gay marriage is based primarily on homophobia. In making this argument, they assert that anti-gay rhetoric from religious leaders and organizations is based on selective and dishonest use of scriptural passages. In addition, gay people such as the author of the following viewpoint believe that "faith-based" opposition to gay marriage is hypocritical and damaging to American society. This viewpoint was written by nationally syndicated sex advice columnist Dan Savage in his 2005 book The Commitment. *Savage and his long-time partner have an adopted son.*

Dan Savage, *The Commitment: Love, Sex, Marriage, and My Family.* New York: Dutton, 2005, pp. 147–52, 156–58, 163–66. Copyright © 2005 by Dan Savage. All rights reserved. In the U.S. reproduced by permission of Penguin Group (USA) Inc. In the U.K. reproduced by permission of the author's agent.

As you read, consider the following questions:

1. When Savage claims that Christian conservatives are always "moving the goalposts," what does he mean?
2. Which scriptural passages does Savage cite to illustrate his belief that opponents of homosexuality are dishonest with their use of biblical passages?
3. What point is Savage making when he mentions a 1994 tornado that destroyed a Methodist church in Piedmont, Alabama?

Think about the way many straight people live today. After college, straight men and women move to the big city. Their first orders of business are landing good jobs and finding cool apartments. Then the hunt for sex begins. Most young straights aren't interested in anything serious, so they avoid dating and look for "friends with benefits," or they just "hook up," a.k.a, engage in no-strings-attached sex with anonymous or nearly anonymous partners. Some want to have relationships, but find it hard to make a commitment, so they engage in what's known as "serial monogamy," i.e., they have a series of sexually exclusive, short-term relationships. When they're not having sex, they're going to gyms, drinking, and dancing. And since they don't have kids, these young, hip, urban straight people have lots of disposable income to spend on art, travel, clothes, restaurants, booze and other recreational drugs.

And do you know what all of that hooking up, drinking, and partying used to be called? "The Gay Lifestyle." Substitute "trick" for "hook-up," and "f— buddies" for "friends with benefits," and "unstable relationships" for "serial monogamy," and straight people all over the United States are living the Gay Lifestyle, circa 1978. The only difference is that social conservatives don't condemn straights for being hedonists or attempt to legislate against the straight version of the Gay Lifestyle.

What prompted so many young straights to run off and live like homos? I have a theory: A lot of the early opposition to the gay lifestyle was motivated by envy. Straight people resented gay people for giving themselves permission to do what a lot of straight people wanted to do but couldn't—have fun while you're young, sleep around while you're hot, and live someplace more interesting than the suburbs. When the first post-Stonewall [reference to the famous 1969 clashes between New York City police and patrons of the Stonewall Inn, a gay bar] generation of young straights came to adulthood, they decided they wanted to get in on the action. They could put off having kids and live a little before they settled down. They could be gay, too.

At the same time that young straights were coveting the gay lifestyle, a growing number of gays were coveting the straight lifestyle. While tricks and f— buddies are fun, even hedonism can lose its appeal after a while—particularly after the AIDS crisis drove home the fact that hedonism can have consequences here on earth, not just in some imagined after-life. As individual gays and lesbians matured along with the gay and lesbian civil rights movement, many of us began to realize that we wanted more out of life than tea dances and club nights. . . . Some of us wanted a commitment, a home, maybe some kids. We wanted the Straight Lifestyle.

You would think that after spending three decades arguing that the Gay Lifestyle was a threat to the traditional family because it was so appealingly hedonistic—yes, appealingly, the fear was that straights would be tempted to live like gays, a fear that was not entirely irrational, as it turned out—social conservatives would be delighted when huge numbers of gays and lesbians decided to embrace the Straight Lifestyle and marry. What a victory for traditional family values! So attractive was commitment, so appealing was the prospect of family life, that even gay men and lesbians were embracing them! But unlike all the good-looking straight guys out there who've come to see being lusted after by gay men as a compliment (hello there, Ashton Kutcher), social conservatives refuse to take the compliment. Gay people who want to settle down and live like straights are not an affirmation of the Straight Lifestyle, they insist, just another attack on it.

You would think conservatives would declare victory and take the freakin' compliment.... But no. Instead, social conservatives moved the goalposts. From Anita Bryant through early Jerry Falwell, gay people were a threat because we didn't live like straight people. Now we've got Rick Santorum and late Jerry Falwell running around arguing that gay people are a threat because some of us do live like straight people. It's not on the hedonism charge that the religious right has attempted to move the goalposts. Anti-gay leaders used to argue that homosexuality was so disgusting a perversion that not even animals engaged in it. When researchers admitted that many other animals—from white-tailed deer to pygmy chimpanzees to hooded warblers—engage in homosexual sex acts and, in some instances, form lasting homosexual bonds, anti-gay leaders declared that gay sex was a disgusting perversion *because* animals engaged in it. I suspect that Kathleen Parker, the conservative commentator who accuses gay parents of being "selfish," would condemn me for being a selfish, self-indulgent gay man if I were childless and spending $1,000 a month on, say, male prostitutes in leather hot pants and not on [son] D.J.'s school tuition.

The religious right moves the goalposts so often that they sometimes forget where they were left last.

The religious right still levels the hedonism charge when it suits them. Robert H. Knight, director of the Culture and Family Institute, a conservative Christian group, attempted to pin the blame for skyrocketing housing costs on gays and lesbians in an interview with a Christian news service. "The homosexual lifestyle is about pleasing oneself," Knight said, "not planning for the future, not setting aside money for the kids, not creating a situation where the generations come together. It's about having fun. It's about indulging in whatever desire you want at any given time." With no kids or generations to worry about, we have more money to spend on housing, and drive up home prices.

Or maybe there are multiple sets of anti-gay goalposts on the field. Homosexuals who do set aside money for the kids and bring the generations together are a threat to the American family; homosexuals who don't do those thing are a threat to the American family's home.

And all those straight people living the Gay Lifestyle in cities like New York, Chicago, Boston, San Francisco, Los Angeles, Atlanta, Miami, Seattle, Portland—basically any city with a population over 250,000? Social conservatives don't have much to say about their hedonism. They want to prevent gay people from acting like straight people (by banning same-sex marriage, gay adoptions, civil unions, and domestic partnerships), but there's no concurrent effort to ban straight people from acting like gay people. This hardly seems fair. If we can't get married, at the very least, all the straight people who've moved into gay neighborhoods should have to go back to the 'burbs, where they should be forced to marry young and make babies. If we can't have marriage, can we at least have our neighborhoods, gyms, bars, and lifestyle back?...

If gays living like straights and straights living like gays proves anything, it's that there really is no such thing as "The Gay Lifestyle"—or "The Straight Lifestyle," for that matter. My life proves there's nothing inherently "straight" about making a commitment or starting a family; my brother Billy's life proves there's nothing inherently gay about being urban and childless and having an "understanding." (Although it is fun to accuse Billy of being a bigger fag than I am.) The Straight Lifestyle was only "straight" because gay people weren't allowed to form lasting relationships, or to have families, things we weren't allowed to do because for centuries straight people insisted we were incapable of it. And how did straight people know we couldn't form lasting relationships? Because we didn't form them. And why didn't we? Because discrimination, hatred, and bigotry warped our lives. Until very recently it was illegal for us to have relationships at all. You could be jailed for being openly gay, your family could have you committed, you could be lobotomized. And our relationships—all conducted under the threat of imprisonment, some conducted post-lobotomy—because *these* relationships weren't perfect in every possible way, that imperfection used to justify the very persecution that warped our lives in the first place. . . .

We also weren't sure we were prepared to sacrifice the one thing gay relationships have always had over straight relationships: their quiet dignity.

Before gay marriage became an option, no one expected a same-sex couple to put on a floor show for our families and friends about how much we really, truly loved each other. Straight couples that want their relationships to be taken seriously have always had to jump through the marital hoop, but not gay couples. We couldn't cut to the front of the take-my-relationship-seriously line by getting married two days or two months or two years after we met. Unlike heterosexuals, we had to do the hard work of building a life together in order to be taken seriously, something we did without any legal entanglements or incentives. Without the option of making a spectacle out of our commitment—no vows, no cakes, no rings, no toasts, no limos, no helicopters—we were forced to simply live our commitments. We might not be able to inherit each other's property or make medical decisions in an emergency or collect each other's pensions, but when our relationships were taken seriously it was by virtue of their *duration*, by virtue of the lives we were living, not by virtue of promises we made before the Solid Gold Dancers jumped out of the wedding cake at the reception.

Copyright 2004 by Mike Keefe and CagleCartoons.com. All rights reserved.

My relationship with Terry has always been our own creation, the product of a love some people believe isn't even supposed to exist. With state and church against us, there's a kind of dignity in loving each other anyway. Sometimes when we're introduced as a couple, straight couples will ask how long we've been together. Often they're shocked and delighted to learn that we've been together such a long time. At first I assumed many were shocked because they believed that gay men weren't good at forming stable relationships. But when I've pried—and I tend to pry—I've found myself listening to straight people explain that it means something different to them when a gay couple hangs in there long enough to get into the double digits. We could walk away from each other at any time, but we don't. That can mean only one thing: We really, truly love each other. Married straight couples don't benefit from the same assumption. They might stay together for love or they might stay together because they take their vows seriously, because they do see themselves as "bound together in holy matrimony." They've tied the knot and the bitch in the house is stuck with the bastard on the couch. Divorce is an option, of course, but the awareness of how awful an experience divorce is works to keep some couples together.

Yes, yes: The quiet dignity of a long-term gay relationship isn't worth the stigma of being treated as second-class citizens. The inability of stable, long-term gay couples to tie the knot is discriminatory and unfair. A straight couple could meet and marry in one drunken evening in Las Vegas (how about a constitutional amendment to put a stop to that?), and their relationship has more legal standing than, say, the fifty-one-year relationship of Phyllis Lyon and Del Martin, the first same-sex couple to marry in San Francisco. Then there's Julie and Hillary Goodridge, one of the same-sex couples who successfully sued the state of Massachusetts for the right to marry. They'd been together seventeen years on their wedding day. If a groom in Las Vegas were to be hit by a car leaving the chapel with his bride, his new wife—not his parents, not his siblings—would have the legal right to direct his medical care and, if necessary, pull the plug. But after fifty-one years, Phyllis and Del may not be able to make those end-of-life decisions for each other. Distant cousins who might be hostile to the surviving partner could blow into town and make all the medical decisions. While the arrival of gay marriage will correct this injustice, something else will be lost, something intangible, something that used to be uniquely our own. . . .

It's not just exhaustion that has many American gays and lesbians eyeing the exits, but a real fear of where the Republican right's never-ending campaign against gays and lesbians will ultimately lead. Republicans tell their religious supporters that the existence of gays and lesbians is a threat to the American family, western civilization, and, as influential conservative Christian leader James Dobson claimed, "the survival of the earth." We're godless commies, marauding Visigoths, and global warming all rolled up into one great big mirrored disco ball.

You typically hear one of two things when you press a Dobson supporter about the threat that homosexuality supposedly presents to the planet. "The practice of homosexuality is potentially lethal to the human race," Rev. Rolfe F. Westendorf wrote in *The Northwest Lutheran*, a religious paper. "It is activity which precludes the possibility of procreation. Hence, if everyone were gay, the human race would be finished in fifty years."

The assumption at the base of the "if everyone were gay . . ." argument is a compliment, if a back-handed one. People like Dobson and Westendorf apparently believe that homosexuality is so tempting that pretty soon no one is going to want to be heterosexual. A sane person might think that the long, sordid history of heterosexuality, and the current human population of six billion, is all the evidence we need that human beings will never tire of heterosexual sex, but not Dobson or Westendorf.

And what of all those straight people out there who live near, work beside, and hang out with gays and lesbians for years without ever succumbing to our charms? I've shared an office with a straight guy for eight years, and he's still sleeping with women; according to *New York* magazine, straight women are still finding husbands in Manhattan; and the last time I was in San Francisco, I actually saw a man and a woman making out in a cab. If heterosexuality can thrive in seemingly inhospitable places like my office, Manhattan, and San Francisco, it's a hardier weed than hysterics like Dobson and Westendorf give it credit for being.

The other argument for the threat homosexuality presents to the planet is harder to refute. God hates gays—it's right there in the Bible, along with "God hates shrimp" (Leviticus 11:9–12), "God hates poly-cotton blends" (Leviticus 19:19), "God approves of slavery" (Exodus 21:20–21; Ephesians 6:5–6), "God wants you to pay your taxes without griping about it" (Matthew 22:17–21), and "God approves of killing women and children" (Deuteronomy 2:33–34). God destroyed Sodom and Gomorrah because of the homos, Christian conservatives insist, and if we're not careful we're going to reach some sort of mincing critical mass and God will lose his shit and destroy the planet. God is already mighty annoyed with current levels of gay and lesbian activity on our planet and, according to prominent Christian conservatives, He's trying to let us know. Sitting in a hotel room in Portland, Oregon, I listened to a "Christian leader" on a cable news shoutfest describe the December 26, 2004, earthquake and tsunami that killed a quarter of a million people in Asia as evidence of God's displeasure. With Asians? No, with same-sex marriage. "We can't allow things that offend God to flourish without expecting to incur the wrath of God," she said. She cited gay and lesbian marriages in Canada, San Francisco, and Massachusetts. "Gay marriage offends God deeply," hence the killer wave.

God may be all-knowing and all-powerful, but He is, it seems, a lousy shot, the [nearsighted 1950s cartoon figure] Mr. Magoo of higher powers. Same-sex couples get married in Boston, Toronto, and San Francisco, and a vengeful, nearsighted God triggers an earthquake that slams a killer wave into Indonesia, Thailand, India, and Sri Lanka, killing a quarter of a million people who weren't even invited to the wedding.

But perhaps I'm being unfair to God: Sometimes He does manage to score a direct hit. The 1993 Northridge Earthquake, measuring 6.7 on the Richter scale, scored a direct hit to the San Fernando Valley in Los Angeles, California. Christian conservative leader Pat Robertson was quick to blame the multi-billion-dollar porn industry, which is based in the San Fernando Valley, for an earthquake that took fifty-seven lives and caused billions of dollars in damage. God doesn't like pornography, you see, and while not one of the people who died that day was a porn star, a porn director, or a porn producer, God's message was clear: Stop making dirty movies in the San Fernando Valley or I'll drop some more houses on innocent bystanders.

The funny thing about God and natural disasters, though, is that He sometimes strikes the faithful, too. So we can only wonder about what, exactly, God's message was on March 27, 1994. Less than three months after God slapped the San Fernando Valley with an earthquake, God slammed a tornado into a church in Piedmont, Alabama. The Goshen Methodist Church was completely destroyed during Palm Sunday services. Twenty people were killed and ninety were injured. Among the dead was the four-year-old daughter of the pastor. The same Christian conservatives who pointed to the earthquake that hit Los Angeles as a condemnation of the porn industry, and a decade later claimed that the Asian tsunami was God's vote against same-sex marriage, get awfully quiet when the subject of the Piedmont Palm Sunday Tornado is raised. The best they can do is this: God was testing the faith of His flock.

How do you even reason with people who believe that, when something bad happens to you, it's God's wrath, but when something bad happens to me, it's God's pop quiz?

> *"There are absolutely no grounds for considering homosexual unions to be in any way similar or even remotely analogous to God's plan for marriage and family."*

Religious Opposition to Gay Marriage Is Based on Scripture

The Vatican (Cardinal Joseph Ratzinger)

Since gay marriage and civil unions first emerged as subjects of debate, the Roman Catholic Church has consistently voiced its opposition to the idea. This viewpoint from the Vatican, released in mid-2003 with the formal approval of then-Pope John Paul II, cites a range of scriptural and practical reasons for opposing homosexual unions. This viewpoint was written by Cardinal Joseph Ratzinger, head of the Vatican's Congregation for the Doctrine of Faith. After Pope John Paul II died on April 2, 2005, Ratzinger was elected to succeed him. The papacy of Ratzinger, who took the name Pope Benedict XVI, began on April 19, 2005.

The Vatican (Cardinal Joseph Ratzinger), "Considerations Regarding Proposals to Give Legal Recognition to Unions Between Homosexual Persons," *Congregation for the Doctrine of the Faith*, June 3, 2003. Reproduced by permission.

As you read, consider the following questions:

1. What scriptural passages does the Vatican cite in describing homosexual acts as "a serious depravity"?

2. What impact would homosexual unions have on the "social order," according to the document?

3. What justifications does the Vatican statement use to oppose the legal arguments for recognition of homosexual unions?

In recent years, various questions relating to homosexuality have been addressed with some frequency by Pope John Paul II and by the relevant Dicasteries of the Holy See [Vatican bodies that assist the Pope and his pastoral mission]. Homosexuality is a troubling moral and social phenomenon, even in those countries where it does not present significant legal issues. It gives rise to greater concern in those countries that have granted or intend to grant—legal recognition to homosexual unions, which may include the possibility of adopting children. The present Considerations do not contain new doctrinal elements; they seek rather to reiterate the essential points on this question and provide arguments drawn from reason which could be used by Bishops in preparing more specific interventions, appropriate to the different situations throughout the world, aimed at protecting and promoting the dignity of marriage, the foundation of the family, and the stability of society, of which this institution is a constitutive element. The present Considerations are also intended to give direction to Catholic politicians by indicating the approaches to proposed legislation in this area which would be consistent with Christian conscience. Since this question relates to the natural moral law, the arguments that follow are addressed not only to those who believe in Christ, but to all persons committed to promoting and defending the common good of society.

The Nature of Marriage

The Church's teaching on marriage and on the complementarity of the sexes reiterates a truth that is evident to right reason and recognized as such by all the major cultures of the world. Marriage is not just any relationship between human beings. It was established by the Creator with its own nature, essential properties and purpose. No ideology can erase from the human spirit the certainty that marriage exists solely between a man and a woman, who by mutual personal gift, proper and exclusive to themselves, tend toward the communion of their persons. In this way, they mutually perfect each other, in order to cooperate with God in the procreation and upbringing of new human lives.

The natural truth about marriage was confirmed by the Revelation contained in the biblical accounts of creation, an expression also of the original human wisdom, in which the voice of nature itself is heard. There are three fundamental elements of the Creator's plan for marriage, as narrated in the Book of Genesis.

In the first place, man, the image of God, was created "male and female" (*Gen* 1:27). Men and women are equal as persons and complementary as male and female. Sexuality is something that pertains to the physical-biological realm and has also been raised to a new level—the personal level—where nature and spirit are united.

Marriage is instituted by the Creator as a form of life in which a communion of persons is realized involving the use of the sexual faculty. "That is why a man leaves his father and mother and clings to his wife and they become one flesh" (*Gen* 2:24).

Third, God has willed to give the union of man and woman a special participation in his work of creation. Thus, he blessed the man and the woman with the words "Be fruitful and multiply" (*Gen* 1:28). Therefore, in the Creator's plan, sexual complementarity and fruitfulness belong to the very nature of marriage.

Furthermore, the marital union of man and woman has been elevated by Christ to the dignity of a sacrament. The Church teaches that Christian marriage is an efficacious [effective] sign of the covenant between Christ and the Church (cf. *Eph* 5:32). This Christian meaning of marriage, far from diminishing the profoundly human value of the marital union between man and woman, confirms and strengthens it (cf. *Mt* 19:3–12; *Mk* 10:6–9).

There are absolutely no grounds for considering homosexual unions to be in any way similar or even remotely analogous to God's plan for marriage and family. Marriage is holy, while homosexual acts go against the natural moral law. Homosexual acts "close the sexual act to the gift of life. They do not proceed from a genuine affective and sexual complementarity. Under no circumstances can they be approved."

Sacred Scripture condemns homosexual acts "as a serious depravity . . . (cf. *Rom* 1:24–27; *1 Cor* 6:10; *1 Tim* 1:10). This judgment of Scripture does not of course permit us to conclude that all those who suffer from this anomaly are personally responsible for it, but it does attest to the fact that homosexual acts are intrinsically disordered." This same moral judgment is found in many Christian writers of the first centuries and is unanimously accepted by Catholic Tradition.

Nonetheless, according to the teaching of the Church, men and women with homosexual tendencies "must be accepted with respect, compassion and sensitivity. Every sign of unjust discrimination in their regard should be avoided." They are called, like other Christians, to live the virtue of chastity. The homosexual inclination is however "objectively disordered" and homosexual practices are "sins gravely contrary to chastity."

God's True Design for Marriage

The advocates of same-sex marriage say they believe in God—most seek to invoke His name in their marriages. I say it's time for everyone to stop—stop and ask ourselves: "Was God wrong?" God's definition of marriage is clearly defined in the account of His creation of this basic human relationship in Genesis 2: 22–24:

> And the rib, which the Lord God had taken from man, made he a woman, and brought her unto the man. And Adam said, "This is now bone of my bones, and flesh of my flesh: she shall be called Woman, because she was taken out of Man. Therefore shall a man leave his father and his mother, and shall cleave unto his wife: and they shall be one flesh.

Was God wrong in creating woman and man for each other? Was he wrong when he established marriage as the institution in which children are to be born?

God's design for marriage is the only one that matters. The evidence . . . also proves that God's design for marriage is the only one that works for mankind.

God loves us—all of us. He created mankind in His own image, and designed a beautiful framework in which we can thrive and multiply and experience true fulfillment in every sense of the word. The laws of nature—created and defined by the Creator—are the indisputable evidence that fundamental to mankind's societal existence is the cornerstone of marriage between one man and one woman.

To say otherwise is to declare God wrong.

Rebecca Hagelin, "Was God Wrong?"
WorldNet Daily, *May 18, 2004, www.worldnetdaily.com.*

The Vatican Position on Homosexual Unions

Faced with the fact of homosexual unions, civil authorities adopt different positions. At times they simply tolerate the phenomenon; at other times they advocate legal recognition of such unions, under the pretext of avoiding, with regard to certain rights, discrimination against persons who live with someone of the same sex. In other cases, they favour giving homosexual unions legal equivalence to marriage properly so-called, along with the legal possibility of adopting children.

Where the government's policy is *de facto* [in fact] tolerance and there is no explicit legal recognition of homosexual unions, it is necessary to distinguish carefully the various aspects of the problem. Moral conscience requires that, in every occasion, Christians give witness to the whole moral truth, which is contradicted both by approval of homosexual acts and unjust discrimination against homosexual persons. Therefore, discreet and prudent actions can be effective; these might involve: unmasking the way in which such tolerance might be exploited or used in the service of ideology; stating clearly the immoral nature of these unions; reminding the government of the need to contain the phenomenon within certain limits so as to safeguard public morality and, above all, to avoid exposing young people to erroneous ideas about sexuality and marriage that would deprive them of their necessary defences and contribute to the spread of the phenomenon. Those who would move from tolerance to the legitimization of specific rights for cohabiting homosexual persons need to be reminded that the approval or legalization of evil is something far different from the toleration of evil.

In those situations where homosexual unions have been legally recognized or have been given the legal status and rights belonging to marriage, clear and emphatic opposition is a duty. One must refrain from any kind of formal cooperation in the enactment or application of such gravely unjust laws and, as far as possible, from material cooperation on the level of their application. In this area, everyone can exercise the right to conscientious objection.

Other Arguments Against Homosexual Unions

To understand why it is necessary to oppose legal recognition of homosexual unions, ethical considerations of different orders need to be taken into consideration.

From the order of right reason

The scope of the civil law is certainly more limited than that of the moral law, but civil law cannot contradict right reason without losing its binding force on conscience. Every humanly created law is legitimate insofar as it is consistent with the natural moral law, recognized by right reason, and insofar as it respects the inalienable rights of every person. Laws in favour of homosexual unions are contrary to right reason because they confer legal guarantees, analogous [roughly the same] to those granted to marriage, to unions between persons of the same sex. Given the values at stake in this question, the State could not grant legal standing to such unions without failing in its duty to promote and defend marriage as an institution essential to the common good.

It might be asked how a law can be contrary to the common good if it does not impose any particular kind of behaviour, but simply gives legal recognition to a *de facto* reality which does not seem to cause injustice to anyone. In this area, one needs first to reflect on the difference between homosexual behaviour as a private phenomenon and the same behaviour as a relationship in society, foreseen and approved by the law, to the point where it becomes one of the institutions in the legal structure. This second phenomenon is not only more serious, but also assumes a more wide-reaching and profound influence, and would result in changes to the entire organization of society, contrary to the common good. Civil laws are structuring principles of man's life in society, for good or for ill. They "play a very important and sometimes decisive role in influencing patterns of thought and behaviour." Lifestyles and the underlying presuppositions these express not only externally shape the life of society, but also tend to modify the younger generation's perception and evaluation of forms of behaviour. Legal recognition of homosexual unions would obscure certain basic moral values and cause a devaluation of the institution of marriage.

From the biological and anthropological order

Homosexual unions are totally lacking in the biological and anthropological elements of marriage and family which would be the basis, on the level of reason, for granting them legal recognition. Such unions are not able to contribute in a proper way to the procreation and survival of the human race. The possibility of using recently discovered methods of artificial reproduction, beyond involving a grave lack of respect for human dignity, does nothing to alter this inadequacy.

Homosexual unions are also totally lacking in the conjugal dimension, which represents the human and ordered form of sexuality. Sexual relations are human when and insofar as they express and promote the mutual assistance of the sexes in marriage and are open to the transmission of new life.

As experience has shown, the absence of sexual complementarity in these unions creates obstacles in the normal development of children who would be placed in the care of such persons. They would be deprived of the experience of either fatherhood or motherhood. Allowing children to be adopted by persons living in such unions would actually mean doing violence to these children, in the sense that their condition of dependency would be used to place them in an environment that is not conducive to their full human development. This is gravely immoral and in open contradiction to the principle, recognized also in the United Nations Convention on the Rights of the Child, that the best interests of the child, as the weaker and more vulnerable party, are to be the paramount consideration in every case.

From the social order

Society owes its continued survival to the family, founded on marriage. The inevitable consequence of legal recognition of homosexual unions would be the redefinition of marriage, which would become, in its legal status, an institution devoid of essential reference to factors linked to heterosexuality, for example, procreation and raising children. If, from the legal standpoint, marriage between a man and a woman were to be considered just one possible form of marriage, the concept of marriage would undergo a radical transformation, with grave detriment to the common good. By putting homosexual unions on a legal plane analogous to that of marriage and the family, the State acts arbitrarily and in contradiction with its duties.

The principles of respect and non-discrimination cannot be invoked to support legal recognition of homosexual unions. Differentiating between persons or refusing social recognition or benefits is unacceptable only when it is contrary to justice. The denial of the social and legal status of marriage to forms of cohabitation that are not and cannot be marital is not opposed to justice; on the contrary, justice requires it.

Nor can the principle of the proper autonomy of the individual be reasonably invoked. It is one thing to maintain that individual citizens may freely engage in those activities that interest them and that this falls within the common civil right to freedom; it is something quite different to hold that activities which do not represent a significant or positive contribution to the development of the human person in society can receive specific and categorical legal recognition by the State. Not even in a remote analogous sense do homosexual unions fulfil the purpose for which marriage and family deserve specific categorical recognition. On the contrary, there are good reasons for holding that such unions are harmful to the proper development of human society, especially if their impact on society were to increase.

From the legal order

Because married couples ensure the succession of generations and are therefore eminently within the public interest, civil law grants them institutional recognition. Homosexual unions, on the other hand, do not need specific attention from the legal standpoint since they do not exercise this function for the common good.

Nor is the argument valid according to which legal recognition of homosexual unions is necessary to avoid situations in which cohabiting homosexual persons, simply because they live together, might be deprived of real recognition of their rights as persons and citizens. In reality, they can always make use of the provisions of law—like all citizens from the standpoint of their private autonomy—to protect their rights in matters of common interest. It would be gravely unjust to sacrifice the common good and just laws on the family in order to protect personal goods that can and must be guaranteed in ways that do not harm the body of society. . . .

The Church teaches that respect for homosexual persons cannot lead in any way to approval of homosexual behaviour or to legal recognition of homosexual unions. The common good requires that laws recognize, promote and protect marriage as the basis of the family, the primary unit of society. Legal recognition of homosexual unions or placing them on the same level as marriage would mean not only the approval of deviant behaviour, with the consequence of making it a model in present-day society, but would also obscure basic values which belong to the common inheritance of humanity. The Church cannot fail to defend these values, for the good of men and women and for the good of society itself.

> "The legal issue of marriage should be separated from the church—as it used to be. . . . That should be left to the civil authorities. . . . Then religious couples, heterosexual or same-sex, could approach the church of their choice to seek a religious blessing."

Civil Unions Are an Acceptable Alternative to Gay Marriage

Jim Wallis

Jim Wallis, who is a theologian, bestselling author, and editor in chief of Sojourners *magazine, claims that both opponents and advocates of gay marriage have staked out unreasonable positions. In the following viewpoint, he asserts that both sides refuse to acknowledge the realities that do not support their positions. Wallis urges both sides to drop their unyielding positions and suggests that civil unions might be an acceptable compromise. He also insists that whatever the outcome of the gay marriage debate, Christians have a moral obligation to welcome gays and lesbians into the "community of faith."*

Jim Wallis, *God's Politics: Why the Right Gets It Wrong and the Left Doesn't Get It.* New York: HarperSanFrancisco, 2005, pp. 329–335. Copyright © 2005 by Jim Wallis. All rights reserved. Reproduced by permission of HarperCollins Publishers Inc.

As you read, consider the following questions:

1. How does the author see the current state of marriage and family life in America?

2. What is Wallis's chief criticism of "the Left" regarding its views of the relationship between family and social problems?

3. What is the author's chief criticism of "the Right" regarding its views of the relationship between family and social problems?

Family and "family values." Seldom has the importance of an issue been so great, and seldom has the political manipulation of it been even greater. The bonds of family that tie together our most important and intimate relationships and provide the critical framework for raising the next generation are too important to be reduced to mere symbols in our most partisan and bitter political wars. Yet that is precisely what has happened. Liberals and conservatives, Democrats and Republicans are all responsible for politicizing the questions of family life and thus contributing to the disastrous weakening of this most basic and important institution.

Each of us, across the political spectrum, must now recognize the crisis of family life in America. The statistics are overwhelming and simply demand our attention. Nearly half of all marriages end in divorce, 1.5 million women a year are assaulted by their current or former husbands or boyfriends, one in three children are born outside marriage (even in poor communities), and so on. Family ties and relationships are growing weaker at an alarming pace, with disastrous consequences—especially for children. And the consequences are also clear for poverty; delinquency and crime; sexual promiscuity; education and employment; physical, emotional, and mental health; spiritual well-being; and social pathologies that transmit themselves intergenerationally. Family breakdown figures into a wide variety of other social problems as a primary causal factor.

But as soon as the issues of family breakdown are raised as a public issue, a very ideological debate quickly ensues about the ideal forms of family life that various cultural, religious, or political constituencies wish to advance. What is soon lost are the "facts" of family life and how those facts can be either weakened or strengthened.

Defining "Family"

There have been many forms of family in history, the most common being the extended family where blood relationships across generations create strong webs of social networks and living arrangements, which provide security and stability for all its members, and multiple role models guide the young. The extended family is arguably the most historically common form of family life and is undoubtedly the form of family operative in ancient biblical cultures, both Jewish and Christian. Of course, forms of extended family life, some stronger and some weaker, continue today as most families have networks of broader relations.

But the more modern phenomenon of "the nuclear family" is what most today refer to as family and is the particular result of a modern industrial and consumer society. Because they have fewer resources to draw upon, nuclear families are more subject to many pressures and tensions that can be more easily absorbed in the extended family model. Today [2005], many forces undermine nuclear families and thus imperil family life as most people in our cultures experience it. And today, there are new forms of family life emerging: single-parent families, families that skip a generation with grandparents having the primary child-rearing responsibilities, some same-sex couples rearing children, and cohabiting couples of unmarried heterosexual adults who choose not to marry but may also be raising children (often from previous marriages). And more people are divorced, widowed, and otherwise living alone than ever before. All of these forms of family have their impact on children.

In the fall of 2003, the Massachusetts Supreme Court ruled that gay and lesbian couples in that state are legally entitled to marry, thereby entitling them to the same "legal, financial, and social benefits" as heterosexual couples. That decision set off a great controversy that played a prominent role in the 2004 election debate. The city of San Francisco and other jurisdictions began issuing marriage licenses to same-sex couples, and President Bush announced his support for a constitutional amendment to stop gay marriages—which were then being performed by the thousands in both San Francisco and Massachusetts. The issue was joined. The topic now seems destined to continue as one of the most controversial issues in America for some time to come.

Over the past decade, this "family values" question has become very difficult and has been polarized by both the religious Right and the cultural Left. To move forward, we must simply refuse the false choices offered by both sides.

As we have already noted, the Left has often misdiagnosed the roots of our present social crisis, mostly leaving out the critical dimension of family breakdown as a fundamental component of problems like poverty and violence. These issues are not important just to the religious Right and are not simply bourgeois [materialistic middle-class] concerns. We do need to rebuild strong and healthy two-parent families. And we desperately need more strong male and female role models in both "nuclear" and extended families.

Today, family breakups, broken promises, marital infidelity, bad parenting, child abuse, male domination, violence against women, lack of living family wages, and the choice of material over family values are all combining to make the family norm in America more and more unhealthy. A critical

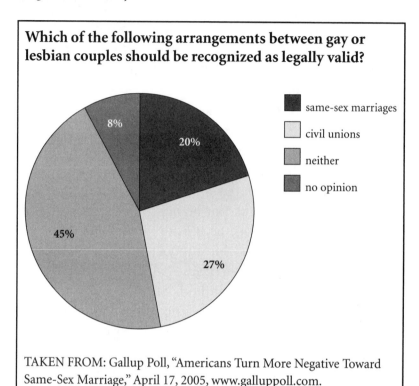

Which of the following arrangements between gay or lesbian couples should be recognized as legally valid?

- same-sex marriages
- civil unions
- neither
- no opinion

20%

8%

27%

45%

TAKEN FROM: Gallup Poll, "Americans Turn More Negative Toward Same-Sex Marriage," April 17, 2005, www.galluppoll.com.

mass of healthy families is absolutely essential to the well-being of any society. That should be clear to us by now, especially in neighborhoods where intact families have all but disappeared.

But the Right has seized upon this agenda and turned it into a mean-spirited crusade. To say gay and lesbian people are responsible for the breakdown of the heterosexual family is simply wrong. That breakdown is causing a great social crisis that affects us all, but it is hardly the fault of gays and lesbians. It has very little to do with them and honestly more to do with heterosexual dysfunction and, yes, "sin." Gay civil and human rights must also be honored, respected, and defended for a society to be good and healthy. It is a question of both justice and compassion. To be both pro-family and pro-gay civil rights could open up some common ground that might take us forward.

Do we really want to deny a gay person's right to be at their loved one's deathbed in a hospital with "family restrictions"? Do we also want to deny that person a voice in the medical treatment of his or her partner? And do we really want all the worldly possessions of a deceased gay person to revert to the family that rejected them thirty years ago, instead of going to their partner of the last twenty years? There are basic issues of fairness here that can be resolved with or without a paradigm shift in our basic definition of marriage.

We can make sure that long-term gay and lesbian partnerships are afforded legitimate legal protections in a pluralistic society no matter what our views on the nature of marriage are. But the question of gay marriage is important; it is a major issue in the religious community, and it is unlikely to be resolved for many years. Many in the churches and the society believe that the long-standing and deeply rooted concept of marriage as being between a man and a woman should not be changed, but same-sex couples should be granted the rights of "civil unions." That's still my own view. For others, only gay marriage fulfills the requirements of equal protection under the law. There are at least three different views being debated in the churches. Most Christians still believe that the sacrament and theology of the church on marriage should not be altered, while others are exploring new rites of church "blessings" for gay and lesbian couples committed to lifelong relationships, and still others want full sacramental inclusion.

The states themselves will ultimately resolve the legal and civil issues through referendums and legislative proceedings. While the issues of gay civil rights are fundamental matters of justice in a democratic society, the legal and ecclesial questions of how to handle the specific marriage issue should not be used to divide the churches, as too many on both the religious Right and religious Left seem eager to do.

In 2004, *Sojourners* published a dialogue between two seminary presidents, Richard Mouw of Fuller Theological

Seminary and Barbara Wheeler of Auburn Theological Seminary. One is more conservative on the issues of homosexuality, the other more liberal. Both are members of the Presbyterian Church USA, which like many other denominations, threatens to divide over the issue. But Mouw and Wheeler believe that would be a mistake.

Richard Mouw says:

> I hope with all my heart that we can avoid the divorce court. I want us to stay together. I do not have a clear sense of what it would take to avoid what many of our fellow Presbyterians apparently are convinced is an inevitable separation. I do sense, however, a strong need to keep talking. The church, some insist, is not some mere voluntary arrangement that we can abandon just because we do not happen to like some of the other people in the group. God calls us to the church, and that means that God requires that we hang in there with each other, even if that goes against our natural inclinations. I agree with that formulation.

> I want with all my heart for this to happen to us in the Presbyterian Church—that we take up our arguments about the issues that divide only after we have knelt and laid our individual and collective burdens of sin at the foot of the cross. Needless to say, if it did happen, I would be surprised. But then, the God whom we worship and serve is nothing if not a God of surprises.

Barbara Wheeler says:

> How's this for a model of the church that we are called to become: "They confessed that they were strangers and foreigners on the earth." What if instead of denying our estrangement, or bemoaning it, we embraced it as a gift from God?

> A church that contains members we think strange, even barbaric, is a healthier setting for us, for our formation as Christians. We like to think that a church of our kind, one

that excludes those who believe incorrectly and behave badly by our lights, would be a better school for goodness than the mixed church we've got. It is not necessarily so. Familiarity and affinity breed bad habits as well as virtues.

The last and most critical reason for all of us Presbyterian strangers to struggle through our disagreements is to show the world that there are alternatives to killing each other over differences. As long as we continue to club the other Presbyterians into submission with constitutional amendments, judicial cases, and economic boycotts, we have no word for a world full of murderous divisions, most of them cloaked in religion.

I believe that the protection of gay civil rights should be a bottom line in the debate, and I try to say that especially in very conservative evangelical circles. On the issues of gay marriage, our *Sojourners* magazine has not taken a "position" but rather an "approach" of civil dialogue between Christians who are committed to justice and compassion but who have different understandings of how best to resolve the question of gay marriage. It is our view that while gay civil rights is a fundamental justice issue, the controversies over gay marriage and the ordination of gay bishops, and so on, should not be seen as "faith breakers." The church is going to have to learn to stay together and talk about these things until we find some resolutions together. Many feel that legal protections can and should be extended to same-sex couples, without necessarily changing our whole definition of marriage. But one could also argue that gay civil marriage is necessary under "equal protection." One could also argue for church blessings of gay unions. I think all those are strong points, even if the churches are unlikely to change their whole theology and sacrament of marriage itself. But this is the good and necessary dialogue. And in the meantime, the church must stand up for gay and lesbian people under attack and must welcome them into the community of faith.

Evangelical leader Tony Campolo offers one proposal. While taking the conservative view that the Bible does not affirm homosexual practice, Campolo denounces homophobia and supports gay civil rights. But he believes that the legal issue of marriage should be separated from the church—as it used to be. Clergy should no longer pronounce marriage blessings "by the authority vested in me by the State of Pennsylvania." That should be left to the civil authorities, and both heterosexual and gay couples should apply to the state for the civil right—be it civil marriage or civil union. Then religious couples, heterosexual or same-sex, could approach the church of their choice to seek a religious blessing. Most churches will only provide marriage ceremonies for the union of a man and a woman. But there are a growing number of local congregations that are open to offering blessings to same-sex couples. It is a solution that might satisfy most, as it preserves the Christian conscience of diverse positions. But for it to work, those congregations that open up to gay couples should not be cut off from their denominations, and neither should more traditional churches be pressured to accept gay marriage by liberal voices in their own denominations.

Conservative Christians should be careful not to draw their primary line in defense of family at the expense of gay couples who want to make a lifelong commitment, instead of standing prophetically against the cultural, moral, and economic forces that are ripping families apart. And liberal Christians should not just argue for gay marriage on the grounds of human rights, but rather should probe more deeply into the theological, biblical, and sacramental issues that are also at stake.

When conservatives seem to suggest that the future of western civilization is at stake in the battle over the legal status of same-sex couples, they seriously overstate the issue. Likewise, when liberals say that resolving the legal issues surrounding gay unions is morally equivalent to the issues of racism, apartheid, and the Holocaust, they make the same mistake. Solutions to the definitional legal issues for gay couples will eventually be found, but this is not the ultimate moral confrontation of our time, as partisans on both sides have tried to make it. It will take many years before we are able to better understand and resolve the many complicated factors surrounding the issue of homosexuality. When we do, we should be able to look back and feel good about the way we conducted our dialogue and our relationships in the process.

"*To offer civil unions as the compromise position is, in effect, to concede that the debate really is about civil rights rather than an aggressive campaign to transform the culture by replacing the traditional family as the cornerstone of social order. . . .*"

Civil Unions Are Not an Acceptable Alternative to Gay Marriage

Peter Wood

In this viewpoint, a conservative scholar argues that civil unions will wreak just as much damage on traditional family structures and American society as gay marriage. Viewpoint author Peter Wood also urges opponents of civil unions to do a better job of explaining how legally recognized unions of same-sex couples constitute a serious threat to future generations of Americans. Wood was a professor of anthropology at Boston University in 2004 when this viewpoint was published. Wood is currently [as of 2007] provost of The King's College in New York City, where he is also professor of anthropology and the humanities.

Peter Wood, "What's So Civil About Civil Unions?" *www.nationalreview.com*, February 17, 2004. Reproduced by permission.

As you read, consider the following questions:

1. What is the basic marriage rule followed by the Miwuyt tribe of aborigines in Australia?

2. According to Wood, the movement to legalize civil unions and gay marriage is not really about gay marriage. What does he think it actually is about?

3. What quote from Michel De Montaigne does the author use to illustrate his belief that compromise is not always wise?

A banner headline in the *Boston Globe* last week [February 2004] was, "Lawmakers Eye Civil Union Provision." The Massachusetts legislature is soon to decide whether to advance a proposed Defense of Marriage Amendment in a compromise form that would allow gay couples civil unions instead of marriage. At issue is whether the amendment proposed by state representative Philip Travis has to be watered down to gain the votes it needs to pass at the constitutional convention that opened last week and resumes in March.

The political temperature is rising in Massachusetts in a drama that may well be replayed in other states as well as in this year's presidential election (including California, if San Francisco's recent exercise in civil disobedience, allowing gay couples to "marry" is any indication). The anti-gay-marriage group Let the People Vote is running advertisements against legislators who support gay marriage. House speaker Thomas Finneran is weighing a decision to defy the Massachusetts Supreme Judicial Court by promoting a bill to prohibit the issuance of same-sex-marriage licenses. And even the *Boston Globe* is finally taking note of critics, such as Princeton University Professor Jeffrey Satinover and Amherst College Professor Hadley Arkes, who have been pressing the point that the establishment of gay marriage will lead the way to further developments such as polygamy.

Where is the sensible moral and political ground on these matters? There is clearly a potential rift between conservatives who oppose both gay marriage *and* civil unions, and those who wish to concentrate on prohibiting gay marriage, more or less conceding on civil unions. The debate over the Federal Marriage Amendment is drawing some conservatives to the position that, in order to build a coalition in support of the amendment, the issue of civil unions should be left to the states. But here in Massachusetts we do not have the option of putting off that day of reckoning. Should the state constitutional convention strike for the compromise? I am edging the other way. I don't think enacting civil-unions laws will prevent the kinds of damage that gay marriage itself would inflict on our society. The unhappy social consequences would be the same either way.

Civil Unions in Scandinavia

Stanley Kurtz's analysis of how gay civil unions in Scandinavian countries have contributed to the decline of heterosexual marriage and the rise of out-of-wedlock births ought to be the foundation of further discussion of these matters. Civil unions in Scandinavia came in the wake of social developments that had already weakened marriage but they added decisive new elements: a final sundering of the connection between "marriage" and having children, and a demoralization of the old institutional supporters of marriage, including many of the churches.

Kurtz has given us a careful prying apart of the many layers of the Scandinavian reality. It is not that, one day, the Scandinavian governments enacted civil-unions laws and the next day heterosexual marriage collapsed. But if we follow Kurtz through his account piece by piece, civil unions emerge as a distinctive force with their own path of social consequences. The Scandinavian countries, in effect, have run an experiment in which they have taken to its logical extreme the idea of the British sociologist Anthony Giddens that modern marriage is simply about elective companionship. If that is all marriage is, why get married? The Swedes, the Danes, and the Norwegians can't seem to think of any compelling reason. The Scandinavian gay civil-unions laws distinguish civil unions from marriage in respect to a handful of rights, such as access to artificial insemination. The Vermont version of civil unions eliminates even those distinctions and offers in effect the definitive declaration by the state that nothing—absolutely *nothing*—distinguishes random sexual coupling from official marriage.

These Scandinavian laws are primarily symbolic since not many Scandinavian gays actually get civil-unionized, but that's not to say that such laws are irrelevant. Culture, as we anthropologists are wont to say, is comprised of symbols. Change the symbols and you change the culture.

The Miwuyt Marriage Rule

While I admire Kurtz's willingness to spend many months sifting through demographic statistics and getting obscure sociological articles translated from Danish and Norwegian, I have been thinking about peoples more remote from traditional Western institutions. On the north coast of Australia in the area known as Arnhem Land live several thousand Australian aborigines. Historically they lacked a collective name for themselves and anthropologists supplied the lack with various terms: the Murngin, the Wulamba, the Miwuyt, and most recently the Yolngu. They made news in the 1970s by successfully suing the Australian government over the appropriation of their land for bauxite mines. Their rich tradition of bark cloth painting has now involved them in the international art market. But they are probably still best known in anthropological circles for their remarkable marriage system.

The basic Miwuyt marriage rule is that a man should marry his mother's mother's brother's daughter's daughter

(MMBDD). When I teach this to my anthropology students, the inevitable first question is, "What if he doesn't have one?" But, of course, he always does. The Miwuyt know perfectly well how to operate their marriage system so that it does what they want it to. Or rather, the older Miwuyt men know how to operate the system—for it turns out that the polygamous Miwuyt elders manage to collect numerous brides. The key is a certain flexibility in classifying relatives as MMBDDs even if they are not literally so. Some men have upwards of ten wives, many of whom are much younger than their husbands. Anthropologists have characterized the system as a kind of gerontocracy.

As far as I know, gay marriage and civil unions aren't anywhere in the Miwuyt scheme of things. The Miwuyt, however, serve as an excellent example of the difference between abstract rules governing marriage ("Marry your MMBDD.") and social realities. And recognition of that difference seems sorely lacking in much of the debate over gay marriage and civil unions.

Gay Marriage as a Civil Right?

When the Massachusetts Supreme Judicial Court decided on November 18 [2003] that the state is obligated to extend the benefits of marriage to gay and lesbian couples, it framed the matter wholly as a set of abstract rights. To a large extent the ensuing debate has pitted defenders of traditional marriage against champions of a new "civil right." The champions of gay marriage, in other words, have immediate access to the powerful ideal and rhetoric of human equality, while the defenders of traditional marriage are equipped mainly with an assortment of religious arguments, appeals to tradition, worries about possible side effects like the rise of polygamy, and a general but vague apprehension that is all too easily caricatured by gay rights proponents as mere prejudice.

Copyright 2003 by Cam Cardow and CagleCartoons.com. All rights reserved.

It is not prejudice at all. That apprehension is an inarticulate insight that gay marriage or civil unions would, in some deep sense, transform marriage for everyone. But exactly how? The Miwuyt, in far-away Arnhem Land, offer a clue. Marriage for the Miwuyt involves complicated reciprocities of clans and generations, organized into a "section" system that has baffled anthropologists for 70 years, along with the prescription of marrying one's MMBDD. But draw back from the precise details and it is plain enough that the system works to benefit the older males and reinforce their dominance over women and younger males.

Unmasking the True Agenda

Likewise, the "civil-rights" issue mainly obscures what gay marriage (and civil unions) would do. The gay-marriage movement isn't really about gay marriage at all. Stable gay and lesbian couples already exist and with only a little inconvenience can arrange for themselves virtually all the "rights" and conveniences that come with marriage. Rather the gay-marriage debate is fundamentally about making homosexual behavior a fully accepted and legitimate part of American life. Gay marriage, like civil unions in Scandinavia, is a symbolic device aimed at transforming this aspect of our culture.

Having to argue this out in the form of a debate on "gay marriage" may be a good thing, in that at least it frames the matter of re-valuing homosexuality as a specific issue. But it is, of course, the battleground and the timing chosen by the Left. Homosexuality has already won cultural approval in the mass media from television shows to the nuptial announcements in the *New York Times,* and in many other contexts, including many churches. The gay-marriage debate is, in that sense, intended as the final battle, after which full normalization of homosexuality will be a matter of cleaning up some details.

And I don't believe conservatives have yet devised a winning defense. Certainly not if we begin with a preemptive surrender on "civil unions." To offer civil unions as the compromise position is, in effect, to concede that the debate really is about civil rights rather than an aggressive campaign to transform the culture by replacing the traditional family as the cornerstone of social order with an amorphous category of sexual liaisons. Eliminate the normative family in the U.S., and who benefits? The Scandinavian situation offers a pretty good clue. Junk the family and its functions will necessarily be transferred to the state: to state day-care centers, welfare bureaucracies, and government agencies. But as long as we continue to debate gay marriage on the grounds preferred by the Left—as a civil-rights issue—the larger assault on the traditional family anchored on the sexual, emotional, and practical complementarity of one man and one woman will remain invisible.

The Perils of Compromise

Conservatives at this juncture seem faced with a choice of strategies: whether to emphasize the recklessness of the proponents of gay marriage in their willingness to jeopardize traditional marriage for what appears to be, at best, a modest social gain; or whether to emphasize the much larger cultural question of the place of homosexuality in our society. The public and political debate, though limited, has been carried on by people like Maggie Gallagher and Stanley Kurtz, almost entirely within the frame of the former position, i.e., "We need to defend marriage." I agree, we do, and Gallagher and Kurtz have made excellent arguments. But I somehow doubt that their arguments are connecting with as a large a public as they hope. Can the other argument ("We should not allow marriage to be used to give full legitimacy to homosexuality.") do better? Can we make both arguments?

Recently, about 4,000 people rallied on the Boston Common in opposition to gay marriage. I talked afterwards to one of the protesters who seemed rather discouraged. He noted that, as he has gone around and talked to people in the state about the issue, he has found many who are diffident [timid]. They have essentially bought the line, "Why should I care? If two gay people get married, how does that hurt me?" In truth, it probably wouldn't. The destructive consequences would fall mainly on the young and the vulnerable who would grow up in a society without the bulwark of traditional marriage protecting them against the excesses of their own immature appetites and the rapacious desire of older males ever eager to expand the zone of sexual permissiveness.

But how do we get that message across? An acquaintance, David Boyajian, who is active in the Massachusetts fight against gay marriage, observed that civil unions are winning support in the polls and from pundits [experts] as the "third way" between gay marriage and outright prohibition. Frame an issue as a three-way choice, he observes, and the middle term almost automatically gets adopted as the moderate, sensible choice. He jests: "Do you favor executing [or] hanging ALL, SOME, or NONE of the people who object to gay marriage?"

All: 23%

Some: 42%

None: 25%

But the Boyajian Principle seems sound. It is not so hard to imagine the poll that will ask, "Do you think polygamy should be prohibited, optional, or mandatory?" But perhaps this game can be turned around. I think we should press for a poll on a question such as, "Should civil unions be available to same-sex couples, organized labor, or Australian marsupials?"

Jesting with calamity has some merit, but it probably won't change the tenor of the debate. As to whether we should cut our losses by accepting civil unions as a step short of gay marriage, I take counsel from Michel De Montaigne. In his essay "On Vain and Cunning Devices," Montaigne warns against the illusion that the middling way is always safest. Rather the middle ground is the natural home of "erroneous opinions" and men who "bring disturbances to the world." I think we are best off facing the harder question squarely. To be generous in spirit and worthy as a culture, do we really need to abandon our commitment to traditional marriage? That's where gay marriage—and civil unions too—will inexorably take us.

Periodical Bibliography

The following articles have been selected to supplement the diverse views presented in this chapter.

Nate Blakeslee — "Family Values," *Texas Monthly*, March 2007.

Bernadette Brooten — "How Our Minds Have Changed: A Historical View of Same-Sex Love," *Conscience*, Spring 2006.

Howard Dean — "Vermont's Lessons on Gay Marriage," *Boston Globe*, May 17, 2004.

Alphonse de Valk — "Same-Sex Marriage: The Battle Against God and Country," *Catholic Insight*, July–August 2006.

Maggie Gallagher — "Banned in Boston: The Coming Conflict Between Same-Sex Marriage and Religious Liberty," *Weekly Standard*, May 15, 2006.

Mary E. Hunt — "A Marriage Proposal: With Gay Marriage Now on the Agenda, It May Be Time to Consider the Institution of Marriage Itself," *Conscience*, Summer 2006.

Christopher Lisotta — "Radical Islam in Your Backyard," *Advocate*, May 23, 2006.

Amy McDougall and Jake Nyberg — "Gay Rights Activists Seek—and Find—Dialogue on (Some) Christian Campuses," *Sojourners*, September–October 2006.

Irene Monroe — "We Who Are Left Behind," *Advocate*, May 9, 2006.

Online NewsHour — "The Battle over Same Sex Marriage," January 2, 2007, www.pbs.org/newshour/bb/law/gay_marriage.

Jonathan Rauch — "A Separate Peace," *Atlantic Monthly*, April 2007.

OPPOSING
VIEWPOINTS®
SERIES

CHAPTER 3

Is a Belief in God Incompatible with Reproductive Rights?

Chapter Preface

On April 18, 2007, the U.S. Supreme Court upheld by a 5–4 vote the first federal law that bans an abortion procedure for all women and all doctors in all states. This court decision upheld the legality and constitutionality of the federal Partial-Birth Abortion Ban Act, which had been mired in Court battles since its passage in 2003. This act banned a rarely used abortion procedure—known as "partial-birth" by abortion foes and "dilation and evacuation" by doctors—that is most often used in pregnancies where the mother's health is judged to be at risk. The U.S. Supreme Court decision overturned the opinions of three lower federal courts that had held that the 2003 act was unconstitutional because it does not provide a "health exception" for pregnant women facing a medical emergency.

Reaction to the U.S. Supreme Court decision was swift and emotional. President George W. Bush spoke for many pro-life organizations and individuals opposed to abortion when he said that the Court's official sanction of the 2003 act "represents a commitment to building a culture of life in America." Pro-choice organizations denounced the decision and echoed the words of dissent from Justice Ruth Bader Ginsburg, who declared that the majority's opinion in the case was "alarming" and could not "be understood as anything other than an effort to chip away a right [to abortion] declared again and again by this Court, and with increasing comprehension of its centrality to women's lives."

Many observers believe that the war of words about the meaning and impact of the federal ban on "partial-birth" abortions will intensify in coming years. Since the 1973 U.S. Supreme Court *Roe v. Wade* decision legalizing abortion in the United States, the abortion issue has polarized political parties, communities, families, and religious organizations. But until relatively recently, *Roe v. Wade* has seemed firmly entrenched in U.S. law. The Supreme Court verdict on the Partial-Birth Abortion Ban Act has shaken that assumption, and both sides of the debate recognize that the next few years are likely to determine the reproductive choices and freedoms available to American women for generations to come. In the following viewpoints, religious men and women from both sides of the abortion debate offer their perspectives of the stakes involved.

> "No woman chooses to be in a situation in which she must consider an abortion, but if that is the decision a woman has to make, I believe firmly that God is with her in that moment."

Christians Should Support Abortion Rights

Reverend Dr. Roselyn Smith-Withers

In the following viewpoint, Baptist minister Roselyn Smith-Withers takes issue with the assumption that most girls and women who decide to have abortions are wracked with guilt afterward. She also explains her deep conviction that God stands with girls and women who have abortions and that pro-choice beliefs are not incompatible with Christian faith. Smith-Withers is a Baptist pastor at the Pavilion of God in Washington, DC, and a member of the Clergy Advisory Committee of the Religious Coalition for Reproductive Choice.

As you read, consider the following questions:

1. According to the author, what is the primary emotion that women feel after an abortion?

Reverend Dr. Roselyn Smith-Withers, "Testimony: Hearing on The Impact of Abortion on Women," *Subcommittee on Science, Technology and Space of the U.S. Senate Committee on Commerce, Science, and Transportation*, March 3, 2004. Reproduced by permission of the author.

2. What is the author's view of Christian denominations and groups that oppose abortion?

3. Why does the author see the consequences of "unintended childbearing" as being so severe?

Thank you for the opportunity to present testimony today on the important issue of the impact of abortion on women. I am Reverend Dr. Roselyn Smith-Withers, Co-Convener of the Clergy Advisory Committee of the Religious Coalition for Reproductive Choice (RCRC) and founder and pastor of The Pavilion of God in Washington D.C. The Religious Coalition for Reproductive Choice (RCRC), founded in 1973, is a national non-profit education and advocacy organization whose members are national bodies from 15 denominations and faith traditions with official positions in support of reproductive choice, including the Episcopal Church, Presbyterian Church (USA), United Church of Christ, United Methodist Church, Unitarian Universalist Association, and Reform and Conservative Judaism.

As an ordained clergyperson and clergy counselor trained in the Religious Coalition model of counseling called All Options Clergy Counseling, I have counseled many women over the last 15 years. Some women have spiritual and religious concerns as they consider their options. My goal in counseling is to help women discern what is right and best for them and their family and to help them come to an understanding that they believe is consistent with their faith and conscience. Women with an unintended or unplanned pregnancy have many different feelings and concerns as they consider their options and after they have decided on a course of action and taken that action. I tell women that there are no easy answers as to what to do, that they must weigh everything involved in this decision—whether they are prepared for parenthood, have the family and financial support they need, are physically and emotionally able to handle the challenges, and many other

A Pro-Choice Message for Jewish Congregations

The Religious Right would like the American public to believe that for one to be religious, one must necessarily also be anti-choice. In reality, many religious leaders worked toward legalizing abortion long before *Roe v. Wade*. During the 1960s, horrified by the injuries and death suffered by women around the country due to illegal, unsafe abortions, they responded as people of faith and conscience must. Reverend Howard Moody and Arlene Carmen organized the first Clergy Consultation Service in New York City, a network of clergy who agreed to help women gain access to safe abortion providers. Similar services soon developed throughout the country.

It was during this time that the progressive movements within Judaism began to advocate for a liberalization of abortion laws. Because Jewish law and tradition allows for abortion, it becomes a matter of religious freedom for American Jews that the secular government not be involved in these personal moral decisions. This one sentence in the United States Constitution, "Congress shall make no law respecting an establishment of religion, or prohibiting the free exercise thereof," has been the foundation of the success of the Jewish community in this country. Without this guarantee, we would be mere guests in this country, as we have been in so many other countries throughout our history, living at the sufferance of the rulers and of our neighbors.

Religious Coalition for Reproductive Choice, "A Sermon for Jewish Congregations," www.rcrc.org/perspectives/sermons/jewish.cfm.

considerations that they know best. I assure them that, while a problem or unintended pregnancy can be devastating, it can also mark the beginning of a more mature life because it requires that they take charge of their own future. In my experience, women become stronger when they are able to make these most personal, morally complex decisions for themselves, without fear and without coercion. No woman chooses to be in a situation in which she must consider an abortion, but if that is the decision a woman has to make, I believe firmly that God is with her in that moment.

The Need for Abortion Rights

Women, both unmarried and married, become pregnant unintentionally for various reasons, including rape and date rape, failed birth control, and lack of information about contraception and sexuality. Many of these women experience a point of low esteem, some even wanting to die. Later, they can come to understand that they can heal and that their faith can be part of that healing.

Research has shown that, while some women may experience sensations of regret, sadness or guilt after an abortion, the overwhelming responses are relief and a feeling of having coped successfully with a difficult situation. Yet the idea persists that women must be guilt-ridden by an abortion and that the decision will haunt them for the rest of their lives. There is an unfounded and unexamined presumption that a woman's conscience guides her not to have an abortion. In my experience as a counselor, I have more often seen women who are guided by their conscience and their sense of responsibility to have an abortion. Because abortion is so stigmatized, they do not express their true feelings and desires. The stigmatization of unplanned pregnancy and abortion can have a coercive effect, causing some women to continue a pregnancy that they prefer to terminate, with lifelong consequences to the woman and her family. Clergy who are trained in the All Options counseling model and who counsel women before and after abortions know that most women believe they have made a responsible decision.

Research studies support what women know in their hearts: that women's emotional responses to legal abortion are largely positive. In 1989, the American Psychological Association (APA) convened a panel of psychologists with extensive experience in this field to review the data. They reported that the studies with the most scientifically rigorous research designs consistently found no trace of "post-abortion syndrome" and furthermore, that no such syndrome was scientifically or medically recognized. The panel concluded that "research with diverse samples, different measures of response, and different times of assessment have come to similar conclusions. The time of greatest distress is likely to be before the abortion. Severe negative reactions after abortions are rare and can best be understood in the framework of coping with normal life stress." Adler pointed out that despite the millions of women who have undergone the procedure since 1973, there has been no accompanying rise in mental illness. "If severe reactions were common, there would be an epidemic of women seeking treatment," she said.

In May 1990, a panel at the American Psychiatric Association conference argued that government restrictions on abortion are far more likely to cause women lasting harm than the procedure itself.

Abortion Is a Moral Choice

To insist, as do groups that oppose abortion in all cases, that women who have an abortion are devastated as a result simplifies the complex nature of each woman's feelings. Even worse, such pronouncements induce and nurture guilt, undermine women's self-respect, and convince women they must be forgiven for a sin, even though abortion might be the most responsible, moral decision.

Religious women who have had abortions have very different feelings from those described by groups that oppose abortion. The book *Abortion, My Choice, God's Grace*, by Anne

Eggebroten, tells the stories of women who have had abortions. Elise Randall, an evangelical Christian and graduate of Wheaton College, who had an unwanted pregnancy, said, "I was filled with resentment and afraid that I might take out my frustrations on the child in ways that would do lasting damage." She and her husband concluded that abortion "was the most responsible alternative for us at this time. The immediate result was an overwhelming sense of relief. Now we were free to deal with the existing problems in our lives instead of being crushed by new ones ... Only God knows what might have been, but I like to think that our decision was ... based on responsibility and discipleship."

Christine Wilson, an active member of a Presbyterian church in suburban Baltimore and attorney, wife and mother of two grown children, became pregnant when she was 16 after having sex for the first time with her boyfriend. At first naïve and then later embarrassed and afraid, she did not tell her parents until she was five months pregnant. Because abortion was illegal at that time, her father took her to England for the abortion. For many years she suffered in silence from guilt and emotional turmoil. Now, she says, "If I had (legal) access in 1969, I know it would not have taken 25 years to attain the peace of mind I have today."

The Campaign to Stigmatize Abortion

The attempt to stigmatize abortion and the women who have had abortions is so far-ranging that it can be considered a campaign. Medical groups calling themselves pro-life, whose purpose is to promote misinformation about abortion, are active and growing; these groups use the professional credibility of doctors to promote a political agenda that includes opposition to emergency contraception and insurance coverage of contraceptives. The campaign is also strong in some Christian denominations, in which groups or caucuses have formed to reverse traditional church policies that support reproductive choice as an act of conscience. The website of the National Organization of Episcopalians for Life (NOEL), for example, which calls itself a "para-church organization within the Anglican tradition," states that the group seeks to change "the growing 'culture of death' in America and the Episcopal Church," in contrast to the resolution adopted by the church's 1994 General Convention that "Human life, therefore, should be initiated only advisedly and in full accord with this understanding of the power to conceive and give birth that is bestowed by God." The National Silent No More Awareness Campaign of NOEL and Priests for Life work to make abortion "unthinkable" while the Episcopal Church, in another statement adopted by its official body, urges there be "special care to see that individual conscience is respected and that the responsibility of individuals to reach informed decisions in this matter is acknowledged and honored."

It is important and heartening to all who care about women's health and lives to know that the consensus in the medical and scientific communities is that most women who have abortions experience little or no psychological harm. The claim that abortion is harmful is not borne out by the scientific literature or by personal experiences of those who counsel women in non-judgmental, supportive modalities such as All Options Clergy Counseling. In fact, scientific data shows that the risk for severe psychological problems after abortion is low and comparable to that of giving birth.

The Negative Impact of Unintended Childbearing

Yet while there is extensive political and media discussion of the supposed harm caused by abortion, the negative effects of unintended childbearing are basically ignored. Yet they have enormous consequences for women, children and families, and society at large. A recent study documents the negative effects of unintended childbearing on both the mother and her family. Women who have had unwanted births sustain lower quality relationship with all of their children, affecting the children's development, self-esteem, personality, educational and occupational attainment, and mental health and future marital relationships. Mothers with unwanted births are substantially more depressed and less happy than mothers with wanted births. The negative effects of unintended and unwanted childbearing persist across the course of life, with mothers with unwanted births having lower quality relationships with their children from late adolescence throughout early adulthood.

In conclusion, as a clergy counselor I believe that women such as Elise Randall and Christine Wilson, whose stories were recounted in Eggebroten's book, deserve respect for making a complex decision. As their experiences indicate, it is not the abortion that can cause harm but the negative attitudes of others, including those who oppose abortion for personal, political, ideological or other reasons. Women who have an unintended pregnancy and decide to have an abortion need our compassion and support. To help women and families, we should work together to reduce unintended pregnancies through increased access to family planning and emergency contraception, comprehensive sexuality education, quality health care, and compassionate counseling.

> *"In ... the fight against abortion, we see displayed with perfect clarity the principle of a single upright truth (that directly killing an unborn child is an evil and a crime) being contested by a rotation of errors. ..."*

Christians Should Not Support Abortion Rights

Todd M. Aglialoro

This viewpoint claims that the pro-choice movement has pursued several strategies to obscure the moral bankruptcy of abortion. The author identifies five specific pro-choice arguments that he sees as irrelevant, cynical, or intellectually dishonest. He asserts, however, that none of these approaches provides convincing arguments that abortion can be a moral choice. The author of this viewpoint is Todd M. Aglialoro, editor of Sophia Institute Press, a publisher of books about Catholicism and the Catholic faith.

As you read, consider the following questions:

1. What impact did the 1980 film *The Silent Scream* have on the abortion debate, according to the author?

Todd M. Aglialoro, " 'Personally Opposed, But . . .' Five Pro-Abortion Dodges," *Crisis Magazine*, vol. 22, April 2004. Copyright © 2004 Crisis Magazine. All rights reserved. Reproduced by permission of *Crisis Magazine* (crisismagazine.com).

2. What is the author's response to Mario Cuomo's arguments?

3. According to the author, which side in the abortion debate most prefers to inject religion into the debate?

In that passage from *Orthodoxy* so familiar that it is almost now cliché, G.K. Chesterton wrote that there are a thousand angles at which a man may fall but only one at which he stands. By this he argued for the unique, enduring character of orthodox Church doctrine, of the one, true, upstanding strand of Right Teaching. Though the same tired heresies may reappear to contest it—mutated, renamed, warmed-over—the old, wild truth remains standing, "reeling but erect."

This well-worn lesson takes on a new freshness, I think, when applied to the culture war. The wild truths that inform Christian ethics—our insistence on a moral universe, on a real human nature with its own teleology, on the transcendent significance of human acts and human relationships—also reel but remain erect in the face of perennial challenges. We are not gods. Moral truth is something we discover, not invent. From the Garden of Eden to the Supreme Court of the United States, we have fought the same battle under different banners.

In what is probably the modern culture battle par excellence, the fight against abortion, we see displayed with perfect clarity the principle of a single upright truth (that directly killing an unborn child is an evil and a crime) being contested by a rotation of errors; taking turns or working in tandem, passing in and out of fashion, each seizing upon the vocabulary, events, and moods of the cultural moment until the next comes along to supplant it.

In some cases cultural developments render one of them obsolete. In the years shortly after *Roe v. Wade* [the 1973 Supreme Court ruling that legalized abortion], abortion debates inevitably featured three words the pro-abortion side considered a trump card: "blob of tissue." This factually empty but sound-bite-perfect catchphrase made a great impact with its implication that the fetus was roughly equivalent to a ball of snot. Which put abortion about on par with picking your nose: bad form, a messy affair that ought to be kept private, but nothing to get overly excited about.

Of course, advances in the study of human embryology, most notably the window to the womb afforded by the sonogram, all but pulled the teeth from the "blob of tissue" canard [misleading story]. The 1980 film *The Silent Scream*, an ultrasound depiction of an abortion at eleven weeks, provided a chilling, graphic look at abortion's inner workings. And today, expectant mothers keep pictures of their "blobs of tissue" on the refrigerator. They make copies and stuff them into Christmas cards.

So that particular line was no longer viable. But it wouldn't be the last. More would follow, and we who are engaged in the culture have surely heard most of them. However, even for those who have heard them all, I think it can be valuable to gather them up and define them; to identify their originators, exemplars, and champions; to understand their appeal; and to consider how to counter them. Let us now look, then, at five (a nice number, though by no means exhaustive) of history's most insidious pro-abortion arguments. . . .

Avoiding the Word "Abortion"

Early last year [2003], in a calculated PR [public relations] move, the National Abortion Rights Action League (NARAL) changed its name to NARAL Pro-Choice America. Amazingly, the new name is even more cumbersome than the old. "NARAL" juts out at the front like "Nokia" before "Sugar Bowl." But this name change was not about streamlining signage and business cards. It was an attempt to deflect notice from the singular object of NARAL's 30-plus years of existence—unlimited access to abortion-on-demand—and toward broader, more high-minded, and less gruesome concepts of gender equality and personal self-determination. The change was timed to coincide with a multimillion-dollar ad campaign depicting the new-and-improved NARAL not so much as an advocate of "abortion rights" as a defender of women's suffrage, satellite TV, and 31 Flavors.

Semantic games have always been part of the battle, of course. No one—*no one*, mind you—is "pro-abortion." Folks are "pro-choice," "pro-reproductive rights," or, slightly more courageously, "pro-abortion rights." In each case, even the last, the emphasis is steered away from the repugnant reality of abortion itself—a sure loser in focus groups time and time again. Whenever we debate abortion or write a letter to the editor, we engage in a struggle for the linguistic high ground. . . .

It can be wearying sometimes, but the counter-strategy is continually to return the debate to where it belongs: the humanity of the unborn child and his right to life. It may also be effective to ask just why abortion is so repugnant to so many.

The "Personally Opposed" Tactic

It is these days thoroughly engrained in abortion discourse, its premises taken for granted and its logic never questioned. It is all too common for a politician, clergyman, or fellow parishioner to claim that he is "personally opposed" to abortion but wouldn't dream of "imposing" that opinion on a public with diverse religious and ethical beliefs—and then sit back, secure in the feeling that his is an ironclad position.

Yet this line about being "personally opposed, but. . ." has only the appearance of reasonableness, acquired through sheer repetition. It also fits perfectly in a society valuing tolerance above all other virtues, conflict-avoidance over tackling unpleasant truths. . . .

In a 1984 speech at the University of Notre Dame titled "Religious Belief and Public Morality," [former governor of New York Mario] Cuomo laid out the basic premises of the "personally opposed, but. . ." line, by way of reconciling his soi-disant [so-called] devout Catholicism with his political support for abortion-on-demand. Skillfully equivocating Catholic teaching on abortion with Catholic teaching on contraception and divorce, as well as a presumed Catholic perspective toward nuclear weapons, he asks, would it be right for a Catholic to make (or sign) laws forbidding divorce? Withholding state funds for contraception? Instituting a unilateral nuclear freeze?

"Should I argue," he asks, "to make my religious value your morality? My rule of conduct your limitation?" Clearly not, is his conclusion. Not, absent a democratic consensus, in a society of varied and sometimes flatly contradictory moral values, a society in which even the collective voice of Christianity is not monolithic on issues but fractured and sectarian. Not, he notes, when "there is no Church teaching that mandates the best political course for making our belief everyone's rule, for spreading this part of our Catholicism."

The forceful case made by Cuomo in his speech (he quotes for support, in places, Michael Novak and even Pope John Paul II; the whole thing makes for fascinating reading) touches only on the context of politics, and mostly from the politician's perspective. But its spirit has crept out of the corridors of power into general society. It is the spirit that makes the saying "If you don't like abortion, don't have one" sound to some ears like a devastating rejoinder. The spirit that gives rise to slogans like "You can't legislate morality," when in fact the morality that protects human rights and thus the common good is the first and best thing worth legislating.

It is also the spirit that animates our next argument.

The True Lesson of Feminism

We insist on informed consent for appendectomies or tooth extractions, but not abortions. As a result, American daughters now coming of age will see only the go-girl aspect of sexual freedom without the whoa-mama revelation of maternal awe.

The latter isn't learned from a textbook, but is experienced during that moment of personal reckoning when one realizes that a fetus is unequivocally a baby. My own transformative thinking—from an unflinching pro-choicer to a disclaiming pro-lifer—came with childbirth and motherhood.

After experiencing the humbling power of creation, it was impossible for me to view abortion as anything but the taking of a life. That is the truer lesson feminism should impart to its little sisters.

Kathleen Parker, "Abortion Chic,"
October 6, 2006, www.townhall.com.

The "Safe, Legal, and Rare" Argument

Among politicians only Bill Clinton could devise a line like this, during his 1996 campaign, brilliantly triangulating liberal abortion-on-demand orthodoxy with Middle America's broad-based distaste for the practice. Ultimately nonsensical yet somehow familiar and reassuring, like a couplet from Dr. Seuss [pen name of Theodor Geisel, author of children's books], this buzz phrase became an instant and enduring success, for two reasons.

First, it validated the internal conflict that the majority of Americans were (and still are) experiencing over the abortion question. They were conscious of a natural sense of revulsion toward abortion itself, yet unwilling for whatever reason to sign on whole-hog with the pro-lifers. Clinton let them know that he felt their pain and that his administration's policy would include a subtle nod toward the general feeling that abortion is a Bad Thing (which ought to be "rare") but would not place restrictions on its availability ("legal") that might send women to back alleys ("safe"). Thus he accomplished an unprecedented political feat: co-opting the vaguely antiabortion sentiments of the masses and mollifying the blood lust of the radical pro-abort left with one simple statement.

"Safe, legal, and rare" also subtly but definitely realigned the terms of the abortion debate. No longer would the question center on whether the aborted fetus was a blob or a baby; no longer would it be necessary to make tortured distinctions between public and private morality. In the first place, safety and legality are conservative concepts, not radical ones. Now the pro-choicer could consider himself a guardian of the status quo—an American tradition, even. In the second place, with the word "rare," the focus shifted away from abortion itself (which we now presumed to be beyond debate) and toward abortion's presumptive root causes. The abortion issue was now *really* a health-care or poverty or education issue—right in the liberal Democrats' wheelhouse.

To be truly pro-life, they could argue, meant to "get over this love affair with the fetus" (as former Surgeon General Jocelyn Elders put it, with typical elegance) and instead pay attention to alleviating the conditions that led women to get abortions in the first place. Implied here, of course, is a kind of false dichotomy: The qualities of justice and mercy are not strained, nor must the interests of the mother and unborn child be necessarily set at odds. But the argument worked by playing into multiple stereotypes: pro-lifers as single-issue fanatics, misogynists, icy-hearted grinches. And it allowed politicians to spin abortion questions into Great Society sermonettes. . . .

Mourning as an Option

In [the 1995 essay] "Our Bodies, Our Souls," [feminist writer Naomi] Wolf called for "a radical shift in the pro-choice movement's rhetoric and consciousness about abortion." Self-deluded by their long practice of dehumanizing the unborn (what she termed "the fetus-is-nothing paradigm of the pro-choice movement"), pro-choicers, she argued, were falling dangerously out of touch with the reality of abortion and women's experiences with it. In order to avert the loss of credibility and thus political influence the abortion movement would suffer thereby (although to her credit, Wolf also cited the need simply "to be faithful to the truth"), she asserted the "need to contextualize the fight to defend abortion rights within a moral framework that admits that the death of a fetus is a real death."

This remarkable essay is liable to engender, in the pro-life observer, the same kind of cognitive dissonance that "safe, legal, and rare" does. In it Wolf admits bluntly that the fetus is a live human being with a certain value and that abortion undoubtedly kills that human being.... She insists that abortion calls for a period of "mourning" and recommends spiritual "mending" ceremonies for women who abort, for vigils outside abortion clinics "commemorating and saying goodbye to the dead."

Yet her practical aim all along is to help other pro-abortionists develop a better strategy for keeping abortion legal.

Wolf avoids adopting conventional pro-life convictions by assigning the significance of the guilt and blood and killing to interior categories only. "If I found myself in circumstances in which I had to make the terrible decision to end this life," she writes, "then that would be between myself and God." For the unhappily pregnant woman, oppressed by patriarchal society and burdened by this fellow-victim inside her womb, abortion is not a social injustice but a personal "failure"; an evil to be borne and acknowledged and slowly atoned for.

For its frank admission (and thus diffusion) of the evidence that abortion kills a living human being, and its conclusion that this evidence doesn't logically require prohibition of abortion—and in fact may even lend its perpetrators a certain tragic nobility—Wolf's argument is a powerful one. Its effects live on in every pro-choice apologist who tries to imbue his position with moral gravity—or, as with our next case, in those who invoke the name of God.

Invoking God in Support of Abortion

Some abortion advocates pick up Wolf's ball and run even farther with it. For some, God might be not merely patiently tolerant, even sympathetic, toward this business of feticide; He may in fact positively endorse it, as the exercise of a mature and devout conscience. For sure, the landscape is dotted with liberal churches and associations of them, each self-defined as "pro-choice." But the biggest and best organizational representation of the religious pro-abortion folk can be found within the Religious Coalition for Reproductive Choice (RCRC), Planned Parenthood's collar-and-chasuble [priestly garment] lackey.

Beginning with the assertion that "most people of faith are pro-choice because of their religious beliefs, not in spite of them," the RCRC attempts to build a case for abortion on both sectarian and interreligious principles. First, compassion: "People who follow Jesus . . . should bring healing and wholeness to those in distress," claims one of the canned sermons the group offers as a resource. This means not forcing them into back alleys for their "healing" abortions and not forbidding them to opt out of the life-threatening ordeal of childbirth. Of course, there's good ol' freedom of conscience, too. Didn't Jesus "emphasize the moral agency of each person"? By this He compels us to believe that a woman's "life, health, and freedom . . . are more important than the potential life in her womb. . . ."

One could spend a great deal of time deconstructing the RCRC—its sophistic mastery of religious vocabulary and concepts; its historical place in the disintegration of American mainline Protestantism; its clever self-positioning as an "equal but opposite" voice in the abortion debate and thus its successful bid to neutralize the natural advantage the pro-life side enjoys in religious contexts.

But I will make just one other observation: *It's the pro-abortion side that always wants to turn this into a religious issue.* Sure, there's no shortage of biblical positivist pro-lifers, but by and large, the pro-life side would like to frame the debate in social-justice terms. One needn't be a Christian to oppose murder or to look at a sonogram. Conversely the pro-abortionists need desperately to paint the issue as a struggle against religious zealotry.

To these folks it is always an effective—and unexpected—rejoinder to ask that they stop talking about God so much.

> *"Jesus's teachings emphasized the religious freedom and moral agency of each person, male or female. Thus I believe that we are called by God to be active in the struggle to preserve and enhance reproductive choice for all people."*

Abortion Can Be Defended on Religious Grounds

Religious Coalition for Reproductive Choice

The Religious Coalition for Reproductive Choice (RCRC) is an organization of national religious organizations from all major religious faiths and traditions. Founded in 1973 to protect the newly won constitutional right to abortion from legal and political challenges, the organization describes itself as "pro-choice, not pro-abortion." It states further: "We do not at any time advocate for abortion but we do advocate for women and men making their own decisions about their reproductive life, in consultation with their faith tradition." The following viewpoint provides a more detailed explanation of the religious underpinnings of the RCRC's position on abortion.

Religious Coalition for Reproductive Choice, "A Sermon for Christian Congregations," *www.rcrc.org*, 2007. Reproduced by permission.

As you read, consider the following questions:

1. According to the author, when did American religious leaders first begin publicly speaking out for abortion rights?

2. Which amendment to the Constitution does the RCRC cite in support of its pro-choice position?

3. How does the RCRC use the example of Jesus's life and teachings to support its pro-choice orientation?

Some time ago, a woman called the Religious Coalition for Reproductive Choice, looking for pastoral counseling. She was 12 weeks pregnant, had a heart condition, was diabetic, and was now on bed rest. The doctor told her that the fetus probably would not make it to term, and there was a strong possibility that she might not, either. She had to make a decision about having an abortion within the week. An abortion any later would be dangerous for her, possibly life-threatening. She came to the Religious Coalition, asking for advice and counseling, and also wanting to know if God would ever forgive her if she "killed the baby."

Many, many women who consider abortion go through the same religious questioning and trauma that this woman experienced, sometimes supported by the love of their partners and family members but often without that support. Stories such as these are doubly tragic not only because of the terrible situations women find themselves in but also because women so often are unable to find comfort in their faith, instead seeing their faith as a source of fear, guilt, and rejection. They are too often unaware that their faith can be a source of comfort, love, compassion, and strength.

The Example of Jesus

The gospel narratives show Jesus as compassionate, forgiving and healing—especially to those in great distress. In the stories from the 5th chapter of Mark we see Jesus even willing to heal under duress, such as when a very ill woman startles him by touching his clothing. According to the laws and practices of the time, Jesus had every reason to ignore her, indeed to stay far away from her. Not only was she a woman, but she had been bleeding for 12 years, making her perpetually unclean. Unable to get control of her own health, she undoubtedly lived at the extreme margins of the society because everyone would be squeamish about having contact with her. Jesus had every right to reject her and rebuke her for what she did, but instead he called her "Daughter" and brought healing to both her body and her spirit. As people who follow Jesus, that's what we should be doing as well—bringing healing and wholeness to those in distress.

The Religious Right would like the American public to believe that to be religious is to be anti-choice. In reality, religious leaders worked toward legalizing abortion for years before *Roe v. Wade*. In the 60s, horrified by the injuries and death suffered by women around the country due to illegal, unsafe abortions, religious leaders responded as people of faith and conscience must. Reverend Howard Moody and Arlene Carmen organized the first Clergy Consultation Service in New York City, a network of clergy who agreed to help women gain access to safe abortion providers. Similar services soon developed throughout the country, and provided thousands of referrals for abortions that were necessary—but illegal—prior to the *Roe* decision.

Many Christians avoid thinking or talking about abortion because it makes them squeamish. But abortion is a topic that we must talk about from time to time, even in the church. And it is a topic that is directly related to freedom, especially religious freedom.

Abortion and Freedom of Religion

All of us, regardless of our denomination, have an interest in protecting the integrity of the First Amendment guarantee of freedom of religion, which says, "Congress shall make no law respecting an establishment of religion, or prohibiting the free exercise thereof." Without this guarantee, we would be in danger of losing a most fundamental human right, living out our faith only with the permission of whoever could gain official sanction for their religious views. And at the center of religious freedom is keeping the government out of personal moral decisions such as terminating a pregnancy.

I want to acknowledge that some Christians believe that life begins at conception and therefore abortion is wrong. They are entitled to that perspective, even though both the biblical basis and the historical basis for it are flimsy. However, having said that they are entitled to that view, we must also acknowledge that millions of Christians—indeed a majority of Protestants in this country—have a different view, believing instead that a fertilized egg is potential life but not actual life. These Christians hold that the life, health, freedom, and moral agency of the pregnant woman are more important than the potential life in her womb. The religious liberty that lies at the bedrock of our free society provides a basis for people with these competing beliefs to live together in one society, assured—we hope—that government will not choose sides.

On January 22, 2004, we observe the 31st anniversary of the landmark Supreme Court decision *Roe v Wade*, which made abortion legal in this country. And as we observe, we celebrate—not because abortion is terrific or wonderful, but because women have the ability to make health care decisions for themselves, and as a result, women's lives are saved.

According to fact sheets from Planned Parenthood and the Center for Reproductive Rights, in the pre-*Roe* year 1965, abortion was so unsafe that 17 percent of all deaths due to pregnancy and childbirth were the result of illegal abortion. It is estimated that illegal abortion led to between 5,000 and 10,000 deaths per year. Today, abortion is 11 times safer than

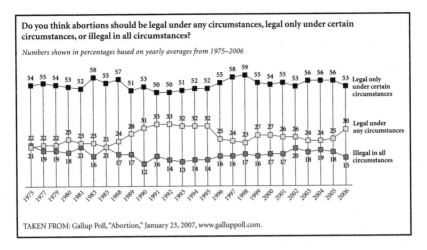

Do you think abortions should be legal under any circumstances, legal only under certain circumstances, or illegal in all circumstances?

Numbers shown in percentages based on yearly averages from 1975–2006

Legal only under certain circumstances

Legal under any circumstances

Illegal in all circumstances

TAKEN FROM: Gallup Poll, "Abortion," January 23, 2007, www.galluppoll.com.

childbirth. Legal abortion has been associated with decreases in both maternal and infant mortality. According to one estimate, 1,500 pregnancy-related deaths were prevented in 1985 alone, because women were able to obtain abortions for difficult pregnancies.

A Step Toward Gender Equality

We also celebrate this anniversary because we embrace the value of full equality for women, and we recognize that true equality can only be fully realized if women have control over their own reproductive lives. Justice Harry Blackmun, who wrote the majority decision in *Roe*, recognized this. He called the decision "a step that had to be taken as we go down the road toward the full emancipation of women."

Unfortunately *Roe v. Wade* came under attack almost from the moment it was decided. Today, 31 years later, *Roe v. Wade* is still under attack and is in real danger of being overturned, or so seriously undermined as to be de facto [in fact] non-existent. Largely due to the efforts of the Religious Right, *Roe v. Wade* has been compromised and diluted and currently hangs by a judicial thread.

The First Amendment guarantee of religious freedom was eroded by the Religious Right's efforts to have its narrow view of when life begins become the law of the land, as in the 1989 Supreme Court case, *Webster v. Reproductive Health Services.* This restrictive abortion law passed in Missouri contained in its preamble the statement that life begins at conception. The Supreme Court allowed that statement to stand in the preamble. Many religious, God-fearing people have a different view. Thus, the *Webster* decision struck at the very heart of the Constitutional guarantee regarding the separation of church and state, as it enshrined into law a religious belief held by some, but by no means all, Americans. Similar attempts by the Religious Right to enshrine in law their idea about the morality of abortion threaten to strip away once and for all our right to believe and practice our own faith.

Threats to Abortion Rights

Roe has been undermined in a host of different ways. In 1992, the Supreme Court decided, in *Planned Parenthood of Southeastern Pennsylvania v. Casey,* that states could impose restrictions on access to abortion, as long as these restrictions did not pose an "undue burden" on women's rights to reproductive freedom. This has opened the floodgates to all kinds of restrictive and even punitive laws, including waiting periods, so-called informed consent laws by which women are made to listen to false and misleading information on abortion that is designed to discourage them from making this choice, and parental consent and parental notification laws, designed to make it extremely difficult for a minor to obtain an abortion.

These are just some of the legal barriers placed on a woman's right to choose. The facts on the ground are in some ways even more disturbing. Today, 87 percent of counties in the United States have no abortion provider at all. And the population of doctors who are willing and trained to perform abortions is aging, with few young doctors being trained to take their places. Religious institutions are taking over public hospitals and HMOs and imposing their religious views on abortion, contraception, and sterilization on the general population whom the hospitals serve, often resulting in an end to these reproductive health services.

The latest, and in some ways most egregious, of the legal challenges to *Roe* is the so-called Partial Birth Abortion Ban, which President [George W.] Bush has signed into law and which is being challenged in the courts. The rhetoric surrounding the debate on this law would have us believe that thousands of women, up to the final moments of pregnancy, are deciding on a whim to terminate their pregnancies and are obtaining abortions. This caricature is nonsense. In fact, 88 percent of abortions occur in the first 12–13 weeks of pregnancy. According to the National Abortion Federation, "Women have access to abortion in the third trimester only in extreme circumstances. Fewer than 2 percent of abortions are performed 21 weeks or after, and they are extremely rare after 26 weeks of pregnancy, generally limited to cases of severe fetal abnormalities or situations when the life or health of the pregnant woman is seriously threatened."

In reality, this legislation arose from a deceptive and corrupt misinformation campaign to inflame the public, confuse the media, criminalize doctors, and strip women of their ability to make medical decisions. Thirty-one years after *Roe v. Wade*, it should be unthinkable that a doctor could be prosecuted as a criminal for performing an abortion procedure, yet that is what would happen under this bill. The absence of a health exception makes it clear that the purpose of this legislation is to undermine the legality of all abortions throughout pregnancy, not to outlaw some procedures.

In 2000, the Supreme Court struck down a similar bill in Nebraska, in the case known as *Stenberg v. Carhart*. The vote was 5–4. This 5–4 vote in *Stenberg* is an ominous sign for *Roe*'s future. The Supreme Court is only one vote away from overturning *Roe*, which would be one of the most radical actions taken in the history of the Court. Without *Roe*, life for

American women would be thrown more than 30 years in reverse, returning them to the days when women could not fully control the number and spacing of their children. Without *Roe*, women will be forced to carry fetuses to full term—even when those fetuses have no brain, no limbs, no heart.

Christian Responsibility

It is our responsibility as Christians who believe that God has given freedom to all of us—including women—to do all in our power to keep *Roe* as the law of the land. You may not choose to have an abortion yourself, but the right of women to obtain an abortion when needed is a right you should care about strongly. We must speak out, we must vote, we must march, picket and protest. We must let our lawmakers know that we will not allow them to take us back to the days of back-alley abortions that threaten women's health and even their very lives.

Abortion is a difficult subject, but it does not arise in a vacuum, and we should never try to think about it in a vacuum. How we think about abortion is inextricably linked to the core values of our faith. Jesus' life among us demonstrated God's compassion and love for every person, as well as God's deep desire for justice and health to prevail. Jesus' teachings emphasized the religious freedom and moral agency of each person, male or female. Thus I believe that we are called by God to be active in the struggle to preserve and enhance reproductive choice for all people. As Christians who strive to follow Jesus, we can and must be both compassionate and pro-choice.

> *"I have always seen the decision not to terminate my pregnancy as the one courageous moment of my life. . . . But lately, I've begun to think it curious that I should have seen not killing my own child as heroic."*

Abortion Should Be Condemned on Religious Grounds

Christine A. Scheller

In this viewpoint, Christine A. Scheller, a religious writer based in southern California who regularly contributes to the evangelical magazine Christianity Today, *recalls her own decisionmaking process when she faced an unplanned pregnancy. Like many other people of faith who oppose abortion, she concludes that the pro-choice movement is based on a materialistic and selfish worldview. She also asserts that abortion is a clear moral wrong and that all of the rhetoric about the importance of "choice" and "reproductive freedom" is really just a disguise for avoiding responsibility for one's actions.*

Christine A. Scheller, "A Laughing Child in Exchange for Sin: What Exactly Does Courage Look Like in an Age of Abortion?" *Christianity Today*, vol. 48, February 2004, pp. 54–57. Reproduced by permission of the author.

As you read, consider the following questions:

1. What is the author's opinion of Kate Michelman, the former president of NARAL Pro-Choice America?
2. How did the author's non-Christian friends respond to her decision to reject abortion?
3. What point is the author making with her use of the scriptural lesson in Psalm 106:13–15?

Exchanging palm trees for stately oaks, I deposited my first-born child at a respected evangelical college this summer. It was an outcome nestled in the farthest reaches of my imagination when I was a pregnant college student 20 years ago. Dark, hopeless thoughts assaulted me throughout that pregnancy. I envisioned myself impoverished and alone or, in rare sunnier moments, as a bohemian heroine of sorts, dragging my grateful child along on my adventures. Still, I decided to keep my biracial baby after the counselor at the home for unwed mothers advised me to put him up for adoption. She said, "You're going to marry a doctor or lawyer someday, and what will his friends think?"

Though I was completely inadequate to the task before me, I didn't ever want my child to think I had given him up for adoption because of the color of his skin. So I determined to become the parent he deserved.

When he was a month old, I was accepted, at my interview, into Moore College of Art and Design in Philadelphia. As the admissions officer urged me never to stop painting, I glimpsed my mother across the street walking the baby in the stroller, and I knew instinctively that I didn't have it in me to both be a mother and pursue a dream in a distant city. These experiences were the seedbed of authentic faith as I began to surrender to love.

A Loving Partner

Not long after, an unlikely prince rode into our lives. I find it nearly impossible to separate the Lord's redemptive work from my husband's powerful love. He didn't make the mess, but he also didn't shrink from entering into the fray the way some men do—those who, despite their own sins, run from the consequences inflicted upon the women and children they leave. His lavish devotion ministered healing year after year until the past largely disappeared. With my mother's help and his support, I earned a bachelor's degree a dozen years after leaving Eastern Mennonite University.

And yet the scar is still there. When my black son explains his white brother to his college dorm mates, it's with the shorthand, "Same mom; different dads." A perfect introduction to another generation's world of woe, and to my family's experience of periodically having my 20-year-old sin laid bare before strangers. The shorthand makes such moments easier for my children as surely as it inflicts a deep lash into both their parents. But as they remind us, they can't pretend our history isn't what it is. In some ways that's a blessing; it forces us out of the shadows.

I have always seen the decision not to terminate my pregnancy as the one courageous moment of my life. I acted with self-abandon for the benefit of the innocent. But lately, I've begun to think it curious that I should have seen not killing my own child as heroic. I could spin a sad tale to make myself look better, but the fact is I failed in my duty to my family, my community, and my Savior. Accepting the consequences of that failure was not heroism. Only in a culture where sex is divorced from meaning and where self-interest trumps everything could such a narrative be produced. Courage would have been to decline that offer of illicit comfort in the first place.

William Blake said of moral insurrectionists, "Mock on, mock on Voltaire, Rousseau; Mock on, mock on: 'tis all in

The Moral Evil of *Roe v. Wade*

"Choice" is a positive concept, and an attractive concept. That's why abortion apologists use it. But the way they use it is a lie and, increasingly, Americans are catching on. There is hope in this development.

There is also hope in the growing popular recognition that the decisions of the Supreme Court can be changed. The assertion of the Supreme Court in its Dred Scott decision (that slaves are not citizens), in time, was changed. The argument of the Court in its "separate-but-equal" *Plessy v. Ferguson* decision, in time, was changed. In each of these cases moral outrage was a decisive factor in the change. So it will be in the case of *Roe v. Wade*.

Increasingly, Americans are recognizing what a moral evil is embodied in *Roe*. Increasingly, they are aware of the vast network of lies that have been spun and fortified to sustain the illusion that abortion is somehow a good, or at least a morally neutral procedure; that it is a standard part of health care and family planning; that it is a proper exercise of a woman's freedom; that it is a solution to intractable social problems. It is, of course, none of these things. What it is, is an unfettered right to take an innocent human life from the mother's womb. All this, more and more Americans are coming to know.

William H. Keeler, Remarks delivered at Basilica of the National Shrine of the Immaculate Conception, reprinted in "The Blood of Innocents Continues to Stain Our Constitution," National Right to Life News, *February 2005.*

vain! You throw the sand against the wind, and the wind blows it back again." Perhaps my foolishness can be traced back to their brood, but I sometimes wonder when the baby boomers who sold me such a wretched bill of goods will at least sweep up the sand.

Maybe they didn't realize they were devouring their own children when they threw off the bonds of traditional morality, but they seem almost oblivious to the depths of their failure. The tired message of women like Kate Michelman, retiring president of NARAL Pro-Choice America, is part of their legacy.

Condemning the NARAL Message

The *New York Times* calls Michelman "one of the grand dames of the reproductive rights debate." She became an abortion activist after her husband abandoned the family when she was pregnant with their fourth child. She was humiliated to discover that she would need his permission and that of an all-male hospital board to obtain a legal abortion. (Imagine allowing a single humiliation to define you.) Michelman is stepping down to care for her ailing husband and their daughter, according to *The Times*. She says, "After nearly 20 years of pouring my heart and soul into this organization I must now put them first." It's an ironic statement from the lips of someone who advocated a utilitarian view of family for so many years.

Michelman says the "true impact" of NARAL can be measured by the "countless women whose lives have been saved and children whose lives have been enriched by our work." Though the lie is smooth as silk, her message is both hopeless and materialistic: hopeless because it says the human spirit cannot overcome devastation (in this case, of unwanted pregnancy), and materialistic because it assigns a family's economic concerns ultimate priority, devaluing the poor—not to mention the unborn—in the process.

My grandmother's experience makes Michelman's (and my own) look like a day at the beach. Abandoned by her husband in the slums of Newark, New Jersey, she raised seven children by herself. Then she raised three of her grandchildren after they too were abandoned. It could be said that this course of action led to an early grave, and she was not a happy woman toward the end of her life. But would any of my cousins or I say one of our parents should have been sacrificed in utero so the others could have had a better life—or so that our grandmother could have? I don't think so. We would all agree, however, that our grandfather should have been wrangled back from his real-estate pursuits in Florida and sentenced to forced labor for their support. My grandmother surrendered her life for her family. That's everyday nobility. It degrades us to sacrifice our children and call it virtue.

Michelman is obviously a resourceful woman. Somehow I think she would have managed to succeed, even with that fourth child. To say others are incapable of the same is nothing more than condescension. And it hardly seems necessary to mention that legalized abortion exponentially reinforces the male tendency toward sexual irresponsibility. The argument that legalizing abortion prevents back-alley abortion tragedies is like saying society ought to dance with the devil because unless we do, those who sleep with him might get torched.

A Worthy Legacy

Two boomer friends of mine provided a sharp contrast to Michelman and her peers. In addition to hosting an annual National Day of Prayer gathering at their expansive home, Jean Peterson ministered to unwed mothers and post-abortive women, while her husband Don counseled repentant substance abusers and financial mismanagers. They went about the work of redeeming a generation of Americans, all the while tethering that work to its source in prayer. They left this world as part of the group of passengers who saved our nation's capital from becoming the third target of terrorists on September 11, 2001. Theirs is the legacy worth emulating.

Oswald Chambers said, "God does not make us holy in the sense of character; he makes us holy in the sense of innocence, and we have to turn that innocence into holy character by a series of moral choices." It was more than I could grasp that Christ would render me innocent of my sin, but then without ever trying, I gained an unexpected moral authority among my non-Christian friends and acquaintances because of the choices I made after I sinned.

Their snickering at my pregnancy and early marriage gradually turned to respect. They would sometimes tell me that when they had moral decisions to make, they would consider what my husband or I might do. Women who had had abortions occasionally reinforced the idea that I had been courageous, particularly white middle class women with education, a group highly represented in abortion statistics.

Women like these identify with my moral failure, and that makes me non-threatening. But they also recognize the hope of redemption and the power of moral absolutes in a world that tells us neither is necessary. That I should gain moral authority after sin is about as mind-boggling as reconciling the sovereignty of God in my son's conception with that same sin. Nonetheless, it is a privileged witness to possess.

Pondering a Different Choice

There is a contrasting Christian witness, though. I write about it only because in our churches we so often talk about abortion as if it were an evil separate from us. But unless we are honest with ourselves about who we are, we cannot hope to turn our own culture on its head, let alone influence the larger one. One story suffices to describe it: My husband and I befriended a young woman years ago when he was a student at Philadelphia Biblical University. I was ripe with my second pregnancy when she abruptly disappeared from our lives. Several months later she reappeared with an explanation. She had had successive sexual relationships with two Bible college students. She had gotten pregnant by a youth leader of a Presbyterian church. He had driven her to the abortion clinic, paid to get rid of the problem—wouldn't even go inside with her—

then dropped her off at her dorm when it was over. She said she thought I would understand, and she knew God would forgive her. She continued serving in various ministries, graduated with her class, and married into a respected Christian family.

I attended her bridal shower, but I didn't "understand" for some time. I was angry at the perceived injustice of others "getting away with" their sin while mine was costly and public. The anger subsided and I began to feel sorry for her as I recalled my exquisite experience of the grace of God: A laughing child in exchange for sin. How incomparable! Those who pile sin on top of sin acquire instead the leanness of soul described in Psalm 106:13–15: "They soon forgot his works; they did not wait for his counsel, but lusted exceedingly in the wilderness, and tested God in the desert. And he gave them their request, but sent leanness into their soul." Think of David during his long-delayed repentance. I've heard it said that he never regained his moral authority because of his shame, thereby sowing destruction into his kingdom. I wonder how many Christians, because of shame over some act of duplicitous cover-up, are unable to speak with voices of moral certitude. And what is it costing our nation?

Using Failure to Strengthen Faith

There was an important distinction between me and the Bible college coed who had an abortion. When I discovered I was pregnant, I knew that, in spite their devastation at my betrayal, my parents loved me more than they cared what the neighbors thought. She didn't know any such thing; her Christian parents had scorned girls like me.

So if there was any hint of courage in my decision to abandon myself to motherhood prematurely, it was this: the exchange of the therapeutic shadow of a faith for an orthodox one. Or, as Puritan writer William Gurnall says in *The Christian in Complete Armour*, "God can, in fact, use his saints' failures to strengthen their faith, which, like a tree, stands stronger for the shaking. . . And here is all the devil gets: Instead of destroying the saint's faith, he is the means of refining it, thereby making it stronger and more precious."

How the next generation needs us to snatch back the victory from the enemy with faith that first rises valiantly from the failures of our own and then speaks with a sturdy voice. The narrative we transfer has to include our own repentance and it has to be more penetrating than the one I heard.

Twenty years of crafting a new narrative for my children came to a close on the lawn of a college much like the one where the sensate tale failed me. So hugging my son one last time before flying back to the palm trees, I left him with an exhortation: "Don't defraud anyone sexually, for God is the defender of all such."

Wryly he answered, "Can't a girl defraud me?"

"Yes," I conceded with a sigh, resisting the temptation to add, "But remember your mother, remember the pain she caused you, and let the wind take the sand far from you."

Periodical Bibliography

The following articles have been selected to supplement the diverse views presented in this chapter.

Erika Bachiochi	"How Abortion Hurts Women: The Hard Proof," *Crisis Magazine Online*, June 2005, www.crisismagazine.com.
Judith A. Baer	"Women's Rights and the Constitution," *Social Science Journal*, vol. 44, no. 1, 2007.
Sam Brownback	"Abortion and the Conscience of the Nation Revisited," *Human Life Review*, Summer 2004.
E.J. Dionne	"A Thorn in Both Their Sides," *Sojourners*, June 2006.
Howard Fineman	"The GOP's Abortion Anxiety," *Newsweek*, March 20, 2006.
Josh Harkinson	"Born-Again Abortion Clinics," *Mother Jones*, March–April 2007.
Charles I. Lugosi	"When Abortion Was a Crime: A Historical Perspective," *University of Detroit Mercy Law Review*, Winter 2006.
Mary Ellen Neill	"The Continued Betrayal of Women: U.S. Culture Exhorts Them to Be Sexual, but Not Pregnant," *National Catholic Reporter*, April 21, 2006.
Cristina Paige	"Contraception Saves Money and Marriages," *AlterNet*, December 21, 2006, www.alternet.org.
Lois M. Powell and Ann L. Hansen	"The Reality of Legalized Abortion: People of Faith Support a Woman's Right to Choose," *United Church of Christ Online*, www.uccc.org.
Donna Schaper	"My Choice," *Tikkun*, July–August 2006.

OPPOSING VIEWPOINTS® SERIES

CHAPTER 4

What Issues of Sexuality Surround Religious Leaders?

Chapter Preface

In the last two decades of the twentieth century, the sexuality of religious leaders has emerged as a leading topic of discussion and study in religious denominations within a wide range of faiths. Various religious institutions and groups are devoting greater attention to the ways in which the sexual activities and beliefs of clergy influence the health and vitality of congregations. This increased attention is due in part to high-profile sex scandals that have profoundly embarrassed some religious groups. But the heightened attention also stems in part from growing recognition of the terrible damage that clergy sexual misconduct can do to churches—and in part from heightened awareness of the unique social pressures that pastors, rabbis, and other church leaders deal with on a regular basis.

This increased attention to clergy sexuality has turned up some interesting data. A 2005 "sex and the church" survey conducted by Christianity Today International, for example, revealed that pastors are much more likely to be happily married than laity, in some measure because of higher levels of satisfaction with their sex lives. But seven out of ten pastors also reported that they had been propositioned to engage in romantic or sexual activity by non-spouses at some point in their career—and nearly one in ten stated that they had to ward off these advances from parishioners or other community members on a regular (more than once a year) basis. Finally, 5 percent of the pastors in the survey confessed to having committed adultery at least once since becoming a pastor.

Other issues of clergy sexuality have also assumed new prominence in recent years. After enduring an onslaught of sex-abuse scandals involving priests, members of the Catholic Church are debating the Vatican's ban on married or female priests with ever greater vigor. Leaders and members of the

Catholic faith are also joining Anglican, Protestant, Jewish, and other religious denominations in spirited debates about the moral and scriptural appropriateness of placing women and homosexuals in church leadership positions. The following viewpoints provide contrasting assessments of some of these issues, but they all reflect a conviction that these issues will dictate the future of U.S. religion and religious faith for generations to come.

> *"The truth of the nonultimacy of sex, family, and worldly relationship can and should be proclaimed through words, but it will be believed only when people can see it."*

Rules of Celibacy Should Be Supported

Robert Barron

In the following viewpoint, Father Robert Barron strongly affirms traditional Catholic rules of celibacy for members of the priesthood. A professor of systematic theology at Mundelein Seminary outside Chicago, Illinois, Barron believes that priestly celibacy is a vital tool in showing Catholic people of faith about the "transcendant form of love" that awaits believers in heaven. He claims that the example of celibate priests is often an inspiration to Catholic worshippers.

As you read, consider the following questions:

1. What does the author think about arguments that sexual contact within marriage would render priests "impure"?
2. What parallels does Barron draw between the sacrament of the Eucharist and priestly celibacy?

Robert Barron, "Why Celibacy Makes Sense," *Commonweal*, August 12, 2005, pp. 17–19. Copyright © 2005 Commonweal Publishing Co., Inc. Reproduced by permission of Commonweal Foundation.

3. Does Barron admit to any personal struggles with celibacy?

There is a very bad argument for celibacy that has appeared from time to time throughout the tradition and is, even today [2005], defended by some. It runs something like this: married life is morally and spiritually suspect; priests, as religious leaders, should be spiritual athletes above reproach; therefore, priests shouldn't be married. I love Augustine [an early Catholic saint], but it's hard to deny that this argument finds support in some of his more unfortunate reflections on sexuality (original sin as a sexually transmitted disease; sex even within marriage is venially sinful; the birth of a baby associated with excretion, etc.). I ran across a recent book in which the author presented a version of this justification, appealing to the purity codes in the book of Leviticus. His implication was that any sort of sexual contact, even within marriage, would render a minister at the altar impure. This approach to the question is not just silly but dangerous, for it rests on assumptions that are repugnant to good Christian metaphysics. . . .

According to the biblical narratives, when God wanted to make a certain truth vividly known to his people, he would, at times, choose a prophet and command him to act out that truth. So, he told Hosea to marry the unfaithful Gomer in order to sacramentalize God's fidelity to wavering Israel. In *The Grammar of Assent*, John Henry Newman reminds us that truth is brought home to the mind when it is represented, not through abstractions, but through something particular, colorful, imaginable. Thus, the truth of the nonultimacy of sex, family, and worldly relationship can and should be proclaimed through words, but it will be believed only when people can see it.

This is why, the church is convinced, God chooses certain people to be celibate in order to witness to a transcendent form of love, the way that we will love in heaven. In God's

Celibacy Symbolizes the Priest's Special Bond with Christ

Above all, the priesthood in the New Testament is a participation in the Priesthood of Our Lord Jesus Christ, the High Priest. And, therefore, the priest has a mysterious and special bond with Christ, in whose name and by whose power he offers the bloodless sacrifice (*in persona Christi*). The most profound reason for priestly celibacy comes from this supernatural bond with the Savior.

Luiz Sérgio Solimeo. "Tracing the Glorious Origins of Celibacy,"
American Society for the Defense of Tradition, Family, and Property,
www.tfp.org.

realm, we will experience a communion (bodily as well as spiritual) more intense than even the most intense forms of communion here below, and celibates make this truth viscerally real for us now. Just as belief in the Real Presence in the Eucharist fades when unaccompanied by devotional practice, so the belief in the impermanence of created love becomes attenuated in the absence of living embodiments of it. Though one can present practical reasons for it, I believe that celibacy only finally makes sense in this eschatological context.

The Priesthood as a Eucharistic Vocation

I realize that you might be following the argument to this point and still feel compelled to ask, "Yes, granted that celibacy is a good thing for the church, but why must all priests be celibate?" The medievals distinguished between arguments from necessity and arguments from "fittingness." I can offer only the latter kind of argument, for even its most ardent defenders admit that celibacy is not essential to the priesthood. After all, married priests have been, at various times and for various reasons, accepted from the beginning of the church to the present day. The appropriateness of linking priesthood and celibacy comes, I think, from the priest's identity as a eucharistic person. All that a priest is radiates from his unique capacity, acting in the person of Christ, to transform the eucharistic elements into the body and blood of Jesus. As the center of a rose window anchors and orders all the other elements in the design, so the eucharistic act of the priest grounds and animates everything else that he does, rendering qualitatively distinctive his way of leading, sanctifying, and teaching. The Eucharist is the eschatological act par excellence, for as Paul says, "every time we eat this bread and drink this cup, we proclaim the death of the Lord until he comes." To proclaim the Paschal Mystery [Jesus Christ's mission of salvation] through the Eucharist is to make present that event by which the new world is opened up to us. It is to make vividly real the transcendent dimension that effectively relativizes (without denying) all the goods of this passing world. And it is therefore fitting that the one who is so intimately conditioned by and related to the Eucharist should be in his form of life an eschatological person.

For years, Andrew Greeley has been arguing—quite rightly—that the priest is fascinating and that a large part of the fascination comes from celibacy. The compelling quality of the priest is not a matter of superficial celebrity or charm; that gets us nowhere. It is something much stranger, deeper, more mystical. It is the fascination for another world, for that mysterious dimension of existence hinted at by the universe here below and revealed to us in the breaking of the bread. I for one am glad that such eschatologically fascinating persons are not simply in monasteries, cloistered convents, and hermits' cells, but in parishes, on the streets, in the pulpits, moving among the people of God.

Struggling with Celibacy

There are, I realize, a couple of major problems with offering arguments for celibacy. First, it can make everything seem so pat, rational, and resolved. I've been a priest for nearly twenty years, and I can assure you that the living of celibacy has been anything but that. As I've gone through different seasons of my life as a priest, I've struggled mightily with celibacy, precisely because the tension between the goodness and ephemerality of creation that I spoke of earlier is no abstraction; rather it runs right through my body. The second problem is that reason goes only so far. As Thomas More said to his daughter in *A Man for All Seasons*, as he was trying to explain why he was being so stubborn: "Finally, Meg, it's not a matter of reason; finally, it's a matter of love."

People in love do strange things: they pledge eternal fidelity; they write poetry and songs; they defy their families and change their life plans; sometimes they go to their deaths. They tend to be over the top, irrational, confounding to the reasonable people around them. Though we can make a case for it—as I have tried to do—celibacy is finally inexplicable, unnatural, fascinating, for it is a form of life adopted by people in love with Jesus Christ.

> *"No doubt there are many great and holy bishops and priests. But we all lack in one basic area—a lived experience of married love. All the good will in the world doesn't make up for this lack of experience."*

Rules of Celibacy
Should Be Abandoned

Alan Phillip

Within today's Roman Catholic Church, a great debate has arisen among leaders and laity about rules of celibacy in the priesthood. In the following article, Father Alan Phillip, a Catholic priest at the Mater Dolorosa Passionist Retreat Center in Sierra Madre, California, urges the Church to discard its celibacy rules. He asserts that longstanding rules forbidding Catholic priests from marrying deprive them of the "human wholeness and spiritual holiness" that can be achieved through the sacrament of marriage. Phillip also stresses that forced celibacy limits priests' ability to provide helpful spiritual guidance to congregants in matters of sex and marriage.

Alan Phillip. "How Father Can Know Best." *U.S. Catholic*, vol. 69, July 1, 2004, pp. 24–28. Copyright © 2004 by Claretian Publications. Reproduced by permission.

As you read, consider the following questions:

1. According to Phillip, what are some of the ways in which modern society shows its anxiety and preoccupation with sex?

2. How do Catholic congregations view the counsel of priests in the areas of sex and marriage, according to Phillip?

3. Which scriptural passages does Phillip rely on to support his arguments?

Last-year's letters to the U.S. bishops from priests in several dioceses brought the issue of optional celibacy into the headlines again. The priests' letters highlighted the serious shortage of priests and the growing lack of available eucharistic celebration for the faithful.

I agree with the contents of the letters. But there is a broader and equally serious reason that needs to be raised.

These days we humans are having real difficulties with our sexuality. A brief glance at TV, the movies, the Internet, and the local magazine rack gives a quick sampling of our unbalance. Advertisers use sex to sell products. Singers use sex to mask their lack of musical talent. Talk shows are obsessed with sexual aberrations.

Considering the extent of prostitution, adultery, group sex, pedophilia, and spousal abuse, one must conclude that our society hasn't got a clue about why we were created male and female.

For much of our society, sex is seen as something people use for entertainment, for selling products, or for manipulating others. The problem is not just sexual aberration and exploitation. The real offense against human sexuality is that it is trivialized.

Many people experience sex as something that is pleasurable but devoid of meaning. Sex for them becomes a shallow activity, intensely involving the body but offering little con-

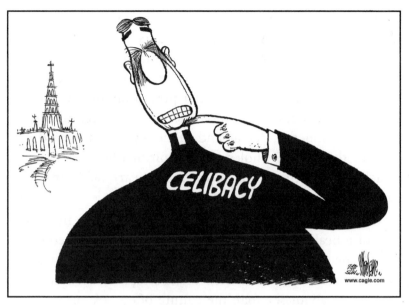

Copyright 2002 by Mike Lane and CagleCartoons.com. All rights reserved.

nection to the soul. Their sexual encounters engage physical organs but not the person. They settle for sex appeal, when what is possible is self-realization. They settle for technique, when what is possible is transcendence.

Very simply, what was designed to reach the very core of the human soul has been relegated to the surface. What was meant to free people from their egos has instead entrapped them in the realm of self-centeredness. There is no commitment. There is no trust. There is no love.

In the midst of this mess, to whom can we turn for help?

Finding Spiritual Guidance

Logically, people should turn to their ordained spiritual leaders for guidance. Ah, here is the problem for Catholics. A medieval law still in force in our Roman Catholic community requires all bishops and priests to be celibate. No doubt there are many great and holy bishops and priests. But we all lack in one basic area—a lived experience of married love.

All the good will in the world doesn't make up for this lack of experience. As spiritual leaders we priests haven't "walked a mile in the shoes" of the married people we are meant to lead. We are lacking the sexual experience that is possible within marriage. We can preach about the shoulds and should nots of sexual morality. And we can certainly say a lot about abstinence, denial, and sublimation. But what do we know of the human wholeness and spiritual holiness that can be achieved in the bonding of body, heart, will, and soul through the sacrament of Marriage?

Our world, perhaps more than ever before, is in critical need of a healthy vision of human sexuality. Young people especially need believable pacesetters in sexual maturity. The church needs to proclaim from the rooftops that it has a better message about sex than the culture offers. We priests, who are the most visible wisdom figures, who are ordained to be teachers and sages, need among our number those who will give prophetic witness to the goodness and beauty of married love.

Approach married couples in a typical Catholic parish and ask them: "When was the last time you heard a Sunday homily about married spirituality?" Most likely, they will scratch their heads, think for awhile, and then respond, "Maybe once last year," or "Along time ago," or even, "Never."

Most of the people in our pews are either married, have been married, or will one day be married. They live much of their life practicing their faith and finding their path to holiness through the sacrament of Marriage. They could certainly use some guidance, direction, and even leadership in their holy vocation.

Unfortunately, they cannot get much help from priests because we are all celibate. Let's be honest. In the eyes of the faithful, we are very limited in what we can preach. Our homilies and other teachings are narrowed to life as seen through the eyes of a celibate.

The result? At best, there is a vast population of married people floundering about with sparse spiritual direction for a major segment of their lives. Many turn to other churches where a married clergy understands their experience and speaks their language. At worst, there are dysfunctional families, a high divorce rate, spousal abuse, and a large array of other problems that are compounded when there is no effective conjugal leadership from our pulpits.

Need for Change

The first moral statement in the Bible proclaims, "It is not good for the man to be alone." Where do we find the church proclaiming by word and example the goodness of God's plan for sexuality? Where does our ordained leadership witness to communion with the Creator through communion with one's spouse?

The Catholic Church needs to give clear spiritual direction, by word and the example of its spiritual leaders, that will guide married couples on their sacramental journey to God.

The Catholic Church needs to promote respect for the human body, teaching by word and the example of its spiritual leaders, the dignity, nobility, and sanctity of human sexuality.

The Catholic Church needs to proclaim to our youth, by word and the example of its spiritual leaders, the power of premarital and marital chastity to shape the human heart for a trust-filled and lifelong union.

The Catholic Church, in stating its position on homosexuality, needs to show, by word and the example of its spiritual leaders, what it truly believes about marriage between a man and woman.

In responding to the crisis of pedophilia, the Catholic Church needs to do more than apologize with words. It needs to declare by the example of its spiritual leaders what a wholesome relationship with children is like, especially in family life.

To fulfill this mission is the urgent challenge before our church today. In the early days of his pontificate, Pope John Paul II wrote eloquently about the "theology of the body." But words alone are not enough. It is time for visible witness. It was St. Francis who advised his followers, "Preach the gospel at all times. If necessary, use words." He knew that people learn by observing.

Our world needs no more words, words, words. It longs for leaders to show us by the power of example what the Creator intended in creating sexual beings. A return to our apostolic roots by opening up ministry to a married clergy would be an eloquent profession of faith by our church that married couples are called to holiness of life.

It would make no more sense to mandate that priests marry than it makes to mandate celibacy. The vocation of marriage should not be imposed but should be a response to a call from the Lord. In view of the reasons above, now would be the perfect time to bring back to active ministry all those ordained who went on to answer a further call to married life.

Reexamine Assumptions

It is not difficult to find people who have the courage of their convictions. What is rare to find are people who have the courage to reexamine their convictions. St. Peter, the first pope, had this second brand of courage. He went through much of his life regarding gentiles as unclean. He thought they were unworthy of his association. This was part of his tradition.

But new circumstances (and a dream) forced Peter to reexamine his convictions. And he came to a new conclusion. "I begin to see how true it is that God shows no partiality" (Acts 10:34). This was such a significant change for Peter that Luke relates it twice in the Acts of the Apostles.

I pray that our American bishops will somehow find the courage to reexamine their convictions. They are being asked to reexamine if they "teach as dogma mere human precepts" (Mark 7:7).

Then, inspired by the bravery of our American bishops, I trust that the next pope will have the courage to reexamine the church's rule requiring celibacy for all priests. Yes, it will take courage to change. But 21st-century pastoral needs cannot be answered with an 11th-century law. A law of mandatory celibacy is powerless to reverse the mentality of our present culture's sexual sickness. It is time for a change.

I believe a new Pentecost for the Catholic Church will soon be realized and a renewed excitement about human sexuality in the context of conjugal love will soon be experienced. Just imagine a time when words preached from the pulpit are spoken in a language and mirrored by an example once again understood by married couples—and young people on the way to marriage.

> *"[Clergywomen have] brought new per-*
> *spectives into the theological discussion,*
> *a more inclusive style, and opened the*
> *doors to worshippers who've felt disen-*
> *gaged from institutional religion."*

The Ordination of Women Is a Positive Development in Religious Communities

Jane Lampman

Although a number of large Christian, Jewish, Muslim, and other religious denominations in the United States remain offi-cially opposed to having women as clergy, many other Christian and Jewish denominations have embraced clergywomen. As this viewpoint details, the growth in women clergy in these denomi-nations has been seen overwhelmingly as a positive development. Clergywomen have been credited with revitalizing church com-munities, bringing fresh perspectives to religious and social out-reach efforts, and creating a more welcoming environment for worshippers. Jane Lampman is a staff writer for the Christian Science Monitor.

Jane Lampman, "Women Clergy Bring a New Sensibility to an Old Calling," *Christian Science Monitor*, July 19, 2006. Copyright © 2006 The Christian Science Publishing Society. All rights reserved. Reproduced by permission from *Christian Science Monitor*, (www.csmonitor.com).

As you read, consider the following questions:

1. In which major Christian denomination do clergy-women comprise the majority of the denomination's clergy?

2. According to the author, what percentage of seminary students in 2006 are women?

3. In what ways are women rabbis influencing Jewish worship practices and beliefs?

The "stained-glass ceiling" was breached in dramatic fashion this summer, when bishops of the US Episcopal Church unexpectedly elected Katharine Jefferts Schori to be the church's leader for the next nine years.

Yet that glass ceiling remains relatively intact, even though the ranks of women clergy and their impact on religious communities continue to grow. It's perhaps no surprise that women's leadership remains controversial, since the two largest Christian denominations in the US—Roman Catholics and Southern Baptists—reject women as pastors. So do Eastern Orthodox, Mormons, some Evangelicals, Muslims, and Orthodox Jews.

Still, thousands of clergywomen are filling rewarding and increasingly influential roles as ministers, priests, bishops, and rabbis. And it's not the numbers or even the level of acceptance that's at the heart of the issue, many say—it's a divine calling.

"God called me, and I have such a sense of that, that it's the defining thing," says the Rev. Nancy Rankin, twice a senior pastor and now director of congregational development for the United Methodist Church (UMC) in western North Carolina.

Growing Ranks of Women Clergy

The UMC and the Presbyterian Church (USA) are currently [in 2006] celebrating 50 years of ordaining women. The Methodists boast some 12,000 clergywomen; and 20 percent of Presbyterian clergy are female. Unitarian Universalists stand out as the one denomination to have a majority of women leaders.

Some Christian and Jewish clergywomen with years of experience—and who've reached the challenging and often-elusive post of senior pastor—say they still encounter resistance. They point to frontiers that remain, but are also encouraged by the strides already made.

"I wanted to be a rabbi long before women could, but I didn't think it would happen in my lifetime," says Rabbi Susan Grossman, who leads Beth Shalom, a Conservative Jewish congregation in Columbia, Md. "There's been more change in women's role in Judaism in the last 30 years than probably all of Jewish history!"

Women of both faiths share the experiences of difficulty in finding jobs, being shunted into smaller, often remote congregations, and receiving lower pay and fewer benefits than their male counterparts, as shown by studies of both Protestant clergy and Conservative Jewish rabbis.

Partly out of necessity and partly out of inclination, women have extended the boundaries of ministry beyond the congregation to serve as both military and hospital chaplains, educators, and counselors for social service agencies, according to a major 1998 study, "Clergy Women: An Uphill Calling."

Trials and Triumphs

Studies also show that clergywomen experience more stress than their male counterparts in a demanding occupation. As a result, a number are leaving the pulpit.

At the same time, clergywomen have been credited with being less interested in hierarchy and more in collegiality. They've brought new perspectives into the theological discus-

Praise for a Female Priest

Janet [the chaplain at the University of Minnesota's Episcopal Center, who has been a priest for ten years] is a priest who does not put on airs. She does not make a point of calling attention to her status by the use of either titles or clerical garb. She is not churchy. She's a natural. Watching her is like watching the seals at the Oregon coast. You know she belongs exactly where she is.

I am sure that God watches Janet with both thumbs up and a big grin, well pleased with this beloved daughter. Otherwise her work would seem disordered or strained, her presence not so life-giving, her ministry less fruitful. In vain would the builder labor.

Anne Marie Wolf, "She's a Natural,"
Commonweal, January 14, 2005.

sion, a more inclusive style, and opened the doors to worshippers who've felt disengaged from institutional religion.

"My mother often said that if there had been women rabbis when she was young, she wouldn't have been alienated from Judaism," says Ms. Grossman.

The role models clergywomen provide are spurring other young women to enter seminaries, where today they make up between 30 and 50 percent of students. "I grew up not ever seeing women in ministry. . . . The girls in this congregation don't think twice about it," says the Rev. Shannon Kershner, senior pastor at Woodhaven Presbyterian Church in Irving, Texas.

Despite the numerous challenges, many women find the profession immensely satisfying and an opportunity to influence their faith communities.

A Woman Rabbi Looks Back

Grossman was in the first class of ordained Conservative rabbis in 1985 and has been in the pulpit for 17 years. She's in an elite class of women who've become senior rabbis leading large congregations.

What means most to her, she says, is bringing comfort and support to people at meaningful moments in their lives. She also prizes "being able to mobilize the community for interfaith work, for peace work, for countering domestic violence. It's tremendously satisfying to do that authentically as a Jewish leader," she says.

And a leader she has become in the Jewish community. Grossman has served as an editor of the Conservative commentary on Scripture (Torah) and as a member of a committee on Jewish law and standards, which enables her to help make Jewish law "more woman-friendly." Her "rabbinic decision" on women serving as witnesses in Jewish law is now an official Conservative position.

Still, even when she took up her latest position, some people left the synagogue because she was a woman. While the difficulties over the years have led her to consider leaving the job several times, "I'm so glad I stuck it out, because now I'm thrilled with the pulpit," she adds.

Jaqueline Ellenson, director of the Women's Rabbinic Network in the Reform Jewish movement, also points to progress. The more liberal Reform denomination was the first, in 1972, to ordain a woman rabbi—the recently retired Sally Priesand. Now 450 women constitute about a quarter of the 1,800 Reform rabbis.

"The walls are down in terms of attitudes toward women rabbis in the movement—getting jobs is no longer an issue," she says. But other challenges remain, particularly bringing about pay and benefit equity. "And women are not moving up in the congregational hierarchy at the same speed as men," she says. Only about a dozen women serve as senior rabbis in large congregations.

A Major Impact

Yet women are having an impact on "conversations about prayer and spirituality, interpretations of text, and recovering of history," she adds. For instance, the project to produce the soon-to-be published revision of the Reform prayer book was headed by a woman.

In Christianity, women's ordination has a long history. American women have pioneered new churches, including Mary Baker Eddy, who founded the Christian Science church, which publishes this newspaper; evangelist Aimee Semple McPherson, the Foursquare Church; and Ellen White, the Seventh-Day Adventist Church.

Still, the continuing debate (among Protestants) over New Testament language about women and the fact that Jesus' disciples were men (for Catholics) shores up the resistance to women leaders.

As Anglicans in the Church of England continue to address the question of women bishops, for example, one Oxford clergyman has written on the distinction between having women priests and bishops. Referring to Genesis, he writes: "God made man in his own image; in the image of God created he male and female ... God's order is that the man is first in order and the woman second (equal in dignity but not in order)."

Ms. Rankin, with 23 years' experience as a pastor and district superintendent in the United Methodist Church, has encountered similar views. In a career that's been "an amazing ride," she has particularly loved preaching and helping nurture disciples. Yet she ponders whether there is a backlash under way.

In her most recent post as senior pastor of a 2,200-member church, she was surprised to "run into walls" over her role with some young congregants. "To see that among a conservative element of a new generation is disheartening," says the mother whose family has been very supportive over the years.

The ministry "is the hardest thing in the world to do and the most rewarding," she adds. "There's been pain and hurtful things, but also glorious moments. I can't imagine doing anything else."

Pioneers Serve as Mentors

Younger pastors have benefited from the work of such pioneers. Reverend Kershner attended Columbia Seminary in Decatur, Ga., where 50 percent of students were women. "I was affirmed in ways that were empowering," she says. After her 1999 ordination, she found an associate pastor post and became a senior pastor before she was 30. That remarkable event occurred in the conservative Texas Bible belt, no less, and after she attended the interview with her newborn baby. Yet she and the Presbyterian congregation of about 325 families seemed to agree her leadership role was what God had in mind.

"No one left as a result of me coming, and actually some folks came because it was something different," Kershner says.

The job has been challenging for a young mother of two (though her husband is a willing stay-at-home dad), who didn't expect the inherent loneliness or the constant emotional weight. "I carry these people around with me all the time, in my head and in my heart," she says. Still, she adds, "I consider it a privilege."

Kershner even takes a bit of mischievous delight in wearing her collar to ecumenical gatherings with conservative Baptists, where it always sparks discussion.

"There are some people concerned with the state of our souls," she says, "but we are OK with that."

> *"The ordination of women is not simply a matter of making a woman a priest. It is much more; it is the ultimate destruction of the Christian faith."*

The Ordination of Women Is a Negative Development in Religious Communities

Father John Morris

According to this viewpoint, the growing acceptance of women's ordination in various Christian denominations is an alarming development that threatens the foundations of traditional Christianity. The author contends that "feminist ideology" is responsible for women's ordination, which in turn has triggered a devaluing of biblical scripture and hallowed religious traditions and principles. The author of this viewpoint is Father John Morris, who serves as pastor of Forty Holy Martyrs of Sebaste Orthodox Mission in Stafford, Texas.

As you read, consider the following questions:

1. According to the author, how do feminists distort the priesthood and other positions of religious leadership?

Father John Morris, "Thoughts on Women's Ordination," *Word Magazine*, January 2004. Reproduced by permission of the author.

2. What church leadership positions does the author believe are acceptable for women?

3. In what ways does the author compare the feminist cause to a political campaign?

During the last part of the twentieth century, Feminism swept through society like a raging forest fire and has become one of the most significant developments in modern history. It is not an exaggeration to state that feminism has redefined almost every aspect of contemporary American culture.

Feminists and their supporters have demanded and received changes in the English language, which, like [author George] Orwell's "Newspeak," more correctly express the prejudices of their movement. Thus, it is no longer acceptable to say "mankind." Instead one must say "humankind." A postman is now a letter carrier. A fireman is now a firefighter and even clergymen are now clergypersons. In schools, young girls learn to be assertive and to reject traditional feminine qualities while boys are urged to "get in touch with their feminine side." In every place where radical feminists have gained a footing, their ideas have overwhelmed traditional beliefs in many different ways including religion. Not only have feminists demanded and received admission of women to the ordained ministry, they have also successfully persuaded many Christians to redefine their understanding of God to conform to the feminist ideology. . . .

If it is necessary to redefine God to conform to a secular ideology such as feminism, it is necessary to redefine everything else, thereby inventing a new, politically correct, feminized religion that only has a superficial similarity to traditional Christianity. In almost every case, one of the first steps in the feminization of religion is the ordination of women. During the last few decades virtually every Christian group, with the exception of a few more conservative Protestant bodies, the Roman Catholic Church and, of course, the Orthodox Church, has yielded to pressure from feminists and has admitted women to the ordained ministry. Significantly, the secular media has fallen into line with feminist ideology and speaks with derision about those Christian groups which still adhere to the ancient prohibition against the ordination of women. However, it is important to understand that the ordination of women is only part of a process that eventually leads to a rejection of Biblical and Traditional Christianity in favor of a new feminized and ultimately heretical religion. . . .

Historical Gender Roles

Although it may not satisfy those who seek a rational explanation, the historical practice of the Church may very well be the best argument against the ordination of women. One might ask, if it is wrong to deny women ordination, why would the Church, which is led by the Holy Spirit to manifest the will of God in society, be guilty of oppression against women by denying them their rightful place in the ranks of the clergy? Christ chose no women Apostles. The Church has never allowed women to become priests or bishops. Indeed, those few "Christian" groups in antiquity that allowed some form of women's ordination were far outside the mainstream of Christianity and were associated with Gnosticism and/or some other major heresy. That should be enough to convince any faithful Orthodox Christian that it would be the height of arrogance for some in the twenty-first century to claim they are qualified to declare that the Church has been wrong for almost 2,000 years.

Indeed, if it is an injustice to deny women ordination, why did not Christ Himself set the example by choosing women Apostles? Neither Christ nor his followers had the slightest inhibition against speaking out against the injustices of their time. If the denial of ordination were an injustice, one would expect that Christ, who criticized so many of the practices of the religious establishment of His day, would have set the example for his followers by naming at least one woman Apostle. . . .

Thus those who approach the priesthood must approach it on God's and His Church's terms, not their own terms or those of a secular ideology such as Feminism. The feminists also distort the priesthood, by turning what should be a ministry of service and self-sacrifice into a position of power and prestige. A priest is a servant, not a master. Indeed, if a man treats his priesthood as a position of power and authority, he has perverted his calling and yielded to the temptation to the greatest sin of all, the sin of pride. Indeed, if the priesthood were a position of power, it would be an injustice to deny it to women. However, the priesthood is only one of many ministries and leadership positions within the Church. Here the words of St. Paul are relevant:

> For by one Spirit we were all baptized into one body—Jews or Greeks, slaves or free—and all were made to drink of one Spirit. For the body does not consist of one member but of many. If the foot should say, "Because I am not a hand, I do not belong to the body," that would not make it any less a part of the body. And if the ear should say, "Because I am not an eye, I do not belong to the body," that would not make it any less a part of the body. If the whole body were an eye, where would be the hearing? If the whole body were an ear, where would be the sense of smell? But as it is, God arranged the organs in the body, each one of them, as he chose. If all were a single organ, where would the body be? As it is, there are many parts, yet one body. . . .

Female Leadership Positions

Despite the male priesthood, women occupy leadership positions within the Church. Women serve on parish councils, attend the conventions of their Archdiocese, and even serve on the Board of Trustees of their Archdiocese. They also are ministers of the Church because the ordained priesthood is but one of many ministries in the Church. The woman who directs a choir or teaches Sunday School is just as much a minister as a priest or bishop. A priest must first of all be humble before God and before those whom he is called to serve. A radical feminist demanding ordination as a "right," is anything but humble and therefore fails to meet one of the most important requirements of the priesthood.

Radical feminism distorts not only the priesthood but also the very nature of humanity by failing to recognize that there are real differences between men and women. A man cannot be a mother, nor a mother a father. By attempting to blur the distinction between the genders, the feminists are distorting the very essence of human nature. They also fail to understand that the roles of the different sexes are complementary and follow the plan of creation designed by God. To act as if men and women are the same in every way is to deny one of the most basic facts of human existence. Because men and women are different, God has decreed as we know through the practice of the Church that men and women should have different, but complementary roles in the Church. That women and men are different and occupy different positions within the Church does not mean that one is superior to the other. This is one of the most basic flaws of the radical feminist argument. They fail to recognize that equality does not require sameness. Men and women can play different roles in the leadership of the Church and still remain equal to one another in every way.

However, perhaps the most important argument against the ordination of women is the results of women's ordination in those Christian groups who have surrendered to the pressure of secular society to ordain women. A priest is not simply a performer or leader; a priest is an image of Christ who in turn is an image of God. Thus, a priest is an icon or symbol of Christ, especially during the Divine Liturgy. Because symbols have real meaning, if the symbol is changed, that

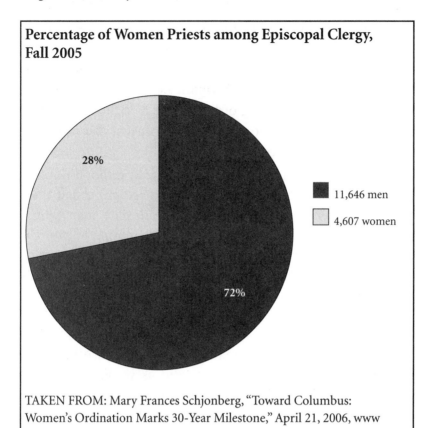

Percentage of Women Priests among Episcopal Clergy, Fall 2005

28%

72%

■ 11,646 men

□ 4,607 women

TAKEN FROM: Mary Frances Schjonberg, "Toward Columbus: Women's Ordination Marks 30-Year Milestone," April 21, 2006, www .episcopalchurch.org.

which is symbolized is also changed. Since a priest represents Christ, who is God, if the priest becomes a priestess, the image of God also changes. This will inevitably lead to a redefinition, or to use their term, "re-imaging" of God. . . .

The Dangers of Feminist Theology

Virtually every Protestant group that has decided to ordain women has to one degree or another begun to reject Biblical language and images of God in favor of images more acceptable to feminist theology.

Thus, God is no longer Father, Son and Holy Spirit, but becomes "Creator, Redeemer, and Sanctifier." On the surface this may seem only a change of terms, but actually, it is much more. It represents a radically different way of looking at God. The new politically correct Trinity is a rejection of divinely revealed language about God and thereby a rejection of the divine inspiration of the Holy Scriptures. It is also heretical because it blurs the important distinction between the Father, Son and Holy Spirit. The Father also creates, redeems and sanctifies, but so does the Son and the Holy Spirit. In reality, the feminized Trinity is actually a form of the ancient heresy of Sabellianism, which portrays Father, Son and Holy Spirit as merely different phases of God rather than different but united persons.

Not only have the feminists redefined God to accommodate their ideology, they have begun to redefine the entire Christian religion in the light of feminism. Thus, they place their secular ideology above the divine revelation of God in the Holy Scriptures and the other manifestations of Holy Tradition. This is the ultimate secularization of the Gospel, because they have subordinated the divinely inspired Scriptures and other manifestations of Holy Tradition to a secular ideology.

Indeed, anyone who has watched the efforts of followers of feminism and its allied ideologies to redefine American Protestantism sees not prayerful contemplation in an effort to discern the will of God, but the very worst aspects of an organized political campaign by one group to gain power over another. Thus, feminists eventually beat down their opponents because they are more persistent and effective political organizers than the opponents.

A Heretical Movement

Borrowing methods from the Civil Rights Movement, these campaigns include rallies, demonstrations, intimidation and civil disobedience. Eventually, although originally a minority, they are able to prevail because the leadership of most American Protestant groups lacks the courage to dismiss or remove anyone who rejects traditional beliefs and practices. Indeed, today it is unacceptable to accuse someone of heresy, much less discipline them or remove them from their office in the Church. This attitude has led to a complete breakdown of anything like traditional Christianity among many American Protestants and even some Roman Catholics.

Thus, the ordination of women is not simply a matter of making a woman a priest. It is much more; it is the ultimate destruction of the Christian Faith. This is because the ordination of women requires the rejection of the clear practice of the Church and thereby of the Holy Scriptures and other manifestations of Holy Tradition. It is also because the movement to ordain women does not come from within the Christian community, but is actually the subordination of the Faith to the secular ideology of Feminism. Once one rationalizes the rejection of something as central to the Faith as the nature of the priesthood, it then becomes easier to reject anything else in the Tradition of the Church that followers of that ideology find offensive. If one takes it upon oneself to decide which beliefs and practices of the Church are acceptable to modern society, the result is the chaos that has engulfed American Protestantism and has even made its influence felt in Roman Catholic circles.

Thus, if one decides that the Church has been wrong to deny the priesthood to women, one might also decide that the Church has been wrong in other beliefs and practices. Indeed, this is precisely what has happened. Despite centuries of opposition to abortion by Christians, almost every major American Protestant group that has ordained women has also adopted a "pro-choice" position on abortion. Recently, the Episcopal Church elected as a bishop a man who left his wife and children to live in a homosexual relationship with another man. There can be no doubt that not only the Holy Scriptures, but also the Fathers and the Ecumenical Councils consider homosexual acts immoral. Indeed, there is also no doubt that until a very few years ago, every Christian group, Protestant, Orthodox, or Roman Catholic, taught that homosexual sexual acts are a fundamental violation of the moral law of God.

A Slippery Slope

However, it is also true that until fairly recently, all Christian groups agreed that only men could be ordained. If Christians can decide that the unanimous opinion of Christians throughout the centuries is wrong on one issue, the ordination of women, it is logical to assume that Christians can also be wrong on other issues such as abortion and homosexuality, especially since the same feminists who demand women's ordination are also frequently sympathetic to so-called gay liberation. Thus, because they see everything in the light of feminism, they no longer accept Traditional images of God. They redefine the Holy Trinity in completely unbiblical language because of the dictates of their ideology.

They also redefine Christian morality to conform to the demands of radical feminism, which has a strong affinity to the gay liberation movement. This eventually leads to a complete perversion of the Gospel. The gospel of feminism and political correctness no longer calls humans to repentance and righteous living, but demands the acceptance of the right to each person to be free to live according to his or her own standards, even if those standards clearly conflict with the standards of Holy Scripture. Indeed, according to this criterion, any demand that one seek any other personal value than self-fulfillment according to one's own needs, is bigoted and to be rejected in favor of inclusiveness.

That is one major reason why every American Protestant group that has begun to ordain women has also begun to feel pressure from many of the same people who successfully campaigned for women's ordination to recognize homosexual and lesbian relationships as equal to heterosexual marriage. Thus, the ordination of women to the priesthood is not simply the acceptance of women priests. It leads to a complete distortion of the Christian Faith and the creation of a new religion that has only a very superficial resemblance to any form of traditional Christianity.

> *"I have come to realize that I am effective in ministry not despite the fact that I am homosexual, but often because I am homosexual."*

Homosexuals Belong in Positions of Religious Leadership

Anonymous

In this viewpoint, a homosexual Catholic priest who has maintained his vow of celibacy laments the refusal of Church leaders to accept openly homosexual priests. He argues that this hostility to homosexual clergy is un-Christian and that it will ultimately have a negative impact on countless Catholic communities. The author of this viewpoint is a Catholic priest who requested anonymity out of concern for potential professional consequences. His request was granted by Commonweal, *the publisher of the viewpoint.*

As you read, consider the following questions:

1. What does the author say is his own mother's attitude toward homosexuals?

Anonymous, "Made in God's Image: A Homosexual Priest Speaks Out," *Commonweal*, vol. 130, April 11, 2003. Copyright © 2003 Commonweal Publishing Co., Inc. Reproduced by permission of Commonweal Foundation.

2. How does the author believe that his homosexual sexual orientation has helped him be a better priest?

3. According to the author, what will be the ultimate result of an outright ban on the ordination of homosexual men, even if they are celibate?

I understand the struggle homosexual people have believing that they are made in God's image, that they are good, that official church teaching can serve as the foundation for a healthy, grace-filled spirituality. I am saddened that it is the authorities of the church I love who have placed the biggest obstacle to acceptance of such goodness, asking that we see ourselves as "disoriented" toward a corrupt end.

I knew that I was called to priesthood before I knew that I was gay. The lure of sacramental mystery that resonated with my young soul, the ready acceptance I found in my home parish community, and the care and attention shown me by priests of all ages and temperaments convinced me at an early age that my life would be spent in service as a priest. The excitement, complexity, and beauty of my sexuality were a later discovery, coming at a time when body, mind, and soul were ready to explore and understand one of God's most profound gifts. Yes, I knew that I was called to priesthood before I knew that I was gay. That is why the recent pronouncements from Rome and elsewhere that homosexuals are not fit for priesthood give me pause and cause me to wonder, "How could that be?"

Though disheartened and angered by the growing number of voices judging me unfit, I am not surprised. It has been my experience that even the most loving people fall prey to intolerance when it comes to the topic of homosexuality. Once when I tried to talk with my mother about my ministry to gay and lesbian students at a local college, her only response was, "I hate those people." And during a time of personal challenge when I "came out" to a pastor I loved like a father, he told me, "Funny, you don't look like one of them."

The Mission Remains the Same

There is not a shred of evidence that lesbians and gay men—whether "out" or not—are any less able or willing to love God and neighbor than heterosexuals; no evidence of their being less adept at feeding the hungry, welcoming the stranger, or visiting the sick; no evidence of less commitment to the weighty matters of justice, mercy, and faith. In relation to ordination, there is no evidence that lesbians and gay men are less capable in service, word, sacrament, and order, nor in conviction and confidence in God's call to ordained ministry.

William M. McElvaney, "Why Should the Church Allow Ordination of Gay Men and Lesbians?" In Finishing the Journey: Questions and Answers from United Methodists of Conviction. *Dallas, TX: Northaven United Methodist Church, 2006.*

No, I am not surprised. I think I have been expecting this to happen for some time. Still, hearing the words that pronounce me unsuitable hurt and confuse me. If Rome decides that homosexuals will not be admitted to the priesthood, then I will be an unwelcome member of a brotherhood whose defining character is the attraction to women. How did I get here? How is it that I now find myself feeling like the guest who entered the wedding feast not properly clothed? Why wasn't I stopped at the door before ordination twenty-five years ago?

Struggles in Seminary

Throughout my seven years of seminary formation, I struggled with the issue of my same-sex attraction and wondered whether it was possible for me to respond to the call to priesthood, given the church's teaching and understanding of the issue. The call to ministry was clear to me and apparently to many others, including family, friends, priests I had known, and seminary personnel. Still, the question remained: Could I live a happy, meaningful celibate life in service to others, knowing that the church I wanted to serve considered an integral part of my person to be "basically disordered"?

As questions emerged each step of the way there was always a spiritual director to guide me, and, for a two-year period, a priest counselor who challenged me to understand the role my sexuality played in my self-appreciation and how I related to others. In the prayer life of the seminary, in the direction I received from spiritual guides and confessors, and in the supportive community of my brother seminarians, I found the strength and acceptance I needed to continue toward ordination.

It puzzles me that those who now oppose the ordination of homosexuals argue that living in a seminary environment might make it more difficult to live chastely (see Andrew R. Baker, "Ordination and Same-Sex Attraction," *America*, September 30, 2002). Every article and book I have read encourages those who want to live in accord with the church's teaching on homosexuality to develop a strong life of prayer, to seek a supportive spiritual director, and to be part of a community that shares the church's teaching. Far from being a source of temptation, the seminary ought to be the optimal place where one can find direction and support in living a chaste life. The assumption that an all-male seminary would be an occasion of temptation for gay men is absurd. Does that mean that hearing confessions in a convent would be an occasion of temptation for a heterosexual priest and thus should be avoided? Of course not. Why is it that sexuality is always reduced to sexual urges rather than being understood in the larger context of how one relates as a whole person—body, mind, and spirit?

A Loving Relationship with God

I also find it disturbing that issues sometimes associated with homosexuals (Baker suggests substance abuse, sexual addiction, and depression) are thought of as intrinsically related to homosexuality, rather than resulting from a poorly formed sexual identity. It would stand to reason: if a homosexual man starts with the assumption that his sexuality is disordered because, as Baker says, it "tends toward a corrupt end" and can "never image God and never contribute to the good of the person or society," he might have to struggle with feelings of maladjustment or depression. Those unhealthy attitudes and potentially self-destructive behaviors stem not from the orientation itself but from the destructive self-image imposed on homosexuals by society and the church. If I were to believe that the God-given gift of my sexuality is disordered, how would I ever establish a trusting, loving relationship with the God who so ordered me? Living a celibate life does not erase one's sexuality. It challenges the celibate to direct all relational energy (heterosexual or homosexual) in loving service to those to whom we minister. That relational energy is more than genital expression; it is the whole self in relation to others. It is a puzzle to me that writers like Baker who voice such strong opinions on this subject reduce sexuality to physical attraction.

The twenty-five years I have spent in priestly ministry have been years of challenge, grace, and a sharing in the mystery of the incarnate God made visible in Jesus, who continues to live in and through his church. The person of the priest is called to mirror the selfless, chaste love of Christ to those he serves. He does so not because he is heterosexual; he does so because he is willing to reaffirm the goodness of people made in God's image and likeness, calling them to live the gospel message in the face of misunderstanding, challenge, and sacrifice. I have come to realize that I am effective in ministry, not despite the fact that I am homosexual, but often because I am homosexual.

I know it is difficult for some to understand that assertion. That may be because writers like George Weigel (*The Courage to Be Catholic*) divide homosexual people into two types: gays ("a man who makes his homoerotic desires the center of his personality and identity") and those who recognize their homosexual desires to be disordered. Such an analysis reduces the choices a homosexual person makes to either promiscuity or self-abnegation. Neither choice leads to a healthy spirituality based on an appreciation of being made in God's image and likeness. Another option is needed, one that defines the multifaceted dimensions of sexuality and reflects the limitless love God has for his beloved. There is no such thing as generic divine love: God's love is always directed in unique, jealous fashion to each person as beloved. So too is the unique response of the individual to God's grace, which builds on one's nature, be it heterosexual or homosexual.

Made in God's Image

Because official church teaching denies such a possibility for homosexuals, I understand the struggle homosexual people have believing that they are made in God's image, that they are good, that official church teaching can serve as the foundation for a healthy, grace-filled spirituality. I am saddened that it is the authorities of the church I love who have placed the biggest obstacle to acceptance of such goodness, asking that we see ourselves as "disoriented" toward a corrupt end. It is one of the heavy burdens, hard to carry, that the church places on many of her sons and daughters. Woe to those who impose such a burden!

It will be a sad day for me if those in authority decide to impose a ban on the ordination of homosexual men, and it will be a sad day for the whole church. Many of us will be lost, for I suspect there will be those who, out of self-respect and a decision not to accept the church's faulty designation, will choose to walk quietly out of the ministry to which God has called them, the ministry that they love. I suspect those in high places will hardly notice or will breathe a sigh of relief.

Those who have trusted and treasured their ministry, however, will notice and be saddened that their own spiritual welfare is being compromised once again by those who have the authority from Christ to make decisions, but lack his mind and heart to make them wisely.

> *"Someone afflicted with S.S.A. [same sex attraction] cannot redirect his inclination toward a complementary 'other' in a spousal relationship, because homosexuality has disordered his sexual attraction toward the opposite sex. It then becomes difficult to be genuinely a sign of Christ's spousal love for the church."*

Homosexuals Do Not Belong in Positions of Religious Leadership

Andrew R. Baker

According to this viewpoint, men and women who harbor "same sex attraction" or "S.S.A." are unsuitable for priesthood in the Catholic Church. The author asserts that people with S.S.A. are more likely to have "personal defects" that can hinder their ability to carry out priestly duties and that their homosexual desires make it impossible for them to partake of the "spousal union" between Christ and the Church. Reverend Andrew R. Baker is a

Andrew R. Baker, "Ordination and Same Sex Attraction," *America*, vol. 187, September 30, 2002. Copyright 2002 www.americamagazine.org. All rights reserved. Reproduced by permission of America Press. For subscription information, visit www.americamagazine.org.

priest of the Diocese of Allentown, Pennsylvania, and a member of the staff of the Congregation for Bishops in Rome.

As you read, consider the following questions:

1. How does the author define homosexuality within the context of suitability for ordination?
2. Does the author view same-sex attraction, in and of itself, as a sin?
3. In what ways does the author see homosexual cliques in seminaries as a serious problem?

Every bishop possesses the sacred duty of discerning the suitability of candidates for holy orders. St. Paul's advice to Timothy is fitting for all bishops, especially today [2002]: "Do not lay hands too readily on anyone" (1 Tim. 5: 22). The church's life and the way it manifests itself as the sacrament of salvation for the entire world leans inextricably on the shoulders of her priests. The supernatural "health," one could say, of the church depends heavily on the fitness of candidates for ordination.

In the aftermath of the scandal of clerical sexual abuse of minors, the church and society have focused partly on the role of homosexuality. The question has arisen as to whether or not it is advisable for a bishop to admit a man with predominantly homosexual tendencies, or what some call "same sex attraction" (S.S.A.), to the seminary and/or present him for holy orders.

Judging Suitability for Ordination

Thanks to a recent *Circular Letter* in 1997 from the Congregation for Divine Worship and the Discipline of the Sacraments concerning the suitability of candidates for holy orders, some guidance and assistance from the Holy See have already been given in order to tackle the thorny and difficult issue of suitability.

The letter says that a vocation is based on "a moral certitude that is founded upon positive reasons regarding the *suitability* of the candidate." Next, it mentions the fundamental reason not to admit a candidate to holy orders. The document says: "Admission may not take place if there exists a prudent doubt regarding the candidate's suitability. By 'prudent doubt' is meant a doubt founded upon facts that are objective and duly verified." Later, the congregation advises that it would seem "more appropriate to dismiss a doubtful candidate" than to lament the sadness and scandal of a cleric abandoning the ministry.

In other words, the congregation seems to suggest that even if there is only a "prudent doubt," based on objective facts, about the suitability of any candidate, the best and safest course of action is not to admit him to holy orders. The church does not ask for certitude that a man does not have a vocation but simply that a doubt has arisen through a prudent examination of evidence. Even though there may be a *lack of certitude* but a *definite prudent doubt*, a proper ecclesiastical authority should judge the candidate to be unsuitable.

What about a candidate with S.S.A.? Does it introduce a prudent doubt about suitability resulting in not admitting an applicant to a formation program or not issuing the call to holy orders?

The Meaning of Homosexuality

In order to determine the existence of a "prudent doubt," it would be helpful to clarify the meaning of the term "homosexuality." The *Catechism of the Catholic Church* describes it as "an exclusive or predominant sexual attraction toward persons of the same sex." Some may experience a wide range of intensity or different types of attractions to persons of the same sex, as some experts propose. Although, in the context of determining suitability for ordination, it would seem appropriate to limit the definition of the term "homosexuality" to describe

The Vatican Comments on "Homosexual Tendencies"

Concerning profoundly deep-rooted homosexual tendencies, that one discovers in a certain number of men and women, these are also objectively disordered and often constitute a trial, even for these men and women. These people must be received with respect and delicacy; one will avoid every mark of unjust discrimination with respect to them. These are called to realize the will of God in their lives and to unite to the Sacrifice of the Lord the difficulties that they may encounter.

In light of this teaching, this department, in agreement with the Congregation for Divine Worship and the Discipline of the Sacraments, holds it necessary clearly to affirm that the Church, while profoundly respecting the persons in question, may not admit to the seminary and Holy Orders those who practice homosexuality, show profoundly deep-rooted homosexual tendencies, or support the so-called gay culture.

The above persons find themselves, in fact, in a situation that gravely obstructs a right way of relating with men and women. The negative consequences that may derive from the Ordination of persons with profoundly deep-rooted homosexual tendencies are by no means to be ignored.

Catholic World News, translation of Vatican document on homosexuality and seminaries by Congregation for Catholic Education, November 4, 2005, www.cwnews.com.

those with *exclusive* or *predominant* tendencies, because a "prudent doubt" can be better verified objectively based on the clear presence of the disorder. With this clear information, a bishop can then make his decision concerning suitability.

Some have described S.S.A. as a sexual "orientation." At first glance, this description may seem to have some merit. The sexual attraction of someone with S.S.A. is "toward" persons of the same sex, and this "tending toward" could easily be described as an "orientation." However, to classify homosexuality as an "orientation" may obfuscate the serious *disorder* that exists and the distortion that has been introduced into a biblically inspired Christian anthropology.

Genesis speaks of God creating an image of himself by making man "male and female." In this dual and complementary relationship of persons, man finds within himself or can, in a certain sense, "read" in his body and in the body of a person of the opposite sex, a tendency to "leave his father and mother" and "cling" to the other (Gen. 2:24). The sexual orientation, the "tending toward" another of the opposite sex, is "written" in man's created constitution. It is part of what Pope John Paul II calls the "nuptial meaning of the body." Any other tendency to "cling" to another (be it to persons of the same sex, children, beasts, objects) is an aberration of the divine economy in which God reveals himself by creating an image of himself in the orientation of male to female and female to male.

The "Disorientation" of Same-Sex Attraction

The "orientation" of those who have another attraction, other than the divinely constituted one, is not a true "orientation." It would be better described as a *"disorientation."* It is fundamentally flawed in its disordered attraction because it can never "image" God and never contribute to the good of the person or society. This is why the Catholic Church teaches that the disorientation of homosexuality is "objectively disordered." Homosexuality may be an inclination, tendency or condition but it is fundamentally "dis-orienting" in that it tends toward a corrupt end. The attraction as such is *not* a sin. Only when one chooses to pursue the attraction in thought or deed does the disordered inclination become a disordered, and therefore sinful, choice.

Nevertheless, homosexual tendencies are aberrations that can and should be addressed by both the individual and by competent experts with the aid of behavioral sciences as well as by spiritual means, including prayer, the sacraments and spiritual direction. According to some experts, S.S.A. can be treated and even prevented with some degree of success. But does it introduce a "prudent doubt" when determining suitability for ordination?

There are a number of significant negative aspects to S.S.A. that contribute to a "prudent doubt" with regard to the suitability of a candidate for holy orders.

First and foremost among them is the possible simultaneous manifestation of other serious problems such as substance abuse, sexual addiction and depression. With more than one serious disorder, a candidate may find it difficult to respond to the demands of formation, and the seminary or religious house may struggle to accommodate the extra needs involved in the healing process of the individual.

Likewise, there is an increased possibility that persons with S.S.A. may be more familiar with certain patterns and techniques of deception and repression, either conscious or subconscious, which were learned in trying to deal with their tendencies in a largely heterosexual environment. After years of hiding or of being confused about their abnormal attractions, it is possible that duplicitous or pretentious behaviors could appear. These kinds of personal defects make the moral formation of the candidate much more difficult and can negatively affect the formation of the other candidates.

Other Problems with Gay Priesthood

Another aspect that would contribute to a "prudent doubt" concerning a candidate with S.S.A. is a question about his adherence to church teaching. There are many men and women with S.S.A. who uphold and defend the church's teaching on homosexuality. But if someone with S.S.A. is insecure about dealing straightforwardly with his disordered attractions or has some doubts about their disordered character, he may tend to possess a distorted and erroneous view of human sexuality. Thus, there exists the risk that such an individual will struggle with or even deny the clear teaching of the church regarding his disordered inclinations and any acts that might flow from these tendencies.

Part of the distortion of S.S.A. is the tendency to view the other person of the same sex as a possible sexual "partner" or even to reduce the other (also a temptation for heterosexuals) to a sexual object. In such a clearly male environment as the seminary and the priesthood, the temptation is ever-present for those with the disorder. This temptation could present very difficult circumstances and the overwhelming presentation of the object of their attraction (men), which is naturally part of an all-male and intensely close community, could make their efforts to live chastely or to be healed of their disorder very difficult.

Furthermore, as has been the unfortunate experience in some seminaries and dioceses, cliques may form based on the disordered attractions. This could hamper the healing process that might be possible for some, because the effeminate affective manners and a certain "acceptability" of the disorder are often promoted in such groups. Also these cliques can confuse young heterosexual men in the growth of their understanding of manhood and in developing skills and virtues to live a celibate life, because they can often see modeled in members of these cliques a disordered view of human sexuality and of proper masculine behavior.

The Question of Celibacy

Another question for determining suitability for a candidate with S.S.A. is whether the individual can live celibacy. Celibacy is a vocational choice to which one is bound by a vow or promise to live chastely for the sake of the kingdom of God by foregoing the good of marriage and family life. It is a sign of one's identification with Christ, one's availability for service to the church and of the spousal union between Christ and the church in the kingdom of God.

People with homosexual tendencies can live certain aspects of celibacy, but their commitment is significantly different from that of heterosexuals because it compromises two fundamental dimensions of celibacy.

On the one hand, celibacy involves a sacrifice of a good for a greater good. It sacrifices ordered and good inclinations toward spouse and family for the sake of the kingdom. For someone with S.S.A., an act of binding oneself by a vow or promise to abstain from something that one is already bound to avoid by the natural law (attractions toward someone of the same sex) seems superfluous. To avoid doing something (heterosexual acts) that one does not have an inclination to do is not a sacrifice. The struggle to live chastely may be extremely difficult for someone with homosexual tendencies, and these struggles would truly be meritorious and virtuous as acts of *chastity*, but not necessarily of celibacy.

Likewise, the spousal dimension of celibacy seems unclear for those with S.S.A. Celibacy is a way of living the spousal character of Christ's relationship with his bride, the church. Through the celibate life, the priest redirects his sexual attraction to the opposite sex toward another "body," the church, which is a "bride" in a complementary spousal relationship. He exercises a spiritual fatherhood and lives a supernatural spousal relationship as a sign to the church of Christ's love for her. Someone afflicted with S.S.A. cannot redirect his inclination toward a complementary "other" in a spousal relationship, because homosexuality has disordered his sexual attraction toward the opposite sex. It then becomes difficult to be genuinely a sign of Christ's spousal love for the church.

Celibacy Is Not Enough

If it can be said that a man with homosexual tendencies can live a celibate life, at the very least it is lacking some important elements due to S.S.A., and it could be another reason to conclude that there exists a prudent doubt as to his suitability for holy orders.

It would seem that if there are firmly established facts, both from an objective psychological evaluation and an examination in the external forum of past and present behavior and choices, that a man does indeed suffer from S.S.A. as an "exclusive or predominant sexual attraction toward persons of the same sex" (*Catechism*, No. 2357), then he should not be admitted to holy orders, and his presence in the seminary would not only give him false hope but it may, in fact, hinder the needed therapy and healing that might come from appropriate psychological and spiritual care. It may be that a man could be healed of such a disorder and then he could be considered for admission to the seminary and possibly to Holy Orders, but not while being afflicted with the disorder.

The Pauline exhortation not to "lay hands too readily on anyone" is a heavy responsibility for any bishop; but if a candidate's suitability is scrutinized with prudence, the act of "laying on of hands" will bear abundant fruit in the lives of those who will be touched by the ministry of a priest.

Periodical Bibliography

The following articles have been selected to supplement the diverse views presented in this chapter.

Jennifer Ferrera and Sarah Hinlicky Wilson	"Ordaining Women: Two Views," *First Things*, April 2003.
John Garvey	"Priests Should Be Married," *Commonweal*, August 12, 2005.
Danielle Harder	"Keeping the Faith," *Herizons*, Spring 2004.
Todd Henneman	"Scared of Sex," *Advocate*, August 17, 2004.
John C. LaRue Jr.	"Pastors, Marriage, and Sexual Temptation," *Your Church*, March–April 2005.
Joe Maxwell	"Devastated by an Affair," *Christianity Today*, January 2007.
Lisa Miller	"Life in Solitary," *Newsweek*, June 20, 2005.
Randall R. Phillips	"Gift or Curse?" *Commonweal*, September 10, 2004.
Anna Quindlen	"Complex and Contradictory," *Newsweek*, April 18, 2005.
Andrew Sullivan	"The Vatican's New Stereotype: Why Its New Rules Barring Gay Priests Turn Jesus' Teaching on Its Head," *Time*, December 12, 2005.
Gerard Thomas [pseud.]	"A Gay Priest Speaks Out," *Commonweal*, January 28, 2005.
Mira Tweti	"Daughters of the Buddha," *Tricycle*, Winter 2006.
Edward Vacek	"Acting More Humanely: Accepting Gays into the Priesthood," *America*, December 16, 2002.
N.T. Wright	"The Biblical Basis for Women's Service in the Church," *Priscilla Papers*, Autumn 2006.

For Further Discussion

Chapter 1

1. Don Lattin and Roger Scruton have starkly different views about whether the so-called "Sexual Revolution" of the 1960s has been good or bad for American morality and attitudes about sexuality. Whose argument do you find more convincing, and why?

2. Pamela Toussaint's essay explains the religious foundations of Lakita Garth's decision to remain abstinent until marriage. Garth's basic philosophy is supported by Lauren F. Winner's essay, but Rabbi Balfour Brickner argues that sexual activity in a loving relationship—even if not a formal marriage—is not sinful. Which viewpoint do you find to be stronger? Explain your reasoning.

Chapter 2

1. The first two essays in this chapter use scriptural passages from the Bible to support their perspective on homosexuality—yet one of the essays condemns homosexuality on moral grounds while the other defends gay sexuality and gay rights. Which arguments carry more weight with you? Why? Which arguments seem misleading or otherwise intellectually dishonest? Explain the reasons behind your view.

2. Dan Savage's essay asserts that opposition to gay marriage is based primarily on homophobia. The Vatican, however, cites scriptural passages in declaring its opposition to same-sex marriage. With these positions in mind, do you think Savage's accusation has merit? Why or why not?

3. Civil unions have been discussed as a possible "compromise" position in the battle between those who support same-sex marriage and those who oppose it. Jim Wallis makes the case for civil unions, but Peter Wood argues against the concept. Wood's opposition, though, stems from his belief that any legal recognition of same-sex couples is morally wrong. What arguments, though, can you think of to oppose civil unions from a *liberal* position? That is, why might advocates of same-sex marriage oppose the idea of civil unions?

Chapter 3

1. In the abortion debate that exists in churches and communities across the United States, each side accuses the other of using dishonest rhetoric to advance its cause. As you read the essays in this chapter, identify two arguments used by each side (four in all) that you believe are misleading, deceptive, exaggerated, or otherwise unfair or untrue. Explain why you believe these arguments are flawed—and whether they detract from the strength of their other arguments. Then identify the two arguments used by each side that you think are strongest. Explain your selections.

2. Christine A. Scheller and the Religious Coalition for Reproductive Choice differ in their perspective on whether abortion should be defended or condemned by Christians and people of other faiths. In what ways do they agree? In what ways do they disagree?

Chapter 4

1. In their essays, Robert Barron and Alan Phillip reach totally different conclusions about whether the Catholic Church should abandon its rules of celibacy for its priests. Which perspective do you find most persuasive? Explain why. What do you think is the weakest argument presented by the opposing essay? Why?

2. The number of women clergy has grown enormously in the last part of the twentieth and first part of the twenty-first centuries in many parts of the country. What factors do you think might account for this increase?

3. The last two essays in this chapter debate whether gay people belong in positions of religious leadership. With which perspective do you most agree? Explain your choice.

Organizations to Contact

The editors have compiled the following list of organizations concerned with the issues debated in this book. The descriptions are derived from materials provided by the organizations. All have publications or information available for interested readers. The list was compiled on the date of publication of the present volume; the information provided here may change. Readers need to remember that many organizations take several weeks or longer to respond to inquiries.

Alan Guttmacher Institute
120 Wall St., New York, NY   10005
(212) 248-1111 • fax: (212) 248-1951
e-mail: info@guttmacher.org
Web site: www.guttmacher.org

The institute works to protect and expand the reproductive choices of all women and men. It strives to ensure that people have access to the information and services they need to exercise their rights and responsibilities concerning sexual activity, reproduction, and family planning. Among the institute's publications are *Abortion in Women's Lives, Adding It Up: The Benefits of Investing in Sexual and Reproductive Health Care,* and the periodical *Perspectives on Sexual and Reproductive Health.*

Catholics for a Free Choice
1436 U St. NW, Ste. 301, Washington, DC   20009-3997
(202) 986-6093 • fax: (202) 332-7995
e-mail: cffc@catholicsforchoice.org
Web site: www.catholicsforchoice.org

Catholics for a Free Choice is an advocacy group for Catholics who support a woman's moral and legal right to follow her conscience in matters of sexuality, reproductive freedom, and reproductive health. It conducts education and advocacy work in the United States, Europe, and Latin America. Publications produced by Catholics for a Free Choice include *Sex in the HIV/AIDS Era* and *You Are Not Alone: Information for Catholic Women on the Abortion Decision.* The organization also produces *Conscience,* a quarterly magazine.

Dignity USA
PO Box 15373, Washington, DC   20003
(202) 861-0017 • fax: (202) 543-5511
e-mail: info@dignityusa.org
Web site: www.dignityusa.org

Dignity USA is a Catholic organization of gay, lesbian, bisexual, and transgender persons who worship together and advocate for increased GLBT rights within the official church and in U.S. society. *Breath of the Spirit* is a weekly electronic newsletter made available to members and friends of Dignity USA.

Family Research Council
810 G St. NW, Washington, DC   20001
(202) 393-2100 • fax: (202) 393-2134
Web site: www.frc.org

The council is a research, resource, and education organization that promotes traditional marriage and traditional family structure as the foundations of a healthy and moral civilization. The organization also believes that government has a duty to promote and protect traditional marriage in law and public policy. The organization's publications include *Getting It Straight: What the Research Shows about Homosexuality; The Bible, the Church, and Homosexuality* and *Protecting Your Child in an X-Rated World.*

Focus on the Family
Colorado Springs, CO   80995
(719) 531-5181 • fax: (719) 531-3424
e-mail: info@family.org
Web site: www.family.org

Focus on the Family is a conservative Christian organization that promotes traditional marriage and Bible-based perspectives on moral issues as part of its larger mission of evangelism. It also actively campaigns against abortion, homosexuality, pornography, sexual activity outside of traditional marriage, divorce, and other perceived threats to Christian society. Organization publications include the *Focus on the Family Marriage Series: A Parents' Guide to Preventing Homosexuality, And the Bride Wore White*, and *Why You Can't Stay Silent: A Biblical Mandate to Shape Our Culture.*

Institute for Marriage and Public Policy (IMAPP)
PO Box 1231, Manassas, VA   20108
(202) 216-9430
e-mail: info@imapp.org
Web site: www.imapp.org

The Institute for Marriage and Public Policy is a nonprofit research and education organization that seeks to find ways in which law and public policy can strengthen traditional marriage as a social institution. Special areas of research and discussion include same-sex marriage, pregnancy outside of marriage, gender roles, and divorce law. IMAPP reports include *Do Mothers and Fathers Matter?* and *Marriage and the Law: A Statement of Principles.*

National Organization for Women (NOW)
1100 H St. NW, Third Floor, Washington, DC   20005
(202) 628-8669 • fax: (202) 785-8576
Web site: www.now.org

The National Organization for Women is the largest organization of feminist activists in the United States, with more than 500,000 contributing members. NOW is dedicated to bringing about social and economic equality for women, and a significant part of its advocacy work is concerned with securing abortion, birth control, and reproductive rights for all women. NOW publishes a quarterly magazine, *National NOW Times.*

National Sexuality Resource Center (NSRC)
2017 Mission St., Ste. 300, San Francisco, CA   94110
(415) 437-5121
e-mail: nsrcinfo@sfsu.edu
Web site: http://nsrcs.sfsu.edu

The NSRC is a project of the Human Sexuality Studies Program at San Francisco State University. The mission of the center is to advance sexual literacy through science, sexuality education, and social policy formation. It also works to counter what it views as negative and distorted representations of sexuality by conservative religious and social organizations and policymakers. Periodicals published by the National Sexuality Resource Center include *Sexual Literacy, American Sexuality,* and *Sexuality Research & Social Policy.*

Planned Parenthood Federation of America (PPFA)
434 West Thirty-Third St., New York, NY   10001
(212) 541-7800 • fax: (212) 245-1845
e-mail: member-services@ppfa.org
Web site: www.plannedparenthood.org

Planned Parenthood believes individuals have the right to make their own reproductive choices without interference from government or other individuals. It promotes comprehensive sex education and provides contraceptive counseling and services through more than 860 centers across the United States. Publications available through the organization include *How to Talk with Your Child About Sex, Human Sexuality: What Children Need to Know,* and *How Abortion Is Provided.*

Religious Coalition for Reproductive Choice (RCRC)
1025 Vermont Ave NW, Ste. 1130, Washington, DC   20005
(202) 628-7700 • fax: (202) 628-7716
e-mail: info@rcrc.org
Web site: www.rcrc.org

The Religious Coalition for Reproductive Choice is an alliance of religious organizations dedicated to using education and advocacy to preserve reproductive choice in the United States.

Special areas of emphasis in RCRC advocacy include representing poor people, people of color, and other "underserved" populations in debates about reproductive issues. Publications offered by the RCRC include *Between a Woman and Her God: Clergy and Women Tell Their Stories* and *Words of Choice: Countering Anti-Choice Rhetoric.*

Religious Institute on Sexual Morality, Justice, and Healing

304 Main Ave., Ste. 335, Norwalk, CT   06851
e-mail: info@religiousinstitute.org
Web site: www.religiousinstitute.org

The institute is an ecumenical, interfaith organization dedicated to advocating for sexual health, education, and justice in religious communities and U.S. society. It seeks to educate lawmakers, religious institutions, clergy, and laypersons about ways in which sex education can be pursued within the context of various faith traditions. Publications offered by the institute include *A Time to Speak: Faith Communities and Sexuality Education* and *A Time to Build: Creating Sexually Healthy Faith Communities.*

Soulforce

PO Box 3195, Lynchburg, VA   24503-0195
e-mail: info@soulforce.org
Web site: www.soulforce.org

The mandate of Soulforce is to help lesbian, gay, bisexual, and transgender people gain greater freedom from perceived persecution at the hands of conservative religious people who, according to the organization, misuse religion to oppress homosexuals. Publications offered by Soulforce include *Religion Gone Bad: The Hidden Dangers of the Christian Right, Christian Youth: An Important Voice in the Present Struggle for Gay Rights in America,* and *What the Bible Says—and Doesn't Say—About Homosexuality.*

U.S. Conference of Catholic Bishops

3211 Fourth St. NE, Washington, DC   20017

(202) 541-3000 • fax: (202) 541-3412
Web site: www.usccb.org

This is the official organization of the Catholic hierarchy in the United States. The purpose of the conference is to promote the programs and Biblical interpretations of the Church and carry out education and advocacy on various social issues based on Church doctrine and guidance. Publications produced by the Conference of Catholic Bishops include *Between Man and Woman, Human Sexuality,* and *Married Love and the Gift of Life.*

Bibliography

Books

Marilyn Bennett Alexander and James Preston — *We Were Baptized Too: Claiming God's Grace of Lesbians and Gays.* Louisville, KY: Westminster John Knox Press, 1996.

Erika Bachiochi, ed. — *The Cost of "Choice": Women Evaluate the Impact of Abortion.* New York: Encounter Books, 2004.

Donald Cozzens — *Freeing Celibacy.* Collegeville, MN: Liturgical Press, 2006.

William J. Doherty, et al. — *Why Marriage Matters: Twenty-One Conclusions from the Social Sciences.* New York: Institute for American Values, 2002.

J. Shoshannah Ehrlich — *Who Decides? The Abortion Rights of Teens.* Westport, CT: Praeger, 2006.

Fran Ferder and John Heagle — *Tender Fires: The Spiritual Promise of Sexuality.* New York: Crossroad, 2002.

Jeffrey Heskins — *Face to Face: Gay and Lesbian Clergy on Holiness and Life Together.* Grand Rapids, MI: William B. Eerdmans, 2006.

Patricia Beattie Jung, Mary E. Hunt, and Radhika Balakrishnan, eds. — *Good Sex: Feminist Perspectives from the World's Religions.* Piscataway, NJ: Rutgers University Press, 2000.

Erwin Lutzer   *The Truth About Same-Sex Marriage.* Chicago: Moody, 2004.

Daniel C. Maguire   *Sacred Choices: The Right to Contraception and Abortion in Ten World Religions.* Minneapolis, MN: Augsburg Fortress, 2001.

Kate Michelman   *With Liberty and Justice for All: A Life Spent Protecting the Right to Choose.* New York: Hudson Street Press, 2005.

Sydna Masse and Joan Phillips   *Her Choice to Heal: Finding Spiritual and Emotional Peace after Abortion.* Colorado Springs, CO: Chariot Victor, 1998.

Lisa Graham McMinn   *Sexuality and Holy Longing: Embracing Intimacy in a Broken World.* San Francisco: Jossey-Bass, 2004.

James Nelson and Sandra Longfellow, eds.   *Sexuality and the Sacred.* Louisville, KY: Westminster John Knox Press, 2006.

Mark D. Regnerus   *Forbidden Fruit: Sex and Religion in the Lives of American Teenagers.* New York: Oxford University Press, 2007.

C.K. Robertson, ed.   *Religion and Sexuality: Passionate Debates.* New York: Peter Lang, 2005.

Jack Rogers   *Jesus, the Bible, and Homosexuality: Explode the Myths, Heal the Church.* Louisville, KY: Westminster John Knox Press, 2005.

Katie Roiphe — *Last Night in Paradise: Sex and Morals at the Century's End.* Boston: Little, Brown, 1997.

Stephen J. Rossetti — *The Joy of Priesthood.* Notre Dame, IN: Ave Maria Press, 2005.

Kathleen M. Sands, ed. — *God Forbid: Religion and Sex in American Public Life.* New York: Oxford University Press, 2000.

Alexander Sanger — *Beyond Choice: Reproductive Freedom in the 21st Century.* New York: Public Affairs, 2004.

Wendy Shalit — *A Return to Modesty: Discovering Lost Virtue.* New York: Free Press, 1999.

David Shallenberger — *Reclaiming the Spirit: Gay Men and Lesbians Come to Terms with Religion.* Piscataway, NJ: Rutgers University Press, 1998.

Glenn T. Stanton — *Marriage on Trial: The Case Against Same-Sex Marriage and Parenting.* Downers Grove, IL: InterVarsity Press, 2004.

Leonore Tiefer — *Sex Is Not a Natural Act and Other Essays.* Colorado Springs, CO: Westview Press, 2004.

Mel White — *Religion Gone Bad: The Hidden Dangers of the Christian Right.* New York: Tarcher, 2006.

Lauren F. Winner   *Real Sex: The Naked Truth about Chastity*. Grand Rapids, MI: Brazos Press, 2006.

Naomi Wolf   *Promiscuities: The Secret Struggle for Womanhood*. New York: Random House, 1997.

Index